**THE OKINAWANS CALLED THEM THE
"TYPHOON OF STEEL"— THE DEVASTATING
AIR STRIKE FORCE THAT PUMMELED THE
TINY ISLAND WITH A DAILY BLAST
OF DESTRUCTION.**

An hour after sunup on October 10, 1944, a flight of twelve dark blue Hellcats wheeled like purposeful hawks over southern Okinawa. On finding no enemy planes in the air, the leader, Commander Fred Bakutis, United States Navy, abruptly tipped his powerful fighter into a seventy-degree dive, screaming from out of the sun at a covey of enemy planes sitting haplessly below on a warm-up apron on Naha airfield, propellers whirling. At a thousand feet Bakutis pressed the firing button on his control stick, coasting a stream of white tracers toward five stubby new Mitsubishi fighters called Thunderbolts.

Yanking back on the stick as his six .50 caliber machine guns continued to flame, Bakutis slumped heavily in his seat from the force of gravity, his vision blurring as his body weight abruptly magnified several times. Looking back a moment later, he saw his squadron mates diving and their targets smoking; no Thunderbolts would rise from Naha airfield this day. . . .

THE BANTAM WAR BOOK SERIES

This series of books is about a world on fire.

The carefully chosen volumes in the Bantam War Book Series cover the full dramatic sweep of World War II. Many are eyewitness accounts by the men who fought in a global conflict as the world's future hung in the balance. Fighter pilots, tank commanders and infantry captains, among many others, recount exploits of individual courage. They present vivid portraits of brave men, true stories of gallantry, moving sagas of survival and stark tragedies of untimely death.

In 1933 Nazi Germany marched to become an empire that was to last a thousand years. In only twelve years that empire was destroyed, and ever since, the country has been bisected by her conquerors. Italy relinquished her colonial lands, as did Japan. These were the losers. The winners also lost the empires they had so painfully seized over the centuries. And one, Russia, lost over twenty million dead.

Those wartime 1940s were a simple, even a hopeful time. Hats came in only two colors, white and black, and after an initial battering the Allied nations started on a long and laborious march toward victory. It was a time when sane men believed the world would evolve into a decent place, but, as with all futures, there was no one then who could really forecast the world that we know now.

There are many ways to think about that war. It has always been hard to understand the motivations and braveries of Axis soldiers fighting to enslave and dominate their neighbors. Yet it is impossible to know the hammer without the anvil, and to comprehend ourselves we must know the people we once fought against.

Through these books we can discover what it was like to take part in the war that was a final experience for nearly fifty million human beings. In so doing we may discover the strength to make a world as good as the one contained in those dreams and aspirations once believed by heroic men. We must understand our past as an honor to those dead who can no longer choose. They exchanged their lives in a hope for this future that we now inhabit. Though the fight took place many years ago, each of us remains as a living part of it.

TYPHOON OF STEEL:
THE BATTLE FOR OKINAWA

JAMES H. BELOTE
AND WILLIAM M. BELOTE

BANTAM BOOKS
TORONTO · NEW YORK · LONDON · SYDNEY · AUCKLAND

*This low-priced Bantam Book
has been completely reset in a type face
designed for easy reading, and was printed
from new plates. It contains the complete
text of the original hard-cover edition.*
NOT ONE WORD HAS BEEN OMITTED.

TYPHOON OF STEEL: THE BATTLE FOR OKINAWA
*A Bantam Book / published by arrangement with
Harper & Row, Publishers, Inc.*

PRINTING HISTORY
*Harper & Row edition published September 1970
A Military Book Club (Doubleday) Selection, April 1971*

*Illustrations by Greg Beecham and Tom Beecham.
Maps by Alan McKnight.*

Bantam edition / September 1984

ISBN 0-553-24372-1

Published simultaneously in the United States and Canada

PRINTED IN THE UNITED STATES OF AMERICA

O   0 9 8 7 6 5 4 3 2 1

...se who served,
...n and Japanese

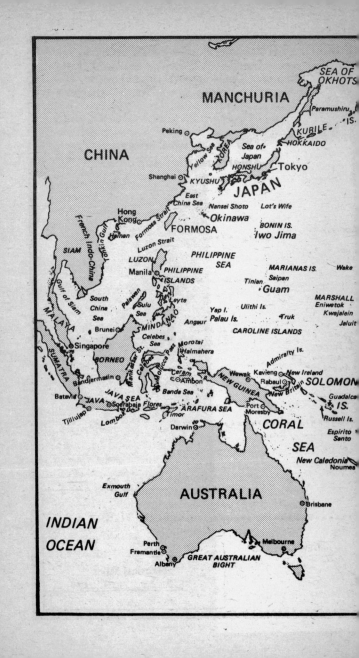

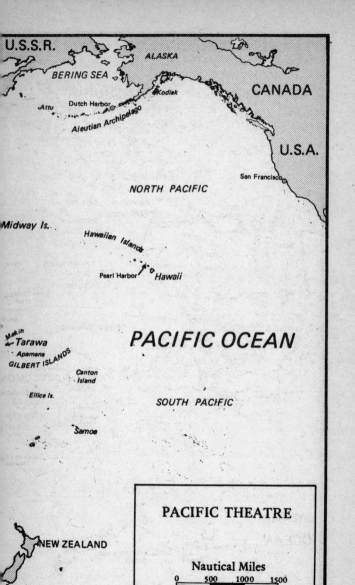

CONTENTS

PREFACE

THE CHALLENGING TASK of bringing into a single volume the complex and fascinating story of Okinawa's seizure by American forces in the waning months of World War II was suggested to the authors by their publisher, Harper & Row. After four years of research, study, and travel, they have produced an account which, while not exhaustive, they hope will provide for the general reader an accurate and authoritative history of Okinawa's "typhoon of steel." Of necessity they have had to be selective. To tell of every hill captured, of every destroyer hit by a kamikaze, even of the details of the planning, would require several volumes.

Although they bear full responsibility for the conclusions drawn in this volume, the debt of the authors to others has been considerable. At the World War II Records Center of the National Archives Mr. Wilbur Nigh, Mrs. Lois Aldridge, and others of the staff have been very helpful. The U.S. Army's chief historian, Dr. Stetson Conn, has been most cooperative as has his staff. Colonel Sisumu Nishiura, head of the War History Office of Japan's Ministry of Defense, helped to arrange interviews in Tokyo with Japanese veterans of the Okinawa campaign, and for this kindness the authors owe the colonel and his staff every thanks. They also are indebted to Mrs. Kyoko Ishikure, who not only acted as their able interpreter in Japan, but also as their "chief of staff."

Colonel James J. Mullen, U.S.A., chief of information at Ft.

Buckner, Okinawa, assisted the authors by every means at his disposal and helped to make their stay on the beautiful island both academically fruitful and enjoyable. To Mr. John Palmer, director of the Ft. Buckner Museum and the U.S. Army's able historian on the scene, they owe a special debt. Several battlefield tours under Mr. Palmer's expert guidance revealed facets of the Okinawa campaign that no archive could have.

For assistance in researching the important naval side of the Okinawa operation the authors wish to thank Rear Admiral Ernest M. Eller, U.S.N. (Ret.), director of naval history, and his executive, Rear Admiral F. Kent Loomis. Dr. Dean Allard, archivist at the Naval History Division, is especially to be thanked. To Mr. Henry I. Shaw and his able personnel at the Historical Branch, Headquarters, U.S. Marine Corps, the authors are indebted for counsel, friendly interest, and numerous photos of the leathernecks in action, as well as access to voluminous documentary material. Mrs. Donna Traxler and her staff at the Still Pictures Branch, Office of Information, U.S. Army, have supplied excellent photos of the Army's role.

The authors owe much to the work of Army historians Roy E. Appleman, James M. Burns, Russell A. Gugeler, and John Stevens, who prepared the Army history, *Okinawa: The Last Battle,* and to Charles S. Nichols and Henry I. Shaw, authors of the standard Marine Corps history, *Okinawa: Victory in the Pacific.* They must also acknowledge their debt to the great naval historian, Samuel Eliot Morison, for his *Victory in the Pacific.* The authors are indebted to many others whose works are listed in the Bibliography and especially to those veterans of the campaign, American and Japanese, who gave of their time to submit to interviews.

For sage counsel from close at hand the authors would like to thank Dr. James B. Becker, professor of philosophy at Principia College, who in 1945 was a "Deadeye" with the 96th Division, and Professor E. B. Potter, chairman of naval history at the U.S. Naval Academy, who served actively in the campaign as a naval officer.

Our editors, Marion S. Wyeth, Jr., and Norbert Slepyan of Harper & Row, have supplied expert assistance throughout in the preparation of this volume.

Finally, as was the case with their previous joint-authored book, *Corregidor: The Saga of a Fortress,* the authors owe more than can be said to Edith W. and Marilyn A. Belote, their wives, and to Mrs. Adelaide Belote, their mother, for constant encouragement, patience, and invaluable assistance in preparing drafts of the manuscript.

JAMES H. BELOTE
Elsah, Illinois

WILLIAM M. BELOTE
Annapolis, Maryland

PROLOGUE

AN HOUR AFTER sunup on October 10, 1944, a flight of twelve dark blue Hellcats wheeled like purposeful hawks over southern Okinawa. On finding no enemy planes in the air, the leader, Commander Fred Bakutis, United States Navy, abruptly tipped his powerful fighter into a seventy-degree dive, screaming from out of the sun at a covey of enemy planes sitting haplessly below on a warm-up apron on Naha airfield, propellers whirling. At a thousand feet Bakutis pressed the firing button on his control stick, coasting a stream of white tracers toward five stubby new Mitsubishi fighters the Japanese called "Raiden" (Thunderbolts) and the Americans "Jacks."

Yanking back on the stick as his six .50 caliber machine guns continued to flame, Bakutis slumped heavily in his seat from the force of gravity, his vision blurring as his body weight abruptly magnified several times. Looking back a moment later, he saw his squadron mates diving and their targets smoking; no Thunderbolts would rise from Naha airfield this day.

After circling further and seeing no more prey, Bakutis headed back toward his carrier, the veteran *Enterprise,* the only flattop in Task Force 38* that had been in commission when the Pacific War began. Behind him planes of Strike Able, making the first

---

* When Admiral Halsey was in command of the Task Force, it was designated Task Force 38. When Admiral Spruance was in command it was called Task Force 58.

Mitsubishi J2M Raiden (Thunderbolt) "Jack"

air raid on Okinawa of World War II, were diving, bombing, strafing, dropping torpedoes, laying waste to airfields at Naha, Kadena, Yomitan, and little Ie Shima Island, lashing at hapless small ships trapped at anchor off Naha Harbor, dueling with light antiaircraft guns tossing up red fireballs from below. Okinawa, an ancient island long accustomed to typhoons sweeping northeastward from the China Sea, was experiencing an ordeal its inhabitants later would call "the typhoon of steel."

The U.S. Navy had been a long time coming to this day, when with nominal aircraft losses it could attack an island that the Japanese had made a prefecture of metropolitan Japan. The surprise attack on Pearl Harbor of December 7, 1941, seemed decades rather than three years past. After destroying the U.S. Fleet Japan had intended to conquer an empire ranging from Manchuria in the north to New Guinea in the south. All had gone well at first. In four months Japan had seized the Philippines,

Borneo, Thailand, Malaya, Indonesia, Burma, and dozens of islands in the Central and South Pacific. Japan's Navy had sunk seven battleships—five at Pearl Harbor—an aircraft carrier, four heavy and three light cruisers, and scores of smaller ships while losing only a handful of destroyers and small craft.

The first faint bright spot for the United States was the Battle of the Coral Sea on May 5–7, 1942, which cost each side a carrier. Then, the following month, at the epochal Battle of Midway on June 4–6, the main fleets collided. Naval aviators from Admiral Chester W. Nimitz's fast carrier forces surprised and sank three, then a fourth, of Admiral Isoroku Yamamoto's large aircraft carriers with a loss of but one U.S. flattop, the *Yorktown*. For the first time the Japanese Navy had been stopped and stunned, and the fast carriers of the rival fleets now mustered an equal number of planes.

Though stopped in the Central Pacific, the Japanese still threatened the last American stronghold in the South Pacific— Australia. Using the troops, land-based planes, ships, and supplies now flowing to Australia, General Douglas MacArthur and Admiral Nimitz decided to forestall the menace to the "down-under" continent by seizing New Guinea's northeast coast and an island in the Solomons chain named Guadalcanal where the Japanese were completing an airfield.* Both campaigns were successful, with Guadalcanal's capture setting the pattern for a long road back for the United States, a succession of island-hopping operations moving ever east and north toward the Japanese main islands. The Gilbert Islands, the Marshall Islands, the Admiralty Islands, and the Marianas Islands fell to MacArthur's and Nimitz's forces in operations lasting into the midsummer of 1944.

With Saipan, Tinian, and Guam in the Marianas secured, lodgments in the south-central Philippines seemed essential in order to command the air over the archipelago, but the primary strategic goal was to secure a sizable land mass astride the focal point of Japan's southward sea communication line, the triangular area bounded by Luzon, Formosa, and the China coast. Because the Japanese had forestalled a China coast landing by

---

* For the full story of this campaign read *The Battle for Guadalcanal* by Samuel B. Griffith II, Brigadier General U.S.M.C. (Ret.). Another volume in The Bantam War Book Series.

driving Chiang Kai-shek's Nationalist Chinese army into the interior, either Luzon or Formosa—take your pick—became the strategic choice. Predictably General MacArthur, being anxious to fulfill his pledge to release the Filipinos from Japanese rule, favored Luzon. Admiral Ernest J. King, the Navy's chief of naval operations, believed Formosa to be the wiser choice. Staff officers serving the Joint Chiefs divided, some favoring the general and others the admiral, but President Roosevelt inclined toward Luzon as did Admiral Nimitz.

As the strategic deadlock continued, Generals George C. Marshall and Henry H. Arnold and Admirals William D. Leahy and Ernest J. King—the Joint Chiefs—settled all but the final Formosa-Luzon choice. They agreed that Nimitz would take Yap, Ulithi, and two of the Palau Islands, while MacArthur took Morotai Island and an airfield site on Mindanao in the southern Philippines. Both forces then would converge on Leyte Island in the central Philippines where the Japanese had only a single infantry division.

In early September Admiral William F. Halsey upset this sequence in a favorable manner. On discovering that Japanese air resistance to his carrier strikes in the Philippines was less strong than anticipated, he recommended that the Yap, Palau, and Morotai landings be dropped and the Leyte operation advanced a full two months. Radio exchanges between headquarters then advanced the Leyte landing from December to October, assigned Leyte to the force scheduled to invade Yap, but retained the Palau and Morotai landings. Morotai proved easy—defenders were not present in large numbers—but at Peleliu Island in the Palau group the 1st Marine Division had a tough, bloody fight in a foretaste of more to come. Angaur Island in the group fell easily and also furnished an airfield. Ulithi Atoll proved the most useful prize; its large protected anchorage served for the remainder of the war as the major advanced base for the fast carrier forces of the Pacific Fleet. Moreover, not a life was lost there, the atoll being undefended.

Their hand forced again, the Japanese acted out of desperation. On learning that MacArthur's forces had landed on Leyte on October 20, 1944, Admiral Soemu Toyoda, the Japanese naval commander, decided to use his powerful force of battleships to destroy MacArthur's transports. Taking into account Admiral Halsey's aggressive nature, Toyoda planned to have Admiral

Ozawa's carrier forces, though without planes, lure Halsey's Task Force 38 away from the Leyte beachhead. Then, he planned to slip battleship and cruiser forces under Vice Admirals Shoji Nishimura and Takeo Kurita into Leyte Gulf from around either end of Leyte Island.

Toyoda alerted his forces too late to catch the transports, and the southernmost wing of his surface forces—Nishimura's—was wiped out. But Admiral Ozawa successfully decoyed Halsey away, and Kurita's main force of Japanese battleships and cruisers, after losing the super-battleship *Musashi* to air attack, nearly reached Leyte Gulf to destroy thirty cargo ships of a supply convoy. A wild fight ensued between the Japanese ships and a force of American escort carriers that found themselves between the enemy and Leyte Gulf until Kurita, not realizing that his way to the gulf was open, turned away from the mauled jeep carriers and ended the Battle for Leyte Gulf. Japanese suicide planes (kamikazes) then made their first appearance in the war to bedevil the U.S. Navy, but on land MacArthur's soldiers won a bitter six-month campaign to subdue the island. With Leyte's conquest the Pacific War entered its final stages, and the United States military and naval leaders faced the decision of where to go next.

1
THE OPERATION BEGINS

SEVEN THOUSAND MILES from Leyte on the morning of September 29, 1944, Mr. Daniel E. London, the manager of the St. Francis Hotel in San Francisco, was standing at the Post Street entrance to the hotel's northeast wing. A chauffeured car pulled to the curb and from it stepped a tall, austere naval officer. Admiral Ernest J. King, Chief of Naval Operations, greeted London cordially and stepped briskly to the private elevator. Accompanied by London, King rode to the top floor suite of Mrs. George A. Pope, widow of the principal owner of the Pope and Talbot Steamship Company, who had lent it to the U.S. Navy for the war's duration. Here, and at the headquarters of the Western Sea Frontier in downtown San Francisco, strategic decisions about where next to carry the war to the enemy after the Leyte invasion scheduled for October 20 would be made.

I

As a member-representative of the Joint Chiefs of Staff, Admiral King had flown to San Francisco to meet with Admiral Nimitz for a final settlement of the lagging Pacific War strategy. Nimitz had brought with him two of his generals, Simon Bolivar Buckner, Jr., and Millard F. Harmon, commanding respectively ground and air force units of his Pacific Ocean Area command. From nearby Monterey had come Ray Spruance, the alternate commander to Bill Halsey of Nimitz's battle fleet, who had been enjoying some well-earned leave. Mrs. Spruance accompanied her husband.

The unspoken purpose of the conference was to sell Admiral King and consequently the Joint Chiefs of Staff on a strategy that Pacific Ocean Area Headquarters had devised to press the war. Given King's nature no one had expected this to be easy. President Roosevelt had once remarked that his naval chief was so tough that "he could chew spikes for breakfast." So far as Nimitz knew, King still was convinced that the next move in the war should be an invasion of Formosa. If Nimitz could persuade King to accept MacArthur's strategy of invading Luzon instead of Formosa everyone would be relieved.

The conferees gradually relaxed as the three days of deliberations got into full swing. Perhaps the luxurious surroundings of their hotel suites had something to do with it. Within the limits of its wartime rationing allowance, the St. Francis served excellent meals in an elegant surrounding of fine oak and mahogany paneling in King's prize suite. Here, and in the plain surroundings of the conference room at Sea Frontier headquarters, Nimitz tactfully presented his chief with a carefully drawn memorandum which demonstrated in precise terms backed by statistical evidence why an attack on Formosa was impossible in the near future. The Japanese had a field army on Formosa too strong to tackle until the war in Europe had ended. Insufficient combat and service troops were on hand in the Pacific and in the United States to support a Formosa invasion, a point stressed by Nimitz's two Army generals in their conversations with King.

There were other problems as well. Based on experience at Saipan, where Nimitz's forces had sustained 17,000 casualties in eliminating 32,000 dug-in Japanese, General Buckner estimated that losses on Formosa might run to 150,000 or more, a figure Pacific Ocean resources could not bear. On the other hand, MacArthur had estimated that he could take Luzon with the men he already had with moderate loss.

Nimitz had learned long ago that merely being a negative critic was not enough. He therefore offered a realistic alternative to the Formosa plan. Let MacArthur, he told King, proceed with his liberation of Luzon and the Philippine capital of Manila; the fast carriers could give the General a hand. Then, using only the combat and support troops already available to his Central

Pacific forces, he would pave the way for a direct invasion of Japan's home islands by seizing Okinawa and Iwo Jima. This would utterly cut Japan off from her oil supply sources in Borneo, Sumatra, and Burma, and without oil her fleet could not operate, her planes fly, her trucks move, or her industrial plants function. From Okinawa and Iwo Jima B-29's could intensify air attacks on Japanese targets. It might well turn out that Japan's leaders would surrender without the need for actually invading Japan.

King listened intently, examined Nimitz's supporting documents, and raised hard, incisive questions. As he told Nimitz at the outset, he had reviewed a logistics report by a committee of the Joint Chiefs that seriously questioned the feasibility of the Formosa invasion. But he challenged the idea of landing on Iwo Jima, seven hundred miles from Japan, and stated his desire to assist the Chinese by a landing at a future date on the China coast. Finally he turned on Spruance: "Haven't you something to say? I understand that Okinawa is your baby." Spruance had informed King three months earlier that he favored attacking Okinawa. But Spruance, never one to grab the limelight or to risk upsetting applecarts, merely rejoined that Nimitz had summarized matters so well that he had nothing to add.

In the end King graciously agreed to set aside Formosa for Luzon, Iwo Jima, and Okinawa. He may have been influenced most strongly by a final advantage to Nimitz's plan: it would not alter the politically sensitive command setup in the Pacific. It delayed the painful dilemma of choosing between Nimitz and MacArthur for the post of Supreme Allied Commander. Both could continue as coequals. As Central Pacific Commander Nimitz could handle the Iwo Jima and Okinawa operations; as Southwest Pacific Commander, MacArthur could deal with Leyte, Luzon, and the rest of the Philippines. Selection of a supreme commander could await the invasion of the Japanese mainland or an earlier surrender of Japan. Target dates for the landings (which the Joint Chiefs realized might be—and were—delayed) were: Luzon, December 20, 1944; Iwo Jima, January 20, 1945; Okinawa, March 1, 1945.

Though neither said so for the record, both King and Nimitz fervently hoped that an invasion of Japan with its frightful loss of American and Japanese life would not prove necessary; that with Okinawa in hand and with a position on the China coast the

3

Navy could blockade Japan into surrender. On this resolve the conference ended, and after bidding Mr. London good-bye and thanks, the conferees departed, King to Washington, D.C., to arrange a formal strategic directive from the Joint Chiefs, Nimitz and his generals to Pearl Harbor to begin planning the new operations.

As Admiral Spruance recalled years afterward, the decisions at San Francisco made such good strategic sense as to be "obvious." But what appeared obvious to him was not so in Tokyo. At the beginning of October the Japanese faced the same dilemma that had plagued them since Guadalcanal in 1942: how to muster their limited resources to protect every important island the Americans might attack. For them Okinawa was but one of many key positions that had to be defended.

II

Little more than a week after the close of the San Francisco conference, Admiral Halsey's Task Force 38 was speeding northwestward, blacked out, to fire the opening shots of the Okinawa operation. Daybreak the next morning revealed a grand spectacle, the task force spread out in four separate groups over a gray ocean flecked with whitecaps. Each group was a task force in itself, with a rear admiral in command, more powerful than the entire force that Admiral Nimitz had deployed to stop Yamamoto at Midway. The carriers formed the central feature of each group and were the object of its solicitude. In circular disposition battleships and cruisers steamed at the quarters of the boxlike carrier formation, which appeared from the air as four toy ships, each streaming a white froth thousands of yards rearward. An outer ring of destroyers, like a circle of busy ants, occasionally took white water over their bows as they performed their screening functions on the fringes of the formation.

On all ships air and surface search radars rotated interminably, feeding information to the nerve center of each ship, its Combat Information Center (CIC) in a darkened compartment below. Ship captains and task group commanders stood by on the navigation bridge of each vessel or in sea cabins immediately adjacent. Emergencies requiring decisions born of long experience could come at any time—and quickly. Hundreds of men stood watch throughout the task force. Lookouts from perches high on masts scanned sea and sky with binoculars, supplementing the electrical impulses of the radar and the sound pings of the sonar.

As the carriers penetrated deeper into the enemy's home waters, they began launching planes—antisubmarine and defensive fighter patrols. When a carrier turned into the wind, the plane guard destroyers closed on either flank to rescue airmen should a plane crash into the sea. The deck officer of each "can" watched carefully the deck angle of the carrier. The flattop might turn without warning to keep the wind dead on the bow; unless the deck officer spotted the angle changing, his destroyer might ram the carrier. This was exacting duty. Not every man plucked from the Navy's V-5 program at a college could do it.

Each carrier had a dual organization, its regular crew and its air group. The air group maintained and flew the planes, about eighty on a 27,000-ton *Essex* class ship, half that number on a small (13,000-ton) *Independence* class carrier converted from a cruiser hull. Air groups came and went as they were regularly rotated from combat for R and R (rest and recreation). The *Bunker Hill*'s Air Group 8 was overdue for rotation and leave.

With Vice Admiral Marc A. Mitscher in tactical command, T.F. 38 would strike with 17 carriers, 6 fast battleships, 14 cruisers, and 58 destroyers. Over a thousand planes—Grumman Hellcat fighters and fighter-bombers, Curtiss Helldiver dive bombers, Grumman Avenger torpedo planes—would overwhelm Japanese Army and Navy planes based on Okinawa's three operational airfields and on little Ie Shima off Okinawa's western shore. Facilities of all sorts would be blasted, and most important, photographic planes would take mosaic strip pictures of the island for study by Admiral Nimitz's staff officers assigned to plan the landing.

Before dawn on October 10, 1944, intelligence officers briefed the aircrews on Okinawa's defenses. Abroad the big carrier *Bunker Hill* the men whistled softly. Just a day or two before, an anonymous Avenger pilot had protested his departure on yet another round of strikes by chalking on the Ready Room blackboard the figure of a crying infant captioned, "My daddy flies for Halsey." Veterans though they were, the airmen's stomachs tightened when they heard the target. As the ship's history put it, "That was the Jap Empire, Bud!"

Grumman TBF Avenger

On all of the seventeen carriers other preparations were underway. Planes moved swiftly up elevators and were muscled into place in the growing packs aft on the teakwood decks. Below, armorers were loading bombs, belts of .50 caliber ammunition, 5-inch rockets, and 21-inch torpedoes.

By 5:30 A.M. all was ready. Plane guard destroyers had taken stations astern of the carriers. The first Hellcats taxied awkwardly to the bow catapults, wobbled like fat chickens into place, then darted abruptly down the decks into the sky. Behind, others roared from the desks to climb away unassisted. The mission of these 130 fighters, led by Commander Fred Bakutis, was to sweep the skies ahead of the fighter-bombers, dive bombers, and torpedo bombers of strikes Able, Baker, and Charlie that would follow.

Between daybreak and dusk of October 10 T.F. 38 flew 1,396 sorties, over a thousand of them aimed at Okinawa, dropping more than five hundred tons of bombs and firing hundreds of rockets. Ensign Ray Baldwin of the *Bunker Hill*'s combat-weary fliers scored the choice hit of the day. He placed a 500-pound bomb from his Hellcat squarely between a pair of midget submarines moored at Unten-ko, blasting one to pieces and sinking the other in a pool of oil and debris. Other pilots attacking Naha port sank the submarine tender *Jingei* and several smaller ships.

Ten "Tony" fighters (Kawasaki Ki. 61's) finally lifted from Yomitan airfield on Okinawa in midmorning, to be overwhelmed by the Hellcats of Strike Baker. Five fell and the rest escaped singly to make precarious landings on their bomb-cratered airfield.

The last strike of the day, an incendiary raid, set Naha afire. With 65,000 people, Naha was the largest town on the island. As he circled overhead afterward, noting that most of the city was burning, Commander Daniel F. ("Dog") Smith, the skipper of *Enterprise*'s Air Group 20, could find nothing profitable left for his squadrons to hit. After he returned T.F. 38 reversed course and steamed quickly southward for Formosa and more strikes.

Halsey could now be certain that Japanese planes could not operate against him from Okinawa until the cratered airfields had been repaired and replacement planes flown in. Task Force 38 had lost twenty-one planes, but many crews would be rescued, some by lifeguard submarine. When the final returns were in, just five pilots and four aircrew would be carried as missing in action. The most important results of the strike were the thousands of aerial photographs being processed aboard the *Enterprise* and the other carriers as the ships retired. Correlated with others taken by B-29's flying from China on September 29, they would enable Admiral Nimitz's map-makers in Hawaii to produce a reasonably accurate 1:25,000 scale map of Okinawa, complete with a military grid suitable for infantry and artillery use.

For the Japanese defenders the most serious consequence of the raid was their loss of shipping. A record kept by the 32nd Army's 62nd Division set down the loss of ten transports and thirty merchant ships, plus about half of the powered sailing and fishing boats on hand, and three-fourths of the small craft attached to the 32nd Army's Shipping Branch Office. In addition to the seaplane tender *Jingei*, an escort destroyer had been sunk, together with four midget submarines, two minesweepers, six patrol boats, and eight flak (antiaircraft) boats.

In Naha's warehouses 300,000 sacks of rice had burned—

enough to feed the defending 32nd Army for a month—plus over 5,000,000 rounds of rifle and machine gun ammunition, 10,000 rounds of small caliber artillery and mortar ammunition, and 400 rounds of 47 mm. antitank gun ammunition. One of the 62nd Division's generals was killed and another wounded. Other military personnel losses totaled about 200 and civilian deaths more than 500.

While this damage done by Halsey's fliers was by no means crippling to the 32nd Army, not even to the airfields, which were made serviceable in just a few hours, yet in the battle for Okinawa the lost supplies would be missed, especially the mortar and antitank gun ammunition. The ships lost could not be replaced. To Miyashita Kuraji, a soldier in a sea-raiding unit, the air attack was an ominous portent. He wrote afterward in his diary, "The enemy is brazenly planning to destroy completely every last ship, cut our supply lines, and attack us." This was exactly what Admiral Nimitz intended to do.

The tragedy of the raid was the loss suffered by the people "in the middle," the Okinawa civilians. Nothing in their experience had prepared them for this terrible day. Believing in their innocence the fanciful reports in their newspapers depicting the war as an unbroken succession of Nipponese victories, they had no reason to suppose that an attack was imminent. Yet their habit of fleeing to their tombs and caves to escape the fury of typhoons stood them in good stead. Fortunately, the Americans did not at first hit their villages and towns and most could escape. Typical was the experience of Miss Chiyoko Higa, seventeen years old and a second-year student in the Naha high school.

At daybreak and without warning, Chiyoko heard a bomb explode and felt the house shake. Outside the mournful wail of the air raid siren mingled with the terrified screams of the people of Naha. With her mother and twenty-five others, she fled to a cave outside the city, to listen fearfully all day to the sounds of antiaircraft guns, bursting bombs, and fires consuming the densely packed city. After dark she and her mother returned to their home, one of the few left standing, to gather their money and some clothes and to prepare for further flight. Carrying a little niece, the pair went first to a friend's house near Urasoe in the country, then to Nago in the northern part of the island. There they waited apprehensively for many long, cruel months for the typhoon of steel to abate.

2
PLANS AND RESOURCES

OKINAWA LIES at the midpoint of the Ryukyu or Nansei-shoto Islands, which form a broad, 750-mile-long arc between Japan's southernmost main island of Kyushu and Formosa (Taiwan). The capital, Naha, bisects the base leg of a triangle whose right and left points touch Kyushu and Formosa and whose upper tip touches the China coast below Shanghai. Altogether, the Rykyus comprise 140 islands in eleven groupings, but only the Okinawa group in the center, the Sakishima group in the south, and the Amami O Shima group in the north contain any considerable land area or population.

I

Anciently the Ryukyus were a dependency of China, paying an annual tribute to the Imperial Court at Peking. The name "Ryukyu" is the Japanese rendering of the Chinese "Liu-chi'u" or "Loo-choo," meaning by one interpretation, "pendant ball," and by another, "rope on the sea." Local kings followed Chinese customs and manners and promulgated Chinese language and learning. Although related to Japanese, the indigenous tongue has always been sufficiently distinct to stand as a separate language. Since Okinawan has no written form, writing was traditionally in Chinese; Japanese replaced it after Japan annexed the Ryukyus in 1879. Racially, Okinawans resemble Japanese,

9

but an influx of Malay, Chinese, Mongol, and other strains in ancient times has left them somewhat shorter and fuller of face than their northern neighbors. A special puzzle is the origin of an enclave of blue-eyed people dwelling in southern Okinawa.

Americans knew little about Okinawa until global war forced a better acquaintance. A colony of Okinawan emigrants dwelt in Hawaii, but those few Americans who had heard of the "Kingdom of the Great Loo-choo" associated Okinawa with the famous expedition commanded by Commodore Matthew Calbraith Perry which opened Japan to foreign intercourse. In the winter of 1853 Perry had anchored at Naha, had established a coaling station there, and had subsequently brought back to the United States with other gifts an ancient bronze bell which today hangs on the grounds of the U.S. Naval Academy.

After Perry's visit, occasional tidings of a particularly destructive Okinawan typhoon reached America, but little else. Being off the usual tourist routes the Ryukyus seldom were visited by outsiders, their poverty and lack of sightseeing attractions or amenities discouraging even inveterate travelers. Nor did the Japanese government after it took over encourage foreigners to come. Even American intelligence dossiers offered little more information than might be found in a good encyclopedia or gazetteer.

II

Although to the Japanese Okinawa was part of the homeland, being a regular prefecture, Tokyo's actual treatment kept the island little better than a colony and a neglected one at that. Despite having acquired the Ryukyus as a protective measure, Tokyo bureaucrats extended to the military sphere a policy of minimal support. As late as 1939 a small naval station at Naha and a Navy airfield just south of the city on the Oroku Peninsula were the sole defense installations. Army troops first came in 1941, and they consisted merely of an artillery outfit equipped with three batteries of 75 mm. and 120 mm. guns—in all about 600 men. These furnished a very skimpy protection for Nakagusuku Bay, a Japanese fleet anchorage on the eastern side of Okinawa. Had Admiral Nimitz's men invaded Okinawa during the winter of 1943-44, the island would have fallen easily. What made such a project unthinkable then, of course, was the still-powerful Japanese Navy and Air Force based in the nearby homeland.

Not until spring, 1944, did Imperial General Headquarters in Tokyo finally decide to arm the Ryukyus effectively by dispatching to Okinawa the 32nd Japanese Army, commanded initially by Lieutenant General Masao Watanabe. But even then Okinawa and its sister islands were regarded as useful chiefly as bases from which Army and Navy aircraft could support other Japanese forces defending the Marianas Islands and the Philippines. The airfields which construction battalions of the 32nd Army would build also would be handy for staging large numbers of aircraft southward to the Philippines, where the Americans were expected to attack. Base construction and guard duty, these were the tasks for General Watanabe to set for his men—so Tokyo viewed it.

On each of the three main Ryukyu islands, Amami O Shima in the north, Okinawa in the middle, and Miyako in the Sakishimas in the south, Imperial Headquarters proposed establishing a brigade—two regiments—of infantrymen plus a regiment of heavy artillerymen for coastal defense. To isolated Minami Dato Shima, an islet approximately two hundred miles east of Okinawa, which the Americans might covet as a forward air base, Tokyo planned to dispatch a regiment. Alerted for movement to Okinawa were the 44th Independent Mixed Brigade and the 7th Heavy Artillery Regiment.

Imperial General Headquarters did not hurry these troop shipments; neither did General Watanabe, now commanding the 32nd Army from Naha, grow impatient to receive them. In ailing health, he found it trying even to perform his routine duties. For Watanabe and his Tokyo superiors the various Ryukyu bases were strictly "rear areas." Men and equipment, therefore, sailed in leisurely fashion. The regiment assigned to the outpost, Minami Dato Shima, went promptly enough—the Americans might try a *coup de main*—but the Amami O Shima garrison did not depart Japan until May and the Okinawa units until June. But by then unexpected disaster had struck; Japan's main defense perimeter had been breached at Saipan in the Marianas. Okinawa would not be a "rear area" after all.

Especially in civilian and naval circles, perceptive Japanese now lost faith in eventual victory. Always a "dove," Japanese version, ex-Premier Prince Fumimaro Konoye later observed, "After Saipan it became even clearer to me that a successful termination of the war was impossible."

Japan's Army firebrands disagreed. Weak defenses in the homeland and in Japan proper* could be strengthened. Americans were predictable, methodical; no immediate rush at Okinawa or the main islands was at all likely. One could count on Yankee planners to wait until they had massed immensely superior forces and then to do the obvious. One must reinforce the most likely points of attack, confident that the "spiritual strength" of Nippon's soldiers—their willingness to perish in battle—somehow would prevail. But a leisurely building-up of Okinawa's defenses was out. Lying northwestward 1,120 nautical miles from Saipan, it was an obvious target.

On June 29, 1944, as the battle on Saipan neared its height and Japanese planners worked diligently to find additional men, guns, and munitions to hurry to the Ryukyus, U.S.S. *Sturgeon*, a veteran submarine that had prowled Japanese sea-lanes since Pearl Harbor, approached at periscope depth the convoy transporting the 44th Independent Mixed Brigade to Okinawa. *Sturgeon*'s skipper, Lieutenant Commander C. L. Murphy, Jr., counted off a large passenger-cargo vessel, five smaller ships, a dozen small craft—sea trucks and the like—and "ten or a dozen" antisubmarine trawlers. Singling out the largest ship as his target, the 6,000 ton *Toyama Maru*, which was carrying all 6,000 men of the 44th Brigade, he fed information into his torpedo data computer, and at 7:25 A.M. *Sturgeon*'s bow tubes spewed four Mark 14 torpedoes on a course converging 3,200 yards distant with the *Toyama Maru*'s expected track. Quickly Murphy began to swing his boat to bring the four Mark 18 electric torpedoes in his stern tubes to bear on a second target. But the wake and smoke from his Mark 14's did him ill. Spotting the torpedoes in the clear air and sea, a seaplane dived in, and two trawlers a thousand yards distant turned toward the submarine. Sweeping his periscope, Murphy spotted them: "Dive! Dive! Dive!"

---

*The terms "Japan proper" and the Japanese "homeland" need clarification. As used in planning and battle orders "Japan proper" referred to the main Japanese islands. The "homeland" included Japan proper, the Bonin Islands, Okinawa, Formosa, Central China, and Korea.

warned the klaxon, and the *Sturgeon* started deep, rigging for depth charges as she went.

Two minutes later, at 7:27 A.M., the ordered routine of the *Toyama Maru* was blown into chaos by the torpex warheads. All four hit, and all four exploded, tearing vast holes in the sides and bottom of the ship, converting her interior into a blazing shambles engulfed almost immediately by inrushing salt water. Sinking at once, the transport carried down with her 5,600 soldiers of the 44th Brigade; about 600 survivors clung to bits of wreckage and to life rafts as other vessels of the convoy, like a covey of partridges whose largest member had been shot, scurried to escape.

A bare minute after the torpedoes had hit, the first depth charges, flung from the Y-guns of the trawlers, lashed the seas about the *Sturgeon*. "For the next hour," recorded Commander Murphy in his patrol report, "escorts made deliberate, accurate runs on us, dropping about 70 ashcans which shook us up quite a bit." Yet damage to the submarine was minor, and Murphy skillfully worked his boat clear of the area after a daylong hunt and rescue operation by the escorts. Single-handedly, he and his crew had disrupted Okinawa's buildup of troops.

To replace this terrible loss, Imperial General Headquarters rounded up transport planes to rush the 15th Independent Infantry Regiment to Naha. If the Americans did the unexpected and attacked Okinawa directly, the 15th Regiment could furnish a semblance of a defense. By sea—this time without loss—Tokyo also hurried the 9th, 24th, and 62nd Infantry Divisions to Okinawa. To Miyako and Ishigaki islands with their favorable sites for airfields, headquarters dispatched the 28th Division plus three independent mixed brigades similar to the ill-fated 44th. Even the world's largest battleships, the superdreadnoughts *Yamato* and *Musashi*, were pressed into service as troop transports. By September of 1944 the Ryukyus were safe, at least for the time being.

It would have made little sense to have left the strengthened 32nd Army with an infirm commander in chief. Consequently, Tokyo ordered to Naha a picked man, Lieutenant General Mitsuru Ushijima, a senior member of its stable of general officers. To support him Imperial Headquarters assembled a young staff, junior in age and rank. Lieutenant General Isamu Cho became chief of staff. A brilliant planner, Colonel Hiromichi Yahara,

13

remained from the old staff as chief planning officer. Together, Ushijima, Cho, and Yahara were to comprise one of the most effective combat teams that the Japanese Army had ever assembled.

Erect, lean-featured, and composed, Ushijima exemplified the best in samurai virtues. Even without noticing his insignia of rank, one would have been aware of his exalted position in Japan's military hierarchy. His General Pershing-style moustache augmented his image as the reserved, austere senior officer. Like many generals, Japanese and other, Ushijima preferred to remain above the pull and haul of issues under consideration by his staff. He played the role of suzerain; the staff must present agreed decisions which he would ratify. Yet he took responsibility for everything done, good or bad. In return the staff revered him, thinking of him as a latter-day Takamori Saigo, one of the military heroes of the period of the Meiji Restoration.

Early in the war Mitsuru Ushijima had been an infantry unit commander in the successful campaign in Burma. At the time of his appointment to Okinawa he had been serving as Commandant of the Japanese Military Academy at Zama, outside Tokyo. For this disciplined, thoroughly experienced officer the Japanese Army was his home. He could be depended on to keep its Okinawa portion in excellent order.

Lieutenant General Isamu Cho, the chief of staff of the 32nd Army, enjoyed a reputation as a stormy petrel. Cho was the opposite of Ushijima in temperament. Deceptively scholarly-looking, with owlish glasses, he was stern of manner, burly of build, and explosive in disposition. He could be convivial off-duty, and unlike the relatively abstemious Ushijima, was a high liver. In his quarters, even late in the battle for Okinawa, could be found the best Scotch whisky, the prettiest of girls, the finest sake. His table exceeded by far the usual talent of a Japanese officer's mess. A stranger neither to war nor to staffwork, Cho could be expected to bully the youthful staff into maximum use of its talents.

In virtually any army except the Japanese, Cho's prewar conduct would have earned him dismissal and disgrace, or more probably a firing squad. In September, 1930, while still a captain, Cho had joined a secret clique of Army officers, the Sakura-kai (Cherry Society), whose members pledged them-selves to purge Japan of all decadent influences which, as they

14

saw it, were sapping ancient virtues. Anti-Western, antidemocratic, anticapitalist, the Cherry Society's hundred-odd members sought to establish a military dictatorship. The selection of the name was significant. To the Japanese, the cherry tree, with its splendid short-lived blossoms, symbolized the warrior—the samurai—ever ready at a moment's notice to yield up his life for his suzerain.

Eagerly courted by several leading generals, each of whom coveted the dictatorial mantle, the Cherry hotheads soon exerted an influence in excess either of their numbers or rank. As one of the society's policy makers and its leading strong-arm advocate, Isamu Cho became involved in two conspiracies.

In January, 1931, Cho joined other Cherry Society members in a plot to murder the prime minister and install a leading general as dictator. This plan fell through when the general they had selected refused at the last minute to cooperate, possibly because he expected to obtain the premiership later by legal means. A few months later, in October, the plotters tried again with Cho acting as the leading advocate of violence. This time the group planned to have some ultranationalists in planes bomb selected targets in Tokyo, including the prime minister's residence. In the confusion the premier would be killed and Emperor Hirohito coerced into naming a suitable general as premier. Cho was to be appointed head of the nation's metropolitan police.

In this notorious "Brocade Banner" plot, as the episode came to be known, Cho exuded zeal during the organization meetings held in the geisha houses in Tokyo's Koyobashi red-light district. According to one conspirator who later turned against the coup, Cho exclaimed that the plot must be made to succeed "... even if it is necessary to threaten the Emperor with a drawn dagger." This was pretty extreme talk even in ultranationalist circles and may have been one reason why the Kempei (the Japanese military police) quietly raided a geisha house on October 16, 1931, arresting the ringleaders and forestalling the coup.

Clearly enough—in Western eyes—Cho had committed high treason and merited at the least imprisonment. But he was not even punished. Instead, the Army leadership appeased him with a congenial assignment to the Kwantung Army, then engaged in wresting Manchuria from China. By this period in Japan's prewar history, even moderate Japanese hesitated to condemn persons who loudly proclaimed themselves to be high-minded patriots. Cho appears to have been more approved than reproved for his conduct.

Although Cho's type of revolutionary ardor became obsolete as military rule became a fact in Japan, he remained a firebrand. In mid-1938 he almost precipitated a war with the Soviet Union by joining another officer in attacking without orders a Russian force just over the Manchurian border. In 1941, while chief of staff of the Japanese Army that had seized Thailand, he appears to have been instrumental in encouraging hostilities between Thai and Vichy French troops along the southern Indochina border.

In 1945, despite his unstable background, he was selected over many other senior generals for assignment to the 32nd Army. The High Command probably hoped he would bring to the Army the same zeal and abandon he had so often exhibited before. If ardor could offset superior American firepower and save Okinawa, then Isamu Cho could be expected to supply it.

More specifically important to Japanese 32nd Army fortunes on Okinawa than Ushijima, its patron and leader, or Cho, its dynamic second-in-command, was Colonel Hiromichi Yahara. It was he who established the 32nd Army's troop dispositions as its Chief Planning Officer. Considerably younger than Cho or Ushijima, Yahara had accumulated at forty-two years of age an impressive variety of professional experience. Graduating in the Japanese Military Academy's Class of 1923, Yahara had been posted to an infantry regiment, had attended the Japanese War College, had spent ten months at Fort Moultrie in the United States as an exchange officer, and had served as a staff officer in successful campaigns in China, Thailand, Malaya, and Burma.

Tall for a Japanese, alert-appearing, poised, Yahara truly looked the intellectual. Distinctly more Western in outlook than the traditionally minded Ushijima, he was almost the antithesis of Isamu Cho. Where Cho was impulsive, Yahara was deliberate; where Cho was almost mystically aggressive in the samurai manner, Yahara was almost maddeningly rational. To him war was primarily a science, only secondarily an exercise of will and abandon in the attack.

Perhaps because of this intellectualism, perhaps because of his habitual aloofness, perhaps also because he caused others to be aware of his superior acumen as a tactician, Hiromichi Yahara

16

remained less popular than others of the 32nd Army staff. But neither friend nor enemy doubted his capacity; "an excellent staff officer," was the assessment of former 32nd Army colleague, Colonel Tusneo Shimura. To the combination of the charismatic leader, Ushijima, and the fiery second-in-command, Cho, the deliberate Yahara added the necessary ingredient of rational sensibility that would complement perfectly the qualities of his two older colleagues.

This blending of personal characteristics was more than an interesting coincidence. It made the 32nd Army's leadership extremely effective, perhaps the best of any Japanese garrison in the Pacific theater of war. It insured that neither excessive zeal nor excessive caution would govern the Army's operations nor its disposal of troops to meet the forthcoming American attack.

III

As chief planning officer of the Japanese 32nd Army, Colonel Yahara had to devise—if he could—some way to prevent the United States forces from conquering Okinawa. He knew that the Americans needed its airfields, its harbors and anchorages, and its space for acres of tent cities, ration dumps, motor pools, and training and maneuver areas to mount a successful invasion of Japan.

In studying a detailed map of the island, Yahara noted that almost everything the enemy needed lay in Okinawa's southern one-third. Here was Naha, the only sizable port, and Nakagusuku Bay, with its expanse of sheltered waters. Here were Kadena and Yomitan, the two best airfields, and enough reasonably level ground for massive base installations. Above the narrow waist of Okinawa at the Ishikawa Isthmus, the island broadened into mountains and valleys too steep and precipitous to be very useful. The Americans would want Ie Shima Island lying just off the Motobu Peninsula, where the 32nd Army had two airstrips under construction, but that was all.

If Yahara positioned the 32nd Army in the rugged northern wilderness, he might insure its survival for some months. But this strategy would avail little if the Americans overran the lower third of the island and then wove a belt of barbed wire and minefields across the two-mile-wide Ishikawa Isthmus. General

Ushijima would find himself in a snare of his own devising. Strong resistance below Ishikawa, on the other hand, would deny to the enemy ground he needed and might delay American preparations to invade Japan.

Where would the Americans land? Probably across the beaches north and south of the village of Hagushi, Yahara concluded. Not only were these the best and most extensive on Okinawa, but the lay just a rifle-shot from Kadena and Yomitan airfields. The Americans might land on the second-best beaches, near Minatoga below the Chinen Peninsula, but high bluffs overlooked these and they were distant from terrain suited to airfield development.

Having decided that the Army must defend the south from attack probably across the Hagushi beaches, Yahara next had to consider how to do it. If he obeyed the instincts of the samurai, he would build strong delaying points at Hagushi at the water's edge and then fling a reckless night counterattack from dug-in positions inland after the enemy had landed. But these tactics had failed repeatedly; always superior American firepower had shattered beach defenses and littered the ground with defenders when they began the fierce "banzai" charge. As drafted by Colonel Yahara one of the first directives of the 32nd Army read: "Hand-to-hand combat with an enemy with superior firepower would be unsuccessful, especially at night." Yahara rejected defense on the beach and the banzai.

Yahara knew that many 32nd Army officers would bitterly contest his determination to avoid counterattacks, most notably Isamu Cho, the firebrand chief of staff, but Yahara's rationality and his understanding of the destructiveness of modern weapons overruled his sentiments and dictated his conclusions.

What the 32nd Army should do, Yahara decided, was to conduct a purely static defense from high ground. With three full divisions and the 44th Brigade, rebuilt after its fiasco at sea, the Army had barely enough troops to man an unbroken perimeter about the south of the island, encompassing a zone between Machinato and Ouki in the north to Mabuni at the southern tip. The perimeter would not compass a hollow shell; rather it would form the outer ring of a defense in depth extending in concentric rings to a central headquarters located under ancient Shuri Castle.

The castle lay on high ground overlooking Naha, and from its thick stone walls the regent of the Great Loo-choo, to whom Commodore Perry had been borne with calculated pomp, had surveyed his kingdom. Beneath the castle an ancient cave system could be extended to provide a completely safe bomb- and shell-proof headquarters for General Ushijima and his staff. Heavy guns emplaced nearby could shell any part of southern Okinawa. As the Americans, with heavy loss, gradually penetrated the outer perimeter of the Shuri defenses, the Japanese troops could retire toward the center. So long as Shuri Castle held, American shipping could not use Naha, and Okinawa could not become an "England" for invading Japan.

Okinawa's soft coral and limestone rock facilitated Yahara's plan. Men could grub it out with pick and shovel. In many places Japanese soldiers and Okinawan levies could enlarge natural caves into shelters for hundreds of men. The 32nd Army must dig so deep underground, Yahara's orders stressed, that even the 16-inch shells of enemy battleships could not reach it. Moreover, it must fight from underground, emerging as infrequently as possible. Only thus could American firepower be nullified.

Certain weak places in the Shuri defense ring worried Yahara. The Chinen Peninsula, jutting from the east side of the island, was vulnerable. If the Americans seized it, then they could advance up the natural corridor leading from Yonabaru to the back side of Shuri and Naha. Ie Shima was a worry, too. The airstrips of this small offshore isle were a great prize and would enable the Americans to install radar and fighter planes to counter air attacks from Kyushu. About all the colonel could do was to dispatch a battalion to hold Ie Shima and another to the nearby Motobu Peninsula, order the defenders to dig in, and hope that the enemy would bungle his attack.

Yahara could think of no certain way to keep the enemy from Yomitan and Kadena airfields. Finally, he resorted to stationing one of his four major combat units a short way inland from the airstrips, in rugged and hilly ground from which the strips could be kept under fire with mortars and light artillery. This left Yahara too few combat troops to cover the Chinen Peninsula as thoroughly as desired, but he had no other choice.

Well did Yahara understand that his strategy was defeatist. He knew the Americans ultimately must take Okinawa and that to a man the 32nd Army must perish. His strategy was intended to make the enemy pay dearly for every foot of soil and coral rock.

IV

At about the time Yahara was completing his plan for Okinawa's defense, American planning for the attack was beginning. On October 3, 1944—Admiral King having returned from the conference at San Francisco—the Joint Chiefs of Staff issued a directive sketching the guidelines for future operations. General MacArthur would capture Luzon, beginning on December 20, 1944; then Admiral Nimitz would land first on Iwo Jima on January 20, 1945, and next on a Ryukyu island on March 1, 1945. The invasion dates were tentative, subject to delay if the usual shipping shortage so dictated.

A few days later Rear Admiral Forrest Sherman, Chief-of-Staff to Admiral Nimitz, began planning the Okinawa attack, codenamed "Operation ICEBERG." Already, lead time for ordering specialized equipment and arranging shipping schedules was terribly short. Material ordered from the United States would take two months to assemble at the Seattle port of embarkation; from there it would go by ship either to Hawaii or directly to Okinawa. Planners would have to order some items before their troop lists were complete. Fortunately, amphibious attacks had by now become almost routine.

Within a week Admiral Sherman had obtained Admiral Nimitz's signature to a directive appointing ICEBERG's commanders, and two weeks later, on October 24, 1944, to a sketch of the procedures to be followed during the assault.

The American chain of command was reasonably simple. Admiral Raymond A. Spruance was named officer-in-charge of ICEBERG. As commander of the Fifth Fleet, with its Task Force 58, his main duty would be to protect the invasion forces and insure their safety before and after arrival. He would review all activity and stand by to make major tactical decisions. Ray Spruance was a happy choice. By nature one of the least excitable officers in the Navy, he had stepped in at short notice to win over a superior Japanese carrier force at Midway in June, 1942. Not once since then had he faltered or lost his calm demeanor. Perhaps, as he maintains, he succeeded because "I picked good subordinates and let them do their jobs," but this slender native of Indiana possessed Hoosier good sense and a confidence that was infectious.

In direct command of the amphibious forces was a rugged and colorful sailor, Vice Admiral Richmond Kelly Turner, who was rumored to possess a mind so retentive that he could memorize an operations plan two inches thick. As an instructor at the Naval War College, he often would read two dozen student officers' papers of an evening, and then discuss each the next morning without further reference and with unerring eye for deficiencies. Turner had controlled virtually every major amphibious landing in the Pacific, starting with Guadalcanal in 1942. He was a difficult personality, but he could get things done, and no one in the world knew more about amphibious operations.

The third of Nimitz's trio of top commanders, Kentucky-bred Lieutenant General Simon Bolivar Buckner, Jr., son of the Confederate hero of the defense of Fort Donnelson during the American Civil War, would lead the troops of the 10th Army assigned to the attack. This ruddy, strikingly handsome, white-haired officer had amassed a lifetime of service experience. He had served in the Philippines during World War I, had been Commandant at West Point—where he had led grumbling cadets on thirty-five-mile marches—and had served in Alaska and Hawaii during World War II. Okinawa was his first chance to lead an army in combat. Somewhat like Turner in personality, he was burly and forceful, but always attentive to his staff. He was not prone to hasty decisions, but on occasion would overrule subordinates without comment or discussion.

Here, then, was the American combat leadership, the challengers to Ushijima, Cho, and Yahara, a team as able—but perhaps no more so—than the trio of Japanese.

On receipt of the go-ahead from Admiral Nimitz, General Buckner's planners set to work at Schofield Barracks on Oahu preparing the land phases of the attack. Because time was pressing, they borrowed as many details as they could from the now-discarded plan to invade Formosa.

After carefully examining aerial photographs of all of Okinawa's possible landing beaches, they came to the same conclusions as had Colonel Yahara: the best beaches were at Hagushi. Over them the Americans could land four divisions abreast to seize a beachhead that would include the Yomitan and Kadena airfields. This proposal was named "Plan Fox."

Because bad weather or other unforeseen circumstances might render "Plan Fox" impossible, the planners drafted an alternative which they named "Plan Baker." Again they seconded Yahara's judgment. This scheme would have utilized the eastern beaches at Minatoga and Nakagusuku Bay. However, the distances of these beaches from the airfields, plus the existence of commanding heights just inland from which defenders could riddle the assault companies with gunfire, gave Buckner good reasons for preferring Plan Fox.

Once the troops had landed, Buckner planned to have them cut across the island, thus splitting the Japanese force in two. Then the troops would overrun the south, including Naha and Shuri, and afterward conquer the sparsely inhabited north and the islet of Ie Shima. Anticipating correctly the general nature of Yahara's dispositions—which aerial photographs had not detected—Buckner's planners guessed that only southern Okinawa would be heavily defended. Regardless of what happened, first priority would go to seizing the Yomitan and Kadena airfields. These were needed so that shore-based fighters could quickly assume a share of the air defense from the carriers.

On November 1, 1944, planning reached the brutal stage. In a classic confrontation the planners of Buckner and Turner, with both commanders present, squared off across a table at Turner's headquarters. The old curmudgeon, gruff Kelly Turner, started the fireworks. He didn't like Plan Fox, he said; he preferred the alternate Plan Baker. The waters off the Hagushi beaches would give him too little room to maneuver his many hundreds of ships, thus inviting heavy losses from enemy mines and submarines. Furthermore, on March 1, the projected landing date, stiff northeast winds probably would kick up a surf too high to beach landing craft. Finally, regardless of whether the Hagushi or other beaches were chosen, he wanted a quiet haven in some small outlying islands where his warships could replenish ammunition in advance of the landing. A day's bombardment would nearly empty their magazines, and Okinawa would require several days of preliminary shelling.

Turner's blunt challenge disconcerted Buckner's planners, but they refused to surrender Plan Fox without a good fight. Retiring in good order to Schofield Barracks, Buckner's supply officers, after some highly sophisticated calculations, concluded that the Hagushi beaches were the only ones in southern Okinawa

"... adequate to take an assault force of four divisions abreast and handle sufficient tonnage of supplies to sustain the operation." Formally, they reiterated to Turner previous arguments favoring the Hagushi beaches: good firm coral, adequate beach exits, gently sloping terrain inland for supply dumps, proximity to the airfields. Informally, they sent Turner their special logistical study, thereby avoiding antagonizing him with another direct confrontation.

Though blunt, Turner was also completely honest intellectually. Immediately he accepted Plan Fox, but in an annex to the basic document, which he dispatched to Buckner, he appended a scheme to capture the Kerama Islands, twelve miles west of Naha, a few days prior to the main landing at Hagushi. Among the Keramas his ships could find the safe anchorage he was sure they would need. Turner knew from Admiral Nimitz's intelligence bulletins that the Keramas were lightly defended, and he believed that a division or less of troops could easily seize them.

As both Turner and Buckner probably had anticipated, the prospect of surf on the Hagushi beaches dissipated of itself. Shipping schedules already had become too tight to permit an L day* on March 1. With Admiral Nimitz's concurrence the landing was postponed first to March 15 and, in early December, to April 1, 1945. This second delay made it reasonably certain that the surf on the Hagushi beaches would be moderate. As the seasons advance on Okinawa the prevailing winds shift clockwise from southward, to northward, to eastward. Thus L day on April 1 should find the Hagushi beaches on the lee shore of Okinawa. A storm might generate a nasty surf, but normal weather would give boat coxswains no trouble.

As finally completed on January 6, 1945, Operation ICE-BERG was satisfactory compromise. Buckner had his beaches, Turner the Keramas for his advanced naval base. Delaying the optimistic target date had taken care of the unfavorable March winds. Only the usual bugbear, logistics, remained troublesome. Admiral Nimitz did not have enough service troops in his command —especially construction engineers and Seabees—even to sup-

---

*After D day in France all other amphibious operations received some other designator. Since the letter L in radio communications jargon was rendered "Love," L day on Okinawa was commonly referred to as "Love Day."

port fully the combat divisions. Ultimately, unit transfers from other areas would make good about seventy percent of the shortage, insuring that the soldiers and marines would receive their K rations and bullets, but work on roads, airfields, and supply bases would be seriously delayed.

The Okinawa landing would exceed in size anything hitherto attempted in the Pacific. Four divisions, two Army and two Marine, would land eight regiments abreast from waves of beaching craft extending nearly ten miles along the Hagushi beaches. Another division would already have seized the Kerama Retto. A Marine division would fake a landing off the Minatoga beaches as a deceptive measure, and another Army division would stand by aboard ships as a reserve. In the South Pacific a fifth Army division would be on alert for movement to Okinawa if needed.

Altogether, 182,821 troops and 746,850 measurement tons of cargo in 433 assault ships would stage from eleven ports reaching across the entire Pacific from Seattle to Leyte. Resupply echelons would bring 87,000 additional troops and thousands more tons of cargo. Combat vessels of all types would add hundreds of ships and tens of thousands of men to those present off Okinawa on L day.

Even as Kelly Turner's and "Buck" Buckner's planners prepared for their confrontation later in the day at Amphibious Force Headquarters on November 1, 1944, a message flashed from the radio towers serving Imperial General Headquarters in Tokyo. Addressed to General Ushijima it asked: Would the 32nd Army agree to release the 9th Division on Okinawa for dispatch to Formosa and thence to the Philippines? A dismayed Ushijima passed the message to Colonel Yahara for immediate reply. Loss of the 9th Division from the 32nd Army would take away more than a quarter of its combat strength.

Into the response Yahara poured his heart as well as his intellectual prowess and cogent logic. If a division were removed from Okinawa, he emphasized, then the 32nd Army could not be responsible for its effective defense. It would be better to remove the 28th Division from Miyako Island than the 9th from Okinawa.

But if it were the irrevocable decision of the Imperial General Staff to "stake the destiny of Japan on a decisive battle in the Philippines," then General Ushijima and the 32nd Army would prefer to accompany the 9th Division to the Philippines and die in battle.

Tokyo remained unmoved. To recall an expression then current among American GI's, for Japan "things were tough all over." Many places besides Okinawa desperately needed troops. Tokyo wanted the battle-experienced 9th Division for the Philippines and early in December the unit sailed. It was not replaced; subsequent appeals by Ushijima and Yahara for another division proved unavailing. At one point Imperial Headquarters seemed ready to dispatch the 84th Division from Kyushu, but at the last moment Lieutenant General Suichi Miyazaki of the Japanese Army's operations section abruptly canceled the order. He had good reason. To defend all of Japan he had only ten divisions and three independent mixed brigades. Plans were being drafted to expand this home defense force to forty-eight divisions and twenty-seven brigades by fall, 1945, but in the meantime Japan proper was almost as vulnerable as Okinawa.

Later, other staff officers in Tokyo arranged to send an infantry regiment to Okinawa from Formosa as a preliminary to further reinforcements from Japan. This unit finally embarked at Keelung for movement to Okinawa on March 20 and then turned back when it became apparent that the American invasion was underway and that it could not proceed safely. The only troops Ushijima received after the departure of the 9th Division consisted of two battalions of construction engineers sent in mid-December.

Without fanfare and swallowing their disappointment, Ushijima and Yahara quietly began forming several thousand engineer construction troops as combat infantry, organizing them into nine infantry battalions. Most were then attached to the 62nd and 24th Divisions and to the 44th Independent Mixed Brigade. These men had been digging cave installations for some hundreds of suicide motorboats (*renrakutei*) in the Keramas and on Okinawa. These were an Army craft designed to sink American ships by releasing close aboard two 264-pound depth charges. At Ushijima's order the engineers turned over their tools to Okinawan levies, formed as infantry, and began intensive training for combat. Thus did Ushijima obtain the equivalent of approximately another brigade of good troops.

Radar Picket 15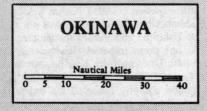

⊙Radar Picket 16A

OKINAWA

Nautical Miles

0 5 10   20   30   40

AGUNI   Radar Picket 13 ⊙

N

W —— E

⊙Radar Picket 11

S

TONAKI

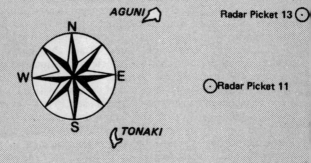

KERAMA RETTO
Zamami
Yakabi   Amuro
Aka   Kaise
Kuba   Tokashiki
Geruma
Hokaji

To Colonel Yahara the 9th Division's withdrawal and Tokyo's refusal to replace it meant just one thing: defense by regular troops of the Kadena and Yomitan airfields would have to be abandoned. In this area the 44th Brigade had been stationed; now, Yahara proposed to withdraw it to the lightly covered Chinen Peninsula. Responsibility for defending the airfields would pass to airfield service troops stationed in the area, reinforced by levies of Okinawan reservists and conscripts (*boetai*) already being mustered by the 32nd Army in considerable numbers.

This proposal, made about January, produced heated debate in staff meetings all the way to Tokyo. Many officers opposed the decision, arguing the folly of allowing the airfields to fall without a good fight. Yahara countered with the dubious contention that the Army's long-range artillery could shell the fields and prevent American planes from flying. Moreover, he argued, expending the 44th Brigade in defense of the airfields would check the Americans only for a day or two. Yahara had his way, and in mid-February the 44th withdrew from the airfield area to the Chinen Peninsula. On landing the American troops would encounter about the airfields only the hastily organized "1st Specially Established Regiment," a body of ill-trained airfield service troops and Okinawans.

Once battle had been joined Ushijima and Yahara intended to employ every man in the 32nd Army as a combat soldier. They meant also to use every able-bodied Okinawan male between the ages of seventeen and forty-five. Beginning in the fall Okinawans who previously had served in the Japanese Army and who were on reserve status were recalled to duty; also called up were Okinawan youths reaching military age. These individuals were assigned to regular combat battalions, given on-the-job training, and accounted as regular troops.

Beginning in January and accelerating as invasion drew near, Ushijima conscripted additional levies of Okinawans. After American forces landed all Okinawan males to about forty-five years of age, regardless of physical condition or prior service, were ordered inducted, bringing the total recruited to about 25,000. Many were assigned to cave-digging, to hauling rations to the front on their backs, and to other menial tasks. These conscripts received little or no military indoctrination.

Adding Okinawan conscripts pushed the 32nd Army's total personnel strength to more than double early American intelligence estimates. In regular troops Ushijima had close to 80,000 men; adding 25,000 Okinawans brought his army to over 100,000. By utilizing to the maximum the Okinawans and all other manpower resources available, Ushijima had wrung out the last possible ounce of combat strength.

VI

The successive disasters that befell the Japanese in the Philippines in the fall of 1944 had produced a mood of black despair at Imperial Headquarters. Almost the only glimmer of hope that Tokyo could detect had been the success during the Leyte campaign of a handful of young Navy pilots organized by Vice Admiral Takijiro Ohnishi to dive their planes and themselves into American warships. This "sure-hit, sure-death" tactic appealed powerfully to the Japanese temperament and recalled the kamikaze, the "divine wind," that had saved Japan two centuries before by scattering a pair of invasion fleets. Imperial Headquarters officers yearned—were almost impelled—to believe that the kamikazes were scoring almost one-hundred-percent hits. Silence in the usually verbose American press on the subject furnished negative evidence that the enemy was being badly hurt.

Viewed in light of the presumed success of the kamikazes, which had indeed been scoring heavily in December and January in the Philippines, the prospects for a successful defense of Okinawa suddenly grew much brighter. Headquarters was by this time convinced that the Americans would invade either Formosa or Okinawa, and if they could be defeated off Okinawa, then Japan might be spared invasion. Navy leaders in particular argued forcefully that the kamikazes offered the only hope for success, though most agreed that volunteers should perform the service. More reserved Army leaders admitted that the kamikazes were worth a try.

At a series of conferences in January and early February, 1945, Imperial Headquarters hammered out a new strategy. Utilizing its last manpower resources, military-age men who had been deferred for essential labor, the Japanese Army would raise new armies to defend Japan proper. When the Americans invaded Okinawa, powerful air attacks launched from Kyushu and featuring *tekko* (kamikaze) units would destroy the invasion force and its naval escort.

Called TEN-Go (TEN or "Heavenly" Operation) this all-out attack would feature more than four thousand planes, conventional and suicide, hundreds of suicide motorboats operating from Okinawa and the Kerama Islands, and a suicide dash by all of the remaining operational warships of the Navy. The readiness date for TEN-Go was set for April 1, the date Imperial Headquarters estimated the American invasion of Okinawa would begin.

By far the strongest element would be the air attacks, for which 4,085 planes were to be assembled. A two-pronged air strike would be launched, the southernmost from Formosa by the Japanese Army's 8th Air Division and the Navy's 1st Air Fleet, the northernmost and more powerful from Kyushu by an amalgamation of several Army and Navy air commands directed by the Navy's 5th Air Fleet. In overall command of the Kyushu wing of the attack would be a veteran Navy airman, Vice Admiral Matome Ugaki.

A joint Army Navy Air Agreement promulgated on February 6 stated the precepts to be followed in executing TEN-Go:

In general Japanese air strength will be conserved until an enemy landing is actually underway or within the defense sphere. The Allied invasion force will then be destroyed, principally by Special Attack [kamikaze] units.... Primary emphasis will be laid on the speedy activation, training, and mass employment of the air Special Attack units.... The main target of Army aircraft will be enemy transports, and of Navy aircraft, carrier attack forces.

These bold guidelines plastered over a basic divergence of outlook at Imperial General Headquarters between Army and Navy staff officers, though none disputed the goals to be attained. Shaken by MacArthur's quick advance through the Philippines, many officers of both services no longer expected that the war could be won. They believed, however, that to inflict severe defeat somewhere on the Americans would modify the Allied demand for unconditional surrender. Japan might be punished severely in a negotiated peace, but national and martial honor might be preserved. For the Navy staff officers TEN-Go offered the last chance to score a major victory. For Army staff officers

TEN-Go would be penultimate; the final showdown would come in Japan proper, probably on Kyushu.

Both services based their reasoning on prior experience. If Japan's airmen could not defeat invading forces off Okinawa, neither could they check them off Kyushu—so the sailors reasoned. For the soldiers the issue was less clear-cut. Even in the Philippines the Americans had not yet fought a really large Japanese field army. On Kyushu they would meet one, and the Army believed that the Yankee, bled first by the kamikazes, might then be repulsed in conventional warfare.

The consequences of this discrepancy of views were important. The Navy's leadership was anxious to muster every ship and every plane to support TEN-Go. The Army's staff chose to withhold reserves of planes and men for the battle for Japan proper. Already it had written off Okinawa.

When Isamu Cho, General Ushijima's chief of staff, arrived in Tokyo for a review of the 32nd Army's defensive positions in mid-January, 1945, he learned of the presumed effectiveness of the kamikazes and was quite taken with their potentialities. Okinawa's role, he was told, would be to lure and hold the American invader within range of the suiciders, airborne and seaborne. If these could score heavily against the enemy fleet and transports, isolating the American ground troops, then the 32nd Army could take the offensive and smash the invasion. Cho returned to Okinawa thirsting for action.

Heartened by the report of his dynamic chief of staff, Ushijima summarized his preparations in three terse fighting slogans published for his troops on February 15, 1945:

> *One plane for every warship.*
> *One [suicide] boat for one ship.*
> *One man for ten of the enemy or one tank.*

3

SOFTENING UP

THE "SOFTENING UP" began on February 16, 1945. Hundreds of Navy and Marine fliers from Task Force 58 blasted aircraft factories and strafed grounded enemy planes on dozens of airfields in the Tokyo area. The next day they struck again, after which they withdrew to their carriers to fly support for three Marine divisions assigned to capture Iwo Jima. After several days near Iwo and another swipe at Tokyo, they would sail west on March 1 to lash the Ryukyus, Okinawa included, to destroy more planes and obtain last-minute aerial photographs demanded by the ICEBERG planners.

I

On February 16 the residents of Tokyo's suburbs had hurried as usual about their business. The 20th Air Force's B-29's concerned them more than did the carrier fighters. The next edition of the *Nippon Times*, Tokyo's English-language newspaper, still printed for propaganda reasons, announced the carrier attack in a front-page header but confined its story to the Imperial General Headquarters communiqué which ended vaguely with, "Our anti-air raid forces obtained considerable results."

The mood of the civilians was as ambiguous as the communiqué. Their beautiful city had not yet been burnt in the terrible fire raids the B-29's would levy in March. Vaguely aware that the

B-29

war was going less well than desired, they were obedient to, but confused by, demands from their leaders for still more sacrifice and effort. Daily, they carried on their routines, trying to cope with increasing shortages even of necessities.

The classified advertising columns of the *Nippon Times* on this February 16 revealed Japan's condition most starkly. Said one ad, "Some pairs of used shoes and six sox, also tennis balls and tennis shoes—apply Box 400." Another, "Cellotex, about 30 sheets...What offers?" A third, "Wanted, *The American Woman's Cook Book,* by Ruth Berolsheimer, copyrighted 1940. Will pay any price or exchange for food." The next day the cookbook was still wanted and the Cellotex unsold, but the clothing had been taken. First things first in the Japan of February, 1945.

Seven thousand miles from Tokyo in Seattle, cranes lowered laden cargo nets into the holds of gray, rust-streaked cargo ships. Although the goods would not arrive on Okinawa until after the troops had landed, Operation ICEBERG was well underway on Seattle's waterfront.

Tokyo's desperate shortages were not matched in Seattle. Without a ration card one could still buy "Ten pounds of spuds, No. 1 Yakima Gems," for 48 cents at the Pike Street Market. Suits—without cuffs, of course, to save materials—were plentiful in the stores, though expensive by prewar standards. Automobiles were another matter; used cars were scarce and new ones had not been made since 1942. "Don't give your car away," pleaded Stratton Motors at 907 East Pike, "See us first!"

On Okinawa on February 16 General Ushijima's 32nd Army combined a mood of bitterness with a grim resolve. The day before some units had received more ammunition, inducing a private of an infantry battalion to exult in his diary, "The feeling that we will crush the enemy is running high!" Earlier, Private Kuraji Miyashita had recorded, "The situation is urgent and we must work more rapidly." Captain Tsuneo Shimura, the commander of a 24th Division infantry battalion, had found it unnecessary to urge his men to dig in above the Minatogoa beaches. Many of them, he recalls, had been missing roll calls because they refused to stop working in the battalion's caves. "They could feel through their skins," comments Shimura, "that an attack was coming, and in digging the caves they felt as if they were digging holes for their corpses."

The attitude of the Okinawans on this February 16 differed substantially from that of Ushijima's metropolitan Japanese soldiers. The Okinawans' primary loyalty was to their households, including the ancestors in the family tombs, their chief desire to survive and carry on as before. Few were ready to perish for a distant emperor who had commanded all of his subjects to fight to the death, although the Okinawans would neither welcome an invader nor refuse to defend their ancient land. Without their willing hands the 32nd Army could not have completed the defense ring about Shuri.

By mid-February both Okinawan civilians and Japanese soldiers had come to expect and to dread attack by American aircraft. After flying two small photo missions in early January, the fast carriers had launched a very heavy strike on January 22, moving one private to write indignantly, "Grumman, Boeing, and North American planes come over continuously, one after another. . . . What the hell kind of bastards are they? Bomb from 6:00 A.M. to 4:00 P.M.!" Then he added, "I have to admit though, that when they were using tracers this morning, it was really pretty." Kuraji Miyashita sorrowfully recorded in his diary, "They attacked every last little boat."

After the carriers had retired, the huge B-29's based in the Marianas took up the slack, sandwiching strikes and photo runs over Okinawa in between missions over Japan. An infantry private noted in his diary on February 28, "Because of the fine weather B-29's visit us daily; no air raid alarm is given. The men call it the 'regular run.' Two planes came over today."

F4U Corsair

On March 1, at Admiral Spruance's order, Vice Admiral Marc A. Mitscher's T.F.-58 carrier air groups hit every airfield in the Ryukyus and attempted to satisfy the planners' seemingly insatiable appetites for photographs. Results were meager. Lieutenant George Murray of VMF 112 in his F4U Corsair fighter found no Japanese planes and shot up a radio tower near Kadena

35

airfield. Only Yomitan yielded a few targets for strafers. Antiaircraft fire was so light that Major Herman Hansen, Murray's commander, reported afterward that the first strafing pass was "strictly on the house—a free ride." Outside Naha harbor the *Bennington's* Corsairs and "Beasts" (SB2C's) battered into wreckage a *Matsu*-class escort destroyer with dozens of bombs and rockets. On other islands in the Ryukyus pilots shot up airfields and sank more shipping. For a total loss of twenty planes and ten airmen T.F. 58 claimed four Japanese planes shot from the air and thirty-three more (some undoubtedly decoys) destroyed on the ground. Photo planes covered eighty percent of Okinawa but missed Ushijima's vitally important defenses north of Shuri which had remained cloud-covered on this as on every other photo mission.

One day of strikes was considered enough. Having reached the end of its prescribed series of missions, T.F. 58 steamed back to Ulithi for rest, beer for the ships' crews at Mog-Mog, upkeep and replacement planes and crews, and to prepare for a new round of strikes.

II

In February, 1945, Operation ICEBERG moved from the planning into the training stage. The two Marine divisions of Major General Roy S. Geiger's 3rd Amphibious Corps already were sweltering in exercises in the fetid heat of the Solomons. Geiger, an old-time airman, had the veteran 1st Marine Division, victor at Guadalcanal, Cape Gloucester, and the Palaus, undergoing reconstitution and training in the Russell Islands. Its commander, Major General Pedro A. del Valle, was filling its depleted ranks with replacements after a bloody fight at Peleliu. At Guadalcanal Major General Lemuel C. Shepherd's newly formed 6th Marine Division brought together three regiments which separately had seen much action. Not a part of Geiger's corps, the 2nd Marine Division under Major General Thomas E. Watson was at Saipan indoctrinating its men for their part in the demonstration landing off the Minatoga beaches.

All three Marine Divisions had plenty of time to indoctrinate recruits and to rehearse their landing, which would put the 1st and 6th Divisions ashore on the northern half of the Hagushi beaches, while the 2nd Division faked at Minatoga to deceive Ushijima.

The 1st Division men, some of whom had to go to Guadalcanal for field exercises, cherished no more love for this pesthole than they had in 1942. Staff Sergeant George J. McMillan recalls that one man "... ran out of his tent at dusk and began to pound his fists against a coconut tree, sobbing angrily, 'I hate you, goddammit, I hate you.' 'Hit it once for me,' came a cry from a nearby tent, the only comment that was offered then or later by the man's buddies." When they learned that their objective was Okinawa, thousands of miles to the north of Guadalcanal, the Marines felt better.

The GI's of the Army's 24th Corps would have understood but hardly would have sympathized with the plight of their marine comrades. Mid-February found Major General John R. Hodge's 7th, 77th, and 96th Divisions still hunting down enemy stragglers in Leyte's jungle-clad mountains. All line companies were depleted by over a hundred days of combat; the men needed rest and rehabilitation more than training. Getting his men free of combat in March, General Hodge kept his Okinawa preparations to the minimum. The men exercised with two new weapons, the sniperscope and snooperscope, infrared gadgets designed to foil Japanese night infiltration tactics, but that was all. Two landing exercises in mid-month were intended primarily for the benefit of divisional and corps staffs and landing-craft coxswains. For the GI's they meant little more than getting their feet wet.

Landing day on Okinawa would see Hodge's 7th and 96th Divisions crossing the southern Hagushi beaches below the Bishi Gawa River. The 77th Division would already be ashore in the Kerama Islands, seizing for Kelly Turner his advance naval base.

Hodge's most experienced division was the 7th, under Major General Archibald V. Arnold. It had seen action in 1943 at Attu in the Aleutians and then at Kwajalein before coming to Leyte. The 77th Division under Major General Andrew D. Bruce had fought on Guam before Leyte. And Major General James C. Bradley's 96th Division, though new to combat at Leyte, had like the others spent 115 days in continuous action. All three divisions were more than a thousand riflemen apiece short of full combat strength, and because the Battle of the Bulge in Europe in December and January had diverted infantry replacements earmarked for the Pacific all three sailed for Okinawa still short.

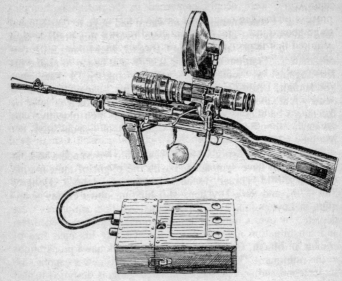

U.S. Carbine M3 (Sniperscope)

Not a part of either the Marine 3rd Amphibious Corps or the Army 24th Corps was Major General George W. Griner's 27th Division, which had seen heavy action on Makin, Eniwetok, and Saipan. This former New York National Guard outfit was designated as the "floating reserve" of the 10th Army, and if all went well would occupy the island after its seizure as the Okinawa garrison division. Nevertheless, anticipating that his men might be called upon for combat, General Griner drove them hard in night maneuvers, absorbing 2,700 replacements as he did so. Because the 27th lacked as many attached units as the other divisions, it numbered only 16,143 men as compared to more than 22,000 each for the other Army divisions and more than 24,000 each for the Marine. The total strength of the 10th Army's seven combat divisions came to 154,000 troops, substantially more than Ushijima's total force of approximately 105,000.

By mid-March officers on the various divisional staffs, Marine and Army, were deeply enmeshed in the infinitely complex process of loading equipment on the transports. Every item had to go aboard just right; the specialized science of combat loading required that items needed last on the beachhead must go aboard ship first—lest some piece of equipment needed by the first wave of troops be buried under tons of stuff of secondary importance. As if by a miracle everything fell into order, mountains of supplies stacked on beaches were lightered out into roadsteads to vanish into the holds of hundreds of ships. Each division would sail with enough weapons, rations, and ammunition to fight, and would carry in addition enough rice and canned fish to feed substantial numbers of civilian refugees. Last of all came the troops, who boarded the ships and settled down in cramped discomfort to sweat out the trip. Operation ICEBERG would not fail because of a snafu in loading; only the kamikazes could foul things up now.

III

To make sure that did not happen T.F. 58 in mid-March once again stood out to sea from its war anchorage at Ulithi. Its target was the Japanese airfield complex on Kyushu, Japan's southernmost island, its mission to destroy the kamikazes and their bases prior to ICEBERG's beginning.

From the Japanese standpoint Spruance's fast carriers could not have appeared at a less opportune time. Preparations to launch the planned massed kamikaze attacks of Operation TEN-Go still were far from complete. Mid-March found only the 5th Air Fleet ready for action, and of its eight air groups, two were capable of flying only one-way suicide missions. The capacity of the pilots to land their planes was considered questionable because they had so few hours in the air. On Kyushu's fifty-five airfields and airstrips Japanese engineers still were tunneling into hills to shelter men, planes, ordnance, and repair facilities, disguising runways and taxi strips as ordinary roads. They were also stripping and abandoning some developed fields and littering them with unserviceable planes and straw dummies to divert attackers from newly built camouflaged operational strips. But their work was as yet incomplete. In particular, communications were inadequate to transmit orders efficiently between the widely scattered fields and Air Fleet Headquarters at Kanoya.

Following the pattern of the Tokyo strikes, Admiral Spruance's staff had divided Kyushu into sectors, assigning one to each of T.F. 58's four carrier groups. Beginning at 5:45 A.M. on March 18 and continuing all that day and the next, the force systematically blasted runways, hangars, and airfield buildings but found comparatively few grounded planes—real ones at any rate—to strafe. Dive bombers hit, but did not seriously hurt, the

Grumman F6F "Hellcat"

40

superbattleship *Yamato*. Hits on other ships, carriers included, hardly mattered.

The appearance of Spruance's carriers had placed Imperial Headquarters in a dilemma. Japanese radio intelligence had detected his departure from Ulithi and warned that he was coming. But should Admiral Matome Ugaki, the Kyushu commander, be allowed to counter? TEN-Go was not yet ready and presumed that attacks would be made only on an invasion force. To strike at T.F. 58 might mean expending the kamikazes on less-important targets, allowing the loaded troop transports to reach Okinawa. But not to attack would risk loss of many planes to the Hellcats and Corsairs swarming over every inch of Kyushu. Following much acrimonious debate at headquarters, Tokyo finally allowed Ugaki to order his 5th Air Fleet to get Spruance.

During the next four days Ugaki threw 193 planes, including 69 kamikazes, at the American task groups. Of these 161—83 percent—were "lost." Another 50 planes were "damaged" on the ground. Ugaki was gratified, however, because his surviving aviators told him that they had hit five carriers, two battleships, three cruisers, and an unidentified ship. The Japanese admiral believed that he had crippled Spruance's ability to cover the Okinawa invasion and so had delayed it.

In fact, T.F. 58 was not crippled, although the claims of Ugaki's flyers were closer to the mark than usual. Bombs had damaged four large carriers, the *Wasp* and the *Franklin* seriously. The *Franklin*'s ordeal began at 7:08 A.M. on March 19 just as the first planes of a strike aimed at Kobe had begun to lift from her flight deck. Without detection by the ship's radar a lone Judy bomber slipped from a low overcast to release two 550-pound bombs from a hundred feet above the flight deck. The first penetrated the wooden flight deck just ahead of a pair of Helldiver bombers preparing to take off. The second struck further aft amid a cluster of twenty-nine armed and fueled Helldivers, Avengers, and Corsairs awaiting their turn to launch. Zooming up, the Judy evaded parting shots from the carrier's light and heavy A-A guns, but was bounced by the *Franklin*'s air-group boss, Commander E. B. Parker, who had been covering the takeoff in his Hellcat fighter. Parker followed the Japanese plane through a half-looping Immelman turn and shot it down. But the damage had been done.

41

Both bombs exploded in the hangar deck, setting afire twenty-three planes, fueled and armed, awaiting their turn to move up the elevators to the flight deck. Most of the sailors and airmen on the hangar deck, including two hundred men lined up to descend to the mess deck below for breakfast, perished instantly from concussion and from a flash of fire that seared the deck. Dense smoke bellowed out, blotting out the *Franklin* from the view of other ships in her task group.

The *Franklin*'s skipper, Captain Leslie H. Gehres, fell sprawling to the deck of the navigation bridge when the bombs exploded. "Immediately regaining my feet," Gehres reported later, "I saw a sheet of flame come out from under the starboard side of the flight deck and envelop the starboard batteries and catwalks and spread aft. . . . The same instant, a great column of flame and black smoke came out of the forward elevator well." To clear the smoke and flame from the carrier, Gehres ordered the helmsman, Quartermaster V. R. Ryan, to swing the ship to the right. Ryan did, only to cause himself, Gehres, and the entire "island" superstructure to be enveloped in hot, oily smoke from the conflagration among the planes spotted aft. Realizing now that his ship had been hit aft also, Gehres passed the word to Ryan to swing the ship the other way. To the engine rooms, still intact, he ordered speed cut two-thirds. The smoke then blew clear of the ship, but the course was embarrassing; the *Franklin* now was headed directly for Japan, less than a hundred miles distant.

Captain Gehres' abortive turn to the right had proved a boon for the aviators manning the planes for the Kobe strike. Ensign W. S. Richardson leapt from his Avenger, groped through the smoke to the "island," and took refuge in the extreme bow of the ship. Machinist's mate Louis A. Vallina felt the shock of the two bomb explosions, and as flame and smoke engulfed the hangar deck, escaped via a route opposite to Ensign Richardson's, aft to the fantail, the extreme stern of the ship. "Then suddenly, as I stood on the fantail, a terrific explosion blew me off the ship and I landed so far out in the water I didn't have to worry about being sucked under." Vallina had had no time to don a life belt, but spotting a powder can that had flown off the ship with him, he grasped it; then, spying a chunk of the flight deck, "I grabbed the wood." A destroyer picked him up later with others who also had been blown clear.

This explosion was the start of a morning-long series of blasts.

In the heat of the flames on the flight and hangar decks, the dozens of bombs and huge Tiny Tim 12-inch rockets mounted on the aircraft had begun to "cook off." The Tiny Tims were especially frightening. As the ship's executive officer, Commander Joe Taylor, reported, "Some screamed by the bridge to starboard, some to port, and some straight up the flight deck. . . . Each time one went off, the fire-fighting crews instinctively hit the deck."

Taylor, like many others, had a narrow escape. Crawling from the flight deck to the bridge he reported to Captain Gehres, to be greeted with "Joe, I'll have to say the same thing that the Admiral told you when you were last bombed; your face is dirty as hell." Taylor, who had been battered by concussion and nearly choked by black smoke from the flames, records, "That apparently light remark relieved whatever tension I was under." Going first to the flight deck, he organized firefighting parties from men who had escaped to the relative safety of the bow, then descended to the hangar deck to organize fire and rescue parties there. A pair of emergency diesel pumps supplied water pressure for the hoses: foam and CO_2 were useless; only saltwater and plenty of it could beat back the inferno that now wracked the ship. Heads dotted the water in twin long strings as dozens of men, trapped by the flames, took the only course possible to save their lives, by leaping into the sea from either side of the ship. As the *Franklin* continued ahead at eight knots, destroyers closed behind her to rescue the straggling lines of swimmers. Eventually they recovered several hundred.

Of mighty assistance to Commander Taylor's fire-fighting and rescue parties and to the survival of the ship generally was the first Navy chaplain to win the Congressional Medal of Honor, Father Joseph T. O'Callahan. To the ship's navigator, Commander Stephen Jurika, who remained on the bridge with Captain Gehres, the chaplain was ". . . a soul-stirring sight. He seemed to be everywhere, giving Extreme Unction to the dead and dying, urging the men on and himself handling hoses, jettisoning ammunition (from gun positions) and doing everything he could to save the ship." With the white cross on his steel helmet showing distinctively through the smoke as he went from place to place ". . . he was conspicuous . . . with his head bowed slightly as if in meditation or prayer." Captain Gehres later added simply, "I never saw a man so completely disregard the danger of being killed."

Early in an eventful morning the question of abandoning the carrier came up, to be decisively rejected by Gehres. From communication lines still open, he knew there were men trapped below: "I had promised these kids I'd get them out." Rear Admiral Davidson, the Task Group commander who was aboard the *Franklin,* realizing that the carrier had become an impossible post from which to command a task force, ordered the cruiser *Santa Fe* to rescue survivors and remove himself and his staff. In a daring bit of seamanship Captain Hal Fitz slammed the *Santa Fe* alongside the *Franklin* to fight fires and take off wounded and injured. Ignoring violent explosions, Captain Fitz held his light cruiser alongside until noon, fighting some of the *Franklin*'s fires with streams of water from his hoses and debarking over eight hundred men.

Gehres' continuing resolution not to abandon ship saved the lives of dozens of officers and men trapped below decks. The largest group of these, about 300 men, were trapped below the blazing hangar deck in a mess compartment. There they remained in suffocating heat, their sole air supply being a hole in the side of the ship large enough to admit a baseball. The trapped men were calmed by a ship's doctor, Lieutenant Commander J. L. Fuelling, who ordered them to sit quietly and avoid talking to conserve oxygen. The men remained in utter blackness until they were rescued in a daring feat of nerve and skill by a young lieutenant junior grade, Donald Gary. Using the knowledge gained in his duties as ship's fuel and water officer, Gary groped through a maze of compartments deep within the ship to locate the men and lead them topside to safety. Like Father O'Callahan, the young officer also received the Medal of Honor. Twenty-four-year-old Holbrook R. Davis said afterward, "We had a slight mental strain when we would hear the explosions above us. But when we finally got out and saw what happened above us, we thought we were lucky."

By noon the worst of the fires were out and explosions had ended, but the ship was dead in the water. Flames and smoke finally had forced the *Franklin*'s engineering staff to abandon engines and boilers. Commander Taylor led a spirited crew of mess attendants in a successful effort to draw in a towline from the cruiser *Pittsburgh* and to commence a slow withdrawal from Japanese home waters at a crawling six knots. Early in the evening officers and men used breathing apparatus to reduce the carrier's dangerous list of thirty degrees, and a volunteer party reached a boiler room to relight a pair of boilers.

The next day with six boilers operating, Captain Gehres was able to drop the tow from the *Pittsburgh* and to increase speed to fifteen knots. At 2:30 in the afternoon bogies showed on radar screens of the *Franklin*'s escorts and a few minutes later the stricken ship was again ambushed by a Judy pilot who made a glide bombing run from out of the sun. Gehres' crew had little left to reply with, but a volunteer crew manually swung round a quadruple 40 mm. mount and shot accurately enough to cause the enemy pilot to swerve upward at his bomb release point. The missile just cleared the port edge of the flight deck to explode in the water two hundred feet from the ship.

A muster showed 603 enlisted men and 103 officers left aboard the *Franklin*. No fewer than 724 men had been killed and 1,428 more were scattered amongst the five destroyers and two cruisers that had picked up survivors. Knowing that he could easily have a crew of psychopaths on his hands if he did not work the survivors mercilessly, Captain Gehres pressed a punishing series of plans of the day which first located, identified, and buried at sea the dead, and then began the massive task of flinging wreckage of all sorts overside and cleaning up burned out compartments. The *Franklin*'s flight deck still resembled "a shredded wheat biscuit" when the carrier arrived at Pearl Harbor, but when Gehres' skeleton crew arrived at New York's Brooklyn Navy Yard, the ship looked "almost presentable." Nevertheless, the *Franklin* was by far the worst damaged carrier on either side to survive the war.

With the *Wasp* and *Franklin* out of action, Admiral Spruance telescoped T.F. 58's carriers into three task groups. Then he retired to fuel, flying farewell sweeps across Kyushu. The American pilots claimed a grand total of over five hundred planes, three hundred shot down in the air, a much too optimistic estimate. Damage to airfield service facilities had been severe, however, seriously reducing Ugaki's capacity to launch TEN-Go. Nor had his loss of planes and pilots been light, particularly in skilled aviators.

IV

On March 19, with a T.F. 58 still cruising off Kyushu, a group of LCI's, LSM's, and LST's stood out from San Pedro Bay, Leyte, under the overall command of Rear Admiral I. N. Kiland. It was Kiland's responsibility to get this brood to the Kerama Retto, onto which they would sprew, across narrow beaches, amphtracs and landing vehicles (LVT's) filled with assault troops of the 77th Division. The remainder of the division would sail two days later in faster ships, while the hundreds of others carrying the bulk of the 10th Army still were assembling at Ulithi.

After a rough, miserable ride in the flat-bottomed landing ships, the force arrived off Kuba Shima in time for M hour, set for 8:00 A.M. on March 26.

Nobody expected much opposition, and, indeed, neither General Ushijima nor Colonel Yahara had anticipated an American *coup de main* in the Keramas. They had believed, rather, that the many suicide boats based in the islands would be able to attack by surprise the ships massed off the Hagushi beaches. They had only 975 soldiers on the four main islands of the group, of whom about 700 were Korean laborers of mediocre fighting worth. The others mostly were members of sea-raiding squadrons assigned to man the 300 *renraku tei,* the Army suicide motorboats. The Japanese had constructed no beach obstacles and had sited few weapons to fire on the beaches.

A heavy preliminary air and naval bombardment preceded the troops, for the precipitous Keramas, rising to heights of several hundred feet, too closely resembled miniature Gibraltars to admit complacency. Gunfire support included a generous ration of 12-inch shells from the thirty-three-year-old battleship *Arkansas.*

Against negligible opposition the 77th's four assault battalions touched down between 8:00 and 9:00 A.M. on four of the nine Keramas. Sergeant Fred A. Meyers of the 305th Infantry's K Company jumped ashore first, followed closely by Lieutenant Robert Berr of Decatur, Illinois. Rapidly the men crossed Aka Island, their target. A little later men from the other three battalions landed on Zamami, Hokaji, and Geruma islands, finding many of the concealed *renraku tei.* The boat operators,

46

assisted by the Korean labor troops, put up a sporadic fire from machine guns and mortars, then retired to high ground to hole up. The troops moved so fast and opposition was so light that General Bruce allowed his reserve battalion to take a fifth island, Yakabi Shima, before pausing for the night. About two hundred Japanese attached to the 2nd Sea Raiding Squadron were on Aka, four hundred of the 1st Squadron on Zamami, and seventy-five others on Geruma. The other two islands had only handfuls of soldiers.

Aka and Zamami furnished most of the resistance. On Aka the invaders blasted their enemies from holes along the eastern side of the tiny island with satchel charges. By 5:00 P.M. on the twenty-sixth fifty-eight defenders had been slain and two-thirds of the ground taken. On Zamami the Japanese commander hid until dark, and then attacked, striking at Company C of the 305th Regiment, whose men had gone into perimeter after placing on their flanks heavy machine guns manned by men from D Company, the weapons company.

From midnight until dawn the GI's beat off repeated counterattacks, some at hand-to-hand range. Sergeant Hurley Gilley, a D Company squad leader, remained in his position despite a deep slash on his arm from a Japanese officer's saber. Private First Class John D. Word, Jr., of C Company, found himself alone with most of the men around him killed or wounded. Picking up the automatic rifle of a fallen comrade, he beat off three attacks, two wounded companions helping him by filling empty magazines from clips of M-1 rifle ammunition. Sergeants Patrick H. Gavin and John J. Galinsky rushed one of their own machine guns which the Japanese had captured and were about to turn on the American positions. Galinsky killed the gunner with his pistol, while Gavin and two others finished off the other five Japanese in hand-to-hand fighting. When daylight came all of the Japanese had gone, except for twenty-seven who lay in and about C Company's positions. The next day the GI's finished sweeping Aka and Zamami, but made no attempt to find and exterminate all of the enemy.

On March 27 the 1st Battalion of the 306th Regiment landed on the largest island, Tokashiki, at 9:11 A.M., followed a few minutes later by the 2nd Battalion. Resistance was light and within three days the two units had completely overrun the island, scattering a hundred defenders of the 3rd Sea Raiding

Squadron, who with four hundred Koreans made up the garrison. They did not try to find all of the enemy troops.

Prior to the landings the Japanese had terrified the six thousand civilian residents of the Keramas, mostly simple fishing folk, by claiming that the Americans would butcher them and rape all of the women if they came. Consequently, the people were afraid to leave the caves in which they had taken shelter. On the night of March 28 GI's of the 306th Infantry, in perimeter for the night near the north tip of Tokashiki, heard explosions and screams. Investigating in the morning they found a valley littered with about 150 dead and injured civilians, many of whom had disemboweled themselves with grenades given to them for that purpose by Japanese soldiers. In some cases fathers had systematically strangled each child and then killed themselves. Horrified soldiers and medics rushed to the scene and did what they could to save the living. On discovering that the Americans intended no harm an old man wept bitterly in remorse; he had killed his daughter.

The reaction was different when word of the mass suicide reached Japan. To official propagandists this was heroism and an object lesson for mainland Japanese. And so the newspaper *Manichi* published a poem in their honor. As translated by American radio monitoring specialists it read:

> *Tears well up, involuntarily*
> *Just to hear of them . . .*
> *Clutching tightly in their tiny palms*
> *Real fire-belching hand grenades . . .*
> *The tiny special-attackers fell admirably,*
> *Like petals of a cherry blossom . . .*
> *The pitter-patter of their small army shoes*
> *Keeps pounding my breast, incessantly.*

Fortunately, relatively few civilians had committed suicide. The 77th Division took 1,195 of them prisoner and other thousands hid out. Most of the 121 military prisoners taken were Koreans. The 77th had killed an estimated 530 of the enemy against 31 of the GI's dead and 81 wounded.

By the evening of March 29, at which time the Keramas were judged sufficiently secure, Kelly Turner's wisdom in insisting on their capture already had become apparent. Two squadrons of flying boats were flying antisub patrols from the Aka anchorage. At the entrance to the larger anchorage, the Kerama Kaiyo, nets in place barred enemy submarines. Specially equipped LST's had found safety and calm water to transfer ammunition to the bombardment ships. Ashore, antiaircraft batteries and radar were

L.S.T.

going in to protect against kamikazes. Most importantly, Ushijima's plan to launch suicide attacks from the Keramas had been completely frustrated. The 77th Division had counted 291 boats on the islands, warships had destroyed three trying to sneak away, and just four had tried unsuccessfully to attack shipping.

A final preliminary operation consisted of the occupation of the Keise Shima, a group of four small, low, sandy islets lying between six and eight miles off Naha. General Buckner wanted to emplace on these islands twenty-four 155 mm. guns to support the main landing. Opposition was negligible and by March 31, L day minus one, the guns were ready to fire.

V

Kelly Turner's descent on the Keramas caught the Japanese air forces on Kyushu in a condition of near impotence as they struggled to recover from the beating delivered by T.F. 58 the week before. Admiral Ozawa, commanding Japan's Combined Fleet, ordered Operation TEN-Go executed on March 26 and placed in overall command Vice Admiral Ugaki, the 5th Air Fleet commander. Ugaki, however, could muster scarcely a dozen planes to throw into the attack. Nor would Spruance leave him alone. Task Force 58 swept Kyushu once more on the twenty-ninth, striking in between two heavy B-29 attacks on the twenty-seventh and thirty-first in which more than three hundred of the huge planes saturated three key airfields with bombs.

Only the Japanese planes based on Formosa or hidden in the Ryukyus managed effective attacks before L day. On March 27 nine Army planes commanded by Lieutenant Hiromori attacked from Kadena airfield. One crashed the battleship *Nevada*, rendering temporarily unserviceable two of the old battlewagon's 14-inch turrets, killing eleven crewmen and wounding forty-nine. Another, either from Hiromori's squadron or from among others flying from Formosa, knocked a hole in the cruiser *Biloxi* near the waterline, but its 1,100-pound bomb failed to explode. A third plane hit the *O'Brien*, killing fifty and wounding seventy-six, sending the destroyer first to the Kerama Retto and then across the Pacific to the U.S. West Coast, the first of a long and dreary procession of cripples. Destroyer *Kimberly* on radar picket duty took a Val, an obsolete Type 99 dive bomber with fixed landing gear, against a 40 mm. gun mount but managed to stay on station. A hit on the destroyer-minesweeper *Dorsey* ended a trying day for the bombardment ships.

March 28 proved to be better. Seven kamikazes from Okinawa expended themselves on small landing craft and hit only one. The twenty-ninth and thirtieth were better yet because no ships were hit. But at 7:07 A.M. on March 31 the kamikazes nearly got Admiral Spruance. Four planes attacked his flagship, the cruiser *Indianapolis*. American carrier planes splashed two and the battleship *New Mexico* got another, but the fourth plummeted into the port side of the heavy cruiser, releasing as it did so a bomb which detonated in an oil bunker and damaged an engine shaft, killing nine men and wounding twenty. Spruance, who had just gone to the bridge, was all right—"It didn't bother me" —but he had to transfer himself and his staff to the *New Mexico* and set up headquarters on the battleship. The *Indianapolis* joined a gathering "binnacle list" in the Keramas and from thence departed for the Mare Island Navy Yard for repairs. The kamikazes had sunk no ships, nor had they in the slightest delayed the invasion, but they had done much damage and had killed or wounded dozens of sailors.

VI

Ugly moored mines also threatened the ships. Ninety mine-sweepers of all types disposed of six minefields planted by the Japanese in Okinawan waters. All the mines were of the contact, not the sophisticated acoustic or magnetic, type, but clearing them still was dangerous, exacting work.

Inevitably ships hit mines. On March 26 a destroyer, the U.S.S. *Halligan,* fouled one near the Keramas which exploded both of her forward magazines in a tremendous blast. Forward of her stack the destroyer simply vanished, along with 150 men, half of her crew. The wreck drifted ashore, to remain a bleak reminder of what mines could do to an invasion fleet. Two days later a medium-sized sweeper, U.S.S. *Skylark,* struck one mine, drifted three hundred yards and hit another, and sank in fifteen minutes. Five men perished. The other minecraft continued sweeping and resweeping until L day and after.

Submarines had worried Turner before the campaign began. American destroyers caught and sank two regular submarines, the RO-41 on March 23 and the I-8 on the thirty-first, but the Japanese Navy had another threat in a midget submarine squadron based at Unten-Ko in northern Okinawa. Carrier planes had attacked this base but had not destroyed all of the subs.

First chance for the midgets came on the morning of the twenty-sixth when the gunfire support ships were moving between the Keramas and Okinawa. The cruiser *Wichita* spotted torpedo wakes, but no ship was hit. The next day the midgets tried again, picking on the destroyer *Callaghan* just after the ship had shot down a plane which first had dropped a bomb and then

51

had tried to kamikaze her. Commander C. M. Bertholf was on his bridge when a lookout shouted, "Periscope!" Bertholf saw the periscope just thirty-five yards away. Immediately he ordered all port side depth charges dropped, even though the ship was idling at eight knots. The commander related afterward, "I thought I had sunk *Callaghan* rather than the submarine." But the midget surfaced, rolled over, and sank.

Based at Unten-Ko with the midget submarines was a squadron of Japanese P.T. boats. These were not suicide craft but carried conventional torpedoes. One of the unit's officers, Navy Lieutenant Hajime Takeshita, undertook to record his unit's activities, although, as he put it, "I am not an Ashihei Hino" (a famous Japanese soldier-historian).

On March 27, Takeshita records, his unit assembled after dark to prepare to attack Admiral W. H. P. Blandy's support ships. The officers and men drank a toast, then boarded their boats, the commander trying a white band about his head and performing the ritual of bowing to the east in the traditional gesture of fealty to the emperor. They then got into a confused fight with some American small craft, sank none, and lost one of their number.

After inconclusive results the next night, the twenty-eighth, when three boats were chased by radar-controlled gunfire, the entire force ventured out again on the night of the twenty-ninth. This time at their ceremony the officers enjoyed whiskey and *yokan*—a sweet jelly made of beans—before taking their boats out to the attack. At sea they encountered the destroyers *Irwin*, *Hall*, and *Tolman*, which sank two boats and drove off the rest. Takeshita's boat ran aground on Saesoko Island off the tip of the Motobu Peninsula. This was the last outing for the P.T.'s. The next day escort carrier planes heavily bombed, rocketed, and strafed their base, wrecking the five remaining boats and forcing Takeshita and the others to join as infantry the Japanese Army on the Motobu Peninsula.

On the morning of March 29 the exotically finned and marked sailors of the U.S. Navy's underwater demolition teams (UDT's) prepared to execute their assignments. Commanded by a "big, rough, tough, red-headed Irishman," Captain Byron H. Hanlon, the teams were to swim from assault boats to reconnoiter the Hagushi landing beaches.

Each team had a dizzying number of chores to accomplish. With knotted fishlines the swimmers would measure the distance from the edge of the reef to shore, and by lead lines and stripes painted at 6-inch intervals on their bodies ascertain water depth above the reef. This was the only certain means of determining whether landing craft could cross the reef. They also had to locate coral heads, potholes, obstacles, defenses on the beach and inland, check the condition of the coral rock, sand, surf, and currents, and measure the width and depth of channels. All this data they inscribed on plexiglass slates. After debriefing them, specialists would prepare detailed charts of the beaches for study by army, corps, and divisional staffs. If a beach was unsuitable for a landing, the UDT boys had to find out.

Although by this stage of the war the UDT's had been bloodied in a dozen operations, strangely, as Rear Admiral Draper Kauffman (then a commander and Hanlon's exec) puts it, "The Japanese acted each time as if they had never seen a team before." This moved Kelly Turner to forbid any mention of them in press reports, agonizing the newsmen, who saw in the teams great copy. But mines exploded offshore could have slain them en masse at Okinawa.

Covered by a heavy bombardment the teams examined twenty beaches at Hagushi and several more off Minatoga. In contrast to the Iwo Jima operation, the swimmers encountered little shooting from the shore, although, as Admiral Kauffman observes, "This was less of an advantage than one might expect. The men had to anticipate fire at any moment and their work was extremely nerve-racking." Furthermore, they became badly chilled in the 68-degree water and suffered from arm and leg cramps. Nevertheless, they finished their jobs and reported that few departures from the landing plan would be needed.

Their task was not yet complete, however. The Japanese had embedded in the reef several thousand heavy wooden stakes. These had to be blown lest the landing craft and landing vehicles snag them and hang up.

The teams swam in again on the morning of March 30 towing small tetyrol charges. Perhaps because the defenders realized what they were up to this time, they received more fire from the beaches. At Beach Yellow 2, where Machinist Frank W. Brittain was attaching a charge, an American 40 mm. round intended for the beach but aimed too low detonated against the post, stunning him but leaving him otherwise uninjured. Ducking from stake to stake, staying underwater as much as they could, the men planted the explosives and rigged primacord between them. After three hours' work, picked team members pulled fuses on the detonators and then swam furiously seaward as, a little later, the posts disintegrated in simultaneous blasts.

From several hundred posts in Team 16's area there was silence. Either—as scuttlebutt in neighboring teams had it—the team had failed to lay all of its charges or the detonators had failed. Captain Hanlon and Commander Kauffman were perturbed, for those posts *had* to be blown before the troops could land, and they ordered their best team, UDT-11, to go back the next morning to complete the demolition. An enlisted team member, Edward Higgins, has recorded the team's dismay. "Going in on the same beaches for the third straight day was asking for it, and we knew it." Nevertheless, without a casualty the men blew the beach as smoothly as if on a practice meneuver.

Admiral Blandy's bombarding warships, some of which had almost scraped the reef in order to support the UDT's, had been shelling Okinawa since the morning of March 26. Starting first at long range, they had moved closer to the beaches as the mine-sweepers cleared the path for them, firing deliberately on targets spotted by observers in floatplanes. Nothing shot back; Imperial Headquarters in Tokyo had directed that shore batteries must remain silent until enemy troops had landed on the beaches.

That the bombardment accomplished much is doubtful. The 32nd Army's troops disliked and feared it, but their killed and wounded probably were confined to those few who ventured into the open. Nevertheless, no American commander would have dared do less than fire the prolonged, six-day preparation laid on at Okinawa. The ships had bombarded only three days at Iwo Jima, and when the marines hit the beach they had received murderous and accurate fire from literally dozens of pillboxes and gun positions that the ships had not touched. Afterward, Marine commanders had complained bitterly that the bombardment had been too short, citing as evidence their 22,000 casualties. Consequently the ships fired over 7,000 tons of shells at Okinawa's beaches ranging in caliber from 40 mm. to 16-inch.

VII

Even prior to the commencement of the bombardment, the 10th Army's combat divisions had begun their "mounting out," as the planners called it. Aboard ship the men could finally be told that their destination was Okinawa—which many had guessed—and be instructed on the island's geography, people, diseases, snakes, and terrain. They were told their landing beaches and given detailed briefings on their Love Day assignments.

Okinawa, they learned, would not be as hot as the jungles to the south, though still warm and humid. Health conditions were reported as bad, with the usual tropical fevers and sundry other diseases. They must beware the nocturnal habu, the big dark snake for whose bite there was no available antidote. They would find umbrella-shaped pines everywhere on the island, low, squat oaks on the higher crests, and also the distinctive cycad, a plant with neat palm fronds whose roots yielded a starch jelly the inhabitants ate in time of famine or typhoon. Though the Okinawans had not been well-treated by the Japanese, the soldiers must not expect them to be friendly toward Americans. Troops should watch out for guerrillas and snipers. Militarily the terrain favored the defense, for the escarpments—ridgelines with steep, clifflike faces—generally ran east-west across the island. Moreover, aerial photographs had revealed inland from the beaches plenty of cave positions which the Japanese undoubtedly would supplement by use of the distinctive lyre-shaped stone burial tombs of the Okinawans. In sum, Okinawa was depicted as no paradise, and the troops told to expect a hard fight.

Radio Tokyo offered less comfort than the briefing officers. Said an announcer on the "Zero Hour" program on March 28, "Here is a good number for you boys off Okinawa, 'Going Home'.... Listen and enjoy it while you can, because when you're dead, you'll be a long time dead.... A little juke-box music for the boys, and make it hot, because the boys are going to catch hell soon, and they might as well get used to it."

On March 31, the day before the landing, the men changed their money for invasion yen, took a last shower, drew two days' supply of K rations, and packed their kits before supper. Wrote Ernie Pyle, the famed correspondent who had forsaken the war in Europe to join with the marines, "We had a huge turkey dinner. Fattening us for the kill, the boys said."

Ushijima's men were waiting for them. The 32nd Army's intelligence had predicted that an invasion in five-division strength would take place in late March or early April. On the evening of March 31 the students of the middle school at Shuri assembled after dark for graduation exercises. Each youth received his military orders with his certificate of graduation. Ushijima had made his last move; both sides were ready.

4

LOVE DAY

IN THE PREDAWN of April 1—Easter Sunday and April Fool's Day—a dull rumbling sound of anchor chains sliding across foredecks disturbed the calm off Okinawa. Among the dim shapes on the water one sprouted a thicket of antennae. This was the U.S.S. *Eldorado*, a converted transport, the amphibious force flagship of Admiral Kelly Turner. Not far distant loomed transports, battleships, cruisers, destroyers, small patrol boats, and LCI's, odd-looking little landing vessels with medieval-style conning towers. The flotilla numbered 1,300 ships.

I

At 4:06 A.M., still in darkness, Turner radioed the traditional, "Land the landing force." Forty-five minutes later, as dawn broke cool and gray, flames stabbed abruptly across the water.

Along eight miles of beach ten battleships were firing. Blasting away with 16-inch guns was the U.S.S. *Colorado,* still clad in prewar rig. Nearby were the handsome, clipper-bowed *Idaho* and *New Mexico,* veterans of convoy duty in the Atlantic, firing 14-inch guns. Pearl Harbor veterans *West Virginia* and *Nevada* were there, rebuilt to resemble in silhouette modern, fast battleships. Also firing 14-inchers were the elderly *Texas* and *New York,* having steamed halfway around the world after the Normandy invasion to join the Pacific fleet off Iwo. Then there was the grand old lady of the battlewagons, the *Arkansas,* commissioned well before World War I and earmarked for scrapping at the outbreak of World War II, bellowing thunder from twelve 12-inchers. Leading them was the flagship *Tennessee,* rebuilt to resemble her sister, the *West Virginia,* firing twelve 14-inch guns and a broadside of 5-inch. All of the old battleships were obsolete, being too beamy and underpowered to keep up with a carrier, but in this last operation of their long careers, they were ideally suited to their main chore, that of shore bombardment.

Interspersed between the battleships were nine prewar heavy cruisers, veterans of every major Pacific action. With them, augmenting the din, were three light cruisers and twenty-three destroyers. With the battleships, they brought to bear the heaviest weight of metal ever fired from the sea in a single campaign. Yet, ironically, on Love Day most of their effort was wasted, directed against hills and draws inland from the beaches that held no enemy, for Ushijima had elected to make his stand elsewhere.

To the trops embarking in the landing craft, the bombardment was at once comforting, frightening, and physically punishing. Each battleship projectile rumbling overhead meant for them less resistance ashore. But the blinding flash of the big rifles, the huge bellow of smoke, and their immense thunder seemed like volcanoes erupting. The slam of the shock wave jarred the stomach. To Ernie Pyle aboard one of the small craft, the concussion of the bombardment ''. . . set up vibrations in the air— a sort of flutter—which pained and pounded the ears as though with invisible drumsticks.'' To Kosuke Matayoshi, an Okinawan civilian who had taken refuge in a cave near Machinato, it was hell itself. ''I drew a blanket over me to shut out the noise. It seems like a bad dream, now.''

Atop the walls of Shuri Castle Leiutenant General Ushijima and his staff also stood watching. An officer later recorded,

The dust, smoke, and flashes of fire from the bombings and shellings in the north [Yomitan] and central [Kadena] airfield areas cover the ground and soar to the sky, presenting a scene of unsurpassed grandeur. Several hundred enemy naval ships are massed, covering the vast sea area from the west coast of Okinawa Island to the Motobu Peninsula and the Kerama Islands.

His foe was doing exactly what Ushijima had expected, landing across the Hagushi beaches.

Aboard the *Tennessee,* which had worked very close to the beach, a lookout yelled, "Here they come!" Led by LCI gunboats the invasion force came slowly, wave following wave, amphibious tanks in the lead, lined up not quite so trimly as Pickett's men at Gettysburg but trailing wakes to their rear straight as highways. Combat had offered no similar spectacle since the mass charges of the French knights in the Hundred Years' War. Here was the finest moment in the history of amphibious operations: an almost unbroken line of landing craft eight miles long simultaneously approaching one beach. With their armored prows pushing curling bow waves like manes, the propellers churning wakes like flowing white tails, the amphtracs became the cataphracts of modern warfare. "Can it be a coincidence," mused the U.S. Navy's great historian, Rear Admiral Samuel Eliot Morison, who watched from the *Tennessee,* "that the control craft for [Beach] Purple 1 is numbered 1066?"

"Amphtrack" (LVT 1)

All along the beach planes now began diving, rocketing, and strafing, two waves of sixty-four carrier planes each. After they finished, the warships, which had checked fire, began bombarding again, this time with every weapon they had. Aboard the *Tennessee* and the other battleships, the 40 mm. antiaircraft guns joined in, flinging out in rapid succession balls of tracer that sailed flat across the water to hit just inland from the beach.

Next, the rocket boats, leading the waves of landing craft, closed to the edge of the reef to discharge their screeching cargo.

Behind them, in the forward landing craft, the faces of the men were grim; they all knew about Iwo Jima and had been told Okinawa would be worse. Back a wave or two the men were less tense. When spray kicked up by another craft splashed over the men in one boat, Corporal Carroll D. Dofflemeyer, a marine from Luray, Virginia, carefully combed his hair. His buddy, Corporal John F. Di Penna, of Somersville, Massachusetts, chaffed him. "What are you parting your hair for—you're not going anywhere." "Hell," replied Dofflemeyer, "it's Easter, isn't it? So I comb my hair." In other boats the men were sitting up on the sides, watching intently the billowing mass of dust and smoke that hid the beach ahead. Others were laughing and joking, to the wonderment of watchers on the warships. Recalls Lieutenant Oscar N. Pederson, then communications officer on the destroyer *Twiggs*, "They all went by us in a very cheerful-like way. Just as if they were going to a ball game, or something. It is hard to understand how they could be that way, with what they expected to hit on the beach."

The weather was in their favor. The sun now was up bright and clear, the wind was light and from the east, and the surf on the reef and beach negligible.

Finally, after what seemed an eternity but in fact was only a few minutes, the amphibious tanks and landing vehicles began climbing onto the flat, shelflike reef that extended all the way to shore, making it easily. Except for a few mortar rounds chugging here and there, opposition was nil. When the craft were very close, about two hundred yards from the beach, the billowing explosions of the bombardment, which had climaxed in intensity moments before, abruptly lifted and shifted well inland, as if in response to an automatic invisible signal.

At exactly 8:30, H hour, the amphibious tanks rumbled dripping from the shallow water of the reef onto the narrow beach. Marines and GI's jumped out hastily, rushed up to the seawall, and crouched under its security. Then, obedient to the yells of their platoon leaders and sergeants, they scrambled up and over, keeping low on their bellies to reduce the hazard of grazing fire skimming the top of the wall, thudding onto the ground on the other side. Ahead, under the lifting smoke and dust of the bombardment, they could see the well-cultivated fields and the gently rising ground. Though cratered from a bombardment designed to place a shell into every twenty-five-yard square of area, the landscape still seemed ordered and neat. The air was cool and brisk. Forming up in skirmish formation, the assault companies moved out, heading across the fields toward their initial objectives. Except for an occasional mortar shell and sniper bullet, they still met no resistance.

Only in one area along the beaches was enemy fire "brisk" but not "real bad," as former Boatswain's Mate Johnnie N. Nelson recalls. A landing boat in his group took a mortar hit on the compass, with heavy casualties to personnel. In all, seven boats from Nelson's group were lost, most to broaching. But overall the landing had more nearly resembled a peacetime exercise than the largest wartime landing in the Pacific.

II

Just inland from the beaches organized confusion developed in the wake of the assault troops. Additional waves of amphtracs splashed across the reef, churned onto the beach, and drove through cuts in the seawall blasted by battleship guns and demolition teams. Then they rumbled inland to unload more troops and "hot" cargo. Behind them came small LCVP's, which with the tide cresting at five feet could just clear the reef and come all the way to the beach to drop their ramps. Later, as the tide fell, the landing craft would transfer their cargo at the reef's edge into tracked vehicles.

All along the shore wandered occasional knots of stragglers, men set ashore on the wrong beach, looking for their outfits. The worst mishap of this sort, inevitable in any amphibious landing, occurred on the 96th Division's beaches. There, Lieutenant Colonel Byron F. King's entire 1st Battalion of the 383rd Infantry Regiment found itself on the wrong beach. Elsewhere, other battalion commanders, Army and Marine Corps lieutenant colonels, huddled about maps with their staffs making certain of their locations, and worrying as military men always will about tying into the adjacent outfit on their flanks. Nearby sprawled their radio operators, resting on the ground the heavy sets strapped to their backs. The lack of opposition made the unwinding of snarls easy.

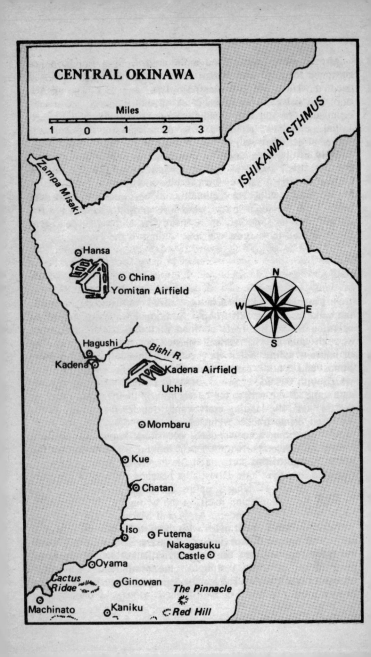

Already some marines had found a small, friendly Okinawan goat, had adopted him forthwith as company mascot, and had put him on a tether. Somebody fed him some K rations, which he happily devoured, cardboard container and all. Nearby "commo" men were running out wires, tying in the regimental CP's. At casualty collection points surgeons sat around smoking, wondering why the dead and wounded had not yet come pouring in. Almost a mile inland Marine Corps combat correspondent Sergeant James Finan was hiking with a forward patrol led by Captain Don P. Wyckoff, the operations officer (S-3) of the 7th Marine Regiment's 1st Battalion. "This is like Indiana and Ohio," the twenty-five-year-old Detroiter told Finan. "It's the prettiest fighting country I've seen this side of Gettysburg. There should be a hell of a battle going on here."

By 10:00 A.M., about an hour and a half after H hour, 6th Marine Division leathernecks held Yomitan airfield. "We had a crap game going," recalls Jack Lyon, who as a member of the 1st War Dog Platoon had landed with his Doberman. By this time, also, patrols from Colonel Francis T. Pachler's 17th Regiment of the Army's veteran 7th Division had reached Kadena airfield. Neither field was defended; installations at Yomitan were virtually intact, although stripped by the Japanese. The two airfields, which nobody had expected would fall before L-plus-three, had been taken virtually without a fight.

Offshore, aboard the U.S.S. *Tennessee,* the hour of 10:00 A.M. found Admiral Morison taking a personal count of the landing craft within range of his vision. His rough total, he recorded, reached "the incredible figure of seven hundred." A few minutes later the seventeenth and eighteenth waves of LCVP's passed the *Tennessee,* carrying regimental reserve troops for the Army's 7th Division.

III

Nearby aboard the U.S.S. *Teton,* Colonel Cecil W. Nist, the senior intelligence officer (G-2) of the Army's 24th Corps, found the radio reports from the beaches unbelievable. Tenth Army planners had assumed that both the marines and GI's would encounter stiff resistance from the high ground just inland from two or more regiments of well-trained troops. As photography had shown and as the troops had found, the positions were there but not the enemy.

Though General Ushijima and Colonel Yahara had planned no more than a delaying action, resistance may have been less than either had anticipated. To defend the airfields and to fight a "prolonged war of resistance"—so the order read—Ushijima had assigned Lieutenant Colonel Tokiharu Aoyanagi's 1st Specially Established Regiment, made up of airfield construction and service troops and Okinawan home guards (*boetai*) many of whom were high school students. Altogether, this scratch outfit numbered 3,473. Of the three battalions of this unit, the first was supposed to be in the Yomitan area, and the second and third between Yomitan and Kadena. The regiment's reserve consisted of just one company of regular troops who numbered about 120 men, First Lieutenant Kezuo Yagi's 2nd Company of the 12th Independent Infantry Battalion.

Although only about half of Aoyanagi's men had rifles, they had enough other weapons, machine guns and mortars, to have seriously delayed both the Marine Divisions and the 7th Division had they stayed in place in well-prepared dugouts and caves east of the airfields. But they were too ill-trained and inexperienced to do this. Many fled when the bombardment began. In what appeared to be a company or battalion headquarters, 1st Division marines found a desk calendar open to March 26, the day when the first American shore bombardment hit the area. Others who stayed, realizing they had no chance, slipped away from their positions when the GI's and marines began landing. Captain Honda, in charge of the defense of Yomitan airfield, got away with thirty of his men to hide out until the war ended, subsisting on sweet potatoes and plant fibers.

Typical of the experiences of those who survived was that of Miyagi Yutaka, an Okinawan *boetai* impressed into the regiment shortly before the invasion. Wounded in both legs by the bombardment, he was taken to the rear by his comrades. Within "a couple of days," he recalls, his company had lost three-fourths of its strength. On recovering sufficiently to walk, he began hiking northward to find his family, only to be overtaken and imprisoned as a POW. He was fortunate; the 1st Marine Division alone counted more than six hundred of his fellows dead in its zone of action.

The marines began encountering Okinawan civilians within a

few minutes after landing. Few had been killed in the bombardment because most had already fled the area or taken refuge in tombs and well-constructed caves. Once again their habit of hiding from typhoons had served them well. The 6th Marine Division encountered its first civilians north of Hanza. Stunted women, old men, and children at first cringed with fear and then smiled shyly and bobbed their heads rapidly when the marines asked, "Okinawa? Okinawa?" using the only word in the local tongue they knew. Others refused to emerge from their caves. Interpreters soon found that Japanese propaganda had convinced most of the population that the Americans would kill them. In most cases they had to enter the caves and "verbally pry the occupants loose." Later in the campaign, when local civilians and Japanese soldiers intermingled in the caves, the troops and interpreters could not enter. Hundreds—perhaps thousands—of civilians smothered needlessly in sealed caves because they believed the propagandists. In truth, the 10th Army command was most anxious to spare and to win the cooperation of the population. In an order read to each small unit by its commander, the troops had been strictly enjoined to spare civilian lives. Most of them tried to do so.

Marching fifteen paces ahead of one group of civilians was a hatless, withered old priest, clad in a gray robe belted with a black sash. Guards quickly surrounded the group and led them to the rear. As Captain L. T. Burcham, an intelligence officer, began to question them through an interpreter, the old man gave an almost imperceptible nod, and all squatted on the ground. Offered a cigarette, the priest accepted it eagerly, and the others, heretofore fearful and apprehensive, all smiled. Among them corpsmen moved, bandaging their scratches and wounds. For this gesture of kindness the old priest bowed to the officers in thanks. Then he bowed to each of the corpsmen in turn, while the others murmured and nodded agreement. The Japanese troops, he said to the interpreter, had left the area two days before. No, he did not know where they had gone; they had headed south. The Japanese had told him the Americans would behead Okinawans, but he had not believed them.

IV

By noontime the advance had gone so well that Major General Shepherd, commander of the 6th Marine Division, decided to transfer his command post to shore. Accompanying him a few minutes later was correspondent Bob Sherrod to whom the beach was ". . . a wonderful sight; no shattered amphtracs and broken boats." From their landing vehicle Sherrod and the general could see tanks probing the hills and amphibious trucks—unarmored DUKW's—delivering supplies along the roads. On the beaches everyone was standing up; Sherrod saw no frantic digging of foxholes as at Iwo.

Throughout the afternoon resistance continued light. At the northern extremity of the beaches, the 22nd and 4th Regiments of the 6th Marine Division kept right on going after crossing Yomitan airfield, moving into the rugged, cut-up ground to the north and east. By nightfall Colonel Merlin F. Schneider's 22nd Marines* had advanced north of Hanza and Colonel Alan Shapley's 4th Marines had passed the town of China, a thousand yards east of the airfield.

Late in the afternoon, while some of Shapley's men were guarding captured Yomitan, without attracting so much as a warning shot a Japanese Zero fighter suddenly dipped down, landed gracefully on the cratered airfield, and taxied toward the still-intact administration building. The pilot clambered out and was walking toward the building before he noticed something unusual and made the mistake of reaching for his pistol. An instant later both he and the plane were well riddled with bullets. Evidently, the pilot had been on either a reconnaissance mission or was escorting kamikazes to the Okinawa area, and apparently had landed on Yomitan under the mistaken notion (probably held at his base at Kyushu) that if low on fuel he could safely replenish there. As a marine said, "There's always one what doesn't get the word."

---

*The marines call their regiments "1st Marines," "4th Marines," "22nd Marines," etc. When reference is made to a division, it is called "1st Marine Division," "6th Marine Division," etc. In this volume "1st Marines" refers always to the regiment, never to the division.

South from the Yomitan airfield the 1st Marine Division, victor at Guadalcanal, but now filled out generously with new recruits, scored equally substantial gains. Evening found Major General Pedro del Valle's men deep in the high ground four thousand yards inland. The men had passed numerous field fortifications, few of which held enemies. On digging in for the night the division found itself tied in on its left flank with the 6th Marine Division but some six hundred yards to the rear of the Army's 7th Division under Major General Archibald V. Arnold.

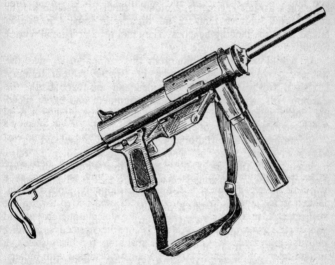

M3 "Grease Gun"

For once the soldiers had outpaced the marines, not because their resistance was lighter—it was negligible for both—but because the GI's had the advantage of being able to move along two roads over fairly level ground eastward from Kadena airfield. Their "find" of the day was a number of intact rocket-powered suicide planes the Japanese called "Oka" (Cherry Blossom). Several of these caught fire and exploded, jarring the 32nd Infantry's regimental headquarters area, but enough remained intact to satisfy Intelligence.

Combat action was sparse. In the late afternoon, in L Company's bivouac area in the 17th Infantry's zone, Staff Sergeant Hugh C. Mathis, a squad leader, found five enemies sleeping in a cave. Charging in, he dispatched them all with an M-3 "grease gun" before they could get to their rifles. His buddies in adjacent K Company ignored scattered sniper fire to seize a precipitous hill just south of the Bishi River which commanded the ground ahead. Said one of them, standing on top, "I've already lived longer than I thought I would."

Nightfall found the leading battalions of both of the 7th Division's assault regiments, Colonel Francis T. Pachler's 17th and Colonel John M. Finn's 32nd, digging in some 4,500 yards inland from the landing beaches. They had set a divisional record for an advance for a single day.

As would become customary in this campaign, it was the soldiers of Major General James L. Bradley's 96th Infantry Division, fresh from Leyte's jungles and a savage battle for Catmon Hill, who had the hardest assignment and experienced the most fighting of the day. Landing in the southernmost part of the beachhead, south of Kadena, were Colonel Michael E. ("Screamin' Mike") Halloran's 381st and Colonel Edwin T. May's ("a hard one, he was, but a good soldier") 383rd regiments. At first the Deadeyes—as the 96th's men called themselves—were tense and nervous. But as the advance rolled on, past one steep hill after another, each with fortifications that could have been formidable if manned, the men began to relax.

Lieutenant Colonel Edward W. Stare's 3rd Battalion of May's 383rd scored the most spectacular advance moving down Route 1, the coastal highway, through the village of Kue, and by noon across an intact bridge over the river estuary north of Chatan. Continuing along the coast for another 1,500 yards, Stare's men seized still another river crossing before halting for the night.

In Halloran's 381st zone, "Item" Company of Lieutenant Colonel Daniel A. Nolan's 3rd Battalion killed a score of enemies in a nest of pillboxes and captured a 5-inch naval gun. Their foes were not the ill-trained men of the 1st Specially Established Regiment. These were the China veterans of the 62nd Division's 12th Independent Infantry Battalion, men averaging twenty-seven years of age, who had the mission of holding scattered outposts in the Shido-Momobaru area, a spot the 10th Army planners had fully expected Ushijima to defend in force and use to mount a powerful counterattack on the beachhead. Near Momobaru, toward the close of day, the infantry encountered a strongly held pillbox. Tanks blasted it, but fire still was coming from it, so the GI's decided to call it quits and dig in for the night.

Elsewhere, all along the front, other soldiers and marines were doing the same. Some still suspected the day's lack of resistance was all a clever Japanese trick, that darkness would bring upon them a screaming, fanatical banzai charge as in the earlier days of the war. Company commanders therefore took care to join their perimeters with adjacent companies. The lieutenant colonels tied in their battalions, and where a flank lay open, bent back the end company to refuse it, dispatching patrols into the vacant area. Other patrols roamed far out front until late in the night. If the Japanese attempted something sneaky, the colonels, the regimental commanders, wanted to catch them at it well in front of the MLR, the main line of resistance. The night passed quietly, however, except for some infiltration in the Marine zone. A few artillery rounds fell into the beachhead and the 96th Division sector without causing significant harm or interrupting the landing of supplies which continued all night.

The main problem for the men during the night was the cold, to which they were not acclimated. With temperatures dropping into the low forties and high thirties and with only their ponchos for cover, their bedrolls being still on the beaches or transports, the men shivered and huddled together for warmth. Staff Sergeant Roy L. Hale recalled that "it got extremely cold, but they wouldn't let us light any fires." Ernie Pyle, who had joined the marines ashore, woke in the morning stiff and uncomfortable. Repeated mosquito bites, he discovered, had caused one of his eyes to swell shut.

Nobody complained too much. Compared to D day on a half-dozen other Pacific battlefronts—most notably on Tarawa and Iwo Jima—"Love" Day on Okinawa had more or less lived up to its communications designator. In the entire 10th Army area only 28 men had been killed, 104 wounded, and 27 reported missing. The only fighting of consequence, and that occasional, had developed in the rugged, hilly ground near Momobaru in the 96th Division zone.

V

While the assault troops were storming ashore on the Hagushi beaches on the west, marines of the 2nd Division had been carrying out successfully their demonstration off the Minatoga beaches on the eastern side of the island. The leathernecks clambered into seven waves of LCVP's, twenty-four in each wave, and headed shoreward just as they would have in a real landing. But at 8:30 A.M., H hour at the Hagushi beaches, as the fourth wave of landing craft was crossing the line of departure, all craft abruptly put about and scurried back to their gray transports behind a thick curtain of smoke. The men then reboarded and prepared to repeat the demonstration the next day.

Although the only Japanese reaction was a single salvo of four rounds of artillery which splashed harmlessly into the water—the defenders on the beaches being under strict orders not to fire until the landing craft had grounded—the Japanese nevertheless believed that they had frightened off a bona fide landing attempt. Colonel Tsuneo Shimura, then a captain and battalion commander in the 24th Division, whose unit was stationed on the cliff above, thought so at the time. He considers the American tactic to have been "very beautiful" and a success. His view is substantiated by a contemporary order of General Ushijima's issued at 4:30 P.M. the following day, after the marines' second demonstration. "... On the Minatoga front," the order read, "the enemy's plans cannot be disregarded. The Army will use the 62nd Division to hold the main line of position over a long period; it will use its main strength [the 24th Division and the 44th Brigade] to annihilate the enemy who plans new landings."

The conclusion seems reasonable that the demonstration landings "cooled off" temporarily some of the hotheads of Ushijima's staff who had disagreed with Yahara's passive strategy and who had wanted to hurl a night counterattack on the beachhead.

VI

The gravest threat to the landing came not from the 32nd Army but from the kamikazes on which Imperial General Headquarters was relying to reverse the tide of the battle. The "hell-bird" units on Kyushu, however, still had not recovered from Spruance's heavy carrier strikes and follow-up B-29 raids. Consequently, although the Japanese had spotted the invasion force en route to the Hagushi beaches, they could not launch powerful strikes against it. The kamikaze and regular air attacks on L day were of the hit-and-run variety and not the sustained, grand-slam blows Tokyo had been intending to hurl.

The most damaging attack came off the demonstration beaches at Minatoga. At 5:49 A.M. a suicide plane plunged into the port quarter of LST-884, killing twenty-four and wounding twenty-one of the more than three hundred sailors and marines aboard. Despite fire and severe damage from exploding ammunition, the landing ship survived to be towed to Kerama Retto, that already indispensable haven for kamikazed ships.

Earlier, a potentially more deadly type of attack had failed off the Hagushi beaches. The Japanese Navy had managed to dispatch twenty-five "Jill 12" torpedo planes from Kyushu Island, each armed with a torpedo able to sink a fairly large ship.

The pilots suffered from inexperience. Typical was Ensign Masatsugu Tsubota, twenty-two years old, who had been flying for about a year, but was on his first combat mission. He had been a student of agriculture when called into the service, had flown torpedo planes for about 140 hours, and had been an instructor, but he had only four hours of instrument flying. Such was his squadron's need for pilots that he was dispatched from Kushira airfield on Kyushu at 10:30 P.M., his plane filled with automobile-grade 87 octane gasoline, for a difficult six-hour night flight to the Hagushi beachhead and—since his squadron leader had not volunteered the unit for kamikaze service—a return at an economical cruising speed of 130 knots. His orders enjoined him to attack troop transports, if he could find any, and, failing that, carriers, battleships, cruisers, and destroyers in that order.

Aided by good weather, Tsubota arrived over the beachhead area at about 1:30 A.M., dropped very low over the dark water, and loosed his heavy "tin fish" at what appeared to be a large ship. Then, without observing the result, he banked steeply away to avoid a U.S. night fighter he had spotted closing from his left. So engrossed was he in watching the fighter that he made the tyro's classic error: he failed to hold his altitude in the turn. The

Jill's tilting wing hooked the water and the plane cartwheeled in. On fighting his way clear of the wreckage, Tsubota found his navigator in the water, but not his radioman, who went down with the plane. After daylight a U.S. destroyer found and rescued them.

The pilots had attacked the ships and destroyer escort of the Northern Tractor Flotilla, a group of LST's and LSM's headed for the northern Hagushi beaches. Twelve of them attacked the destroyer *Hugh W. Hadley*, which shot down one and drove off the rest. One plane attacked the tractor flotilla but its torpedo passed under the shoal-draft LST's. Though the pilots on return to Kyushu claimed three cruisers sunk, they had, in fact, hit nothing.

The Japanese reserved their heaviest attacks of the day for Task Force 57, the British carrier squadron under Vice Admiral Sir Bernard Rawlings, R.N., which had joined Admiral Spruance in mid-March. With his four fast carriers, two new battleships, five cruisers, and fifteen new destroyers, Rawlings had assumed the mission of pounding down Japanese airfields at Miyako Jima, used as staging bases for kamikazes from Formosa. On March 26 Rawlings' ships had launched their first strikes, and on the thirty-first, L day minus one, they had returned to strike again.

At 6:40 on Love Day, twenty minutes after daybreak at Okinawa, Rawlings launched a sweep of fighters. Ten minutes later the radar picked up enemy aircraft approaching, distance seventy-five miles, and the sweep was vectored to intercept. Forty miles distant from the ships the formations met, with the British Hellcats, Corsairs, and Seafires (a carrier version of the Spitfire) bouncing the oncoming Japanese. At 7:05 a low-flying fighter strafed the *Indomitable* causing seven casualties, but caused no loss aboard the battleship *King George V.* Moments later came a kamikaze that crashed the carrier H.M.S. *Indefatigable* near its island superstructure. Such a hit on an American carrier would have caused serious damage, but this Britisher, though fourteen of her crew were killed and sixteen wounded, remained capable of launching and recovering planes, though on a reduced basis.

Among naval experts "in the know" the British carriers were controversial ships. Because of stability problems they carried only 49 planes apiece, just half as many as American carriers, although they displaced 23,000 tons against 27,000 for the *Essex* class. But the reason for their light plane complement was also their great asset in kamikaze waters. The *Indefatigable* and its sister ships had armored flight decks of steel instead of teakwood mounted on a metal frame as on the American ships. This feature greatly increased their topweight and forced the British designers to reduce the size of their hangar decks and to limit the number of planes carried. But the armor of the flight deck was thick enough to stop a kamikaze. The bomb of the attacking plane might penetrate the armor but the plane with its load of fuel would not. Thus the *Indefatigable* suffered only a deck fire, easily extinguished, and a small hole in the flight deck which its crew quickly patched.

Damage caused to the destroyer H.M.S. *Ulster* in this attack was of another order. A Japanese pilot, bombing conventionally, managed to accomplish what every airman since Billy Mitchell had hoped planes would do regularly in warfare—and which they rarely did. He barely missed the British "can," but his 550-pound bomb exploded alongside and flooded the fire and engine rooms. The destroyer did not sink from this "mining effect," but lost all power and had to be towed to the British operating base at Leyte by the New Zealand cruiser *Gambia*.

In the evening a kamikaze evaded two Hellcats in the clouds and dove on the H.M.S. *Illustrious,* which had joined the others in launching a bombing strike at noon. The carrier heeled over sharply on sighting the plane, and the plane's wing just touched the ship. Plane and bomb blew up harmlessly in the water alongside, the explosion tossing the pilot's written instructions onto the carrier. These, which contained the Japanese priority list of targets, failed to surprise Admiral Rawlings. He and every tar in the British force already knew that aircraft carriers headed the list.

This time the *Illustrious* was lucky. Earlier in the war German Stukas had heavily damaged her in the Mediterranean, but she had survived to undergo repairs in an American shipyard. Now, in Pacific waters, this famous ship was finishing out five hard years of wartime service. As well as dishing it out with her planes, *Illustrious* was offering herself as a "hell-bird" decoy, thus diverting the kamikazes from more important game off the Hagushi beaches.

The suicide attacks on L day closed spectacularly—but relatively ineffectively—at 7:13 P.M. off the Hagushi beaches. A steep-diving plane, masked by the twilight, plummeted into the old battleship *West Virginia* while Admiral Deyo's fire-support ships were withdrawing from the bombardment area. As was usually the case aboard a battleship, casualties were relatively light, with four killed and twenty-three injured, and damage was confined to the galley and ship's laundry, allowing the *West Virginia* to stay in action. This was the only hit.

Love Day mightily advanced the Allied cause, notwithstanding Ushijima's decision to defer combat and the tragic events that occurred later. The kamikazes had not touched the landing ships and transports massed off the beaches. The resistance ashore was so light that the marines and GI's possessed by nightfall a beachhead more than two miles deep and eight miles long, one that contained an asset beyond price—two relatively undamaged airfields.

Consternation reigned at Imperial Headquarters when it learned from American broadcasts that these fields had fallen. Kamikazes could not sink airfields, and Tokyo remembered Henderson Field on Guadalcanal whose seizure on D day in 1942 had meant for the Americans the difference between victory and defeat. Some Army leaders now mentally wrote off Okinawa, concentrating their attention on measures to protect Japan from invasion. The Navy's leaders, though sorely disappointed, continued to hope that the kamikazes could succeed even though shore-based American fighters would soon augment the carrier fighter patrols.

Aloof in his underground headquarters beneath the imposing walls of Shuri Castle General Ushijima retained his composure. Not in the least was he disturbed by the day's events. For him the battle would begin in earnest only when the enemy ground troops closed the 62nd Division's defense lines three-and-a-half miles to the northward. The next morning, L-plus-one, would find him at the entrance to his cavern, performing the traditional samurai exercises with his sword, a daily rite he never failed to observe.

5

AN EASY TRIUMPH?

THE FIRST DAY on the beachhead had seen a good start, but only a start. To be really secure from counterattack and free to develop a solid logistical base, General Buckner's troops had to reach the narrow Ishikawa Isthmus in the north and in the south a line running across the waist of the island from approximately Chatan through Kishaba. In the next two days the troops pushed well below Chatan and almost reached the Ishikawa Isthmus, taking ground the planners had not expected would fall for ten to fifteen days.

For most of the troops the advance on April 2 and 3 was mainly a foot-wearying forced march, interrupted by frequent pauses to tie in flanks, locate positions, or—occasionally—to root out isolated enemy elements. The Bishi River divided the Marine and Army sectors, the Marine 3rd Amphibious Corps taking care of everything northward from it on a line due inland from the river's mouth, the Army's 24th Corps everything south of that. In terms of walking distance the marines had farther to go over rougher terrain with fewer roads, but the GI's encountered the stronger enemy positions.

I

All units of the 6th Marine Division jumped off on April 2 between 7:30 and 8:00 A.M. Colonel Victor F. Bleasdale's 29th

Marines led the attack in the north, advancing rapidly into the Zampa Point region. East of them, also advancing north, were the 22nd Marines under Colonel Merlin F. Schneider. The 22nd hiked all day against only light opposition and halted well north of the L-plus-five phase line of the planners at 4:00 P.M. But Colonel Alan Shapley's 4th Marines, striking eastward from Yomitan airfield, early began running into enemy strongpoints.

Captain Nelson C. Dale, Jr.'s Company L caught it—and dished it out—in a ravine cut by a small stream. Its second platoon had barely cleared the neck of the ravine when small-arms fire burst from scores of well-camouflaged caves dug horizontally into the side of the ravine. Captain Dale fell badly wounded with six other marines. His executive officer, Lieutenant Marvin D. Perskie, took over as the men recoiled and took cover.

There could be no thought of abandoning the attack. As Perskie recalled later, "We had to get those men out of there." After various outflanking maneuvers had failed, Perskie yelled, "Let's go, men," leaped to his feet, and ran down the ravine followed by the company. This time the attack burst right through, with the flamethrower men dousing the caves with liquid fire as they passed. Emerging Japanese toppled to the riflemen. One cried weakly, "Banzai." "Banza, hell," a marine retorted, knocking him sprawling with a burst from his Browning Automatic Rifle (BAR).

While L Company was having trouble, companies of Major Bernard W. Green's battalion were clearing up a similarly held strongpoint. This ravine was less V-shaped and more approachable, enabling a platoon of M-4 tanks to work its way up the bottom, shooting up caves as it went. This attack, plus L Company's, cost the Japanese about 250 men.

At the day's end, despite the resistance, Shapley's regiment, worthy successors to the leathernecks of the old 4th Marines, who had fought to glory on Corregidor early in the war, had advanced about three miles inland. At 6:30 P.M. all units stopped and began digging foxholes in rapidly gathering darkness.

For the marines of General del Valle's 1st Marine Division, April 2 was a long, hard walk interrupted only by occasional shooting by forward patrols. This lack of opposition had astonished General del Valle, who still suspected Japanese trickery. Late in the afternoon he ordered a "reconnaissance in force" by two

Browning Automatic Rifle (BAR)

battalions of the 1st Marines, who moved out ahead of the lines and marched until 9:30 P.M. before digging foxholes and forming perimeters in the vicinity of Chibana. Their lunge had carried them halfway across the island.

With the veteran 7th Division again leading, the soldiers on April 2 recorded gains as spectacular as the marines'. Moving out at 8:00 A.M. GI's of the "Hourglass Division"—so-called because of the shape of their shoulder patches—met only a few mines and roadblocks. But in the early morning a misdirected Navy air strike hit the command post of Captain Willis A. Fornacre's Company I of the 32nd Infantry, killing four men and wounding seventeen others, including most of the company headquarters. Such tragic episodes were to occur frequently during the campaign and cause hundreds of casualties. Around

1:00 P.M. this same company caught it again, this time from Japanese 81 mm. mortars, but nobody was hurt. Evening found I Company and the others of the two assault regiments, the 32nd and 17th, digging in along a ridgeline overlooking the thousand-yard-wide coastal flatland skirting the shoreline of the Nakagusuku (later renamed Buckner) Bay. The troops could see their advance patrols below hiking upright along the seawall at the water's edge, furnishing visual evidence of the absence of enemies.

Evening found the 7th Division's GI's lounging outside their foxholes, gabbing after the manner of soldiers. Some recalled Kiska, which the Japanese had elected not to defend. Others passed along the rumor that the Japanese had shipped the Okinawa garrison off to the Philippines. But the majority of the Hourglass veterans, mistrustful both of the Japanese and the rumors, dug their foxholes a little deeper.

For the Deadeyes of the 96th Division, April 2 had been a somewhat different story. In the difficult terrain of the Shido-Momobaru-Futema area the infantry had to cross heavily forested pine ridges and pass empty caves and dugouts, each of which had to be investigated cautiously. When they found the enemy, intense fire fights developed.

In one of these First Lieutenant John Restuccia of Company B—at the cost of his life—won the first Distinguished Service Cross of the Okinawa campaign. Finding his unit pinned down by fire from the flank, Restuccia jumped to his feet and followed by his platoon charged the hillock from which the fire was coming. Bleeding freely from two wounds, he continued to direct the attack until he and his men had cleaned out the hill. In supervising the evacuation of some wounded, Restuccia took two more bullets and died a few minutes later.

The Deadeyes gained up to 3,000 yards that day. In most places the advance had been swift, helped markedly by tanks and air strikes. The 2nd Battalion of Colonel May's 383rd Infantry alone killed 214 of the enemy and took a road junction that 10th Army planners had not expected to have before L-plus-ten. But in and around the town of Momobaru, defending infantry of Colonel Yokichi Kaya's 12th Independent Infantry Battalion, reinforced with machine gunners, held a salient. Though enveloped on the north and south at the end of the day, the defenders stubbornly refused to retreat, forcing their enemies to dig in on the spot for the night.

The overall gains of April 2, Love-Day-plus-one, had been enough to secure the entire 10th Army beachhead from counterattack by local forces. Territorial gains had been substantial, even spectacular, against very light American losses.

At sea, after the infantry had settled into their foxholes for the night, the big loss of the day occurred. At 6:38 P.M. a kamikaze pilot plummeted his "Frances" bomber into the *Henrico*, an assault transport containing the victorious troops of the 77th Division, now re-embarked and held in 10th Army floating reserve following their rapid seizure of the Keramas. The plane smashed through the commodore's cabin and into the transport's second deck, where its bombs exploded, killing several high-ranking officers. Casualties from this devastating hit totaled thirty killed, six missing, and fifty injured. Among the latter was Major Winthrop Rockefeller, the future governor of the State of Arkansas.

II

For the Deadeyes the going was much easier on April 3 than on the previous day. Altogether, they advanced 2,000 yards on their left, 4,000 yards in the center, and 3,000 yards on their right. They reached the L-plus-ten phase line of the planners, which crossed the island from Isa on the west coast to the vicinity of Hill 165 near Kuba on the east coast, where they tied in with advancing 7th Division regiments.

For the 7th Division April 3 was the easiest day of the campaign. Combat action was negligible until late in the afternoon. The 32nd Infantry reached and seized Kuba and then began getting fire from Hill 165 which a company of Kaya's Japanese was holding. That night the regiment dug in below the hill, welcoming into its perimeter a Deadeye company which had strayed too far left into the 7th Division's zone. The 184th Regiment also had a quiet day, slowed only by numerous encounters with mines on the roads that necessitated detours and delays. Late in the afternoon the 2nd Battalion, leading the advance, took its place on the L-plus-ten line. This brought both Army divisions abreast, poised, and ready to begin a coordinated push southward the next morning.

Some of the Hourglass Division's soldiers had found Okinawan ponies, had tied their packs onto them, and had walked along the easy way. Other soldiers had munched long Okinawan cabbages they had plucked from the neat, intensely cultivated fields along the coast. All had encountered civilians, especially the 17th Regiment patrolling and mopping up to the rear.

Thus far not much had been learned from POW's. The first one taken, on April 2, may have been a deliberate plant by Ushijima's intelligence. Claiming to be a former Tokyo University student who had deserted from his unit five days before Love Day and professing complete willingness to cooperate with his captors, he incorrectly identified several 32nd Army units and insisted that General Ushijima had four Japanese infantry divisions on Okinawa. The only correct statement he appears to have made to his captors was that Japanese morale was high.

In contrast another POW, an Okinawan reservist from a guard unit assigned to defend Kadena airfield and who had fled when the American bombardment began, accurately reported that both the 62nd and 24th Divisions were on Okinawa, with the 24th in the south. He also reported correctly that only a few troops defended the northern part of the island. But aside from the number of his company and its commander, he knew little else about the 32nd Army and was entirely ignorant of the existence of the 1st Specially Established Regiment to which his unit belonged.

The most pressing need in the American high command on April 3 still was to answer the question, "Where is the enemy?" Colonel Nist, intelligence officer of the 24th Corps, knew only that the bulk of the Japanese forces were in the south. But in Captain John Gaillard he had one of the best order-of-battle specialists in the business. Nist and Gaillard were confident of their precampaign intelligence as to the units and strength of the 32nd Army and were willing to stand behind their estimates, but they badly needed POW and documentary confirmation. Above all, they needed to know the precise location of each major enemy unit.

The light enemy resistance in the Marine Corps zone of action induced General Buckner on April 3 to authorize a significant modification of the original ICEBERG plan which had called first for the conquest of southern Okinawa and then of the north. Now, he removed all restrictions on the northward advance of the

6th Marine Division. Instead of stopping at the L-plus-fifteen phase line across the Ishikawa Isthmus, General Shepherd's leathernecks would keep right on going to the north tip of the island. Buckner intended to take advantage of Ushijima's concentration in the south to overrun northern Okinawa as quickly as possible and forestall the possibility his enemy might try to slip in reinforcements from the northern Ryukyus.

April 3 thus witnessed the beginning of the northward dash of the 6th Marine Division, while the 1st Marine Division secured the east coast and mopped up in the beachhead area to the rear. Neither encountered organized resistance. Dusk on April 3 found the 1st Division firmly anchored on the east coast, ready to advance into the Katchin Peninsula, while the 6th Division neared Ishikawa at Okinawa's narrow waist. The only real problem either division encountered was a shortage of food and water.

The leathernecks of Colonel John H. Griebel's 5th Marine Regiment were too tired to eat by the evening of April 3. They had walked steadily over rugged and hilly country since 8:00 A.M. Another unit, the 3rd Battalion of the 7th Marines, had made a forced march of three miles after receiving orders to push on at 4:30 in the afternoon. The regimental commanders had thrown away caution in exploiting the enemy's weakness.

III

By the close of April 3 U.S. forces held a beachhead 20,000 yards long straddling the island. Two airfields had been taken virtually intact, the beaches were reasonably good, and behind them was plenty of ground free from enemy artillery fire for the enormous quantities of war materiel pouring from the huge gray fleet offshore. Preinvasion fears that the bloodletting of the Iwo Jima campaign would be repeated had begun to subside. Cautiously, American commanders began to hope that perhaps all of Okinawa might be had with light losses.

General Geiger, commanding the marines, voiced his optimism to *New York Times* correspondent George E. Jones. "We have secured our beachhead. Don't ask me why we haven't had more opposition . . . I don't understand it. . . . [But] now we're in a position to work over the Jap forces at our leisure at the least possible loss to ourselves.'' One of Geiger's young lieutenants, Lawrence Bangser, put the matter more bluntly: "Either this Jap general is the world's greatest tactician, or the world's most stupid man.'' From Guam, reflecting the growing optimism at Admiral Nimitz's advanced headquarters, correspondent Bruce Rae reported, "There is every indication that American casualties may be a record low for Pacific operations even if the enemy should attempt to turn and make a stand.''

As the troops advanced many caught the same spirit of optimism that buoyed their officers. Even nature seemed kinder than anticipated. The crisp, cool weather reminded many men of their early spring training days at military camps on the American West Coast. Okinawa belied the preinvasion intelligence that had depicted the island as a sinister place, with the air laden with pestilence and the ground crawling with venomous serpents. When some Marines finally found a habu, after days of living on K rations, they promptly cut the thick, dark snake into fillets, broiled, and ate it. Before the campaign had ended Okinawa's fleas proved more of a nuisance than the habu, which was rarely encountered. Mosquitoes also were controllable, and as the weeks went by cases of malaria dropped well below the average of other Pacific War operations. No known cases of schistosomiasis— "liver fluke"—developed, and fewer than a hundred men caught dengue fever, a scourge of the Saipan operation. Only the fleas, which were carried by the goat herds, became a serious nuisance.

Already it had become apparent that Okinawa would make a much better military base than the planners had anticipated. Said Major General Fred C. Wallace, who would execute the base development plan with his Island Garrison Force, "Somehow, our previous information seemed to stress the unhappy aspects of the island.''

Reconnaissance by UDT's and engineers during the first two days had revealed that Nakagusuku Bay would be a fine naval anchorage. Coral and limestone deposits found near the east coast would build up the light Japanese airfield runways and widen and strengthen what one American officer aptly called Okinawa's "excellent network of poor roads.''

Of possibly greater importance than the favorable climate and terrain was the attitude of the Okinawan civilians in custody. Very few had resisted or had tried to escape north. When a correspondent asked an old Okinawan standing in a ration line to whom he owed allegiance the man replied, "I haven't thought about it. So long as you are here, we expect we will have to do as we are told."

6

THE GOING GETS ROUGH

TO WATCH PASSIVELY from the ramparts of Shuri Castle while his enemy seized a beachhead had been galling yet tolerable for Colonel Yahara. He had been disappointed but not surprised by the feeble performance of the 1st Specially Established Regiment. But he had been pleased by the work of Lieutenant Colonel Kaya's 12th Independent Infantry Battalion. Kaya's men had fought stubbornly in their outposts, had suffered heavy losses, and now were falling back to the main defense zone still in disciplined fighting order. Lieutenant Kinsaku Yamazoe's 2nd Company, cut off during the fighting, had managed to infiltrate by threes and fours to the east coast, and traveling by night and hiding by day, to reach the main defense line with three-fourths of its personnel.

I

As dusk settled over the island on April 3, Yahara's chief concern was not the 10th Army's rapid occupation of central Okinawa; rather, it was the possibility that General Buckner might race an armored task force down the east coast shoreline to Yonabaru and outflank the Shuri line. In truth, Buckner had neither the armored strength nor the intention of making so bold a move.

In contrast to Yahara, Lieutenant General Cho had chafed

restlessly during the first three days of the campaign. Never had he approved of Yahara's defensive strategy. Now, on the night of April 3, he moved boldly and abruptly to reverse it, laying before the assembled 32nd Army staff a daring proposal to attack. He knew he would have the support of the 62nd Division's commander, Lieutenant General Takao Fujioka. Though quiet and undemonstrative, Fujioka was, like Cho, a thoroughgoing samurai in spirit.

The time had come, Cho told the assembled officers, to smash the enemy. The Japanese Army's point of superiority, he claimed, was in hand-to-hand combat; at this the individual Japanese could best the individual American. If Japanese attackers could infiltrate the enemy's line to very close range, they could negate his superior artillery and air power. The entire front would crumble into disorder and man-to-man combat would follow as in Japan's medieval past. Cho proposed to bring up to the front the 24th Division, the 44th Brigade, and all of the major artillery units, and infiltrate the infantry completely through the 10th Army beachhead to high ground north of Yomitan airfield.

To many of the staff's youthful fire-eaters, Cho's proposal seemed eminently sound. It appealed to their romantic spirit, to their conviction that the reckless offensive was the surest way to win in battle. With exuberance they voiced their approval. The gloom of their cavern meeting place beneath Shuri Castle enhanced their ardor to burst from the underground fortress in which the 32nd Army was self-confined.

Yahara found Cho's plan utter nonsense. He liked Cho personally and admired his courage and abandon but summoned his intellectual prowess to vigorously assail the proposal. Even if the attack should succeed initially, he argued, since no dug-in positions awaited them the Japanese infantry on arrival at their objectives would be at the mercy of American air and naval power. Moreover, to abandon the south of the island would invite a second enemy landing. Also, even if driven back the Americans could always establish a defense line across the island and conquer the north, putting off indefinitely the reduction of the south.

During the ensuing discussion, which grew heated, General Ushijima listened passively. At the conclusion of the meeting, he rose and quietly approved Cho's attack plan. The staff could begin preparing an offensive.

But Ushijima was by no means completely sold. He greatly respected Yahara's ability and knew that his chief planning officer understood the tactics of modern warfare better than any other of his officers. Accordingly, the next night, April 4, when a strong concentration of enemy ships was reported off the coast, he abruptly canceled the offensive, accepting Yahara's warning that the Army must guard against a second enemy landing. For the moment Yahara had triumphed and Cho and the fire-eaters were quieted.

II

On the American side of the battle line, at 24th Corps headquarters, stocky, crew-cut Major General John R. Hodge already had stopped worrying about the possibility of a successful enemy counteroffensive. Even though the attacking regiments of his 7th and 96th Divisions were spread quite thin, each had continuous radio communication with both land- and sea-based artillery. If the Japanese advanced the battalions could recoil into perimeters and summon a ferocious concentration of shellfire the likes of which Cho and the fire-eaters of the 32nd Army staff had neither experienced nor could imagine.

Hodge's main concern, therefore, was to sustain the momentum of the advance. On the afternoon of April 3 he gave to the Deadeyes the mission of seizing the Urasoe-Mura escarpment that dominated the western side of the line, and to the Hourglass veterans the assignment of taking the equally dominating mass of Hill 178 and the coastal area in the vicinity of Ouki on the eastern side of the island. This done, both divisions would pause, consolidate, and await further orders. The attack would jump off at 0800 hours, April 4.

When issuing his attack order Hodge had no idea that he was sending his men against Ushijima's main Shuri defenses. Encouraged by the pace of the advance of the first three days, Hodge hoped, rather, that the infantry could sweep through the high ground of the Shuri area, seize the vitally needed port of Naha, and clean up Okinawa in record time.

Across the trio of lane-and-a-half paved highways leading southward to Shuri, Highways 1, 5, and 13, the Urasoe-Mura escarpment and Hill 178 were the principal obstacles. The escarpment lay like a long, narrow ship athwart the line of advance along Routes 1 and 5. Its stern dominated the coastal town of Machinato; its jagged prow loomed above Route 5, which looped to the left to swing around the escarpment's east end. Eastward from the escarpment to about 2,000 yards from the east coast, Hill 178 dominated surrounding hillocks. A ridge—Skyline Ridge—extended east from it almost to Route 13 on the east coast flat. To use Route 13 the Americans would have to take both Hill 178 and its appendage, Skyline Ridge, just as they would have to take the escarpment before Routes 1 and 5 could be used. Hodge needed all three roads to supply an attack southward.

Only a landing in the south could outflank these positions, but this strategy already had been ruled out. Plans called to assault simultaneously the Urasoe-Mura escarpment, Hill 178, and Skyline; hence Hodge's April 3 order.

To oppose Hodge's attack were three of the independent infantry battalions of Lieutenant General Fujioka's 62nd Division. In front of the Deadeyes of the 96th stood the 13th Battalion; in the center was the 14th; and on the right before the 7th Division was the 11th. Still manning some outposts were remnants of the 12th Battalion, which had lost about half of its personnel in the fighting of the first three days. Some of its elements already had reached Kochi, where the battalion had been ordered to re-form and consolidate.

The odds against the determined Japanese unit commanders were great enough; two full divisions of well-equipped, experienced American troops. But the Japanese had certain advantages which helped to offset American numerical superiority. All units had dug-in positions, skillfully camouflaged and completely integrated from shore to shore across the island. Their 47 mm. antitank guns, for example, were hidden so carefully as to be undetectable at two paces. Each battalion had five rifle companies armed with standard infantry weapons, including in each company nine Nambu light machine guns and nine Model 89 50 mm. so-called "knee" mortars, a light grenade-launcher fired with its baseplate resting on the ground. Backing these up were ten Hotchkiss heavy machine guns of the battalion machine gun company and two squat Type 92 70 mm. infantry howitzers of the battalion gun company. Extra mortar platoons detached from several independent mortar battalions further augmented firepower, while to the rear dug into individual caves for protection was the plentiful artillery attached to the 32nd Army's 5th Artillery Command. Ushijima had concentrated most of the 32nd Army's artillery on Okinawa rather than distributing it evenly through his entire command in the Ryukyu chain.

Type 92 70 mm. Infantry Howitzer

In numbers the independent infantry battalions had authorized strengths of nine hundred men, but each had been reinforced with about three hundred Okinawan conscripts and reservists. The independent battalion was actually a small regiment, well armed, well indoctrinated, experienced, and most important, determined to fight to the death of every last man from the commander to the lowliest private. The attached Okinawans appear to have caught the universal determination; the absence of Okinawan prisoners during the early stages of the campaign suggests that their morale, too, was high.

III

When issuing his attack order on April 3 General Hodge did not suspect the difficulties he would have even in approaching the roadblocks to his advance. At first the assault companies of the 96th and 7th Divisions moved fairly rapidly, but sharp fights for a number of outposts soon ran up casualties. When April 4 ended losses had risen to the highest one-day total thus far in the campaign. As the 96th Division's history put it, "The honeymoon was over."

In the Deadeye sector on the west on April 4, Company C of the 763rd Tank Battalion attached to the 96th Division had suffered. Twenty rounds from a concealed 47 mm. antitank gun had set afire three M-4 Sherman tanks and routed several others. A 47 mm. round from this 1941 model gun could penetrate a 35-ton Sherman's armor at several hundred yards' range. No U.S. tank available to the 10th Army could approach a Japanese position with impunity.*

Action in the 7th Division zone on Okinawa's east side consisted primarily of attempts by the 184th Infantry Regiment to seize the ruins of Nakagusuku Castle, an ancient fortress built by a medieval lord to dominate the narrow coastal plain fronting on Nakagusuku Bay. A company of infantry from the 14th Independent Infantry Battalion defended it. Attacking were three companies from Lieutenant Colonel Delbert L. Bjork's 2nd Battalion. The Americans overran a bowl-shaped area before and to the right of the castle's terraced twenty-foot-thick stone walls, but heavy fire from the defenders barred them from the castle proper. G Company men, trying a frontal assault, "ran like hell" across an open area to shelter beneath its base, each man receiving at least one rifle shot as he crossed. Pfc Duane A. German, an assistant bazookaman (rocket-launcher assistant), had a sole ripped from his shoe by a bullet. No one had been hit, but the men could not approach the defenders above them.

Colonel Bjork next sent Companies E and F to the right flank. They did seize high ground adjacent to the castle, but E Company lost its commander, Captain Wilbur M. Byrne, to a sniper who singled him out and shot him dead just as he stepped atop a small rise.

The next day was an anticlimax. Because the castle had been partially surrounded, and because he believed his men had done

---

*The 45-ton M-46 tank was not yet in service in the Pacific. All American units recommended its immediate adoption at the conclusion of the campaign.

well enough, Colonel Yukio Uchiyama withdrew the 14th Battalion during the night. Early on April 5 G Company mounted the castle's terraces and moved almost two miles along the hillcrest before machine gun fire from the next strongpoint—a fortified coral promontory rising thirty feet above a ridge—drove the men to cover.

Nasty as this and other actions had been for the infantry involved, they were but a warm-up for two stiff battles fought on April 5 and 6. One in the 96th zone involved "Cactus Ridge," a long, low hill which flanked Route 1 on the west coast. The second involved the coral outcrop which had stopped Company G and its fellows, a landmark the 7th Division referred to as "the Pinnacle." Like Nakagusuku Castle, the Pinnacle barred safe movement along Route 13 and the east side coastal plain below.

The Pinnacle may have been the promontory on which Commodore Perry's exploring party had raised the Stars and Stripes in 1853. Atop and under its 40-foot height were a hundred defenders of 1st Lieutenant Senji Tanigawa's 1st Company of the 14th Independent Infantry Battalion. From the top Tanigawa could see northward to Yomitan airfield and southward to the end of the island. It was his mission to deny this visibility to the Americans for as long as possible. Well dug and wired in, Tanigawa's men deployed ten machine guns and seven 50 mm. knee mortars and awaited in place the approach of the GI's. Colonel Uchiyama had ordered Tanigawa not to retreat.

This time the 1st Battalion of Colonel Green's 184th Infantry went in to do the job. Its commander, Lieutenant Colonel Daniel C. Maybury, dispatched Companies B and C to overrun Tanigawa. Neither could do much before night fell on April 5 because a Navy plane accidentally strafed and disorganized Company B, killing a man and wounding eleven others.

Early the next morning Lieutenant Allen H. Butler's B Company stepped off toward the Pinnacle close behind a ten-minute artillery preparation. Captain Daniel F. Sullivan's C Company followed on the right, ready to support the attack with fire. Three times B Company attacked and failed, the last time after reaching the base of the Pinnacle. Its men could not endure the shower of grenades and knee mortar shells falling from above. A TNT charge tossed from the top wounded Lieutenant Butler.

With the failure of Butler's third attack, Lieutenant Colonel

Maybury decided to send Sullivan's C Company around the flank of the enemy up a rugged but covered route from the west. Preoccupied with a B Company demonstration across the ground in front of him, Lieutenant Tanigawa failed to spot Sullivan's men coming. Scrambling up on top of the Pinnacle, the GI's found the Japanese literally under their feet in holes and caves. Staff Sergeant Walter Peters finally spotted the head of one sticking from a cave and turned a flamethrower on him. Tanigawa and his men then poured out and charged, while the C Company men crouched and blasted them with BAR's. Only about twenty Japanese escaped, Tanigawa not among them, against American losses of one killed and ten wounded in B Company. C Company had no losses.

The Pinnacle had been as foreboding and dangerous as any position on Okinawa, but it fell relatively easily because it stood alone, unsupported, and was vulnerable from one of its flanks. Its fall enabled the 7th Division GI's to continue their advance on high ground along the east coast.

That night, while Maybury's men were dug in on their prize, Japanese 150 mm. guns located in the Shuri heights shelled the Pinnacle. Though Tanigawa had radioed for artillery support, they had been silent while the position was under attack. Now, too late, they fired, with little harm to the infantry in their foxholes.

Unlike the isolated Pinnacle, Cactus Ridge in the 96th Division's west coast sector could not be outflanked. As the Deadeyes of Colonel May's 383rd Infantry stared sourly at its fissured slopes on the morning of April 5, they realized there was no easy way to assault it. Mines, an antitank ditch, and barbed wire protected its full 1,500-foot length. Even getting close to the ridge through the hail of mortar shells and bullets coming from it took the GI's most of the day.

On the morning of the sixth a glide-bomber attack by Navy Avenger planes struck squarely on the ridge without reducing the defending fire from its gun pits. Nevertheless, the infantry assault companies closed, trying to envelop the ridge from its northern end. In a typical encounter on the lower slopes Pfc Lloyd R. Smith of Major Prosser Clark's attacking 2nd Battalion killed three Japanese in a pillbox, then charged to slay another who had been hurling grenades at him. On examining the body of his last opponent for dog tags and documents, Smith was

91

jolted to discover that his adversary was a woman. Some civilians evidently had donned uniforms and joined Lieutenant Colonel Hara's defenders. Other nasty encounters, fatal to many on both sides, erupted along the northern slope.

To end it Companies E and G of Clark's battalion teamed up to make an old-fashioned World War I style infantry charge against the crest. "We stood up in waves," recalled Staff Sergeant Francis M. Rall, "firing everything we had and throwing hand grenades by the dozen and charged. I guess that was too much for the Nips, because when we got to their first line of defense they pulled out except for a few who blew themselves up." Clark's men had knocked out at least 15 pillboxes, many mortar positions, and against 30 killed or wounded, had killed an estimated 150 of the enemy. That night Lieutenant Colonel Munetatsu Hara's defenders of the 13th Battalion threw a counterattack at Clark's companies, only to lose 58 more soldiers. In compensation Japanese artillery at Shuri shelled Cactus the rest of the night.

Cactus Ridge and the Pinnacle were but the strongest of the enemy outposts. Many lesser ones in the center of the island had also required elaborate maneuver and considerable loss to subdue. The sharply increased overall resistance in the south of Okinawa on April 4, 5, and 6 had dispelled illusions that the island would fall with only light American losses, though General Hodge still hoped that his men could keep moving rapidly.

Events of the next two days dashed Hodge's hopes. Enemy artillery shells of all calibers up to 155 mm. rained down on both the 7th and 96th Division fronts. Attacks on a series of unimpressive-appearing little hills across the island gained little. Hodge now realized that all were heavily garrisoned; all were defended by interlocking bands of fire; none had a vulnerable flank. It was time for Hodge to mass his artillery and planes to soften up Ushijima's defenses. Attacks from here on out would have to be strong affairs, launched against specific objectives for short gains.

Keeping moving had been no problem for the marines. The 6th Marine Division had hiked easily northward on April 4 for 7,000 yards to bivouac astride the narrow waist of Okinawa between Yadaka and Kin Bay. It continued to advance the next two days, pushing a regiment up each coast. The method of attack ordered by General Shepherd was to rush ahead units spearheaded by tanks and a company of engineers to reduce strong points and repair bridges, while the infantry peeled off patrols up to the source of each trail and track penetrating the brush- and tree-covered interior. Except for chance encounters with a few *boetai* and Japanese Navy stragglers, enemy resistance was nil.

The hardest work fell to the engineers. American carrier planes had blown many of the bridges, the Japanese the rest, and to keep the advance rolling Major Paul F. Sackett's 6th Engineer Battalion had either to lay portable bridges across the ruins of each destroyed bridge or have a bulldozer hastily fill in a temporary bypass. To ease the problem of running supplies up the narrow coastal roads, the marines pushed landing craft into every likely bay and cove, reducing the burden on their overworked trucks, jeeps, weasels, and amphtracs.

By April 7 the 6th Division was in Nago, Okinawa's second largest town, and General Shepherd was ready to pause for a bit, reconnoiter the Motobu Peninsula, and build up his supplies for a further push to Hedo Misaki at Okinawa's northernmost tip.

IV

A dividend of the rapid Marine advance had been the overrunning of two more of the Japanese suicide boat bases. These, located on Kin Bay, were the home of the Japanese Navy's version of the suicide boats. Navy boats differed from similar Army craft in that, whereas the Army boats carried a depth charge, intended to be dropped alongside an enemy ship, after which the boat operator theoretically would put about and escape, the Navy boat carried a 300-kilogram charge in the bow rigged to explode on contact with an enemy ship. The Navy boat was thus a true kamikaze craft. Officially, the Navy boats were supposed to make 20 knots from the power supplied by an automobile-type gasoline engine, but at sea 6 or 7 knots was more usual. They were called *shinyo* boats, *shin* meaning "shake" and *yo*, "ocean." To "shake the ocean" in such craft was deemed an honor in Japan comparable to piloting a suicide plane.

The commander of the larger of two *shinyo* boat squadrons at Kin Bay was twenty-two-year-old Toyohiro Minoru, the youngest full captain in the Japanese Navy. Slim and tall by Japanese

Suicide Motorboat (Shinyo)

standards, this intense young man had been trained as a navigator and flyer. He had served on the destroyer *Hamanami* until its loss in Philippine waters. On his return to Japan he had volunteered for suicide boat duty, and, after training, had taken 50 boats and 130 men to a base near Kin village in January, 1945. His boat crews had been recruited from a naval coxswain's school and were youths eighteen to twenty-one years of age. As a naval officer Captain Minoru was not subject to General Ushijima's order transferring suicide boat base personnel to the infantry. He could use his boats and men as he saw fit.

Although it might seem easy for a dedicated youth to sneak up to and ram a ship off Okinawa, actually it was not. The boats had so little freeboard as to be marginally seaworthy, even in calm water. Any sort of gunfire would wreck them, and in an ocean swell they sat so low as to make it difficult for the operator to pick up targets. Except for a compass they totally lacked navigational aids. Their gasoline engines were unreliable. Moreover, being deployed at Kin Bay, they were on the wrong side of Okinawa;

the Hagushi beaches and the most lucrative targets were on the opposite coast. Finally, the boats were vulnerable to strafing because their base had no cave protection and no antiaircraft guns. Captain Minoru had not even a marine railway to ferry the *shinyo*'s to and from the water; his crews had to manhandle them across the beach from brush-covered hideaways.

Despite these drawbacks Minoru managed to dispatch twelve of his youthful crews, two men to a boat, on the night of L day. Believing that he had sent heroic youngsters to their death, he found it difficult to sleep. When they returned the next morning, having failed to spot targets in an empty Kin Bay, Minoru thought at first he was seeing ghosts. The next night, he ordered out ten more boats, but once again the crews could locate no ships. Minoru did not know it, but because his enemies believed Kin Bay was mined, American vessels had orders to keep well out to sea, beyond the 100-fathom line.

By the evening of April 3 Minoru's command was coming apart. Marauding Hellcat fighters had detected his base, had strafed and wrecked most of his boats. Of the ten that had returned the evening before, all had been destroyed; pulled hastily up a creek because their crews had lacked time to drag them to cover behind the beach, they had been seen and shot to pieces.

Anguished by these failures and determined to accomplish some positive result, Minoru personally manned a guide boat to escort the three remaining *shinyo*'s on the night of April 3. One dropped out. Sleepy to the point of exhaustion as he led out the remaining pair, Minoru told himself his condition did not matter. Soon he would sleep forever.

Far out in Kin Bay the young captain spotted a line of patrolling warships about 10,000 yards away and ordered his two *shinyo*'s to attack. The first boat, manned by Seamen Akio Iwata and Nei Nakamura, closed the enemy at full speed—and missed! Iwata had apparently closed his eyes when nearing the target. Unable to see the American ship from the trough of the heavy ground swell running offshore, he circled in the wrong direction, then inadvertently grounded on an island which in the gloom looked like a ship.

The other *shinyo* was manned by Shokichi Ichikawa and Otomatsu Suzuki. Young Ichikawa was born to tragedy. First his father had died; then a typhoon had taken his entire family save only himself. Very determined, he had been among the most vehement of those who had affirmed that they lived only to destroy an enemy ship. Suzuki, his partner, shared his zeal.

As Minoru recalls, the two made "a beautiful run" to smash squarely against a warship which their watching commanding officer took to be a destroyer. Minoru watched the ship burn, then appear to break in two, and, satisfied at last that his command had accomplished a positive result, he put about for Kin Bay, hoping to repair and take out later the last boat himself.

Yet the victim was not a destroyer, but a humble landing craft gunboat, LCI (G) 82, which with five other similar craft had been manning a patrol line off Kin Bay. The gunboat's skipper, Lieutenant (jg) Theodore Arnow, was, like Minoru, short in years and aged in war. He had taken his ship through many amphibious operations, beginning in Alaska in 1943. This night he and his men had just finished investigating a downed enemy torpedo plane, when, as Arnow described it, ". . . There was just a big 'boom!' . . . and I found myself lying on the deck."

The explosion of the *shinyo* had blasted a twenty-foot hole in the craft's amidships troop compartment, killed an officer and eight men who had been berthing there, and injured many others. No one had fired a shot. The 40 mm. gunner, who had seen the approaching suicide boat, had swung his gun on it, but his gun pointer had failed to depress the firing pedal.

When Arnow reached the deck he found that the explosion had wrecked almost every piece of machinery on the LCI. All pumps and firemains were smashed, the diesel generator was out, and a fire was raging in the demolished troop compartment and no means existed to put it out. Abandoned by its crew who were picked up by another LCI, the gunboat burned all night and into the next day, finally buckling and sinking in the afternoon. LCI (G) 82 was the victim of one of the few successful suicide boat attacks off Okinawa. The other suicide boat unit based at Kin Bay had failed to score.

For Minoru war at sea was over. His last *shinyo* having proven inoperable, he collected his men, retired to northern Okinawa, and operated as a guerrilla until wounds in the elbow and upper arm disabled him. He was still a convalescent when the war's end terminated his career and forced him into captivity.

7

THE FLOATING CHRYSANTHEMUMS

ON APRIL 6 the full fury of the kamikazes exploded in the opening phase of the TEN-Go operation which the Japanese called "Kikusui Number 1." Kikusui meant "Floating Chrysanthemums," and the designation "Number 1" implied that other massed attacks would follow the first.

I

The Joint Army-Navy Air Agreement of the preceding February authorizing TEN-Go had specified that 4,085 planes should be assembled by April 1 to counter an invasion of Okinawa. American forces offshore of the island were to be hit from south and north, with the Army's 8th Air Division and the Navy's 1st Air Fleet attacking from Formosa and Admiral Ugaki's 5th Air Fleet striking from Kyushu. Ugaki would have under his jurisdiction two more Navy air fleets, the 3rd and 10th, and nominally the Japanese Army's 6th Air Army. The 3rd and 10th Air Fleets were training organizations, and their assignment to kamikaze duty was indicative of the Navy's determination to expend if need be every available plane to repel the Okinawa invasion. Lieutenant General Michio Sugahara, however, commanding the 6th Air Army, could expend up to about 2,000 Army planes at Okinawa but that would be all. The remainder of the Army Air

Force, the General Staff had decreed, would be withheld for combat in Japan proper. By mid-March Ugaki had on hand a considerable force to throw at the Americans, but General Sugahara had merely a handful of planes, less than a hundred. Nor had his strength been greatly augmented by the time of the American landing at Hagushi.

Although they probably were better integrated for Okinawa than for any previous operation, the Japanese still lacked true command unity. Subordinate Army and Navy commanders on Formosa and Kyushu neither cooperated with each other nor followed directives from Combined Fleet Headquarters in Tokyo in the way that—say—Admiral Turner cooperated with General Buckner and followed orders issued by Admiral Nimitz. On Formosa the 1st Air Fleet and the 8th Air Army paid little attention either to each other or to Tokyo. On Kyushu coordination was better between the 5th Air Fleet and the 6th Air Army but still incomplete. To get the 6th Air Army to take action, Admiral Ugaki could not issue a direct order; he had either to send an officer to General Sugahara's headquarters—a time-consuming process since he was at Kanoya and Sugahara at Chiran—or to ask Combined Fleet Headquarters to issue a directive binding both on himself and General Sugahara. Neither method worked well. Ugaki could, however, send orders directly to the pair of Army air divisions that carried out most Okinawa attacks, a process that appears usually to have worked, though on occasion their commanders ignored an order.

The man who seems to have actually directed the kamikaze attacks from Kyushu was Ugaki's chief of staff, Rear Admiral Toshiyuki Yokoi, a veteran airman who had been commanding a naval air flotilla based at Kanoya Naval Air Station. Yokoi had demanded and tacitly had received a prerogative that no American subordinate would have been given, namely, complete leeway to conduct the Navy's Kikusui attacks when, where, and how he pleased. Orders from Combined Fleet Headquarters thus were reduced almost to suggestions. From his superior, Ugaki, he enjoyed complete confidence and backing.

In preparing for kamikaze attacks the Japanese had to strike a delicate balance between too much and too little training for their pilots in plane handling and aerial navigation. To overtrain a suicide flyer would be wasted effort; to undertrain him might mean he would not reach his target. To the layman it might seem deceptively easy for a neophyte pilot to dive an obsolescent plane into a ship. But in a season of changeable weather when ceilings often were low, visibility poor, and wind currents uncertain, it was common for experienced flyers en route from Kyushu to Okinawa to drift off course and become lost. A student pilot barely able to hold a laden plane straight and level on a given bearing would have little chance of finding a target. This factor, plus unreliable engines that often necessitated a plane's return, made it desirable to train a suicide pilot well enough so that he could return and successfully land his aircraft. This necessity slowed the aerial build-up.

If, therefore, Admiral Soemu Toyoda, commander of the Combined Fleet, had expected to strike Okinawa's attackers en masse with the 4,000 planes earmarked for TEN-Go, he was overly optimistic. The series of attacks in March by Task Force 58 had seriously depleted Ugaki's 5th Air Fleet, and Sugahara's 6th Air Army was not ready. Toyoda made a brave show of alerting all forces for TEN-Go on March 25, but not until April 1 did Toyoda order Kikusui 1 to be launched, and then he waited two more days before designating the date, April 6.

II

April 6 dawned overcast and ominous. A northeast wind whipped waves into whitecaps and briskly propelled layers of clouds that scudded along at heights of 3,000 to 7,000 feet—good cover for kamikazes and no great hindrance to air navigation. This day neophyte airmen could find their way down the Ryuku chain to Okinawa.

Actually, Admiral Ugaki had begun Kikusui 1 the night before. Twenty-nine planes of four different types, dispatched to attack shipping off the Hagushi beaches, had encountered bad weather and had accomplished little. A dozen or so found the destroyer *Colhoun* on duty north of Okinawa and gave her a busy time but failed to hit her. An intrepid pilot of a Jill torpedo plane strafed the Yomitan airfield, drawing wrath from several antiaircraft gun battalions, but neither he nor the "ack-ack" did more than waste ammunition. Sublieutenant Tetsuji Kashimoto and several other pilots claimed to have attacked the Kerama anchorage, telling a Domei News Agency reporter of fierce enemy fire and "tracers glowing like some translucent candy," but the "battleship" they claimed to have attacked was not hit, nor was any other ship, according to American records.

Rear Admiral Yokoi, Admiral Ugaki's chief of staff, planned to tie up T.F. 58 with a series of attacks while the main portion of his force struck the beachhead. He delayed takeoff of most of his planes until around noon or a little later hoping to catch patrolling American fighters refueling on the decks of their carriers or on the aprons of Yomitan and Kadena airfields. A good idea, but Admiral Spruance's task force commanders had long ago adopted the practice of maintaining defensive fighter patrols from sunup to sundown, and Marine Corsairs en route to Yomitan and Kadena airfields still were aboard their ferrying escort carriers and not due at Okinawa until the next day. As a deception measure Yokoi dispatched three fast "Saiun" (Myrt) reconnaissance planes to drop quantities of "window" (aluminum strips which reflected radar emissions) off Minami Dato Shima, hoping to divert American fighters away from the actual attack. Task Force 58's radar operators picked them up at 11:30 A.M. but, as the blips faded from the radar oscilloscopes in the Combat Information Centers, the ruse became evident.

Neither Spruance nor Turner expected an easy day despite the relatively low-key beginning. Broken Japanese codes had revealed to American intelligence officers what common sense would have told them anyhow: that a full-scale kamikaze attack would come as soon as the enemy could assemble forces. Accordingly, Turner had disposed radar picket destroyers on sixteen different stations that extended like irregular spokes in a wheel from "Point Bolo," a reference point on the Zampa Peninsula north and west of Yomitan airfield. Each radar picket, as the name implied, could give early warning of an attack, and aboard each ship was a five-member radar direction team trained to vector patrolling fighters to "bogies," unidentified targets. A control officer, "Delegate," supervised all fighter patrols about Okinawa from Turner's command ship, the *Eldorado*. Hot spots were Radar Picket Stations 1 through 4, guarding an arc a dozen miles north of Okinawa's northern tip on the most likely approach for enemy planes from Kyushu.

III

Most of the action generated by Kikusui 1 on April 6 developed in three areas: over two of the task groups of Task Force 58, operating about a hundred miles northeast of Okinawa, over Radar Picket Stations 1, 2, and 3 off northwestern Okinawa, and within a 50-mile radius of the Hagushi beaches. Other battles raged over Kikai Jima, an islet near Amami O Shima, which the Japanese used as an emergency strip and navigational reference point for kamikazes and their escorts.

To hit T.F. 58 Admirals Ugaki and Yokoi dispatched about 120 naval planes, half from kamikaze units. After taking off sporadically from several Kyushu airfields about half failed to find their targets and flew on to Okinawa instead. The others zeroed in on the task force. Flagship *Bennington* of Rear Admiral Joseph J. "Jocko" Clark's Task Group 58.1 had a typical time in dealing with them.

At 10:52 the *Bennington* had begun to launch her fifth combat air patrol of the morning, and fifty-nine minutes later her radar picked up the first of several bogies that heckled her until midafternoon. She was launching her sixth patrol at 12:17 P.M. when Ugaki's flyers arrived. A destroyer on her port quarter opened fire, and for the next hour ships posted on the outer ring of the circular screen about the big carrier fired at miscellaneous targets. *Bennington*'s only close call came at 12:53 P.M. when a Judy dive bomber plunged from astern at her flight deck in a suicide attempt. All guns that would bear fired; the plane hit and exploded just twenty yards astern, the blast flinging engine fragments onto the deck and temporarily disabling the ship's rudder. Afterward the *Bennington*'s crew could brag about the near miss, but this unknown but valiant member of the 5th Air Fleet had nearly accomplished a major purpose of Kikusui 1, knocking out a fleet carrier. Nor was *Bennington*'s the only near-miss. Elsewhere in the task group light carrier *Belleau Wood* narrowly evaded a plummeting "Ginga" (Frances) light bomber.

Above and around the task force the combat air patrols had a busy afternoon. The *Bennington*'s sister carrier, U.S.S. *Hornet*, at 12:20 P.M. launched eight Grumman Hellcats under Lieutenant Commander M. U. Beebe, the commander of its fighting squadrons. On reaching their assigned patrol station at 10,000 feet (patrols were "stacked" at various altitudes and bearings), they were immediately vectored fifteen miles due south to intercept two bomb-carrying Judys detected sneaking up on the task group from the rear. Lieutenant T. E. Pool saw them first; the entire patrol dropped down, and Pool and his wingman, Ensign R. F. Cunningham, set ablaze first the one, and then the other.

Beebe had just rounded up his pilots and was heading back to the ship when he got another vector, this time to the northeast. Soon his flight spotted a tight vee of three fighters approaching, blood-red rising suns gleaming on their wings. Swinging into a 180-degree turn, Beebe and his mates dropped on their tails. Selecting an opponent who broke sharply to the right, Beebe stayed with him and fired a 20-degree deflection burst squarely into his cockpit, finishing him. Beebe's mates burned the other two.

A fourth Japanese fighter, too low for radar, almost slipped by Beebe's flight. Lieutenant T. S. Harris spotted him low on the water running north at high speed. He maneuvered onto the enemy pilot's tail and followed him through a split-S turn, the favorite Japanese method of breaking contact. Putting his nose straight down, the Japanese pilot tried to dive away, but Harris followed until both pulled out only two hundred feet above the water. Harris fired and the enemy pilot, apparently hit, nosed down and in.

This series of air battles was fairly typical of many others that day. Action over T.F. 58 had been a lopsided victory for Spruance's flyers. No carrier had been hit.

IV

Radar Picket Station 1, 2, and 3, lying on a fairly narrow arc north of Okinawa's tip, enclosed the most viciously prolonged fighting. Taking off at about noon from Kanoya Naval Air Station and other bases, 104 late-model Zero fighters (Zeke 52's) took to the air in four waves. Theirs was not a kamikaze mission, although some possibly made suicide dives. Drawn from the best remaining pilots in the Japanese Navy, this group had orders to clear the air of defending American fighters to open the way for the suicide and conventional bombers following. Somewhat later 15 Judy dive bombers, 30 Kate torpedo planes, 46 Val dive bombers, and—the number is uncertain—about 55 bomb-laden older model Zeros took off: target, the beachhead; mission, special attack. The 6th Air Army planned to contribute many more suicide planes of various makes but had difficulty getting them ready. Fifty-six, straggling off in no particular order, mingled with the Navy planes. The Army Formosa command contributed 27 Type 99 reconnaissance planes (Idas), which were similar in appearance to the Vals. Formosa's 1st Air Fleet added ten planes, of which four were fast Frances twin-engine bombers that made a particularly deadly suicide plane.

Shortly after the first of this miscellany had been waved off the usual stragglers began returning, plagued with engine and other malfunctions. About a quarter of the striking force aborted the mission, but the remaining planes, 180 of them kamikaze, constituted a formidable threat. Conventional bombers and reconnaissance planes followed the fighter and suicide pilots. If all held to the course plotted by 5th Air Fleet headquarters, their route would bring them directly over the destroyers *Bush, Colhoun,* and *Cassin Young* manning Radar Picket Stations 1, 2, and 3.

Over Station 1 the attackers picked up the *Bush* first. About forty Zeros and dive bombers orbited over Commander Rollin Westholm's destroyer and organized an attack. At 2:55 P.M. a fast Judy—its nickname was Suisei or Comet—zigzagged expertly just off the water through the desperate barrage from the *Bush*'s 5-inch and 40 and 20 mm. batteries. The Judy slashed into the destroyer's side amidships, its bomb killing the forward engine room watch and wrecking both boilers. Bereft of propulsion Westholm's ship drifted to a stop, her best defense—speed and maneuver—gone. Besides disabling engines and boilers the bomb had dealt terrible damage topside, blasting the torpedo tubes overboard, ripping away all deck plating except for a three-foot strip, and starting many fires. Westholm ordered his sailors to fight the fires, control flooding, and succor the many burned and injured. With reason he feared that his ship might break in two. Over the assigned voice radio circuit an operator called, "Help, help, anyone on this circuit, help." Providentially a combat air patrol appeared, driving the attackers away.

A dozen more of Ugaki's flyers had moved eastward to heckle

the *Cassin Young* on Station 3, but *Colhoun* on Station 2 had been overlooked, though visibility was unlimited and "bogies" showed on the entire 360-degree sweep of her air-search radar scopes. Commander George R. Wilson swung his ship to assist the *Bush,* having intercepted her call for help. He attempted to vector to Station 1 another combat air patrol, but the Hellcats encountered so many Japanese en route that they quickly expended their ammunition and fuel. When *Bush*'s protectors also left, being low on fuel, both destroyers were on their own.

When Wilson found Westholm's *Bush* dead in the water at Station 1 an hour later—4:35 P.M.—two attached support gunboats were circling nervously about her, all hands warily eyeing a dozen Vals and Zeros orbiting just out of range. Wilson tried to steam between the enemy and the *Bush,* and four quickly singled him out as a target. Using a conventional glide bombing technique a Zero released a bomb that missed. The pilot might as well have tried a suicide dive; his plane splashed between the two destroyers. Next, three Zeros, kamikazes, began a loosely coordinated attack, one off either bow of the *Colhoun* and one off the starboard quarter. Good shooting and maneuvering frustrated two, but the third hit the *Colhoun*'s deck alongside a 40 mm. mount, slaying every man at this position and the next. The engine and bomb of the plane penetrated to the after fireroom, killing the entire watch and destroying boilers and machinery, but Commander Wilson continued maneuvering at fifteen knots on one engine and his other set of boilers.

The sailors had scarcely begun to fight the flames when a new trio of suiciders came in, two Val dive bombers and another Zero, using the same technique as the previous set. Again it worked. On nearby *Bush* Westholm's 40 mm. gunners dropped the first plane after *Colhoun*'s 5-inchers had staggered it; a second Val splashed also, but the speedy fighter plunged into the *Colhoun*'s forward fireroom and wrecked it, leaving Wilson's destroyer without power. Now both destroyers were in desperate peril as seamen fought fires with portable "handy billy" pumps, bucket lines, and foam and CO_2 extinguishers.

After a 15-minute lull another trio of planes bore in at 5:25 P.M., again a fighter accompanying two slower Vals. With only sailor-power left to train the heavy 5-inch mounts, the gunners of the *Bush* and *Colhoun* were badly handicapped; even so they got the fighter in time. But with deadly aim the two Vals crashed both destroyers. One glanced from the *Colhoun*'s upper works, freeing a bomb which detonated alongside the ship aft, opening a three-foot square hole below the waterline. The other skimmed the *Colhoun*, pulled up, and winged over to hit the *Bush* amidships, breaking her keel and all but severing the destroyer. Only thin plating and not much of that held her together. Another lull followed, and then two Kates (although eyewitnesses have cited three different makes) appeared, bombing the destroyers in conventional attack. Both missed. One hauled out for Japan, but the other nosed down to crash, turning the *Bush*'s wardroom into flaming chaos. Because wounded had been collected there loss of life was grievous.

Above the destroyers a three-plane combat air patrol from the U.S.S. *Hornet* commanded by Lieutenant G. W. McFedries saw the melee from 9,000 feet while returning to their carrier. They saw the Kate hit the *Bush* and the second pull out and head for Kyushu. Promptly they fell in behind, closing the obsolete torpedo plane at high speed. The first two Hellcats overshot, but Ensign F. R. Chapman lowered his flaps, slowed abruptly, and fired at very close range. The Kate flamed, and, nosing down into the sea, exploded. Turning back over the *Bush* at 1,500 feet, Chapman spotted another Kate diving on the ship at right angles to his course. Skidding about he tried a full deflection shot from the beam, then pulled behind to riddle the Kate, which smoked at the wing roots, blazed, and crashed.

Meanwhile a second *Hornet* fighter division of four Hellcats under Lieutenant C. E. Watts had been vectored to the area by the still-functioning controller team on the *Colhoun*. At 3,000 feet Watt's four caught two Vals closing the destroyers at 1,500 feet. Pulling into scattered clouds for concealment Watts led his section in a diving attack from the rear. The Vals split, one peeling away, one still heading for the destroyers. Watts and his wingman blasted the last one, flaming it in the cockpit, and the other two fighters followed the first Val into a diving turn and shot it down.

With this last plunge no attackers remained. By this time, however, the *Colhoun* was flooding steadily and the *Bush* was threatening to break apart on the next large swell. Suddenly, as if from nowhere, a Japanese fighter—possibly one of the escort

Zeros headed homeward—delivered a Parthian shot which almost got Commander Wilson. Alone on the *Colhoun*'s bridge, he was near-missed by the plunging fighter which hit the ship but fortunately carried no bomb. Several men were knocked unconscious by concussion but nobody was killed. The ship already had been so badly hurt that this pilot's final gesture made little difference.

Marine pilot First Lieutenant Junie B. Lohan of Charleston, West Virginia, whose squadron was assigned to the *Bennington*, had been an interested and frequently alarmed observer of the afternoon's events. His Corsair being disabled by flak over Tokuno Shima, about sixty miles north of Okinawa, he had crash-landed in a rough sea on June 5 just offshore. A *Bennington* squadron mate had flown south, located the *Colhoun*, and brought her to Lohan's rescue. Before Lohan had had a chance to be transferred back to his carrier he had found himself in the thick of the "can's" fight with Ugaki's kamikazes.

When the first kamikaze hit Lohan stood transfixed. Everyone else ducked, but "... I was too fascinated to move an inch. I just stood by the rail and watched him come racing toward us. I wasn't afraid. Guess I wanted to see what another pilot was going to do. I reckon I figured he couldn't hit us, but he did." Attaching himself to Lieutenant "Doc" Casey's first aid crew, Lohan worked furiously the rest of the afternoon, giving plasma, pulling aboard a sailor blown overboard, and—paradoxically—wondering if he would catch cold from getting his feet wet. "I prayed and prayed." Later, after a rescuing landing craft had taken survivors to a larger ship, "I broke down and cried. I looked around. Lots of others were crying too."

The *Bush* sank first, breaking apart just as darkness fell at 6:30 P.M. Commander Westholm left last after seeing to it that his men had gathered into two groups on rafts and floater nets. The water, he noted, did not seem particularly cold. Spying an overturned whaleboat he swam toward it—"I was surprised how hard it was to swim in a straight line"—but could not right it. Unable to join the others he managed to signal a support gunboat by using the emergency light on his life jacket. Others, less fortunate or less clear-headed, drifted away and were lost. LCS-64 picked up the two main groupings of survivors.

By this time the destroyer *Cassin Young* had arrived from

Station 3 along with a tug, but neither could do much for the *Colhoun*. Commander Wilson thought of constructing a coffer-dam about the hole aft, which was causing the worst flooding, but lacked the lumber to do it. Mattresses and other stuffing rammed into the hole simply washed through. Regretfully Wilson concluded that he had better get the men off, and at about 9:00 P.M. LCS-87 came alongside to transfer all remaining hands except for the skipper and a small salvage crew. About two hours later the ship flooded completely aft, the keel snapped, and the *Cassin Young* sank the derelict. Loss of life on the *Colhoun* had been thirty-five; on the *Bush* ninety-four officers and men were killed or missing. An extra supply of blood plasma that Wilson had stored on his destroyer enabled Lieutenant Casey to save many who had been terribly burned.

V

Action in the fifty-mile radius about the Hagushi beachhead began twenty minutes after the show had started over the radar pickets. Six small minesweepers covered by two "big protectors," destroyer-mine-sweepers *Emmons* and *Rodman,* were sweeping the channel between Iheya Shima and northern Okinawa. When the kamikaze swarm homed in on the protectors as targets, an ordeal began for both that equaled that of the *Bush* and *Colhoun* thirty miles north.

At 3:15 P.M. two planes dropped from the clouds. One bombed and missed the *Rodman*, but the other crashed her forecastle, starting nasty fires beneath her superstructure. Boilers and engines remained intact, and Commander William H. Kirvan, the *Rodman*'s skipper, retained power for his 5-inch mounts. Immediately, Commander Eugene N. Foss turned his *Emmons* toward the stricken vessel, preparatory to helping her fight her fires. When his combat information center reported bogies all around the horizon, Foss broke off, circling the *Rodman* to furnish antiaircraft protection. A patrol of Marine Corsairs dove in to help, and although they shot down several planes more remained to dive at both ships.

Fast-shooting gunners claimed six attackers, but then no fewer than five kamikazes hit the *Emmons* successively and four others near-missed. Two more struck the damaged *Rodman*. Flames engulfed both ships, though—amazingly—neither completely lost power. At least one set of boilers and an engine remained in each. Nevertheless the *Emmons* was hopelessly crippled. The first two kamikazes had struck the fantail, blasting off the rudder. Later, her port engine failed. With the ship aflame from her rear guns to her bridge, an abandon-ship order was mistakenly circulated, and many crew members left off fighting fires to go overside. An unusual incident prevented Commander Foss from immediately countermanding the order. When the fourth plane hit, gutting the Combat Information Center and slaying all there, including Lieutenant Temple J. Lynds, his "exec," Foss had ducked to cover into the pilot house behind the bridge. Now flames drove him out again—but there was no bridge and over the side he tumbled into the sea to be rescued later. Scrambling down from the main gun director, Lieutenant John J. Griffen found himself in command. "I immediately gave orders or rather countermanded orders to abandon ship." In the *Emmons'* forward mounts the 5-inch gunners ran out of antiaircraft shells, so they loaded common and even star shells in the guns to fire at circling planes, burning their hands as they did so on blazing nose cones on the shells and cork rings on the powder charges.

During this time sixteen Hellcats from the *Hornet* had arrived over the ships, taking up the covering task from Corsairs. They got into a tremendous melee, lost no planes, claimed thirty-six opponents, and saved both minesweepers from immediate destruction. The leader, Lieutenant (jg) R. D. Cowger, got the first plane. After losing a Val which ducked through the clouds, he spotted another low down, dove, chopped his throttle to avoid overshooting, and dropped this Val from dead astern. Similar one-sided engagements took place all around the *Emmons* and *Rodman*. Ensign W. J. Kostik had already destroyed two Vals and had just bagged an escorting Zero when he saw a fast bomb-carrying *Saiun* ("Painted Cloud" to its Japanese pilot, "Myrt" to Kostik) head for one of the destroyer-minesweepers. Young Kostik fired a long-range burst to turn the plane away from the ship enclosed. With one gun functioning he hit the Myrt in the wing, then charged his guns and fired again. This time three of the six worked, the Myrt's wing dropped, and side-slipping into the sea the plane exploded.

Cowger, Kostik, and their *Hornet* companions had merely

prolonged the *Emmons*' life and that briefly. Although she had not been hit while the Hellcats covered her, Lieutenant Griffen found that he could not extinguish the fires that now threatened the magazines. Reluctantly, he ordered those still aboard to leave, departing himself in a small landing craft at about 7:30 P.M. The ship floated, a blazing hulk, until sunk the next day by gunfire. Aboard the *Rodman* Commander Kirvan had better success with his many fires, and worked his ship to the haven of the Kerama anchorage during the night. Commander Foss was picked up from the sea injured, but sixty-six of his crew died during the action or later.

Although the battle around Iheya Channel had attracted many attackers, enough flew on southward to strike at other ships off the beachhead. An aerial brawl of epic proportions erupted over Ie Shima when fighters from T.F. 58 and from escort carriers intercepted the main force of Kyushu-based planes as they infiltrated in twos and threes. The *Bennington*'s intelligence officer, Lieutenant J. Davis Scott, pulled all stops in the ship's action report. Describing what happened when Lieutenant Richard E. Britson led eleven Hellcats to the scene, Scott wrote, ". . . At about 1630 [4:30 P.M.] the flight participated in what every pilot dreams about. For the next hour and fifty minutes Jap planes by the score [came] in just right for nice runs on them." Of the thirty-five to forty encountered, Scott recorded, the *Bennington*'s pilots shot down at least twenty-five, mostly at altitudes of 1,000 feet or less. *"Not one returned fire,"* he emphasized. "The only evasive action taken was jinking [weaving from side to side] and the majority of the aircraft were obsolete models."

Again, though the *Bennington* pilots did exceedingly well, too many kamikazes slipped through and dove. Two destroyers near Ie Shima attracted the most attention, each being hit once. Sailors on Commander Rollo N. Norgaard's U.S.S. *Hyman* had been watching the big dogfight as the ship steamed five miles off Ie Shima. At about 4:00 P.M., with a 5-inch shell, they disintegrated a fighter, then a second, then a third at closer range. A minute and forty-two seconds later the automatic weapons gunners sawed the wing from a fourth 800 yards out, but it continued in to hook the torpedo tubes amidships and explode the warheads in a tremendous blast that ripped the deck from the forward engine room. Four more suiciders dove, one missing by inches, one pulling up, and two splashing close by. Commander Norgaard's spirited crew—they had shouted "Hurray for the *Hyman*!" when the first plane splashed—at once began a successful fight against bad fires amidships. The skipper limped his ship back to the Kerama anchorage, but like most destroyers hit by suicide attack, the *Hyman* required extensive Stateside repair.

The plane which had pulled up found another victim. The destroyer *Howorth* had been firing, claiming five planes. Probably deciding that one hit per destroyer was enough, the pilot who had passed up the *Hyman* flew over and dove onto the gun director of the *Howorth*, killing nine men and wounding fourteen. Fires were not too bad, and Commander Edward S. Burns got his ship to the Keramas without much difficulty.

While the air battle raged unabated around Ie Shima, some of Admiral Ugaki's pilots, and possibly a few from Formosa, broke into the transport area to threaten Admiral Turner's transports, cargo vessels, and landing craft discharging supplies onto the Hagushi beaches. Antiaircraft gunners on dozens of ships blackened the sky with shell bursts. Several planes, two of them friendly, were destroyed, and rounds that failed to detonate in the air destroyed a pair of supply dumps ashore, killed soldiers, and hit a number of ships. "Delegate," the air control officer, ceased even trying to report new bogies. To those watching the barrage and listening in on voice radio circuits, it seemed certain that the Divine Wind flyers must disrupt Okinawa's logistical buildup.

Nevertheless, alert American pilots, aided by the controllers, shifted southward with the kamikazes, continuing the slaughter of these ill-trained innocents. "The primary danger to our pilots," declared the *Bennington*'s action report, "was collision or getting in the path of a friendly plane's fire." Lieutenant Haydin A. Gregory kept a score on his plotting board of the planes he saw fall; there were twenty-eight marks on it when he returned to base. The Lubbock, Texas, flyer himself had fired at from twelve to fifteen planes.

The only significant damage was inflicted by a handful of planes that penetrated the Kerama anchorage. At 4:30 P.M. three approached the southern entrance, looking for victims. LST-447, captained by Lieutenant Paul J. Schmitz, opened up on them with its 40 mm. battery. Two swerved toward the landing ship, one breaking off to continue toward the Keramas, the other charging the LST. "From about 3,000 yards out . . . he was our boy," recalls Lieutenant Schmitz. The gunners hit him several times. "I didn't think he was going to make it." But the damaged plane did, striking the LST amidships at the waterline. This landing ship was loaded with fuel intended for small craft, and now its entire load exploded into flames and smoke in a spectacular display. The LST was finished, sinking later, but only five men died. The other two planes selected three ammunition ships as targets. An alert gun crew on the *Las Vegas Victory* shot down their attacker, but the other crashed the *Logan Victory*. The nearby *Hobbs Victory* weighed anchor and moved out, only to sustain a hit from still another intruder an hour later. Blazing and exploding, both ammunition ships drifted into the roadstead to be gunned and sunk for safety's sake the next day. Neither suffered great loss of life, the crews having abandoned these floating powder kegs posthaste.

Kikusui 1 entered its most dangerous phase as dusk approached. The protecting carrier fighters had to be back aboard their ships by dark, and T.F. 58's night fighters were too few in number to cover much more than their own carriers. Ugaki's pilots thus had the best opportunity of the day to break through, but once more screening vessels, not vulnerable transports, lured the special attack flyers.

The destroyer *Mullany,* commanded by Commander Albert O. Momm, had been patrolling for several days off Okinawa's east coast. At about 5:25 P.M. a fighter appeared, strafing the late-model vessel from a long, shallow dive. Hits around the engine cowling failed to deflect the hurtling plane. Writes Momm,

The plane crashed into the ship at the after deckhouse between the two high 5-inch gun mounts, and exploding with a spray of gasoline started huge fires, leaving the deckhouse, gun mounts, and gun directors a mass of torn wreckage. We lost steering control and communications abaft the after deckhouse. Attempts to sprinkle the after magazines and ammunition handling rooms were useless; the fire mains had been pierced and sprinkler valves destroyed by the crash and explosions that followed it.

More planes attacked as the ship lay dead in the water, but gunnery officer Lieutenant Oliver Hazard Perry, Jr., (a distant relative of the hero of the Battle of Lake Erie in the War of 1812 and direct descendant of Matthew Calbraith Perry, opener of Japan) expertly laid his weapons on the attackers to destroy three and drive off another. By this time, however, plating next to the magazines was glowing red hot, and depth charges and shells in the wrecked handling rooms had begun "cooking off" in the heat. Momm ordered the ship abandoned.

Plenty of nearby help and daring fire fighting saved the ship. Destroyer *Purdy* closed to hose down the fires aft, and Momm, organizing a salvage party from a small landing craft, led a successful effort to dampen flames near the magazines by using portable pumps. After the fires were out he sailed the *Mullany* first to the Keramas and then to San Francisco, using the forward engines. Losses had been thirty dead, thirty-six wounded.

On Okinawa's west side Admiral Deyo had been rounding up his heavy warships which during the day had continued to bombard the shore. At 6:00 P.M. as his circular formation moved toward Ie Shima in usual nighttime retirement, the destroyer *Leutze*'s lookouts spotted a dozen enemies approaching low over the water. Singling out the destroyer division flagship, the *Newcomb*, four of the enemy pilots crashed her one after the other. At first the skipper, Commander Ira E. McMillan, and the destroyer division commander, Captain Roland N. Smoot, scarcely realized the ship was hit, but the other three hits were unmistakable. A door flung open by concussion walloped Smoot in the backside. "It is a wonder to me," he recalls, "that the ship didn't break in two." One of the planes, a Kate, had carried a large bomb into the ship's bowels, blasting to wreckage a fireroom and the engine rooms. From the battleship *New Mexico* it appeared to naval historian Samuel Eliot Morison that the *Newcomb* had sunk, so completely was she hidden in smoke and spray. But when she emerged, though aflame from well aft to her bridge, Lieutenant Leon Grabowski, the skipper of the nearby *Leutze*, ordered his ship alongside to extinguish the conflagration.

Grabowski and his crew had only just begun to battle the *Newcomb*'s fires when a fifth kamikaze dove at the two ships, aiming directly for the *Newcomb*'s bridge. "He would have hit us squarely . . . and I wouldn't be telling this story," relates Admiral Smoot, "but a proximity fused shell went off under the left wing of the oncoming plane and lifted it just enough to tip it aft. . . ." Barely skimming the *Newcomb*, the plane crashed the fantail of the *Leutze* alongside, blasting out the destroyer's steering control and blowing many holes in her bottom. "Then it was the blind leading the blind," continues Smooth. "It was a question of who was going to sink first."

Neither did. Eventually Grabowski and his crew controlled the flooding on the *Leutze*, and some very heroic fire fighting— Lieutenant D. W. Owens led men into a magazine fire and quenched it—saved McMillan's *Newcomb*. Towed to the Keramas both ships were out of the campaign and out of the war.

The last ship severely hit was the small destroyer *Morris*. Though crashed between her fore turrets by a kamikaze, her crew successfully battled a hot and dangerous fire near her magazines. This little hero of the Guadalcanal campaign early in the war then withdrew to the Keramas to join the covey of victims.

About 289 kamikazes had taken off from fields on Kyushu and Formosa. Of these some 223 actually had entered the Okinawa area, most to be shot down by defending fighters before they could make suicide dives. At least as many more conventional

Nakajima Ki-84 Hayate (Gale) "Frank"

bombers, reconnaissance planes, and fighters on sweep missions had accompanied the special attack flyers. The kamikazes struck nineteen ships for thirty-three recorded hits. About fifteen percent of the pilots who reached the target area scored, a percentage which decidedly bettered previous rates for conventional bombing and torpedo attacks.

As usual, American claims of aircraft destroyed greatly exceeded the number of enemy planes actually present. Turner's ships claimed to have bagged 108 of 182 attacking; T.F. 58 claimed 249 of which 136 were believed shot down near Okinawa. Pilots from the large carrier *Essex* reported 65 enemies splashed; Ensign Carl Foster of the light carrier *Belleau Wood* was credited with six planes to become individual high scorer. Task Force 58 lost two planes, both in battle for air supremacy over Kikai Jima, where thirty Japanese Tojos, Franks, and Georges, protecting the kamikaze reference point, had tangled with Hellcats and Corsairs forming a barrier patrol across the Japanese advance. The Japanese claimed seven Americans, like their foes overestimating enemy losses.

Kikusui 1 had been rough on the radar picket and screening destroyers. Three had been sunk and eight damaged, a loss rate which if continued would cause serious trouble. But when correspondent Robert Sherrod asked Kelly Turner the next day if he thought that his ships could best the Special Attack Corps, the Admiral raised bushy eyebrows in surprise. "Sure, we're going to take heavy losses in ships and men. We knew we'd have to take on the whole Jap air force when we came here. But we'll be all right." Turner took a somewhat different tack when Commander Westholm, fresh from the sunken *Bush,* braced him a few days later to request greater fire support for destroyers on the picket stations. When he came in Turner greeted him with a cordial, "Nice to see you, Westholm," and then delivered a ten-minute monologue on various subjects. At the end, lifting a hand, he said, "I know why you are here, but we just don't have enough destroyers to spare more than one for each picket station." He might have added—but didn't—that it was better to have the kamikazes expend themselves on the radar pickets rather than against shipping off the beachhead. He might have added—but didn't—that Captain Arleigh Burke had urged him to add an entire division of four destroyers (at least) to Station 1, but that he had settled for a single ship per station.

The Japanese assessment of the operation differed markedly from Turner's. On the basis of optimistic reports from 32nd Army observers at Shuri and from returning escort and observer pilots, Admiral Ugaki's 5th Air Fleet headquarters initially recorded two battleships and seven other warships sunk, plus five transports. Many more ships were claimed damaged. A little later the staff raised the ante to add three cruisers and eight destroyers (on the basis of ships seen under tow to the Keramas). "The above results," the staff concluded, "show clearly that Kikusui Operation Number 1 was successful."

8

YAMATO: THE MIGHTIEST KAMIKAZE

THE KIKUSUI 1 operation had contained a decoy, the First Diversion Attack Force, intended to lure American aircraft away from Okinawan waters. This consisted of the battleship *Yamato*, the light cruiser *Yahagi*, and eight destroyers, whose mission was to draw away Spruance's aviators of Task Force 58 from the beachhead to allow the kamikazes to slip through. If by some chance the warships survived they were to close the beachhead to shoot up U.S. transports and the Kadena and Yomitan airfields. None, not even the *Yamato*, was to return; the ships carried only enough fuel oil to reach Okinawa.

I

The battleship *Yamato* was one of the most graceful capital ships ever built. Though unmistakably Japanese in appearance, with a clipper bow, high superstructure, and raked funnel, she did not have the top-heavy pagoda look that had characterized many of Japan's battleships and heavy cruisers. Her decks were sweeping, her superstructure massive and yet compact, her stern high, commanding, and graceful. Three turrets, two forward and one aft, each equaled a light cruiser in weight. Her clean lines differed from the porcupine appearance of many contemporary

American heavy ships, littered as they were with antenna masts and A-A batteries. Yet she carried radar both for air-warning and gun-laying purposes, and her hundred A-A weapons, from 25 to 155 mm., mostly were massed neatly about her superstructure.

The *Yamato* was the largest battleship in the world, larger by far than America's *Missouri* or Germany's late *Bismarck*. On 69,100 tons standard displacement* she carried nine 460 mm. (18.1-inch) guns in three triple turrets, was 863 feet long, and was the most extensively armored vessel ever built. Her main side armor measured 410 mm. (16.1 inches) in thickness and her decks 200 mm. (7.87 inches). Her magazines and even her stacks had additional armor protection. With her sister ship, the *Musashi*, she had been secretly begun prior to the war in a specially constructed and screened off drydock to best any American battleship in a conventional big-gun action. Only in speed (27 knots or 5 knots slower) and in draught (35 as compared to 40 feet) was the *Yamato* inferior to America's *Missouri*-class ships. Japan's admirals had expected her to bring sure victory in a Pacific Ocean Jutland, at which the rival battleships of Japan and the United States would fight it out for control of the seas. But like battleship-minded admirals the world over they had underestimated the future of air power. Despite her bulk and strength the *Yamato* was vulnerable, as the sunken *Musashi* had been six months earlier, to the bombs and especially the torpedoes of carrier aircraft.

Though present with Japanese forces in many battles from Midway onward in the Pacific War, the *Yamato* had seldom fired her big rifles in anger. Even during the Battle of Leyte Gulf she had failed to close with her prey. In this, the twilight of her career, she had one last chance, though a faint one, to fulfill the role for which she had been designed and built, engaging enemy capital ships.

Yet when she sailed, at 3:20 P.M. on April 6 from Tokuyama Bay, the *Yamato* was already too late to fully accomplish her mission of diverting American aviators. The best that Vice Admiral Seiichi Ito, the attack force commander, could hope for was that the *Yamato* and her consorts might draw away many U.S. fighter planes from the second day's strikes of Kikusui 1.

---

*The *Missouri* displaced 45,000 tons, the *Bismarck* nearly 42,000 tons.

Nevertheless it was unthinkable that the ship bearing the name of the ancient province around which Japan's nationhood had been built should expire quietly in port.

It would have been contrary to tradition and to the custom of the service for the *Yamato*'s crew to have departed without ceremony. Accordingly, on the night before departure the officers of each division in the ship held drinking jamborees "in solemn gaiety," as former Ensign Mitsuru Yoshida writes. The enlisted men shared in the festivities, each receiving the esteemed *Onshi no tabako,* cigarettes of the imperial brand.

At 2:00 A.M. on the morning of April 6, Captain Jiro Nomura, the executive officer, ordered ashore the ship's midshipmen trainees to preserve them for the future of Japan. Men assigned to other stations also left. The *Yamato*'s junior officers implored Captain Nomura to put ashore family men past the age of forty, and after a conference of senior officers some were ordered to leave. Those remaining were resolute, though aware that they had but slight chance of survival. Sakae Katano, former damage control officer on the *Yamato*, remarks, "Some of my friends must have felt that they would not see their families again . . . , but I was not married, did not have a fiancée, and was the last child of the family. I had no special feelings about going away."

Shortly after the *Yamato* slipped from her moorings, Executive Officer Nomura assembled the crew, all hands sang the national anthem and gave three banzais for the emperor. Then careful watch was set for American planes and submarines and speed raised to twenty-two knots, standard for the entire force. The *Yamato* and her consorts steamed at maximum watertight integrity; the battleship's crew had buttoned up even the escape scuttles.

At 8:00 P.M. on April 6 the *Yamato,* accompanied by the *Yahagi* and the destroyers, steamed through Bungo Strait into the Pacific. At Admiral Ito's order the ships took up their Number 1 Alert Cruising Disposition, designed to protect against submarines, which put the destroyer *Isokaze* at the head of the formation, the other destroyers and the *Yahagi* to the flank on the right and left, and the *Yamato* in the center at the rear.

Already the task force had been discovered. Radio intercept stations throughout the Pacific had been transmitting coded messages to the cryptanalysis center at Pearl Harbor for some days. There, experts had pieced together a complete picture of Japanese intentions down to the precise composition of Admiral

Ito's force. Confirmation of the intelligence had come even before the task force reached open ocean. The submarines *Threadfin* and *Hackleback*, posted at Bungo Strait for this very purpose, had reported Admiral Ito's passage at 5:45 P.M. Admiral Mitscher in Task Force 58 intercepted the message and began steaming his carriers northward to get into position to attack Ito after daylight the next morning. Admiral Spruance, from his flagship off the Okinawa Beachhead, approved Mitscher's action and also ordered Admiral Deyo's Okinawa bombardment force, Task Force 54, to prepare for surface action. T.F. 58 and to Admiral Deyo's Okinawa bombardment flotilla, T.F. 54. If Mitscher's planes and fast battleships somehow missed the *Yamato*, then Deyo's old battlewagons would have to defy Ito's 18-inch guns.

By the gray predawn of April 7, her four great turbine engines whining softly, the *Yamato* and her nine escorts had reached the tip of Kyushu Island, steering westward to open the distance from T.F. 58 before turning south for Okinawa. Admiral Ito hoped to arrive at the Hagushi anchorage and off the Kadena and Yomitan airfields by the evening of April 7.

A handsome sight the ships were as they assumed at 6:00 A.M. their Number 3 Alert Cruising Disposition, a circular formation designed to repel air attack, which put the *Yahagi* in the lead and the destroyers spaced evenly about the *Yamato*, steaming majestically in the center. All ships zigzagged together, using a preset time interval, still maintaining their steady 22 knots. With this maneuver Admiral Ito had done all that he could.

II

This same morning found Admiral Mitscher mustering three groups of his carrier force. He planned a one-two punch; as soon as he was reasonably sure of Ito's whereabouts he would strike first with two task groups, then with a third. Planes from eight large and four light carriers would stalk the *Yamato*.

Already fighter planes were lifting from the decks of several carriers, their mission being to fan out along various search sectors from T.F. 58's position eastward of Okinawa's northern tip. At 8:32 A.M. *Essex* pilot Ensign Jack Lyons reported the enemy: course 300 degrees, speed 12 knots. He was wrong about the speed; Ito's task force still was making 22 knots. But the position report gave Admiral Mitscher what he was looking for. Eight minutes later the *Yamato*'s radar discovered Lyon, reporting him on a bearing of 150 degrees, distance 40 kilometers. On learning the news Admiral Ito merely nodded. But when two PBM amphibious flying boats from the Keramas began shadowing the force, he changed course and ordered the *Yamato* to fire. He could not afford to have his position continuously reported. The PBM's nevertheless remained in contact, flying in and out of clouds and dodging the *Yamato*'s antiaircraft.

At 10:00 A.M. Mitscher's main strikes took off, heading first toward the estimated location of the *Yamato* based on Ensign Lyons' initial sighting, then homing on the orbiting PBM's. The strikes were shy of fighters; the need for using Hellcats for search and for combat air patrols—Mitscher intended to take no chances with kamikazes—cut deeply into the numbers available. But his dive bombers and torpedo planes were out in full strength, more than 180 Helldivers and Avengers. Many of the accompanying fighters also carried bombs. In all, 386 U.S. planes stalked the *Yamato*.

Ito had hoped, without really expecting it, that friendly fighters from Kyushu would give him some cover against Mitscher's planes. A few did but left about 10:00 A.M. At Kanoya Admirals Ugaki and Yokoi knew of Ito's departure but lacked enough planes and pilots to maintain a proper cover. So Ito's lookouts on the *Yamato* could only eye the irritating PBM's and await whatever fate had to offer.

At about 11:00 A.M. the weather, which had been lowering all morning, turned to intermittent showers from a 2,500 foot ceiling. Ito's spirits brightened a little. When the Americans came—as he knew they would—they would have trouble coordinating and lining up their attacks. At 12:32 P.M. the *Yamato*'s radars picked up the flyers; Ito ordered his force to steam into the worst of the weather and await attack. Visibility dropped to five miles or less; that would help.

Mitscher's first two attack waves, from T.G.'s 58.1 and 58.3, had had a long, boring flight. At first the weather was fairly good and the pilots drummed ahead in a huge formation just under clouds hanging at about 2,000 feet. Seventy-five miles from the target the weather cleared and the formation began a slow climb to 6,000 feet. ASB radar sets in the planes then picked up the enemy, but the weather turned bad again, the ceiling falling to 2,000 feet with nine-tenths cloud cover. A little later a loud hum in their radio earphones told the airmen that Ito's radio operators were attempting to jam their transmissions. Belches of colored smoke—bursts from the *Yamato*'s guns—told them they had reached the radius of her antiaircraft.

The strike commanders found it impossible to arrange a coordinated attack. Task Group 58.1 went in first, followed by 58.3, and an hour later by 58.4.

Probably attacking first (though the honor was hotly disputed among pilots later) were the bomb-carrying Hellcats of Lieutenant Commander Beebe's *Hornet* fighter squadron. Roaring down from 5,000 feet, Beebe's pilots broke through the overcast a mile short, pulled up again into the murk, lost formation, then broke through to dive individually at the destroyers scattered about the *Yamato,* claiming two hits. Beebe, whose plane carried no bomb, strafed the Yahagi which was maneuvering astern of a destroyer.

Right behind Beebe, Commander Edward W. Hessell led six *Bennington* Hellcats in a 400-knot plunge. Bursting abruptly from the overcast, Hessell lined up on a destroyer, then found to his fury that his bomb would not release. Radioing angrily to his wingman that he had not brought a bomb this far to drop it in the ocean, Hessell braved the flak and dived again. This time his bomb released, landed within twenty-five feet of a destroyer, and failed to explode. Other pilots had better luck. Ensign Melvin R. Carter hit a big destroyer and his wingman, Lieutenant Clarence Davies, near-missed another. Flak erupted in vast purple bursts, but hit none of the fast Hellcats.

The fighter attacks had forced Ito's entire force into violent individual maneuvering, completely disrupting its neat, circular formation. Yet the huge bulk of the *Yamato* still dominated the mass of turning ships.

Commander Hugh Wood's Helldivers from the *Bennington* followed the fighters in, hearing strike commander E. G. Konrad order, "Take the big boy!" This was not easy. Dive bomber tactics called for a near-vertical plunge from at least 10,000 feet. Wood's eleven Helldivers had to dive through clouds from half that height. Catching a fleeting glimpse of the *Yamato* just ahead, Wood and four others nosed into 50-degree dives. Hastily lining up, they hurtled through red balls of light flak, dropped their thousand pounders, and abruptly pulled up with engines howling. All claimed to have hit, and the *Yamato*'s log records two bomb strikes at this time, 12:41 P.M. Both exploded near the after mast, knocking out an A-A gun, a radar, and a fire control station. But no vital harm was done; the thousand pounders could not penetrate the heavy deck armor to reach the ship's vitals.

Wood's seven other Helldivers dove on other ships in the force. Someone saw a wing flutter down; that would have been from Ensign Jack Carl Fuller's plane, hit by flak. Meanwhile, the *Hornet*'s Helldivers were also plunging through the overcast, scoring damaging hits.

Coming in below the Helldivers, just off the water, were the Avenger torpedo planes of the *Hornet, Bennington,* and two light carriers, the *Belleau Wood* and *San Jacinto.* The murky weather bothered them less. Leading the first group was Lieutenant Commander Edward E. DiGarmo with nine planes, each of which carried a stubby Mark 13 aerial torpedo. Through an oversight the torpedoes were set to run only twelve feet under the water, rendering them useless against the *Yamato* whose thick armor belt extended below that depth. Unable to reset them to run deeper, DiGarmo decided to attack the smaller ships, against which a twelve-foot depth setting was ideal.

Dipping beneath the overcast, DiGarmo's pilots broke right and left to catch the Japanese ships broadside whichever way they turned. Selecting the *Yahagi* and a close-by destroyer, they attacked from either flank, dropping the Mark 13's from 800 feet. Several ran hot and true, and a gunner looking back watched a column of water rise against the light cruiser. At 12:41 the *Yahagi* went dead in the water, the result of this hit and another from a bomb.

Lieutenant Robert L. Mini, losing the rest of the formation in the overcast, selected a stray destroyer as his victim. Releasing his torpedo through puff balls of flak, he jinked away, to hear a loud, "Bingo!" over his intercom from his gunner, Aviation Machinist's Mate 3/c William A. Raker of Shamokin, Pennsylvania. Raker had seen the fish blast the "can" amidships and the ship sag in the middle and begin to sink. This probably was the *Hamikaze,* which broke in two during the first attack.

Lieutenant Norman A. Weise inadvertently flew too close to

the *Yamato*. Then 25 mm. antiaircraft shells began hitting his plane just as he dropped his torpedo at a destroyer. As the tracers flashed by he ducked his head in a reflex action that saved his life. A shell penetrated his windscreen and instrument panel, drove a splinter into his scalp on exploding, and temporarily blinded him with 100-octane gasoline from his shattered fuel gauge. Another shell detonated in his radio compartment and wounded his gunner. Two more shredded his rudder and vertical stabilizer. He made it back to his carrier but probably missed the destroyer.

To this point in the action the *Yamato* had come off easily. Its light and heavy antiaircraft guns had been firing at targets ringing the ship. The turret gunners in the 18-inch batteries were loading shrapnel shells fused to burst in the air into the huge rifles, hastily pointing, and firing at more distant targets. Picking up targets in close were the 25 mm. gunners, manning triple and quadruple mounts, who swung their weapons to track like ducks the screaming Hellcats, Helldivers, and Avengers. They had shot down at least one plane, a Helldiver.

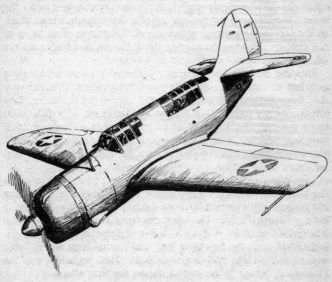

SB2C Curtiss "Helldiver"

Following in DiGarmo's torpedo planes were Avengers from the *Hornet* from VT-17. They, too, had taken off with wrong depth settings on their torpedoes, but because they took off a little later, each plane could reduce its fuel load enough to carry three men. This third crewman could, if the pilot thought of it, change the depth setting in midflight. Of eight planes which attacked the *Yamato*, four had reset their Mark 12's to run deep. As they bored in, flak from the huge battleship hurtled out in sheets, dropping the plane of Ensign Lee O'Brien into the sea. Another plane "hung" its torpedo and could not drop it but the other six did drop, and while some of the fish may have detonated harmlessly against the *Yamato*'s armor belt, one, running at twenty feet or deeper, hit the port side forward at 12:45 P.M.

One torpedo hit did not much bother the *Yamato*. "So at last a torpedo got us, eh?" remarked the navigator, smiling. Admiral Ito did not smile. He was contemplating three bodies being littered from the bridge, victims of the planes' machine guns, and knew that the action had hardly begun. Ensign Yoshida, learning that his former duty station, the after radio room, had been wrecked by a bomb, ran back to find nothing left of his comrades who had been manning the post. Then, spotting a second wave of planes approaching, he ran back to the bridge.

III

This second attack wave came right after the first. Planes from the *Essex* and *Bunker Hill* and from the light carrier *Bataan* (*Hancock*'s planes, launched fifteen minutes late, missed the target in the overcast) had been orbiting, waiting for the initial attackers to clear. At about 1:00 P.M. the squadrons began descending through the overcast.

Lieutenant Commander Chandler W. Swanson, commanding the *Bunker Hill*'s VT-84, was determined to torpedo the *Yamato*. At the briefing before takeoff he had insisted, "This squadron will attack the battleship, and only in case of necessity will any pilot drop on any other target." He did not overlook the torpedo depth settings. The fourteen Avengers carried Mark 13's set to explode at 18 to 22 feet, below the protective armor but high enough up the ship's 35-foot draught to cause stability problems when the torpedoes let in floods of salt water.

Swanson's squadron orbited with the rest of T.G. 58.3's planes twelve miles north of the *Yamato*. At 12:50 P.M. Swanson got the signal to attack and led his formation down, using his radar to track the battleship as the fourteen planes bumped and swayed through the overcast. Breaking from the clouds at 2,000 feet, Swanson spotted the battleship through the gloom and rain still making 22 knots in a sweeping starboard turn. Yelling "Break!" over his radio, he split his formation, his own flight of eight planes bearing straight ahead for the ship, the second of six planes under Lieutenant B. F. Berry banking left to catch the *Yamato* on its other flank in an "anvil" attack. Whichever way the *Yamato* now turned it must present its broadside to a group of attackers. Spotting the torpedo planes at 1:33 P.M., the battleship's captain, Rear Admiral Kosaku Ariga, elected to stay in his starboard turn. Each division of planes now approached the ship from the stern, Swanson's eight on the outside and Berry's six on the inside of the battleship's wide turn, making a miss virtually impossible.

At a second command each flight broke into three and two plane segments, separating widely to make the job of the *Yamato*'s automatic gunners more difficult. As they closed each of the five attacking sections again separated, spreading the distance between planes, giving each pilot room to jink right or left to throw off the A-A controllers. As the now widely spaced planes approached in two ragged waves, one to port and one to starboard, the *Yamato*'s gunners threw out every caliber of shell in the magazines, from 18.1-inch to 25 mm. Suddenly, flames spurted from Lieutenant R. J. Walsh's Avenger, which nosed down and exploded in the sea before Walsh could release its torpedo. At an altitude of 500 feet, speed 214 knots, the remaining pilots pressed on, some using their ASB radar to read off range to the *Yamato*. At an average of 1,570 yards from the battleship they released. The torpedoes splashed into the water, seemed to hesitate a moment, and then sped toward the still turning battlewagon trailing strings of bubbles in their wakes.

For all of the torpedoes to miss was impossible. At 1:37 P.M. three hit the port side amidship and a few minutes later, two more. Now the *Yamato* was gravely hurt. Six hits on the same side had wrecked or drowned out much machinery, including the auxiliary steering gear, and had caused power to fail, crippling the battleship's electrically operated turrets. But worst of all, as Swanson had hoped, the ship began to flood unevenly with a steadily increasing list to port.

With torpedoes away, all of Commander Swanson's Avenger pilots concentrated on survival, kicking rudders and banking violently to throw off the vengeful gunners. Many headed for the safest place, right over the battleship (A-A guns cannot normally fire straight up), and then flew away to the south. Lieutenant J. O. Davis perfectly expressed their sentiments. "On the way in I was working for the Navy; on the way out I was working for myself and my crew." He made it, but two pilots nearly didn't. Ensign O. R. Webster's Avenger was holed in the right wing root and caught fire. Incredibly, the flames died out, but the right wheel dropped, forcing Webster to increase his power setting to hold the formation. He landed on the *Bunker Hill* with just five gallons of gas left, a mere thimbleful for his big Wright Cyclone engine. Lieutenant D. F. Ray had been unable to retract a wheel after takeoff, but continued the attack anyway, afterward tossing from the plane everything except his two crewmen. He landed with fifteen gallons of fuel.

After Swanson's attack torpedo squadrons from the other ships also made approaches from either side. A torpedo hit at 2:07 to starboard and three more struck the wounded port side between 2:12 and 2:17 and rapidly increased the list. Helldivers added to the chaos, blowing overside machine gun mounts with several direct hits. The *Yamato*'s gunners fought back valiantly, but amid the shock of explosions and flying shrapnel they found it difficult to train their guns.

Seaman First Class Nobuyuki Kobayashi, a loader on a 25 mm. triple machine cannon, took the gun aimer's place when a bullet chopped down the man, then had his center gun smashed by a piece of shrapnel from a near-miss by a Helldiver. "At this time I got a splinter in my brow," he recalls, "but I pulled it out, wrapped a towel around my head and kept shooting." Lookouts reported that two Helldivers had been shot down, but the attack continued relentlessly. One after another the *Yamato*'s guns fell silent as each bomb blast left her more vulnerable than before.

The necessity of correcting the *Yamato*'s list, now fifteen degrees, became imperative lest she capsize. From the bridge came Admiral Ariga's order to flood the starboard engine and boiler rooms. "I hastily phoned these rooms to warn the occupants of the flooding order, but it was too late," writes Mitsuru Yoshida. "Water, both from the torpedo hits and the flood valves, snuffed out the lives of the men at their posts, several hundred in all." With only one propeller revolving to move the *Yamato*'s massive bulk, speed fell off still more.

The planes of the first two attack groups had also been pummeling the cruiser *Yahagi* and the escorting destroyers. At 1:45 P.M. they ganged up on the light cruiser, dive bombers lining up for attacks, torpedo bombers hitting from both sides. In twenty minutes they had done her in with seven torpedo and twelve bomb hits. Two bombs had wrecked the destroyer *Kasumi,* and a near-miss had flooded the *Isokaze.* The remaining destroyers had suffered damage in varying degrees; a dud torpedo had passed completely through the *Fuyutsuki.*

After a brief pause planes from T.G. 58.4 arrived at 2:00 P.M. The need to fly support missions at Okinawa had limited this force to a half-strike, 109 planes, but the weakened condition of Admiral Ito's defenses made their attack horribly effective. Helldivers and Avengers were able to make deliberate, careful runs, picking on the wounded port side of the battleship. The *Yamato*'s list increased, causing men and guns to slide into the sea. Nobuyuki Kobayashi took a piece of bullet in his knee; he found it impossible now to fire at the planes.

In the bowels of the ship, in the seventh section aft on the starboard side, Sakae Katano strove to carry on his damage control duties. "I left one of my men in Section 7 and took the rest to do repair work. But while we were running a torpedo hit the starboard side. So I closed the hatch and our belongings were floating about." Katano went to the bridge but found the ship listing hopelessly. Returning to his station he called his men—all now had to swim to the escape hatch. More torpedo hits—the ship's log records five hits in ten minutes but there may have been more—flooded still more compartments, further increasing the list.

On the bridge Admiral Ito resolutely entered his sea cabin and closed the door. The *Yamato* was capsizing and he meant to go down with her. Seaman Kobayashi got his ditty box, scrambled to the high side of the ship, sat down, and broke out his ration of cigarettes of the imperial gift, sharing them with others. "I knew there was hardly any hope of survival whether one jumped into the sea or stayed with the ship, so I wanted to stay with the ship and die with her." He heard the captain, Rear Admiral Ariga, shouting that the young men must leave the *Yamato* and preserve their lives for Japan's future, but he did not move. Just then a magazine exploded in the fore part of the ship. "I was blown away and lost consciousness, but just before passing out the image of my mother calling my name appeared before my eyes. . . . I think I was blown 200 or 300 meters and was truly lucky." Kobayashi, who was only eighteen, came to, swimming.

In the stern Katano heard the order to abandon ship. "I told my men to jump into the sea but they did not have the courage to follow my order. [So] I jumped into the sea first—it was really a matter of sliding down the side of the ship—and my men followed me."

Ensign Yoshida crawled out a port on the bridge as the *Yamato* rolled onto her beam's ends at 2:20 P.M. Explosions rent her interior as ammunition detonated, then she slid under, more blasts sending sheets of flame into the air. Yoshida was battered about, and then expelled to the surface.

The *Yamato* was no more, the mission of the First Diversion Attack Force had ended in the China Sea 240 nautical miles short of the Hagushi beachhead. Two destroyers, relatively intact, remained on the scene to pick up survivors. Two more were badly damaged and crawled back to Kyushu. A third, separated from the others, had been sunk by the Helldivers. The *Yahagi* and three more destroyers had perished in the main attack. Only twelve U.S. airmen had been lost, plus four Helldivers, three Avengers, and three Hellcats.

IV

For hundreds of men in the water a battle for survival was beginning. Sakae Katano peered about nearsightedly—he had lost his glasses—but could see no ships. "I had a bad feeling because I knew there were sharks in the sea." After the planes had left, Japanese destroyers returned, but a tidal current carried Katano away. "Finally we gave up. . . . Then I heard people talking and found a destroyer in front of me." Katano and the others swam to the ship, the *Yukikaze*, but he found himself too weak to climb a rope ladder. Finally he tied a line about his waist and, gripping the bitter end in his teeth, was drawn aboard.

Katano had been lucky. Many sank from wounds or weakness; others went mad or lost consciousness. "I found other men floating or swimming around me," recalls Nobuyuki Kobayashi. "I started to swim, encouraging others, and whenever U.S. planes came near to strafe us, I remained under water for a minute or so." Taking off his waistcloth he tossed it to a man who was weakening, tying one end to a floating object. "I tried to rescue others, too, but in the end it was not possible to save them. About thirty men died around me while we were swimming for four-and-one-half hours." At a little past 6:00 P.M. the other rescuing destroyer, the *Fuyutzuki,* hove to near the twelve or thirteen men of Kobayashi's group who remained alive. "When I was rescued I noticed for the first time that my left arm was fractured." This destroyer also picked up Ensign Yoshida, who had survived the long ordeal despite a severe gash on his head. The highest-ranking officer to survive was Captain Jiro Nomura, the executive officer. Admiral Ito had perished, as had Rear Admiral Ariga. Of the men on the *Yamato,* only 269 survived; 2,498 officers and men had died. Loss of life on the other ships also had been heavy.

At noon on April 7 radio operators at the Kanoya Naval Air Station had picked up a message from Admiral Ito's *Yamato* force. It read, "We are under attack by carrier planes." Officers at 5th Air Fleet headquarters were mildly surprised; they had hoped that the great attack of the previous day had largely knocked out Admiral Mitscher's T.F. 58. But Admiral Ugaki and Yokoi could do nothing for Ito and his men. They had hurled nearly all their remaining strength, seventy-eight escorting fighters and forty-one kamikazes, at what they hoped would be the remnants of shattered U.S. carrier forces. They could only pray that these attacks would avenge the *Yamato,* if, as they believed likely, she were to be sunk.

As in the attacks of the previous day, combat air patrols expertly intercepted incoming Japanese attackers. A quartet of F6F's launched at 9:08 A.M. from the *Bennington* saved T.G. 58.1 from a lot of trouble. Led by Lieutenant Ray B. Dalton of Arkadelphia, Arkansas, the four went after a target fifteen miles distant and coming in fast at an altitude of 1,000 feet. The Hellcats closed, then bounced three late-model fighters they identified as a George and two Franks. None returned fire and all were destroyed. Glancing about, Lieutenant Armand G. Manston, one of Dalton's four, saw two more Franks diving in, and with his wingman, Lieutenant (jg) Lloyd B. Murray, attacked both and shot them down. All planes downed burned on the water. The action had been lightning quick, just a few seconds. So it went elsewhere, T.F. 58 fighters claiming twenty-four.

Carrier *Hancock* was the hard-luck ship of this April 7. Going astray in the poor weather her air group had missed the *Yamato*. Now, at 12:12 P.M. the big carrier opened fire on a plane which appeared at 3,000 feet, moving fast. Its pilot dove, dropped a bomb which hit the flight deck forward, then crashed the carrier astern, cartwheeling into several Hellcats on the after deck. Flames shot up, and the *Hancock*'s captain, Robert F. Hickey, turned his ship broadside to the wind, enabling the ship's fire crew to attack flames on the flight and hangar decks. They did this to such good purpose that fires soon were out, but over seventy men had been killed, and although the deck was patched sufficiently to permit the strayed air group to land, the *Hancock* had to retire to Ulithi for repairs.

Most of the attacks thrown at the Okinawa beachhead on April 7 came from General Sugahara's 6th Air Army. At dawn eleven special attack planes took off for Okinawa from Tokuno Shima and six more followed a little later. Making up for the lapse the previous day, when only fifty-four kamikazes had taken off, twenty Army flyers left Bansei on Kyushu in the morning and thirty left Chiran in the afternoon. Even from much-battered Wan airfield on Kikai Jima, favorite target of American pilots, nine planes that had been hidden away took off for Okinawa. Ugaki's naval command contributed twelve Frances bombers. The same bad weather that had hampered Mitscher's American airmen bothered the attackers; only thirteen of the Kyushu Army planes got through and nine of the Navy kamikazes.

Though a pale shadow of the previous day, they were sufficiently deadly. One plane plummeted squarely into the old battleship *Maryland* as she steamed in formation with others of Admiral Deyo's support ships in case the *Yamato* broke through. Another crashed the destroyer *Bennett* on radar picket station, killing three crewmen. A third hit a destroyer-escort. About twenty planes approached the Hagushi area but hit no transports or cargo ships.

Kikusui 1 and its appendage, the First Diversion Attack Force, alias the *Yamato* and her consorts, had sputtered out. A combination of good training, excellent shooting, and fine work by American pilots, especially those of the *Bunker Hill*'s torpedo squadron, and above all the desperate valor of the radar pickets had frustrated the primary Japanese threat to the Okinawa operation. Not that it was over. Even as American staffs at Spruance's floating headquarters evaluated the results of April 6 and 7, Combined Fleet Headquarters in Tokyo flashed an order to Kanoya Air Station: "Prepare for Kikusui Operation Number 2." As soon as enough planes and pilots had been assembled the hell-birds would fly again in force.

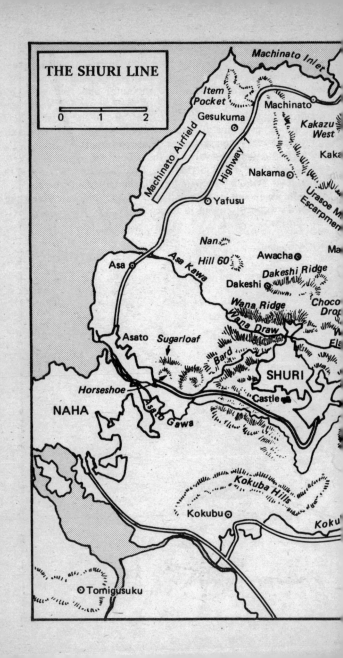

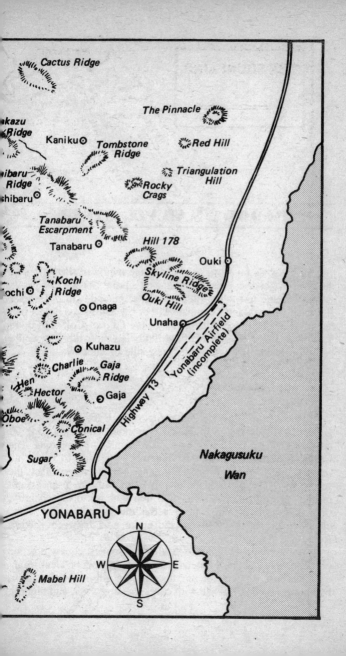

9

BLOODY KAKAZU RIDGE

THE KAMIKAZES on April 6 had tried the mettle of the sailors of the radar picket destroyers. Beginning on April 9 General Ushijima's infantry would test to the fullest the courage and skill of General Buckner's line infantry companies. For the sailors the ordeal had begun at Radar Picket Station 1; for the GI's of Colonel Edwin T. May's 383rd Regiment of the 96th Division the test would begin on Kakazu Ridge on the west side of Okinawa.

I

As seen from May's command post on Cactus Ridge, eight hundred yards to the north, Kakazu (pronounced cock-a-zoo) did not appear high, nor was it especially steep and precipitous. The Urasoe-Mura escarpment three-quarters of a mile to the south seemed much more formidable, and May assumed that the seizure of Kakazu would be merely a preliminary to an assault on the escarpment. His maps told him nothing to the contrary; they had been prepared from aerial photographs taken when cloud cover had blanked out the entire area between Kakazu Ridge and Shuri.

In truth, May was about to tackle the strongest enemy position on Okinawa. Colonel Munetatsu Hara's 13th Independent Infantry Battalion, digging for months with the aid of civilian labor, had honeycombed Kakazu with caves, passageways, and tunnels, some of which ran completely through the ridge. To man Kakazu's defenses Hara had his own 13th Battalion, replenished after heavy losses on Cactus Ridge, and elements of the 2nd Light Mortar Battalion, the 4th Independent Machine Gun Battalion, and the 1st Artillery Mortar Regiment manning several 320 mm. spigot mortars which could lob a huge shell from a piston mount more than a thousand yards. Hara's positions were not essentially different from others American forces had encountered; what was remarkable about them was their complete camouflage, their deft selection, their abundance, their mutually interlocking firepower, and their impregnability even to the 1,900-pound shells being fired daily from the U.S.S. *Colorado* lurking offshore.

Kakazu Ridge was a rough coral hogback about a thousand yards long, running from the edge of the coastal flat in the northwest to Highway 5 in the southeast. Two hills made up the ridge. The larger, rising to a maximum height of 280 feet above sea level, was about 500 yards long with a rounded hilltop averaging 25 yards in width. A draw separated it from the smaller hill, later called "Kakazu West" by the Americans, which lay at a right angle, north-south, to the main part of the ridge. Its length was about 250 yards and its summit consisted of two knolls facing north-south with a slight depression or saddle in between. Just over the main ridge, invisible to the attackers, lay the tile-roofed hamlet of Kakazu.

Colonel Hara had buried his headquarters in a deep, impregnable cavern dug into the south base of the main ridge. His only real problem was communications. Passageways connected many tunnels and voice tubes others, but some were isolated, forcing Hara to rely on runners who would have to expose themselves to shrapnel from American artillery and mortar fire. Hara had no worry about tanks. Before the ridge, running for its entire length, was a deep gorge cut into the coral rock by a small stream, a natural antitank ditch. Tanks could not traverse it, nor could they skirt either end of Kakazu without exposing themselves fatally to artillery and antitank fire.

On the northern face of Kakazu and on its crest, Hara had emplaced outposts in tombs and concrete positions. On the southern reverse slope, defiladed from artillery and invisible to an attacker, were concentrated most of his infantry and all of his mortars. If the Americans attacked, Hara could lay down a heavy barrage along the top and northern face of the ridge, supplemented by mortars, artillery, and heavy machine guns firing from the Urasoe-Mura escarpment to his rear. Every cave, every position, was covered by others. Few American troops ever have faced a more difficult chore than Colonel May's GI's, who were as unaware as their commander of how thoroughly Hara had organized his ground.

320 mm. Spigot Mortar

II

For his attack on Kakazu, set for April 9, Colonel May decided to commit two battalions of his 383rd Infantry; his 1st commanded by Lieutenant Colonel Byron F. King, and his 3rd under Lieutenant Colonel Edward W. Stare. King's A and C companies would attack Kakazu Ridge proper; Stare's I and L companies would seize Kakazu West. Taking a leaf from the book of tactics of his enemy, May ordered the men to move out before daylight. He hoped they would seize the top of Kakazu and Kakazu West by dawn. To insure total surprise the artillery would remain silent.

An hour before daybreak May's infantry jumped off, Captain Jack A. Royster's A Company and First Lieutenant Dave Belman's C Company hiking toward the main ridge and First Lieutenant Willard M. "Hoss" Mitchell's L Company toward Kakazu West. Captain Alvin E. Von Holle's I Company was late getting started and was caught by daybreak and pinned down short of Kakazu West, missing the action. The other three companies, moving according to plan, scrambled into and out of the steep gorge, and began climbing Kakazu and Kakazu West. By daybreak, an hour after jump-off, Hara's defenders still were unsuspecting though Mitchell's men had already bayoneted several Japanese pickets in outposts and Royster's and Belman's leading platoons were nearing the top of the ridge.

Then it happened. As he reached the top of the northernmost knoll that formed the initial crest of Kakazu West, Sergeant Alvin Becker of Company L saw a Japanese on the rearward knoll. Waving reassuringly to him, Becker saw him laugh and wave back; then "I opened up with my automatic rifle and all hell started popping." Emerging from their caves behind the rearward knoll, Colonel Hara's defenders prepared to expel the Americans from their lodgment.

Quickly Lieutenant Mitchell formed his men into a perimeter in the saddle between the two knolls. The saddle was just deep enough to shelter a man if he lay down. Mitchell's strategy was to let the Japanese expose themselves to fire as they charged over the rearward knoll. A fight now began which was epic by any standard of warfare.

Company L's best asset was Mitchell himself. A stocky, level-headed, easygoing Southerner who had played basketball and football at Mississippi State University, Mitchell was famous throughout May's 383rd Regiment because of his war cry: "Watch out! Here comes 'the Hoss' and God's on the Hoss's side!" Although he was still a lieutenant, his men—who adored him—called him "Captain Hoss." "He's a hoss," they would say. In turn he affectionately referred to them as his "lardtails." This day the "Hoss" and his "lardtails" would need every bit of support, divine included, they could get. It was a case of hold or die for L Company. The men knew that I Company had been pinned down below them and could not help. Retreat was infeasible; enemy machine guns covered the open ground below Kakazu West with a curtain of fire. Only Mitchell's leadership and their own weapons stood between the "lardtails" and destruction.

All morning a furious battle raged, with grenades and even satchel charges flying back and forth over the southernmost knoll beyond the saddle. Mitchell's deep bass voice boomed his war cry again and again as he encouraged his men. His First Sergeant, William L. Holbrow, took a fragment of metal but refused to leave the perimeter. Sergeant John A. Bradley, leading the first platoon, took a Japanese slug in the shoulder. Refusing to let the bullet stop him, he rallied his platoon when it was cut off from the rest of the company, then counterattacked enemy infiltrators. Hit in the leg he again rallied his men as the enemy recoiled, advanced, then recoiled again leaving behind twenty-six dead, victims of the platoon's fire. On the left flank of the perimeter Pfc Billy W. Stubbs wielded a machine gun to silence an enemy mortar and repel two enemy rushes. Technical Sergeant Milton Shepsky, L Company's "narrow escape kid," constantly exposed himself to Japanese fire as he sought out new positions for his platoon. In the process he picked off seven foes with his M-1. Hoss Mitchell was everywhere about the saddle, tossing grenades and dueling with Hara's defenders with his carbine. On one occasion he, Pfc Joseph I. Solch, and several other men spotted a 320 mm. spigot mortar on Kakazu West's southernmost knoll. Realizing that its huge shells could slay everyone in the saddle, Mitchell and his group blasted its cave position with grenades, destroying the weapon and its nine-man crew.

Sensing at about noon that Mitchell had only a small force controlling the northern knoll and the saddle of Kakazu West, Colonel Hara's defenders hurled the first of four general counterattacks, charging recklessly through their own mortar fire over the southern knoll. Lieutenant Bill Curran shot and killed the two Japanese leaders. Hoss killed an officer. Three times more the "lardtails" hurled back the enemy as casualties mounted in their dwindling ranks. In one attack Private Solch rose to his haunches to spray Hara's men with fire, emptying three BAR clips and driving a full company to cover. The coral rock of the saddle was too hard for the men to dig foxholes. "We just had to lie there and take it," commented Private Louis Novak later. Each attack depleted the limited supply of ammunition.

The last attack nearly overran the company. Recalled Sergeant Marshall W. Weaver, "The charging Japanese came within three feet of us and threw satchel charges that looked as big as boxes of apples." Billy Stubbs distinguished himself again "yelling like an Indian" and blazing away from the hip with his BAR.

III

Like Company L, the GI's of Royster's Company A and Belman's Company C had reached the top of Kakazu Ridge—in their case the main part of the ridge overlooking the Highway 5 road cut—before Hara's men spotted them. Then a lone Japanese in a pillbox saw Royster's men coming and opened fire. Within moments the Japanese defenders had piled from cave positions on Kakazu's reverse slopes, had set up mortars, and were pummeling the top of the ridge and its northern slopes with 50 mm. missiles. Heavier weapons hammered the gorge, too, trapping the heavy-weapons platoons, wounding a forward artillery observer, and driving all in the gorge to cover. Caught on open terraced ground between gorge and ridge, the mortarmen and heavy machine gunners had to hit the dirt and crawl into tombs to survive.

Atop the ridge Royster had only two of his three platoons, the other having joined Belman's company with which Royster had no contact. He and his GI's were squarely amid the Japanese positions with Hara's infantry popping up all about from cave openings. Other Japanese charged up the reverse slope of the hill, braving their own mortar fire. At points fighting swirled hand-to-hand.

In Belman's area nearby heroism was of necessity commonplace. On finding his platoon pinned down by a pair of Hara's machine guns emplanted farther along the ridge, Pfc Edward J. Moskala, a 23-year-old BAR man from Chicago, started crawling toward the enemy from rock to rock. When near enough he threw several grenades, following the last with a rush. A staccato burst from his automatic rifle and both Japanese guns went silent. Moskala's company commander, young Dave Belman, already had been hit. Refusing evacuation despite weakness from loss of blood, he retained command, aided by his veteran Regular Army First Sergeant, Walter Cendrowski. His and Cendrowski's main concern was how to keep a group of Japanese from slipping around C Company's exposed left flank.

The fight was going no better in Royster's sector. A mortar burst had wounded Royster in the face and left him in great pain and nearly blind, but like Belman he refused evacuation. One of his platoon leaders, First Lieutenant Stephen M. Macey, deliberately crawled forward into an exposed area to draw fire and to locate targets. Another platoon leader, First Lieutenant John F. Casey, continued crawling from group to group of his men despite a serious leg wound. The company's lead scout and first man up the ridge, Pfc Gervase D. Birster, broke up a counterattack by fifteen enemies, killing four and wounding one with his rifle. Birster's move was an exception; lacking the protection of the saddle that had sheltered L Company, most of the A and C Company GI's could merely hug open ground until they were hit.

By about an hour and a half after the action began, Royster knew that he and Belman could not stay on the ridge much longer. Already many men had edged back off the crest to huddle in niches and holes on Kakazu's northern slope, seeking some cover from flying shrapnel. Others further down the slope had found shelter in Okinawan tombs. Still others, wounded and helpless where they had been hit, lay hugging the earth. Casualties mounted steadily, mostly from mortar fire. Desperately Captain Royster radioed at 7:45 A.M. to Lieutenant Colonel King, his battalion commander:

Have 50 men on ridge. Support elements pinned down. Heavy concentration of mortars and artillery being laid down on troops besides MG crossfire. If we do not get reinforcements, we will have to withdraw.

King's response was—hold on. He would send up B Company as reinforcement. But Colonel King's promised reinforcement got nowhere in its attempt to approach Kakazu. Captain John C. Van Vulpin and his B Company men were pinned down short of the gorge.

North of the gorge where his own command post was under shellfire, Colonel King's feeling grew that his entire 1st Battalion was in serious trouble. Learning that his reinforcing company had failed to reach the gorge, he radioed at 8:40 A.M. to his regimental commander, Colonel May:

We are in a serious predicament. There are only 50 men left on the ridge. . . . Furthermore there is an estimated battalion of Japs moving up for counterattack.

But May would not hear of withdrawal. He replied,

I am sending G Company [of his 2nd Battalion, located back on Cactus Ridge] to reinforce you. Hold the hill at all costs. You will lose just as many men if you try to withdraw and . . . will lose the high ground. If . . . [you are] jumpy, have the executive officer take over.

Hard-boiled Eddie May still believed that Kakazu was not all that difficult. He needed its high ground to use as a jumping-off point for the Urasoe-Mura escarpment three-quarters of a mile beyond and evidently believed that King had, indeed, become excessively "jumpy."

Captain Royster, up on Kakazu, could have set May straight. Though suffering terribly from his facial wounds, he was still rational enough to know that one of Colonel Hara's counterattacks must soon overrun him. But to retreat under observed enemy fire would be suicidal. He therefore radioed the 88th Chemical Mortar Battalion to fire concealing smoke shells with its 4.2-inch mortars to blind the Japanese gunners and to permit his men to escape. The mortars fired, but the wind blew the smoke back into Royster's face. It was almost 10:00 A.M. before Royster judged the smoke thick enough to allow his men and Belman's to withdraw. Then both A and C Companies began working down Kakazu's northern slope toward the gorge, pulling and carrying their wounded with them.

A small covering force in both companies—Royster included—stayed on the ridge to protect the wounded and to prevent the enemy from interfering with the withdrawal. Many took chances to save their wounded buddies. Pfc Charles L. Wagner guarded four wounded men until they could be pulled to safety one by one. Pfc Edward C. Basset of Company C abandoned his radio to help carry wounded; then, realizing the radio could be vital to the survival of all, he crawled back up the ridge to retrieve it. The last man down was Ed Moskala, who on learning that a wounded man remained on the ridge went back up to get him.

When the first men reached the gorge at about 10:30 A.M., they found John Van Vulpen, B Company's commander, in charge. Though pinned down, Captain Van Vulpen and a few of his men had managed to reach the gorge after a desperate crawl under enemy mortar and artillery fire. They found the gorge only relatively safer. Japanese mortar fire was dropping into it, forcing the men into caves and holes on the steep south side for protection. Machine gun fire from Japanese who had reoccupied portions of the Kakazu's crest was raking the gorge's south rim. Van Vulpen could count only forty-six of an initial three hundred able-bodied men in the 1st Battalion, but on radioing Lieutenant Colonel King he found that he was expected to reoccupy Kakazu. Dutifully, he led the men out, only to be pinned down with seven casualties before he and they had gone more than a few feet beyond the lip of the gorge. All crawled back to safety, dragging the wounded.

Now the entire battalion—what was left of it—was trapped in the gorge. How to escape? Several hundred yards of exposed ground to the rear prevented a direct withdrawal. A small ravine leading northwestward toward the American lines seemed the best route, and so Lieutenant William R. Nieman and T/Sgt Hilton Shults led a crouching file of men up the ravine. Before they had gone far a Japanese machine gunner cut them off, forcing them to pull eleven wounded men into an abandoned pillbox. Later, when the firing died down, they crawled the remaining 300 yards to the 1st Division command post.

In the gorge Van Vulpen, seeing his men were trapped, decided to try to get back himself and arrange for an artillery barrage to silence the Japanese machine gunners and mortarmen on the ridge. Then litter bearers could reach the gorge to carry out the wounded. Leaving Second Lieutenant Leo Ford in charge, he crawled back, accompanied by T/Sgt John J. Summers. After successfully running the gauntlet of fire, they were so shaken by concussion that neither was rational. But they did make clear the need for litter bearers.

Responsibility now fell on young Leo Ford, an Oklahoman. Both Royster and Belman were suffering too intensely from their wounds to command further. Ford knew that he would need smoke cover to get the wounded out, but when he radioed to the 1st Battalion command post, he learned that the mortarmen were almost out of smoke ammunition. Nevertheless, he risked his life peering over the south rim of the gorge directing fire until the supply was expended. Then all seemed lost. "Leo," Captain Hugh D. Young, the battalion operations officer (S-3), radioed him in a voice choked with emotion, "I hope I'll see you again, but I don't understand how you can make it. God help the bunch of you."

Ford's best chance for escape now seemed to be to retire down the gorge toward the jump-off point of Hoss Mitchell's men earlier in the day. By 4:00 P.M. he and his men had inched their way westward with their casualties to a point approximately opposite the north slope of Kakazu West.

Bringing up the rear was Ed Moskala, who again had volunteered to act as rear guard. Twice he helped carry wounded buddies, paying for his courage with his life on the second trip. None of the men might have made it had not Pfc Louis H. Thornton of Company C charged a hundred yards down the gorge to knock out an enemy machine gun blocking further retreat.

When an American air strike hit the ridge, knocking down debris and boulders, Ford decided to chance it and told his men what the 96th Division's history has described as "a magnificent falsehood." "Smoke will be coming up soon and we can make a break for it." Many did, slipping out with Ford in twos and threes.

Others—some wounded—still crouched in caves and dugouts along the gorge. It still was necessary to give them first aid and get them out. At 1st Battalion headquarters a dozen men volunteered to cross the fire-swept ground and litter out the wounded. They left the American lines and moved forward, but one was killed and others were pinned down. Only six, including Private Tom

Yei, crawled to the gorge where they ducked into caves to escape the continuing mortar fire. There they remained until dark.

Early the next morning the six volunteers moved down the gorge, calling out to the wounded. Sergeant Arthur Dubin, a C Company man, heard Yei shout and with others helped him carry the injured to the lower end of the gorge from where they could be dragged on ponchos to the American lines. At about 5:00 A.M., with Yei in the lead, the party headed back. Said Yei later, "Halfway across snipers opened up, but I made it. I wasn't scared, but afterward I was shaky."

IV

In contrast to the painful retreat of the 1st Battalion survivors, Mitchell's "lardtails" of L Company left Kakazu West in good order. After the repulse of Hara's fourth counterattack, the Hoss realized that one more would finish him and his men. He had very few left unwounded, his machine gun ammunition was gone, and his mortars had long since expended their last shells. On contacting his battalion headquarters by radio, he learned that more smoke ammunition had reached the chemical mortars. He directed the concealing fire skillfully, the wind was right, and after ten long hours of battle, he and his men slipped back down Kakazu West to the gorge, and from there under the cover of smoke to their own lines. Of eighty-nine men who had started out that morning just three remained unscathed. Thirty-seven wounded had to be carried, and 17 more were killed or missing, but the "Hoss" estimated that 165 of Hara's infantry had perished, mostly during their fierce but futile counterattacks. Solch and Mitchell received Distinguished Service Crosses. Virtually every other man won either a Silver or a Bronze Star, and L Company as a unit received a Distinguished Unit Citation. Ed Moskala received a Congressional Medal of Honor, and Leo Ford a Silver Star.

For the 383rd Regimental Combat Team the Kakazu Ridge attack of April 9 had been a frightful disaster. The regiment had suffered 326 casualties, of which 23 were killed, 256 wounded, and 47 missing, mostly from the 1st Battalion, now so depleted in its line companies as to be considered ineffective. Colonel

May had relieved its commander, Lieutenant Colonel King, after King had continued to plead for permission to withdraw, and at 1:30 P.M. had placed King's executive officer, Major Kenny W. Erickson, in command. This he had done although failure of the attack could in no way be considered King's fault. May's only consolation was his G-2's estimate that about 420 of the enemy had fallen. Although this figure may have been somewhat exaggerated, Japanese records confirm that by April 10 Hara's 13th Independent Infantry Battalion mustered but 600 men, about one-half of its original strength.

The Kakazu attack taught American commanders at all levels their most sobering lesson of the campaign. The key to victory, they now realized, lay on the reverse slopes of the chain of ridges lying between Kakazu and Shuri. Seizing the forward slope of each ridge and its crest would be but the easiest task. The infantry would somehow have to endure enemy mortars, artillery, and machine guns to work their way down the reverse slopes and blast or burn out the interlocking system of tunnels, pillboxes, caves, and trenches below. Progress would be, as one officer foresaw, "damn slow, and not cheap." In one sense it could be said that the battle for Okinawa had begun with the attack on Kakazu Ridge.

V

Even before the attack on Kakazu had failed, Brigadier General Claudius M. Easley,* the assistant division commander of the 96th, was up front conferring with all three of his regimental commanders, Eddie May, Mike Halloran, and Marcey Dill. None was discouraged despite the events of the day, least of all May, the infantryman of the old school. More firepower, they decided, was the answer to the challenge of Kakazu Ridge. They well knew that General Hodge wanted to keep his 24th Corps offensive moving and agreed that the price would have to be accepted.

This time surprise was out. Easley, who would personally

---

*It was General Easley who was responsible for the division's nickname, "The Deadeyes." A champion rifle shot himself, Easley had placed unusual stress on marksmanship in training in Oregon.

direct the attack of four battalions of infantry, proposed to blast out the Japanese with artillery and bombs. Eight battalions of 105 mm. and 155 mm. guns, supplemented by air strikes and fire from Navy warships, including the battleship *New York,* would unleash a devastating concentration intended to stun Hara's men and bury them in their holes. Then two regiments would overwhelm Kakazu Ridge and Kakazu West. May's 2nd and 3rd Battalions of his 383rd Regiment would attack the main ridge across the infamous gorge; Holloran's 381st would attack Kakazu West. The infantry would go it alone; tanks could not cross the gorge to help.

Attacking Kakazu West about 7:15 A.M. on April 10, two companies of Lieutenant Colonel Russell Graybill's 2nd Battalion managed to reach the gorge, cross, take cover from the fierce mortar barrage the Japanese immediately laid down between themselves and the Americans as on the day before. The savage preattack bombardment had in no degree diminished it. At 8:05 A.M. in a skirmish line the Americans moved up the north face of Kakazu West. Captain Willard G. Bollinger's Company F and First Lieutenant John D. Blair's Company E occupied the northern knoll and face of the hill. Staff Sergeants Robert L. Kulp and Arvil M. Brewer, with three privates, had outflanked and grenaded a pair of enemy machine guns on the northern knoll, killing ten Japanese. By 9:30 F Company held an arc in the shallow saddle where Mitchell had held out the day before; E Company, below, occupied the hill's northern face. Already Colonel Graybill had called up his reserve, G Company, to reinforce them. He knew only too well what had happened the day before to "Hoss" Mitchell and his company.

In the meantime, on Kakazu proper, Colonel May's 2nd and 3rd Battalions were getting a near-repeat of what his 1st Battalion had suffered the day before. His 2nd Battalion failed even to reach the ridge. Suffering terribly from enemy mortar, machine gun, and artillery fire, it had to settle for positions astride the gorge near Highway 5 at the east end of Kakazu Ridge. The 3rd Battalion and K Company managed to reach the main ridge further to the west near the narrow draw between Kakazu and Kakazu West. With them was Lieutenant Colonel Edward W. Stare, the battalion commander, who soon was fretting over the heavy losses enemy mortars and machine guns were inflicting on his men. At 1:05 P.M. Stare reported his position, adding that he was short of men and that the Japanese were counterattacking. In response General Easley dispatched three companies to his aid. All made it, stopped Hara's counterattack, and dug in for the night below the crest of the ridge. They might have taken it had one of Hara's light machine gunners not jumped onto the crest to spray them with his Nambu and drive them to cover.

Rain, which had begun falling at noon, combined with steady Japanese artillery fire from Shuri to generate a bad night for the line infantry companies of the 381st and 383rd, huddling miserably on Kakazu and Kakazu West under foxholes covered with shelter halves. Nevertheless, they appreciated the efforts of their cooks and mail clerks, who, with volunteers from other headquarters organizations, braved the rain and artillery to haul up heavy boxes of ammunition and rations and to evacuate wounded.

VI

It required two more days to convince General Easley that Kakazu was too tough for the Deadeyes. On April 11 Colonel John G. Cassidy's battalion of the 381st attacked again and failed to seize the top of the main ridge. Twice the Japanese counterattacked First Lieutenant Julius B. Anderson's Company A, clinging just below the crest; twice they were driven off, mostly by the efforts of Technical Sergeant Alfred C. Robertson. A half-Sioux Indian, "Chief" Robertson used an automatic rifle, his M-1, grenades, bayonet, and even his trench knife to knock out two machine guns and kill twenty-eight enemies single-handed. Then he took over a radio, crawled up to the crest, and directed close-in mortar fire on Hara's positions. One of his buddies remarked, "Just a good day's work for the Chief." He received a Silver Star.

In another episode Captain Irven T. Larsen, of Laramie, Wyoming, commanding Company F of the 383rd Regiment, led four privates in an attack on a Japanese strongpoint built around one heavy and three light machine guns. With grenades and his M-1 Larsen killed the heavy machine gun crew, then turned the Japanese weapon on the light machine guns, pinning down the gunners until his men could grenade them. Later, he flushed an enemy sniper with a smoke grenade, then got him with his rifle. But as he rose to move forward once more, a concealed machine gun killed him with a single burst. In the end this attack also failed. Despite the bravery of Larsen and others, the Japanese counterattacked again, and the Americans, carrying their casualties with them, had to return under smoke cover to their starting point near the gorge. Everywhere, the Deadeye attack had failed to achieve significant gains.

The night of April 11–12 featured not only the usual Japanese mortar fire but also bombardment of the Kakazu area with 320 mm. spigot mortar shells. One of these 674-pound monsters brought down a landslide across a cave being used as an aid station by the 381st, killing thirteen and wounding nine. Had the weapon been capable of accurate fire, Deadeye losses before Kakazu would have been much higher.

The morning of the twelfth witnessed the last Deadeye try at Kakazu. General Easley ordered heavy air strikes on Kakazu's crest and reverse slope, but these were so ineffective that when Colonel Cassidy's 1st Battalion attacked early in the morning it was pelted for an hour by mortar shells falling at a rate of better than sixty a minute. Understandably, the attack failed, with a loss of forty-five more men.

VII

Eastward from Kakazu Ridge, from Highway 5 to the shores of Nakagusuku Bay, the 7th Division made the only significant American advance of the period April 9–12. From Triangulation Hill to Ouki on Nakagusuku Bay, the division gained up to 1,000 yards. Ouki proved tough; the 32nd Infantry entered the town on April 11 and was promptly driven out. The night of April 12 found all units of the 7th stalled a few hundred yards north of Hill 178, a towering height and important Japanese artillery observation point.

M1 Garand

Immediately east of Kakazu the Deadeye 382nd Regiment failed to gain against stubborn Tombstone Ridge. It went over to the defensive on April 11 and consolidated its positions, mopping up Japanese stragglers to its rear. Tombstone obviously rivaled Kakazu in defensive power and like Kakazu would have to wait.

Casualties to the 7th and 96th divisions totaled approximately 2,880 between April 9 and 12, with 451 dead. An additional 241 men were missing and 2,198 were wounded. Estimated enemy losses, all KIA (killed in action), totaled 5,750, which was probably an overestimate by at least a third. Nevertheless, the 13th Independent Infantry Battalion had suffered very heavily, and the 14th was down to two-thirds of its strength.

The Kakazu battle had been heartbreaking for the commander of the 96th Division, Major General Jim Bradley. Usually an affable man, inclined to joke and to laugh with his men when he visited them, his "inevitable cigarette" in its "inevitable holder," Bradley had become grim and silent as the action proceeded. He knew what his men were suffering; worse, he could read the dwindling strength reports and note the alarming decline in the combat strength of his division. He knew his men were questioning the worth of it all, but until his orders were changed Bradley had to keep his infantry on Kakazu, subjecting them to steady attrition.

At 24th Corps headquarters General Hodge and his intelligence officer, Colonel Nist, understood thoroughly why the attacks had failed. On April 9 they had received a captured Japanese map which showed in detail the strength of the defensive positions before Shuri. The map convinced Hodge and Nist that the Shuri positions were the strongest yet encountered in the Pacific.

Hodge's main concern was ammunition. Only artillery and plenty of it would soften those enemy positions. Renewed offensive operations against Kakazu would have to wait until enough 105 and 155 mm. shells had come across the beaches to sustain a really heavy daily expenditure. As the 24th Corps official report noted, an age-old truth of warfare had once again been borne out; the Okinawa campaign was ninety percent logistics and ten percent fighting.

149

10

USHIJIMA STRIKES BACK

IN THE FIRST dozen days of the Okinawan campaign General Ushijima had adhered rigidly to his present strategy of making his enemy come to him, had inflicted heavy losses on his foe, and had preserved intact his tight perimeter about southern Okinawa. His Kakazu line had not been seriously weakened.

I

Yet, to remain so passive had been all but intolerable for Ushijima's restless chief of staff, Lieutenant General Cho. Though bested once by the rational Colonel Yahara, Cho had not ceased to press for an offensive. To this end he soon received reinforcement in the form of a telegraphic order from Imperial Headquarters urging the 32nd Army to overrun Kadera and Yomitan airfields. Seizing on this, Cho succeeded in persuading Ushijima at 2:00 P.M. on April 6 to order preparations for an attack on April 8. But once again he had to see his plan canceled. In his turn Colonel Yahara had used the sudden appearance of a 110-ship convoy offshore of Urasoe-Mura escarpment on April 7 to warn of a threat to the flank of the 62nd Division and induce Ushijima to cancel the attack order.

During the next two days, on April 8 and 9, while the 96th Division was hammering in vain against Kakazu Ridge, Cho and

Ushijima became convinced that the great kamikaze attacks of Kikusui 1 had achieved "remarkable" results. Their optimism was enhanced by a "stirring telegraph order"—as the 32nd Army's historical report described it—from Japanese Naval headquarters in Tokyo to all commands. The "TEN-Go" operation, the order suggested, had been very successful. ". . . There are signs of uneasiness among enemy forces and odds are seven to three in our favor." All forces—including Navy units on Okinawa—were to engage in "a general pursuit operation."

This message was heaven-sent to Cho, who accepted a reduction in the number of American ships visible from the ramparts of Shuri Castle as confirmation of the Navy estimate and took reduced American air activity on April 10 as a token of kamikaze success against U.S. carriers. In truth, a turn of rainy and cloudy weather had forced the cancellation of air strikes on April 10, and the reduced number of ships was normal because many had unloaded and started for home. Ushijima was nevertheless convinced, and over the protests of a glum and unhappy Yahara ordered an attack by "powerful" units for the night of April 12–13.

In essence, Cho's plan called for a mass infiltration of General Hodge's lines across almost the entire front. Three battalions of the 22nd Regiment of the 24th Division would attack the U.S. 7th Division on the east; three of the Japanese 62nd Division would attack the weakened 96th Division on the west. The troops would break through the line infantry on the American perimeter, then infiltrate the rear area as far north as Kishaba, four miles southeast of Kadena airfield. Each battalion then would take cover in an assigned area in caves and tombs, to emerge on the morning of April 13 and fall on 10th Army rear echelon units. Since American and Japanese troops would be hopelessly entangled, Yankee artillery and air power would be silenced. In the meantime, troops remaining in the line would attack the forward American positions, forcing an American retreat, while the infiltration battalions shot up the rear. The attack order did not spell out where the line would be stabilized. Presumably, Cho's intent was to hand General Buckner a severe jolt by mauling and disorganizing his two forward divisions.

Since the 22nd Regiment was stationed on the Oroku Peninsula, it underwent an ordeal just to reach the front. Its men had to march for two nights in the rain with 110-pound packs "in a sinuous eel line." By day they hid in sugarcane fields to escape American planes and naval guns. Another unit, the 272nd Independent Infantry Battalion of the 62nd Division, found itself hampered by rain and slippery roads but reached its attack position on the south side of Kakazu Ridge at midnight on April 10. The next day it entered deep caves at the base of the hill where its two companies rested and waited.

As the time neared to launch the attack, Hiromichi Yahara grew more and more apprehensive. He was certain that the only result would be unnecessary losses, and he feared that General Buckner might attempt a surprise landing at Yonabaru, taking the 32nd Army on its flank. In a display of personal initiative that would not have been tolerated in the U.S. Army, he contacted Lieutenant General Takeo Fujioka, the commander of the 62nd Division, and Lieutenant General Tatsumi Amamiya, commander of the 24th Division, urging them to reduce the scale of the offensive. As a result the attack force was reduced from six to four battalions.

II

The weird light from three Japanese flares glowing over the fighting line on April 12 gave General Hodge's GI's their first hint that an attack was coming. Consulting a captured Japanese signal code book, 7th Division intelligence officers discovered that the two red flares meant either "We are attacking with full strength tonight" or "Commence artillery fire." The third flare, which resembled a dragon, meant "Make all-out attack." Confirmation that the Japanese had not changed their signal book came about 7:00 P.M. when the heaviest artillery barrage to date during the Pacific War began falling on the American positions. In the 96th Division's sector more than a thousand rounds fell on the 381st Infantry and twelve hundred more on Colonel May's battered 383rd. Losses were slight because the men were deeply dug in. In the 7th Division's sector some two hundred shells fell on the 184th Infantry in five minutes. These caused no casualties because the men were in foxholes they described as "dry and deep."

The attackers in the 7th Division sector hit first in twos and threes, then in groups of a squad or two. Their efforts were so weak, unsuccessful, and poorly coordinated that the Americans remained innocent that they had been targets of a major attack, believing instead that the Japanese had been practicing normal nighttime infiltration. Incomplete preparations, unfamiliar terrain, and a lack of precise knowledge had thoroughly confused Lieutenant Colonel Masaru Yoshida and his company commanders of the 22nd Infantry Regiment. "The main body of the Regiment," acknowledges the 32nd Army report, "did not participate in the action. . . ."

The heaviest fighting in the 7th Division sector began at 11:23 P.M. when three green star shells burst over the hilltop positions of First Lieutenant Daniel R. Leffel's G Company of the 184th Infantry. About ten minutes later a hundred Japanese of Captain Keisuke Tagawa's 3rd Battalion of the 22nd Infantry Regiment began mounting the hill. Hearing them, Pfc Lloyd H. Coos, a BAR man, left his foxhole, crawled to the top of a knoll offering a better view, and sprayed the dark shapes below. Other GI's fired with rifles and machine guns, sending Tagawa's men scurrying into caves and tombs. Mortars then pounded them relentlessly until daybreak. When full daylight came Coos and his buddies counted thirty bodies below and from dog tags identified members of the 22nd Regiment's 7th, 9th, and 11th companies.

In the 96th Division sector the Japanese attack was much heavier in places, sustained, and well organized. It began at 10:30 P.M. when a platoon-sized force hit Lieutenant Colonel Cyril W. Sterner's 2nd Battalion of Colonel Dill's 382nd Regiment. More attacks developed as the Japanese progressively shifted their preparatory artillery fire from east to west across the front.

At about midnight the GI's of Eddie May's 383rd Infantry spotted a file of soldiers marching boldly down Highway 5 in a column of twos at the east end of Kakazu Ridge. Assuming they were from the neighboring 382nd Infantry, the men let twenty pass before realizing they were Japanese. Then everyone started firing at once, the entire column was trapped, and after daybreak the still-amazed soldiers counted fifty-eight dead enemies of Colonel Kaya's 12th Independent Infantry and six Nambu light machine guns and a knee mortar lying on the road. Kaya had dispatched a reinforced platoon down Highway 5 to divert

Model 89 "Knee" mortar

attention from the assault battalions. A few hundred yards westward Colonel Hara's 13th Battalion launched two supporting attacks, one of two platoons and the other of company strength, against the Deadeyes astride the gorge before Kakazu. Neither dislodged the GI's.

In the early hours of April 13, following the diversionary attacks, General Fujioka, the 62nd Division's commander, threw his Sunday punch, the blow intended to crack the western hinge of the Deadeye's Kakazu line. To envelop and overwhelm the Americans, he dispatched two companies of Captain Shimoda's 272nd Independent Infantry Battalion in a two-pronged attack on Kakazu West. Starting from Kakazu village a small force would attack around the end of Kakazu West, while the main force burst through the draw between Kakazu and Kakazu West.

In no sense was this to be a banzai charge. The infantry would follow behind a mortar and artillery barrage along routes carefully plotted beforehand. Each man wore a heavy pack with enough ammunition for several days and every fourth man carried a sack of food. All had clean, new uniforms.

At 3:00 A.M. the Japanese harassing barrage, which had continued all night, suddenly intensified. A few minutes later the enemy's fire shifted to the rear as Shimoda's infantry moved out.

The first man they met was Pfc William W. Dailey of a weapons platoon guarding the draw between Kakazu and Kakazu West. Unable to depress his heavy machine gun sufficiently, Dailey began tossing grenades. A few minutes later Staff Sergeant Beauford T. (Snuffy) Anderson, holed up with his mortar section in a tomb at the northwest corner of the draw, heard the Japanese coming. Anderson ordered his squad to cover in the rear of the tomb, stepped onto a ledge above the enemy, threw all his grenades, and then emptied his carbine. Looking about frantically for something more lethal, he spotted a Japanese mortar dud and spiraled it like a football into the draw, to be rewarded by an explosion. Rushing back into the tomb, he grabbed one of his own mortar rounds, wrenched the projectile from its casing, yanked out the safety pin, slammed the shell against a rock to release the setback pin, and spiraled it into the draw. Fifteen times he repeated this operation, reducing the screams of Shimoda's infantry below to moans. Then, still refusing to let his men join him, he stood guard above the draw until morning. At daybreak he counted twenty-five dead enemies below and seven 50 mm. knee mortars and four machine guns.

Anderson had stopped one group of attackers, but at least one other either had broken through the draw or found its way over Kakazu West. This unit advanced into the tomb positions occupied by the machine gun and mortar platoons attached to E

Company of the 381st Infantry. There, as Herman A. Puryear, a machine gunner, recalls, a quiet had prevailed when the attack began, interrupted only by rifle fire from other areas and the bursting overhead of star shells fired from warships offshore to illuminate the battlefield. Suddenly, Puryear's buddy, Gerald Warner, a cook, whispered, "I see one," and raised his carbine and fired, hitting the Japanese in the throat and dropping him. Immediately after Warner's shot, a Japanese officer yelled a command, and grenades showered the Americans, wounding several including Sergeant John D. Becker, Puryear's foxhole buddy since induction days.

Squatting on a wall nearby was Sergeant Sassaman, firing his M-1 rifle and yelling. A grenade bounced directly under him and exploded, injuring him horribly and causing him frightful suffering until the company's overworked medic could give him a shot of morphine. In a nearby tomb serving as an aid station another wounded boy kept complaining that his foot hurt. The medic dressing his wound did not have the heart to tell him that he had no foot; that a mortar shell had blown it completely off.

Somehow the weapons platoon managed to beat off the attackers, and dawn came. Dead Japanese lay everywhere, and two feet from the muzzle of Puryear's heavy machine gun stood a rifle, bayonet driven into the ground, its lifeless wielder sprawled behind it. E Company's losses were relatively heavy though mostly in wounded and not in dead.

The Japanese also had suffered heavy losses before the foxholes of B and C companies of the 381st located on Kakazu Ridge proper. One reason was the risky tactics adopted by American 81 mm. mortar crews firing in support from 400 yards to the rear. On learning that forty Japanese had penetrated to the vicinity of the 1st Battalion's O.P. (observation post), the mortarmen laid around it a concentration of 800 "HE light" mortar shells, hoping that the American infantry would be deep in their foxholes and the Japanese approaching in the open. Marine Corps artillery also fired, dropping their shells to within 150 yards of the American positions—much too near for safety. The scheme worked; neither American company lost a man, and an anonymous Japanese diarist of the 272nd Independent Battalion recorded later that mortar fire had pinned down his unit with heavy losses before it could cross Kakazu. Besides himself just three other members of his squad survived. American patrols, peeking over the hill after daybreak, reported enemy dead "stacked like cordwood" on the reverse slope below.

On guard on a rocky knoll atop Kakazu West was Pfc Troy O'Neill, a BAR man. Early in the action a Japanese officer approached him and asked him if he were a Japanese. O'Neill said, "No," and then shot him and his ten men following in Indian file.

Other Japanese, trying to slip across more exposed ground around the west flank of Kakazu West, had the misfortune to be spotted by Pfc Ruben Johnson, a machine gunner. Johnson got twenty-three of them. Still others, despairing over their helplessness in an exposed position, committed suicide.

The 272nd Battalion's counterattack had been a near-total disaster. First Lieutenant Kanematsu Akiyama's company was wiped out and First Lieutenant Shimizu's decimated. The 381st Infantry Regiment counted 196 enemy bodies against very light losses to its 1st Battalion and moderate losses to its 2nd. It also boasted a new hero; for his one-man stand in Kakazu draw, Staff Sergeant "Snuffy" Anderson received the Congressional Medal of Honor.

For General Ushijima and his staff just one hope glimmered faintly from the result. In the thinly held Nishibaru-Kaniku-Tombstone Ridge sector, where the lines of the 96th Division's 382nd Regiment were paper-thin, an entire battalion—the 22nd Regiment's 2nd under Major Yamamato—had slipped through undetected into the Ginowan area. But when daylight came Yamamato found his troops too isolated, scattered, and few in numbers to carry out their assignment of shooting up the American rear echelon. The men hid all day, and about half managed to escape to their own lines after dark.

Two small counterattacks on the next night, April 13–14, closed out General Ushijima's counteroffensive. Its total failure demonstrated the tactical disadvantage the Japanese faced and which Colonel Yahara had foreseen. When holed up in caves dug into reverse slopes, the infantry could fight very effectively, inflicting heavy losses by making the Americans come to them in the open. But outside the caves, attempting to form up under heavy American mortar, artillery, and Navy gunfire, beset with extremely difficult communications problems, and forced to move at night across unfamiliar terrain, the Japanese lost every advantage. As in other battles of the Pacific War, beginning with the Guadalcanal campaign of 1942, superior American supporting firepower provided the decisive margin of difference.

III

Though aware of Ushijima's counterattack, Imperial Headquarters in Tokyo was much more interested in the prospects of its continuation of Operation TEN-Go, Kikusui Number 2, the second of its series of suicide attacks. Ushijima could not win the Okinawan struggle but the kamikazes might. Originally scheduled for April 10, Kikusui 2 had to be postponed because of bad weather until April 12.

Both Admiral Ugaki and General Sugahara realized that this time they faced a harder task than in the first attacks of April 6 and 7. For one thing, neither the 5th Air Fleet nor the 6th Air Army could muster as many planes as before. For another, photographs taken by high-flying Type 100 Headquarters Reconnaissance planes (Dinahs) had told them that Marine Corsair fighters had arrived at Yomitan and Kadena. Planes reaching the beachhead now could expect interception by ground-based fighters. Ugaki still thought that his planes had seriously weakened T.F. 58, a viewpoint General Sugahara did not share. "Despite many attacks," Sugahara's headquarters staff concluded, "the Navy cannot block the enemy's carrier force, which still is operating east of Okinawa." Both headquarters planned a series of bombing raids on Yomitan and Kadena on the night before the operation, and the Army added a scheme to dispatch a decoy force of fighters to lure T.F. 58's Hellcats and Corsairs away from the kamikazes. As before, the naval staff planned to split the kamikazes, sending some against carrier, the remainder against shipping off Okinawa.

The preliminary attacks on the Kadena and Yomitan airfields on the night of April 11–12 did little more than give the defending gun batteries good practice. Fourteen Navy Judy and eight Army bombers took off at 2:30 A.M. and created a considerable uproar in the beachhead area on arrival shortly before dawn. Two well-placed bombs damaged five planes. The 40 mm.

gunners claimed four planes that searchlights illuminated; the 90 mm. U.S. Army and Marine Corps crews another.

At 3:30 A.M. fifteen Army fighters flew off to lure American carrier pilots from the route of the kamikaze attack. This proved a wasted effort; they encountered nothing and drew out nothing.

U.S. 90 mm. A.A.

Starting at 11:00 A.M. the main event began. Fighters took off first to sweep the way, 49 late-model Army and Navy types to engage barrier patrol Hellcats over Kikai Jima, 72 Zeros to battle Corsairs and Wildcats over the Okinawa anchorage. Special attackers followed, 42 Kates and Vals aiming for the beachhead, 34 planes, 12 fast Frances bombers included, looking for T.F. 58. The Army kamikazes waited a little, timing their flight to arrive after defending carrier planes (which the less-optimistic 6th Air Army staff still expected to be present at Okinawa in force) had left Okinawa shortly before dusk. Between 2:30 and 3:30 P.M. 74 Army planes—all kamikazes—took off, mostly from the Chiran and Bansei fields. The Formosa commands contributed eight Army and twelve Navy suicide aircraft.

A shortage of fighters impelled Admiral Ugaki to add a bit of spice to the kamikaze hell-brew. Eight "Betty" bombers roared from Kanoya's main runway, each carrying a queer-looking object under its belly, the "Oka"—"Cherry Blossom"—a tiny, rocket-boosted suicide glide bomb that packed a tremendous wallop, 2,645 pounds of tri-nitroanisol. The Oka was ferried to within a dozen miles or so of an enemy force by its mother plane, usually a "Betty" or "Peggy" heavy bomber. The pilot then manned it, on release directing it with rocket-power speed— up to 500 knots—directly into his target. United States Intelligence had known of these weapons before and gave them the derisive name of Baka, or "fool." Previous attempts to use these 16½-foot horrors off Kyushu had failed when their "Betty" mother planes had fallen victim to Hellcats and Corsairs. Oka had been the brainchild of a Navy junior officer, Ensign Mitsuo Ota, a year before. He had designed the piloted missile and had seen his project accepted by higher authority. Now his remarkable weapon would have another chance to prove itself.

At 2:30 P.M., two-and-a-half hours after the first planes took off, a slam-bang air battle erupted over Kikai Jima. High-performance Frank Army fighters and "Violet Lightning" (George) Navy fighters tangled with Hellcats and Corsairs of the barrier patrol. Only their better training and greater experience gave the American flyers the edge. Commander Beebe led twelve Hellcats from the *Hornet* into a wild melee, his men claiming fifteen enemies. As they approached Kikai Jima an Army fighter bounced Beebe's section of four planes. Skillfully Beebe turned into his enemy, hitting him in the cowling with a deflection shot. The enemy pilot then tried to dive out, but Beebe followed him down, firing bursts at his wing root and tail. This plane was no flimsy Zero—it refused to burn and armor plate protected its pilot. Sideslipping to the right Beebe fired a 20-degree deflection shot into the plane's engine, setting it on fire. Lurching, the enemy plane hit the sea, scattering flames and wreckage along a 500-foot path on the water. In the meantime two pilots, Lieutenants T. S. Harris and H. J. Sundberg, by good shooting had bagged a George apiece. Sundberg's victim bailed out. Less fortunate was an Okinawa-bound Kate that blundered into the middle of the fight. Sundberg promptly shot it to pieces.

It was not all one-sided, as Ensign Terry Mills from the *Bennington*'s fighter squadron discovered. In company with Lieutenant Lloyd B. Murray he gave chase to two Zeros. Mills had one boresighted and was about to fire when bullets suddenly ripped his Hellcat from the port side. A George or Frank had riddled his oil tank with a good deflection burst. Knowing his plane probably would catch fire, Mills shoved back his canopy to jump but wind pressure held him in. So he rolled his Hellcat upside down at 300 knots and tumbled out. Not knowing how much altitude he had lost, he immediately pulled his ripcord and momentarily lost consciousness from the shock of the sudden deceleration. On coming to he found himself descending toward the water a mile-and-a-half off Kikai Jima. Following doctrine he unbuckled his chest and leg straps on his parachute harness and dropped free just as he touched. He had no life raft but friendly fighters saw him and dropped one. Two hours later a Kingfisher floatplane from the cruiser *Miami* appeared and landed to pick him up. The low-powered plane had to bounce across the water a half-mile to get airborne, but Mills was saved. Others on both sides were less fortunate.

In this case the Japanese pilots, aided by higher-performance planes, had done better than usual, claiming twenty Hellcats and Corsairs, but their attempt to protect the attacking kamikazes as they passed over Kikai Jima and Amami O Shima on their way to the beachhead had not been successful. Major Herman Hansen, commander of the Marine Wolfpack squadron on the *Bennington*, simultaneously celebrated his twenty-fifth birthday and became an ace by destroying an escorting Zero and a suicide-bound Kate torpedo plane, the Kate being kill number five. For good measure he shot down another plane which he identified as an Army Tojo, and his wingman, Lieutenant George Murray, successfully followed a Zero through a difficult split-S turn and

161

destroyed it. Task Force 58 pilots claimed 126 enemy planes on sweeps, an obvious exaggeration but indicative of the scale and intensity of the fighting.

The kamikazes that had escaped the ministrations of Commander Beebe, Major Hansen, and the other Navy and Marine pilots continued southward. The first ships they encountered were the destroyers and gunboats on Radar Picket Stations 1, 2, 12, and 14. Profiting from their bitter experience of April 6, Admiral Turner's staff had established an eight-plane combat air patrol over "hot" stations, half to orbit in immediate protection of the ships, half to be vectored out to intercept attackers by the fighter-direction team at each picket station. Turner also had added another destroyer to each station by drawing ships from patrol and antisubmarine duty.

At Station 1—still the hottest spot—was Commander J. W. Arles' *Cassin Young* with Commander Frank L. Johnson's *Purdy* in antiaircraft support. Four small gunboats backed up the two destroyers. Radar operators picked up the incoming suicide flyers at 1:13 P.M., noting eight different blips on their radar scopes. Blips seven and eight merged into thirty planes closing Station 1 rapidly. At about 1:40 P.M., both destroyers opened fire using full radar control on a fighter which released a bomb at the *Cassin Young*. The pilot then banked about to make a low-level suicide run on the ship, but crashed close aboard under a hail of 40 mm. shells. Five Vals then showed up and were promptly bounced by the defending quartet of fighters which destroyed two but let two slip through. One just missed *Cassin Young*, but the other smashed into the destroyer's starboard quarter and blew apart, killing one man, burning or otherwise injuring another fifty, and knocking out the forward fireroom. Commander Arles withdrew from the station, leaving Johnson in the *Purdy* to carry on with the gunboats.

The *Purdy* and the four gunboats faced an unpleasant prospect. Bogies continued to show on the radar scopes as Ugaki's attackers straggled down from Kyushu. It was only too likely that their hopped-up pilots, anxious to die, would dive at the first ships they saw—in this case *Purdy* and company. The fighters splashed would-be suiciders left and right, but there were too many to bag them all.

Four broke through to make runs at the destroyer, and several more—mistaking minnows for whales apparently—dove at the support gunboats. At exactly 3:00 P.M. after shooting down two Vals and probably a third, the *Purdy*'s 5-inch mounts engaged another. The plane bounced off the water twenty feet from the ship and ricocheted into its side, releasing a bomb which smashed through and exploded.

In the forward fireroom Water Tender First Class Rodney L. Hall had the watch with five other men. One man died instantly; the others were knocked flat. Struggling to his feet Hall closed valves, cutting off smashed steam lines, then led his remaining four men to safety amid a chaos of debris, pouring fuel oil, soot, smoke, and hot steam. Commander Johnson's well-drilled crew isolated damaged areas, cross-connected steam lines to permit the engines to function on the after boilers, and kept up an effective fire at remaining planes. Fortunately, the bomb had started only a small fire which a broken steam line extinguished.

A kamikaze hit on a destroyer was bad enough, but on the 158-foot gunboat LCS(L)-33 it was disaster. Almost simultaneously with the strike on the *Purdy* another suicide-bound pilot dove at the gunboat, which blazed away with everything it had. Lieutenant Carroll J. Boone's craft already had shot down three, but this one hit its port side amidships with a tremendous bang. Everyone fell sprawling, Boone suffering a displaced vertebra. Gasoline set the vessel aflame throughout the midsection, forcing men to leap into the sea to escape. Boone ordered all hands overboard as the LCS, its rudder jammed, heeled into a tight circle. In the water the men helped each other. Radarman Robert E. Reese gave his life jacket to a nonswimmer, then rounded up several more men who were becoming panicky, gathering them around an overturned waste can, encouraging them until rescue came. The blazing craft circled out of control until another ship sank it with 5-inch fire. At 3:30 P.M. all ships retired southward.

On Picket Station 14 the new destroyer *Mannert L. Abele* was steaming about thirty miles westward of the *Cassin Young* and *Purdy* and seventy-five miles northwest of Okinawa. Like them she picked up the attackers a little after 1:00 P.M. and attracted suicide-bent pilots. At about 2:45 P.M. a pair of Vals selected the ship as a target, coming in wing on wing off the starboard bow. "Each burst," recalls the *Abele*'s skipper, Alton E. Parker, "gave the feeling the planes had been hit, but they reappeared through the smoke an instant later.'' One broke course and splashed from a hit, and the other drifted aft and looked as if it would miss, but, banking slightly, it swerved directly into the after engine room of the destroyer. ''The shock was terrific,'' writes Captain Parker. ''Parts of the deckhouse aft and the deck plating were blown from the ship. The keel and starboard propeller shaft were broken. The 40 mm. gun crew directly over the impact was wiped out and others in the vicinity were injured.'' He adds that the hit wrecked the after engine room and fireroom and that the ship visibly buckled in the middle.

Parker and his men already had noticed and shot at two slowly circling Betty bombers. One now disgorged an Oka which screeched at the stricken destroyer at 500 knots. The pilot's aim was perfect; he hit the *Abele* at the waterline amidships. The tremendous blast heaved the already weakened ship and slammed it down into the water. Within a minute the *Abele* broke in two. Bow and propellers lifted out of water as both halves began to sink. The crew could only cut loose life rafts and rescue as many wounded as possible. The ship's First Lieutenant, George Wray, had been blown overside by the first hit. After the second he swam back and, climbing aboard, fought open a jammed escape hatch to the forward engine room. The engineering officer and his entire watch scrambled to safety. A second or two later would have been too late. In five minutes the *Abele* had disappeared.

In the meantime a support LSM also had been hit, but with another, closed to rescue survivors despite continuing attacks. They recovered most of *Abele*'s crew, but even so the loss was very heavy, six killed and seventy-three missing.

This success was not the only one for Oka on April 12. As the destroyers *Stanly* and *Lang* steamed from Station 2 to assist the *Cassin Young* and *Purdy,* a Betty cast off an Oka which flashed through a group of American fighters at pistol-bullet speed. *Stanly*'s crew had remarkably good fortune. The missile hit the ship in the extreme bow, blasting away the lower portion. Ten minutes later another flashed down, and ripping the ship's flag from the stern gaff, skipped like a stone from the water and disintegrated into bits. The *Stanly* was patched up at the Kerama base. Somewhat further south on Station 12, the crew of the destroyer-minesweeper *Jeffers* was jolted by an Oka which narrowly missed. The blinding speed of Oka gave it virtual immunity from

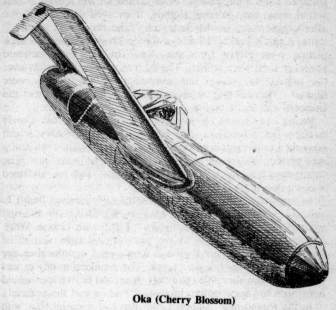

Oka (Cherry Blossom)

gunfire but also apparently gave its pilots great difficulty aligning their machines on target. Nevertheless, the Okas had scored hits in their debut at Okinawa, and the sheer terror induced by this frightful weapon scared every bluejacket afloat.

Simultaneous to the attack of the Okas, a group of conventional kamikazes found Rear Admiral Deyo's gunfire and supporting force operating within sight of the Motobu Peninsula. Alerted by intelligence of the impending attack, Deyo had not dispersed his ships this day, instead keeping them together in a formation best disposed to repel air attack. It was fortunate he did. Boring in from the formation's left came a kamikaze that slammed into the side of the destroyer *Zellers*, touching off powder and ammunition and starting a great fire. Partly concealed by the smoke pall came five more, one of which crashed a 40 mm. quadruple antiaircraft gun mount on the *Tennessee* and tumbled aft spewing gasoline that caused terrible injury from burns. "One sailor," records naval historian Morison, who was aboard the battleship, "blown into the air, landed on top of a 5-inch gun turret, where he calmly stripped off his burning, gasoline-soaked clothes while awaiting a stream of water from the nearest fire hose." Marine Corporal W. H. Putnam fell overside, came up, found himself near a big life raft and climbed in. With him in the raft was the headless corpse of the kamikaze pilot, flung into it by the explosion. He remained in this "grisly company" for several hours, writes Morison, before being rescued by a destroyer and returned to the *Tennessee*. The venerable battlewagon was only slightly damaged, but twenty-three officers and men perished, another thirty-three suffered horrible burns, and seventy-three others suffered lesser burns or injuries.

Admiral Ugaki's attempt to knock off the "remnant" of T.F. 58 had actually begun on April 11 when the 5th Air Fleet hurled against it a daylight suicide attack of fifty-two planes which reportedly "sank" three carriers, set a cruiser afire, and holed another cruiser and two destroyers with torpedoes. The next day the war diary of the 5th Air Fleet recorded sinking a light carrier and two battleships. Actually, not much damage was done to Admiral Mitscher's ships either day. The carrier *Essex* took a very close miss that damaged fuel tanks and steam lines and killed thirty-three men, but did not put her out of action. The edge of veteran *Enterprise*'s flight deck was sideswiped by a Judy; another exploded under her bows, starting a flight-deck fire which flared briefly, forcing suspension of air operations for two days. A lone Zero had the effrontery to crash the side of the majestic new battleship *Missouri*, doing little more harm than to scratch and scorch paint. The destroyer *Kidd* took the worst damage and losses—thirty-eight killed, fifty-five wounded—when a kamikaze struck her forward fireroom at waterline level. This ship had the hot spot for T.F. 58, picket duty thirty miles ahead of the main formation in the expected direction of the attacks. (After this episode some waggish sailors on a T.F. 58 picket destroyer set up a huge arrow-shaped sign pointing rearward and reading "Carriers this way." Half-a-dozen ships claimed the honor, but naval historian Henry H. Adams swears it was his destroyer.) The fast carrier force had gotten off much more easily than in the first Kikusui raid, though by the narrowest of margins.

Once again the kamikazes had failed. In no way had this second major kamikaze blow affected the course of the Okinawa operation. Nevertheless, the devil-birds had inflicted heavy losses on the American Navy. Though only destroyer *Mannert L. Abele* had sunk, eight other destroyers, a destroyer-escort, and several smaller craft took damaging hits and high casualties. The second kamikaze attack confirmed what the first one already had demonstrated, that the Okinawa campaign at sea would rival in ferocity the fighting on land.

11

DEATH OF THE CHIEF

EARLY ON the morning of April 13, while the crews of the American warships offshore of Okinawa were at breakfast, recalling the kamikazes and the appearance of the Okas the day before, their already jangled nerves received another jolt. This one came from far-off Washington, D.C.: "Attention! Attention! All Hands! President Roosevelt is dead. Repeat, our Supreme Commander, President Roosevelt, is dead." Minutes later, the news had reached the Army ashore, filtering by noon to the forward foxholes.

I

Though he had been in poor health for many months, end for "the Chief" had come suddenly on the afternoon of April 12 at Warm Springs, Georgia, while he was sitting for a portrait for the noted artist, Mrs. Elizabeth Shoumatoff.

Up front with Japanese artillery whistling in and death commonplace, men accepted the word with a nod and little more. Their own immediate personal danger stifled their normal reactions. But to the rear and aboard the ships shock and grief were universal. For many of the younger servicemen F.D.R. was the only president they could remember. Marine Sergeant Major Walter L. Snyder later told a correspondent with the 1st Marine Division, "I thought the report was Jap propaganda." Similar skepticism prevailed afloat until Admiral Turner confirmed the news in a special message to his ships. The sorrow quickly deepened, and many men approached their officers, always with a variant of the same question, "What will happen to us now?" A special edition of the 96th Division's mimeographed newsletter, the "Deadeye Dispatch," summarized the feelings of most, soldiers and sailors alike. "We have lost . . . a man whom every soldier has felt to be his friend—a personal friend—one who has cared for the soldier's needs and protected his future."

In memoriam, units held services throughout Okinawa and on most ships off the island. Where they could, all officers and men donned Class A uniform—their best service dress—and paid tribute in simple ceremony. Sadness prevailed for several days. Marine Private John Nenley of Harriman, Tennessee, said, "The only other time I felt like this was when Will Rogers died. The President seemed close to me—just like Rogers."

In the United States an 85-hour dirge was still underway on April 14, designated by the new President, Harry S. Truman, as a day of national mourning. At 9:58 A.M. the U.S. Army Air Force Band met a special train at Washington, D.C.'s Union Station. On hand was a bodyguard of eight noncomissioned officers of the Army, Navy, Marines, and Coast Guard commanded by Army Master Sergeant James Powder. Gently and slowly they lifted Mr. Roosevelt's casket, flag-draped, to a four-wheeled caisson drawn by seven white horses. Then, at the rear of a long procession followed by national and presidential color bearers, they marched with steady and purposeful dignity along Delaware and Constitution Avenues and up Pennsylvania Avenue to the White House. Before went the U.S. Marine Corps Band, the U.S. Navy Band, a battalion of midshipmen from Annapolis, a squadron of armored cars, a battalion of field artillery, another of marines, one of Army service forces and air force, and a mixed battalion of Wacs, Waves, Spars, and women marines. Overhead droned twenty-five B-24 bombers, followed by forty-eight more. Following the color bearers, immediately behind the caisson, were autos carrying Mrs. Roosevelt, the Roosevelt family, President Truman, government officials, and the diplomatic colony. Hundreds of thousands lined the funeral route, many in tears.

At 11:17 A.M. the caisson stopped before the White House. As the Navy Band softly played "Lead Kindly Light," and two squirrels played on the lawn, Mr. Roosevelt, who had been elected to an unprecedented four terms, entered the Executive Mansion for the last time.

At 4:00 P.M. in the East Room of the White House Episcopal Bishop Angus Dun conducted a twenty-minute private service, assisted by the Reverend John C. Magee of St. John's Episcopal Church, where the late President had frequently attended services. Guarded by four noncommissioned officers and an officer, the body lay in state until 9:00 P.M., whence it left by motor coach for transfer to the train carrying it to its burial place at the Roosevelt estate at Hyde Park, New York.

Like the Okinawa campaign itself, President Roosevelt's death marked the last stage of World War II and foreshadowed an uncertain peace. Hence the deep anxiety it aroused both on Okinawa and in the United States, where fear underlay grief. Even the Japanese on Okinawa did not gloat. A propaganda leaflet found later at the front recorded, "We must express our deep regret over the death of President Roosevelt. The 'American Tragedy' is now raised here on Okinawa with his death."

II

In Europe the war was reaching a climax. Russian armies stood poised to push west from the Oder River in eastern Germany, while from across the Rhine, American and British forces were advancing to the Elbe River. Hitler, caught in Berlin in between, was directing a last-ditch defense that would not end until V-E Day on May 8, more than a week after his own suicide in his headquarters bunker in the German capital.

News of such drama, combined with the shock of Roosevelt's death and lurid photographs of Nazi concentration camps, effectively kept details of the Okinawa fighting from reaching the American public. The busy staff of correspondents continued to file lengthy stories, particularly of the bitter struggle still raging for Kakazu Ridge, but the pencils of the editors bit deeply into the volume of copy. The casual reader of the leading American newspapers, leafing through pages of material on the events in Europe, might well have been pardoned for overlooking entirely the brief, inside-page stories. Even a thorough reader might have failed to understand just how bitter the Okinawan campaign was destined to be.

The Honolulu *Advertiser,* for example, which might have been expected to feature Pacific War news ahead of European, joined all others in devoting headlines and front-page stories to Germany's hastening collapse. Except for isolated slips here and there, censorship still blanked out the activities of the kamikazes, and journalists' references to "heavy fighting" and "slow going" by the 96th Division at Kakazu Ridge were offset by highly personalized stories recording the "sweeping gains" of the 1st and 6th Marine Divisions in northern Okinawa. A few writers—Homer Bigart of the *New York Herald Tribune* was an outstanding example—made clear to their readers the strategy of the campaign and the tactical problems facing the divisions before the Shuri line, but not until mid-May did the Okinawa battle finally come into its own in the American press and in the consciousness of the American people.

III

One generally overlooked aspect of the Okinawa campaign was the logistics problem.

To sustain its forces so far from home the United States faced two unprecedented challenges. First, it had to supply the largest amphibious operation of the Pacific War—the last great amphibious operation of world history—at a distance of seven thousand miles from the United States. Second, it had to keep a powerful fleet at sea for a period of several weeks while supplying it with ammunition, food, fuel, planes, and all of the thousands of lesser items necessary for daily operations.

Responsibility for supplying the 10th Army across the Hagushi beaches and new beaches opened at Nakagusuku Bay centered largely on one man, Commander John Huntington, who served as port director for Okinawa and controlled all shipping off the beachhead from a floating "office" in a converted landing craft. His skill and the hard-won experience of the Navy and Army landing-boat crews resulted in the beaching between April 1 and 16 of 577,000 measurement tons of cargo from hundreds of ships, some 47,000 tons more than the ICEBERG planners had expected. The crews achieved this goal despite a pair of storms on April 4–5 and 10–11 which generated thirty-knot northeast winds and a six- to ten-foot surf on the beaches, enough to wreck or sink twenty-two landing craft and force suspension of operations for many hours.

Other delays, annoying but not serious, resulted from the rapid advance of the troops in the first four days of the campaign, forcing DUKW's and amphibious tractors hauling supplies to front-line units to roll far inland to unload. The combat units needed their own trucks and jeeps, but since the unloading plan had placed vehicles beneath other stores normally needed first—such as ammunition and rations—the landing crews had to heap these stocks on the beaches, breaking down the elaborate plans for establishing supply dumps. Night unloading, begun on April 2 under floodlights and suspended only during red air raid alerts, helped to empty the ships but added to beach congestion.

On April 13 a potentially serious problem surfaced when General Buckner learned that only 640 tons of ammunition had crossed the beaches in the past 24 hours. This amount was totally inadequate to supply the artillery, which was firing many more shells daily than the planners had estimated. At Buckner's order the landing crews gave priority to ammunition, and in the next few days unloaded 3,000 tons daily, enough to keep the artillery firing and to build up a slender reserve.

Erection of pontoon causeways from the shore to the edge of the hard, flat reef aided the hardworking shore parties. To the small ones LSM's and LCT's could tie up at all levels of tide and transfer cargo directly into trucks. Onto the larger ones cargo ships could unload with the aid of their own cargo booms. Red Beach 1, opposite Yomitan airfield, supported the largest causeway, an L-shaped affair 1,428 feet long, with a pierhead 45 by 175 feet. More than 60,000 men and 110,000 tons of cargo crossed the piers in the first few days.

Though well laid out the Japanese road network on Okinawa was too narrow and too lightly surfaced for the heavy American armored tractors and six-by-six cargo trucks. Rains generated by the two storms of early April softened the light surfacing, forcing the engineers to hastily cover them with loads of coral mixed with sand. The coral was hard to dig. When blasted it frequently came out in great chunks, which were dumped along with finer material and sand onto the road. Major Roy D. Appleman, the 24th Corps's historian, records, "Any one who traveled the Okinawan roads . . . will not soon forget the huge coral boulders that bellied up jeeps and trucks and bounced vehicles about like rubber balls." General Hodge, the corps commander, recalling Leyte's mud, constantly worried about the ditches as he toured the front, reminding the engineers of the need for good drainage. So long as rain was occasional the roads were passable, though terribly dusty when dry. To put them in all-weather shape would have required more engineers than the 10th Army possessed and the services of a rock crusher.

Only one serious materiel shortage developed, of 81 mm. mortar ammunition, the direct result of the loss of ammunition ships *Hobbs Victory* and *Logan Victory* to kamikazes on April 6. A hurried request by Admiral Turner for 81 mm. shells from Guam resulted in airlift of 117 tons, enough to alleviate the shortage until more could arrive by ship. In late April a shortage of aviation gas developed at Yomitan and Kadena airfields, but enough remained in stock to fly all missions; no plane stayed on the ground for lack of fuel.

Supply of the Fifth Fleet and T.F. 58 rested largely with a logistics support group of oilers and supply ships under Rear Admiral D. B. Beary, who commanded from the U.S.S. *Detroit*, an old light cruiser with adequate communications facilities. When a carrier task group needed oil and ammunition, Beary would dispatch a unit of replacement ships that would make contact at first light and rush the chore to completion as rapidly as possible. Early in the war the Navy had perfected the art of refueling at sea, and later all sorts of other provisions passed from replenishment ships to the carriers and their escorts, including such bulky items as crated aircraft engines and even jeeps, needed on the large flight decks. In the Okinawa campaign bombs and ammunition were added, thus making T.F. 58 almost totally sustainable on the high seas. The limiting factor was not know-how or even weather conditions; rather, it was a shortage of 3½- and 4-inch Manila line used to make the transfers from one ship to another. Until General MacArthur had completed his conquest of the Philippines, no more would be available.

Thanks to Admiral Turner's foresight in demanding the seizure of the Keramas, supply of the bombardment ships off the Okinawa beachhead was easier than keeping T.F. 58 operating. A special force of Landing Ship Tank (LST) ammunition ships, each equipped with a mobile crane, shuttled between Ulithi and the Marianas and the Kerama roadstead. There, they could unload their potent cargo directly into the bombardment ships.

Many LST's were "type loaded," that is, they carried ammunition for just one class of ship—for example, a destroyer. Fuel was supplied both by Beary's force and by fleet tankers shuttling between Guam and the Keramas. So great was oil consumption that two large fleet tankers had to be dispatched from Guam every three days. Between them, T.F. 58 and the invasion and bombardment fleet used a daily average of 167,000 barrels of fuel oil and 385,000 gallons of aviation gasoline during the peak period between April 4 and 24. By May 27 nearly 9,000,000 barrels of fuel oil and over 21,000,000 gallons of aviation gasoline had been consumed. Other items supplied included 2,700,000 packages of cigarettes, 1,200,000 candy bars, and over 24,000,000 pieces of mail. By way of contrast the supply of 854 replacement planes and 207 pilots in the same period seemed almost petty, even though the effort required four escort carriers constantly shuttling planes from Ulithi and Guam and seventeen more steaming back and forth between the Marianas and the American West Coast.

Aside from the sinking of the two ammunition ships, the Japanese accomplished little by way of harassing this logistical effort. Because Rear Admiral Beary's force normally operated some 200 miles south of Okinawa with air cover from two escort carriers, it seldom was attacked. Just one kamikaze scored a hit, on the bridge of fleet oiler *Taluga* which was quickly repaired.

Nothing could better illustrate the degree of American mobilization for war than this truly massive logistical effort, made at a time when the country was supporting more than four million troops in Europe, a continuing campaign to conquer Luzon and the remainder of the Philippines, and a B-29 offensive against Japan that required the full-time service of a hundred cargo ships. The effect was also indicative of the massive responsibility that had lain on Franklin Delano Roosevelt and had made him a casualty of war as surely as any Deadeye killed at Kakazu Ridge or sailor burned to death at sea.

12

MOTOBU: THE MARINES DRIVE NORTH

IN THEIR BRIEF accounts of the Okinawa campaign, America's newspapers scarcely mentioned a small but important action underway in early April about the rim of Nakagusuku Bay. The Navy needed this splendid anchorage and harbor, but before it could be used safely the enemy had to be cleared from a chain of small islands across its mouth. Admiral Turner was so anxious to have the bay that he was prepared to use his entire floating reserve, the 27th Division, to seize the islands, but reconnaissance soon disclosed that only one was defended.

On this island, Tsugen Shima, General Ushijima had placed a picked force of 250 troops manning a pair of 6-inch and 4.7-inch coast defense guns. Primarily to destroy these the 3rd Battalion of the 27th Division's 105th Infantry landed early on April 10, covered by the U.S.S. *Pensacola,* a heavy cruiser. Though hindered by a driving rain all day, its GI's, half of them National Guardsmen from New York State, plugged doggedly ahead to overrun all of the island except for a single fortified ridge. The next morning they resumed the fight, and by 3:30 P.M. had reduced all but a single strongpoint. This being deemed unworthy of another day's attention, they withdrew leaving the enemy's guns destroyed and 234 of his men counted dead. The 3rd Battalion had eleven killed and eighty wounded. The Japanese commander and thirty of his men remained alive, but with nothing left to fire at enemy ships withdrew from the island to join Ushijima in his southern bastion. The Tsugen operation was not a major battle, but nevertheless it was a key element in the complex seizure of Okinawa.

I

In his campaign to clear northern Okinawa, General Shepherd had originally intended to use his 29th Regiment to fan into and overrun the Motobu Peninsula while his 4th and 22nd Regiments cleared the enemy from the remainder of the mountainous north. The slight resistance his leathernecks had been encountering had initially led him to believe the enemy had no strongly held positions. But mounting intelligence accumulating as his men neared Motobu induced him to change his mind by about April 7. Several Okinawan civilians had reported that most of the Japanese in northern Okinawa had retired into Motobu and were planning to make their stand there. Aerial photographs pinpointed numerous caves and fresh diggings about the Yae Take hill mass in the center of the peninsula to verify their testimony.

In truth the Japanese position on Motobu was much stronger than Shepherd at first suspected. Into a redoubt on and about three-headed Yae Take mountain towering to 1,500 feet, Colonel Takehido Udo had concentrated a force built about his 2nd Infantry Unit of the 44th Brigade. This Udo force, as it was called, consisted of two full battalions of trained infantry supplemented by an artillery unit with 150 mm. and 75 mm. guns, a naval unit manning a pair of 6.1-inch coastal guns, and about 150 Navy personnel from the 27th Motor Torpedo Boat Unit and the 33rd Midget Submarine Unit which had been stationed at Unten Ko. Udo also had two units of Okinawan reservists and conscripts to bring his total numbers to between 1,500 and 2,000 men. His headquarters consisted of a cave complex on Yae Take with elaborate means for an effective defense, including a good radio and telephone communications system and horses to carry his supplies up the extremely steep slopes. A plentiful supply of mortars, of Nambu and Hotchkiss-type light and heavy machine guns, and of 20 mm. and 25 mm. aircraft and antiaircraft weapons converted for land warfare use gave Udo considerable firepower. With the equivalent of about a regiment, he had to limit his centers of resistance to just two prominent mountaintops, including the Yae Take itself.

Of the precise nature of Udo's dispositions General Shepherd knew little, other than that somewhere in the tangled wilderness of Motobu's mountains, ridges, brush, and pines he would find his enemy. To locate Udo he dispatched the 29th Marines into the peninsula, the 1st Battalion striking into the center of the island toward Itomi, a town immediately east of the Yae Take hill mass, and the 2nd Battalion moving along the north coast road toward the small base at Unten Ko. Shepherd dispatched the 3rd Battalion along the south coast road to Togushi, a coastal town just north and west of the Yae Take.

Initially no unit met much resistance. The 2nd Battalion easily seized the abandoned P.T. boat and midget submarine base at Unten Ko, finding four scuttled midget subs and some wrecked P.T. boats. But near the town of Itomi the 1st Battalion late in the day uncovered a hornet's nest and dug in. The next day the 2nd found more of the same in trying to advance along an inland road running between Togushi and Itomi westward and to the rear of Udo's Yae Take redoubt. And in the next two days patrol and probing actions by all three battalions proved to Shepherd that Udo had established an all-around defense anchored on the Yae Take. So long as Udo held out Motobu could not be secured.

From any direction an American attack appeared to be a bad deal; Shepherd's infantry would have to fight up steep slopes against a dug-in enemy with superior observation. The Marine general's answer was to devise a two-pronged assault, launched from two sides of the Yae Take, bolstered by maximum use of artillery, air strikes, and naval gunfire. The plan was unusual, Shepherd afterward explained, in that it provided for an attack by two regiments "in opposing directions" but without "great danger of overlapping supporting fire." The hill mass of the Yae Take, lying in between, would absorb shot and shell hurled from either side.

The attack jumped off at 8:00 A.M. on April 14, with two battalions of the 4th Marines joining the 3rd Battalion of the 29th in an advance from the west, while the 1st and 2nd Battalions of the 29th attacked from the east on the opposite side of the Yae Take. For the marines on the west side, heading for a 700-foot ridge, the first of several rising toward the heights of Yae Take, the going was not bad at first. But the battalions attacking on the east side ran into trouble at the outset, stalled, and played little part in the fighting of the next two days.

On the west side the 4th Marines kept running into enemy small groups using shoot-and-run tactics. Utilizing teams built around machine gunners armed with a heavy and several light machine guns, Udo's men often would wait in concealment until most of a company had passed before firing. One team waited for half an hour to identify Major Bernard W. Green as the commander of the 1st Battalion of the 4th Marines; then it chopped him down with a short burst while he was standing between two of his staff officers.

Countering these shoot-and-run tactics proved difficult. "It was," said one officer, "like fighting a phantom enemy." An enlisted leatherneck put it more colloquially: "Jeez, they've all got Nambus, but where are they?" Only occasional bloodstains in the brush after a firefight bore testimony.

After a trying day, the 4th Marines and the 3rd Battalion, 29th Marines, reached their phase lines and began digging in. Ahead lay a ridge with two heavily fortified hills. One, designated Hill 200, lay in front of the 4th Marines; the other, Green Hill, barred the approach of the 3rd Battalion. Both would have to be cleared and support weapons emplaced before the west slope of the Yae Take proper could be mounted.

The next morning initial resistance was of the same shoot-and-run variety of the day before, but by noon it had stiffened. Particularly troublesome was a Japanese 75 mm. gun that kept popping from a cave to lay accurate rounds on the advancing marines. A liberal application of naval gunfire, artillery, and even 500-pound bombs and tanks of napalm failed to silence it, because the Japanese crew would withdraw the gun deep inside and pull it out to fire again when an attack ended. Company G of the 4th Marines took sixty-five casualties from this gun and other fire, nearly half its strength, and lost three commanders, but its sister companies, E and F, took Hill 200 by 4:30 P.M. Not far away the 3rd Battalion was digging in just below the summit of Green Hill. It had advanced 900 yards through intense machine gun, mortar, and artillery fire. All three assault battalions were desperately tired.

In assessing the day's events, General Shepherd, who had

repeatedly come forward to review progress, concluded that Udo had at least two companies. But he knew that Udo could not be strong everywhere and decided to attack again in the morning despite the weariness of the 4th and 29th regiments, supplementing them with strong patrols from the 22nd, which would advance from the south to take Udo's flank. As an officer later put it, Shepherd would use "school solutions" to overcome the enemy. Udo lacked the manpower to create a flankless front as at Kakazu Ridge.

The next morning, April 16, the attack began at 9:00 A.M. with the 3rd Battalion attacking the top of Green Hill. By noon its "gyrenes" had it, counting 147 Japanese bodies in and about the caves and in trenches on top. Success lay in a flanking maneuver and skillful marine use of supporting artillery, which kept the Japanese infantry down until the marines could scramble up and blast and burn caves and dugouts with grenades, satchel charges, and flame throwers.

Advancing from Hill 200, the 1st Battalion of the 4th Regiment moved directly up the nose of the Yae Take itself. Near the main summit Captain Clinton B. Casement's Company A began exchanging grenades with its Japanese defenders in close and fierce fighting. Once the marines withdrew below an overhang, but then, joined by Lieutenant William H. Carlson's Company C, Casement's men drove to the top and won the crest. Together, the companies had suffered fifty casualties and were short of ammunition but had triumphed.

Corporal Richard E. Bush of C Company had exemplified the courage of every man. Lying badly wounded beneath the hillcrest with others at an improvised aid station, he reached out and seized a Japanese grenade that fell nearby. Drawing it to his body he smothered it, saving the lives of the others at the cost of three of his own fingers and additional wounds in his stomach. He somehow survived to receive the Congressional Medal of Honor.

After nightfall Colonel Udo's defenders attacked in a desperate effort to recover their lost high ground, closing to hand-to-hand range, but the 4th Marines held on. The next morning they found the Yae Take summit area abandoned except for 347 Japanese dead. Udo's Motobu bastion was finished.

Having given up trying to climb the east side of the Yae Take, the two battalions of the 29th Marines meanwhile had shifted their attack down the Itomi-Toguchi road, thereby cutting off those Japanese who tried to flee deeper into Motobu's wilderness. A hundred defenders fell victim to the 14-inch shells of the U.S.S. *Tennessee* rendering offshore gunfire support. But several hundred men, Colonel Udo among them, slipped eastward from the Motobu Peninsula into northern Okinawa.

In the next four days, from April 17 through April 20, the 6th Division completed the occupation of Motobu. Yae Take was scouted and cleared and in the high mountains west of the Itomi-Toguchi road well-prepared defenses were taken without a fight. Here the marines found trenches littered with enemy dead, presumably victims either of naval gunfire or air strikes.

Altogether, the Motobu battle cost the 6th Marine Division 213 killed or missing and 757 wounded, against the loss to the enemy of more than 2,000 counted dead. Looking back on the action Colonel Alan Shapley, commander of the 4th Marines, commented, "[It] was as difficult as I can conceive an operation to be. . . . It was an uphill fight all the way." And he voiced what every Marine who survived thought, ". . . I wonder how it was all accomplished."

Had Colonel Udo possessed the sophistication in the art of guerrilla warfare of Mao Tse-tung, then operating a few hundred miles distant in China, his American enemies might well have found the pacification of the remainder of northern Okinawa a much more difficult proposition than it turned out to be. Udo did leave Motobu with the intent of conducting guerrilla war. But before the Motobu campaign had fully developed, the 2nd Battalion of the 22nd Marines had raced up the west coast road to seize Hedo Misaki at Okinawa's northern tip on April 13. In so doing the battalion reached the L-plus-120 phase line of the ICEBERG planners without suffering a casualty. From Hedo Misaki patrols worked around the tip of the island, meeting units advancing up the east coast road on April 19.

Being forced to rely on a limited number of hastily prepared sanctuaries, Udo was subject to detection and attrition. Even so, he forced his adversaries to retain a full division of troops in northern Okinawa for the remainder of the war.

II

The fate of Colonel Udo's embattled troops scarcely concerned Admiral Ugaki's 5th Air Fleet planners at Kanoya Air Station. Believing that the first two kamikaze attacks had seriously weakened T.F. 58 and Turner's supporting warships off Okinawa, they were working feverishly on a third major offensive, Kikusui Number 3. By mustering every available plane and pilot, they planned to hit hard at what they believed were remnants of Spruance's carrier forces and at the Okinawa beachhead; readiness date of Kikusui 3, early morning of April 16.

By chance Buckner's 10th Army command supplied Ugaki with a prime target, the transports carrying Major General Andrew D. Bruce's 77th Infantry Division to Ie Shima Island. If the GI's and the kamikazes arrived off Ie simultaneously, or nearly so, Ugaki's flyers would have their best opportunity to date to impose a setback on the Americans.

For Kikusui 3, Ugaki's staff simply lacked the wherewithal to sustain an attack on the same scale as before. Admiral Yukoi estimated that of the 2,000 Navy planes committed to the Okinawa operation between March 23 and April 16 six hundred had been destroyed. By straining every resource the command mustered 160 kamikaze and 246 regular attacking planes, and although this strength equaled Kikusui 2, it fell well short of the numbers committed in Kikusui 1. Furthermore, the last reserve of planes and pilots had been tapped, and Kikusui 3 would be the last big attack until replacement planes and pilots could be drawn from the training commands in Japan proper.

As before, Ugaki split the attackers between T.F. 58 and the beachhead. He now added one new wrinkle. The attacks on the beachhead would come at dusk when the defending fighters would be landing on Okinawa's airfields or orbiting their carriers far at sea.

Fortunately for the GI's of the 77th Division, their superiors were disinclined to take needless risks with troops. From his Guam headquarters Admiral Nimitz took strong action to keep Ugaki's aviators busy in their own backyard. On April 15 T.F. 58 fighters flew sweeps over southern Kyushu, and on the sixteenth

B-29's of the 20th Air Force from the Marianas left off their city-busting to join the fighters in hitting at various Kyushu airfields. Nimitz had arranged for the B-29 attacks under special emergency powers granted to him by the Joint Chiefs of Staff. Army medium bombers and long range P-51 fighters from Iwo Jima supplemented the B-29's.

P-51

The Navy and Marine fighter pilots from T.F. 58 enjoyed complete surprise on the April 15 sweeps. At Kanoya airfield, the target of Hellcats and Corsairs from T.G. 58.1, the pilots found 200 planes on the parking strips, including a "Tabby" (Japanese DC-3) transport with a file of troops boarding it. For once the ground-strafers had a field day, since most of the planes appeared to be operational types and not propped-up wrecks or dummies. Aerial fighting picked up when Japanese planes from other fields intercepted some American formations on their way home. Over Ariake Bay a Hellcat flight led by Lieutenant Robert H. Jennings of a *Bennington* fighter squadron turned the tables on three Tojos, jumping them from the rear. Lieutenant Omer J. Donahoe hit an opponent with a ten-degree deflection burst and set him afire. The pilot shoved back his canopy, waved away the amazed Donahoe, and bailed out.

Perhaps thinking "There but for the grace of God go I," Donahoe let his foe drift earthward in peace. Donahoe's victory brought to twenty the claim of planes destroyed in the air; fifty-one more were believed destroyed on the ground, mostly at Kanoya.

The results of the carrier strikes, when combined with the Army Air Force's contribution, were very gratifying to Nimitz. Admiral Ugaki's 5th Air Fleet managed to fly off several missions in the early morning of April 16 and 17, but his projected evening strikes had to be scratched.

Ugaki's enfeebled attacks fell on T.F. 58 on April 14, 16, and 17. One hit only was serious. At 1:36 P.M. on the sixteenth a kamikaze slipped through defending fighters and A-A gunners to start bad fires on the hangar deck of the big carrier *Intrepid*. After an hour the crew quenched the flames, and although personnel casualties had been light for a hit on a carrier—ten killed and eighty-seven wounded—the ship required a Navy yard overhaul in the United States. Ugaki's intelligence officers thought the attackers had done better than that, recording three large and two small flattops as sunk or damaged. Once again they were victims of overoptimism. Nimitz's spoiling attacks had succeeded brilliantly, weakening Kikusui 3 before Ugaki could launch an attack in force against Okinawa.

THE ORDEAL OF THE *LAFFEY*

"RODGER PETER ONE." By the time Kikusui 3 was launched these words were enough to give any U.S. bluejacket the shudders. In radio voice jargon they stood for Radar Picket Station 1, now on its third set of station ships. This time the destroyer in the hot seat was Commander F. Julian Becton's U.S.S. *Laffey,* a new ship whose combat career had begun the year before at Normandy. On April 14 the *Laffey* relieved the fast minelayer *J. William Ditter* at Station 1 thirty-five miles north of Okinawa's tip and stood ready for whatever the kamikaze corps might offer.

With few exceptions the *Laffey*'s crew were not sanguine about their assignment. Beginning at Leyte Gulf they had seen many suicide attacks on close-by ships, the deliberate, calculated dives, the ball of fire roll up as bomb and plane exploded. Recalls Aristides Phoutrides, then a nineteen-year-old second-class quartermaster, "After a while it kind of got to you. We realized that it would happen to us, eventually." The crew kept up a brave front, pridefully adopting an insignia painted on the bridge showing a black panther chewing up a Japanese plane. But while lying-to under smoke cover off the Hagushi beachhead awaiting assignment, forbidden to fire at the Japanese planes circling overhead, the men had had time to ruminate about their future and were not reassured.

The clincher came on Friday, April 13, when the *Laffey* received orders to depart for Station 1. A superstitious crewman quickly pointed out the date, then added the clincher: The numbers of the ship's official designation, DD 724, when added totaled thirteen. Observes Phoutrides, "The consensus was: we've had it now!"

Like all ships the *Laffey* contained a few confirmed optimists who refused to listen to the pessimists. Commander Becton heard one say, "Nothing's going to happen to us! Maybe to other ships, but not to the *Laffey*. We're too lucky!"

Becton's experience—he had been aboard the destroyer *Aaron Ward* when she was sunk off Guadalcanal in 1943—told him otherwise. "I knew our chances of not being hit were slim," he writes. But so long as the *Laffey* remained afloat and had a gun to fire he intended to carry on his mission of giving early warning and absorbing attacks. He knew, too, that his sailors shared his determination. "They knew what they were up against. They knew it was a life or death duel with fanatical pilots. . . ."

The crew had the utmost confidence in their skipper. They respected his professionalism—"He was Annapolis"—and his concern for their welfare, which he always placed ahead of his own. They liked the ship, too, three-fourths of them being "plankowners," having served on her since her commissioning.

The *Laffey* was launched on November 21, 1943, at the long-established shipyard of the Bath Iron Works, Bath, Maine. Like all ships built by that firm, she exemplified fine workmanship and was a worthy successor to an earlier ship of the same name sunk in 1942 off Savo Island near Guadalcanal. In type she was of the *Allen M. Sumner* class, a standard design very successful in wartime service. On 2,200 tons displacement the *Laffey* mounted six 5-inch guns adapted to both surface and antiaircraft use, ten torpedo tubes, and more than twenty 40 and 20 mm. light antiaircraft guns. Twin propellers connected to four steam turbines totaling 60,000 horsepower could drive her to a top speed of 36 knots. Besides manning her engines and guns her 320 crew members ran a miniature city afloat, including voice and wireless radio equipment, radar, three restaurants (the officers', chiefs', and crews', messes to the sailors), a post office, a hospital clinic, a well-equipped machine shop, several stores, and even a small library.

Though functional, with a sweeping flush deck and squared off stern, the *Laffey* exhibited lean grace when underway at high speed, a long wake trailing for hundreds of yards behind her. Her

376-foot length, twin low stacks, and three twin turrets—two forward and one aft—made her resemble a light cruiser; from the air a neophyte airman who failed to note her slender beam might even confuse her with a heavy cruiser or a fast battleship of the *Washington* or *New Jersey* classes. Like others of her class she rolled badly in a heavy sea when low on fuel. Her turrets, A-A guns, "commo" gear, and radars added up to so much topside weight as to give her a stability problem.

After commissioning the *Laffey* in February, 1944, Skipper Becton had taken her to Normandy for a brush with German P.T. boats and a shore battery near Cherbourg. She had one close call. While screening battleship *Texas*, a shell from a German 240 mm. gun splashed nearby, skipped across the water, and socked her in the bow near the anchor without exploding. The Normandy campaign over, Becton and crew left for the Pacific, arriving in time to get into the last stages of the Leyte campaign. After supporting aircraft carriers off Iwo Jima, *Laffey* then left for Okinawa and screening and gunfire support duty before embarking a fighter-director team and heading for Rodger Peter 1.

Arriving at Station 1, Becton's ship quickly fell into the routine of picket duty. This consisted primarily of patrolling a smallish square chunk of ocean at economical speed while the Combat Information Center's radar watch swept the sky for bogies. When an enemy flight was picked up, the direction team, using information supplied by the ship's radar, would vector fighter patrols attached to the picket station to intercept the incoming enemy. Since between massed Kikusui attacks a few scouts and suiciders flew in singles, pairs, or treys almost every day, some activity by the direction team was normal.

So it proved with the *Laffey*'s first two days on station. On the fourteenth, within three hours of its arrival, the *Laffey*'s radar had picked up bogies, and with the assistance of the destroyer *Bryant* on a nearby station, the fighter-director team had coached fighters to an intercept in which three Zeros fell. The fifteenth, which saw no intercepts, was nevertheless busy. The crew lowered a whaleboat in midafternoon to investigate wreckage lookouts had spotted in the water, identifying a ditched enemy Judy. A search of the corpses of the crewmen revealed logbooks and other items of interest to the intelligence staff on the flagship *Eldorado*. The evening hours brought a dozen radar contacts with bogies near the ship, causing the crew to believe that the enemy's purpose was to deprive them of sleep and vitiate their alertness. At a little before 5 A.M. a contact looked sufficiently menacing as to induce Commander Becton to bring the crew to general quarters, but nothing developed.

As the midwatch passed into the morning watch, the day dawned fair and bright, bringing muttered imprecations from sailors on the navigation bridge. Good visibility with high scattered clouds made it simple for Japanese pilots to slip down the Ryukyu chain and spot the *Laffey*. The early morning watch continued as before with the ship at Readiness Condition One, a step removed from General Quarters, keeping two-thirds of the crew at battle stations. Radars scanned the ocean for air and surface targets, but all that showed on the scopes in the darkened CIC compartment were the blips identifying the *Laffey*'s two support gunboats patrolling on either flank.

Nobody talked much. A few men rehashed once more the shocking news of a few days before, agreeing it was too bad that President Roosevelt had not lived to see the European war through. But with this exchange, talk flagged. Gunners and loaders sat at their guns; water tenders checked the feed water supply to the boilers; oilers plied their long cans to the machinery; chiefs kept watchful eyes on their youthful charges.

Because the *Laffey* had to be kept ready to go to full speed at literally a moment's notice, the "black gang" below had to keep the superheaters cut in. These raised temperatures to well over a hundred degrees in the boiler and engineering spaces. Though he knew this was very hard on the crew, Commander Becton could do nothing about it. If attacked he intended to go to flank speed at once.

At 7:35 A.M. a single bogie, identified as a Val dive bomber, appeared from the south sixteen miles distant and circled the *Laffey*. Then it closed to 3,500 yards only to be bounced and destroyed by the two-plane combat air patrol attached to the ship's air controllers. Because the controllers were having trouble contacting the planes—the shoot-down had been a fortunate break—the control team asked for a new patrol to replace the pair overhead.

Almost immediately the *Laffey*'s CIC men realized that the lone Val pilot had been the advance man for a considerable kamikaze circus to follow. Four Vals appeared next, were spotted by the patrol, intercepted, and chased for forty miles. Three of them were shot down. Then, at exactly 8:27 A.M., *Laffey*'s radar oscilloscopes became cluttered with blips, fifty planes or more closing Station 1 in an arc northward of the ship. Swinging his ship broadside to the attackers to bring his mounts to bear, Commander Becton took them on.

In three minutes four Vals, leaders of the approaching swarm, closed to eight miles of the ship, then split, one pair circling to attack from the stern, the other two approaching from the front. Lieutenant Paul B. Smith, the *Laffey*'s gunnery officer, laid his main battery fire director on the bow pair and opened fire with the forward gun mounts. The stern mount, shifting to local control, shot VT projectiles equipped with radar proximity fuses at the rear pair. First blood for the *Laffey;* all four Vals splashed, two falling victim to the forward guns, two to the rear, one of which also had been hit by the guns of little LCS 51, which had been clinging to the destroyer's port stern quarter.

Almost simultaneously a pair of Judy dive bombers, taking advantage of the distraction imposed by the hapless Vals, tried to ambush the destroyer from either side. Both were splashed at the same moment by the 40 and 20 mm. pieces of the port and starboard automatic gunners, hitting the water on either flank 3,000 yards from the ship.

So far ten planes had fallen and not even the *Laffey*'s paint had been scratched, but four minutes later her fortunes changed. Describing what happened next Commander Becton told a reporter:

Then another one [a Val] came in from way to heck and gone out. They try to hit the bridge if they can, and that's what he was after. I kept the ship turning on him to spoil his [attack] angle, and finally he must have said, "Oh, the hell with it," because he came down and hit the top of the after gun mount, killing a man, and went on to splash overside.

By using high speed, 32 knots, and a heeling turn to port with a 25-degree angle on the rudder, Commander Becton had kept the kamikaze aft, away from the engineering plant and bridge. Damage had been minor.

But now a series of disastrous blows came one after the other. Two Judy dive bombers plunged in from either side. Seaman K. D. Jones swung his 40 mm. mount to get one, but the other, banking around the port motor whaleboat, hit the after deckhouse.

Flaming gasoline splashed everywhere, searing the sailors manning three 20 and 40 mm. mounts and putting them out of action. In the next five minutes four more planes hit aft, two on the deckhouse and two on the after mount, killing or blowing overside many men manning the after batteries. One young seaman, ducking against the corner of a bulkhead, crouched with his hands knotted against his face as the flames enveloped him. Nine men at Group 25, a pair of 20 mm. weapons near the after mount, had fired at the second suicider until it wrecked the mount and killed them.

In the midst of this series of blows another plane skimmed over the *Laffey*'s stern and releasing a bomb at the fantail made off. In Commander Becton's words, "The explosion from this bomb disabled our steering gear. . . . Our rudder was hard over and our movements after this were strictly circular. We weren't quite a sitting duck, but we felt like one." The destroyer was now in bad shape. As she steamed in uncontrolled high-speed circles fires blazed in the three after crew compartments and near the after 5-inch magazine. Despite the combat air patrol, which had bagged several, too many kamikazes still circled overhead preparatory to making runs on the ship.

That the *Laffey* did not blow up was due primarily to the efforts of Ensign Robert C. Thomson, the radar officer. Thomson went aft to deal with the fires about the 5-inch magazine. Using foam extinguishers he was making good progress when another hit killed him and others in the group fighting the flames.

Gunner's Mate M.S. Matthews had joined Thomson in fighting fires. A hit blew him into the water where he was nearly sucked into one of the propellers. But he fought clear and, seeing another man, Seaman Rex Vest, who had been blown off with him, he grasped him and supported him until both were rescued.

The action continued another hour, adding to the ship's injuries and casualties. With a Marine Corsair in hot pursuit, an Oscar fighter charged the *Laffey*'s port quarter, hit the mast, knocking out all but two radio transmitters, and splattered into the sea. The Corsair hit the port yardarm, knocking it off, but the pilot retained sufficient control to pull up his fighter, roll it over, and parachute. He was rescued with minor injuries. The impact of the Oscar having ripped off the ship's ensign, a second-class signalman from Brooklyn, Thomas McCarthy, shouted, "We've got to get that flag back up there." Seizing another from the flag locker he shinnied up the swaying mast and tied the new ensign in place with a piece of line.

Other Corsairs shot down several attackers before they could crash the ship, but two more damaging blows followed. A Judy dive bomber exploded close to the port side, and shrapnel from its bomb knocked out power leads to a forward mount and the main battery gun director. Both forward mounts now had to aim and fire manually which they did with sufficient effect to drop an Oscar and a Val 500 yards from the ship. Said Commander Becton, "I'd never seen a plane take a direct hit from a 5-inch shell. It was a pleasure to see the Oscar poised in space a few feet above the water, and then just disintegrate into nothingness."

The second-to-the-last attacker released a bomb visible to the gunners in the forward 20 mm. batteries. Seaman Jack Ondrasek leapt into the harness of a gun at Mount 21 and tried to deflect its trajectory with a stream of 20 mm. bullets. He failed, and the bomb hit nearby, killing him outright. Recalled his buddy, Seaman Fred Gemmell, "He didn't have to get into those gun straps, but he did." A man at another gun had fired his weapon until the blast tore off both of his legs. He murmured to Aristides Phoutrides and others who rushed up to him, "Please, please get me out of here." Before they could release him from the harness he was dead.

The last plane, a Judy dive bomber, hit near the ship, but not close enough to inflict further damage. It was the final attacker of twenty-two planes that had tried to send the *Laffey* to the bottom.

In the wardroom, used as the clearing station to treat casualties on a destroyer, Lieutenant Matthew Driscoll, the ship's doctor, was treating the sixty officers and men injured in the attack, half of them seriously. The final bomb had wounded him in the hand and killed his assistant, but Driscoll continued to work with one hand, while verbally instructing volunteers in the art of administering plasma to burn and shrapnel cases.

Now all hands turned to fighting numerous fires and flooding in the after part of the ship. Lieutenant Theodore Runk led a repair party to free the rudder, but that effort failed. However, he accomplished something more worthwhile by finding an unexploded bomb on the deck and rolling it overside. Gradually the crewmen got the fires and flooding under control. Because the worst hits had been on the stern, the *Laffey* had retained full engine power throughout the attack, a big factor in her survival.

The jammed rudder frustrated Commander Becton's efforts to steer a straight course. The support landing craft had their own troubles and could not help. One had taken a kamikaze on an after 40 mm. mount; the other had splashed a plane that exploded twenty-five feet from its side, tossing the engine through the craft's hull. Finally, a minesweeper came to Becton's aid and towed the *Laffey* to the Kerama anchorage.

Other picket stations north of Okinawa also had trouble with Kikusui 3. On Station 2 the destroyer *Bryant* was hit as she steamed to succor the *Laffey*, losing thirty-four killed and thirty-three wounded. At Station 14 destroyer *Pringle* took a Val that must have been carrying a huge bomb. Hit abaft the first stack the ship buckled, broke in two, and sank in five minutes, losing sixty-five killed or drowned. Fast minesweeper *Hobson*, which had been supporting the *Pringle*, also took a hit, though damage was fairly light and only four were killed. Two other ships steaming north of Ie Shima were damaged. One, the destroyer-minesweeper *Harding*, had her keel so badly warped by a near-miss that Lieutenant Commander D. B. Ramage had to back his ship to the Kerama refuge.

But around Okinawa that was it. Thanks largely to the detemination, tenacity, and endurance of crews like those of the *Laffey* and her two support gunboats, no kamikazes had attacked the 77th Division's transports off Ie Shima or any ship off the Hagushi beaches. The *Laffey* had also made the greatest utility of the radar picket destroyer dreadfully apparent. Though useful in giving early warning, its main utility was as a gambit, a pawn to absorb the impact of the suiciders before they reached the tender-skinned transports and cargo vessels. In this role *Laffey* had absorbed the bulk of Ugaki's airmen of Kikusui Number 3.

14

IE SHIMA: "WHERE WE LOST ERNIE PYLE"

THE PRINCIPAL REASON for Colonel Udo's stubborn defense of the Motobu Peninsula came to light after the marines had overrun his redoubt. Hidden snugly in a cave in a narrow valley, sited to fire directly on the airfield on nearby Ie Shima, were two 150 mm. guns. Anticipating that General Buckner might try to seize Ie before overrunning Motobu, Udo had emplaced the guns to interdict the airfield from 17,600 yards. The untimely arrival of Lemuel Shepherd's 6th Marine Division had forestalled that. Now the defense of Ie would devolve on Udo's subordinate, Major Masashi Igawa, who garrisoned the island with his 2nd Battalion of the 44th Brigade's Second Unit.

I

To defend Ie Shima, Igawa adopted a strategy somewhat similar to that used by Japanese forces on Iwo Jima. On Ie was a miniature mountain, Iegusugu Yama, rising to 587 feet on the island's eastern end. Igawa elected to center his defense on the mountain and in adjacent Ie town. So long as they remained in place, dug deeply into the rock, his regular infantry, bolstered by service troops, *boetai,* and impressed civilians, could prevent the Americans from using the airfield. From Iegusugu Yama and Ie town every part of Ie Shima could be kept under fire, for the rest of the island was mostly flat and measured only two-and-one-half by five miles.

Igawa and his men prepared a defense in depth. Beneath the houses of the village they dug pillboxes; under a prominent ridge and into Iegusugu Yama's limestone rock they hollowed out elaborate caves and tunnels, some being three stories deep with outlets at each level. Mortars, sited to bombard roads, beaches, the airfield, and other preselected targets, they sunk in pits twenty feet deep. On the airfield, on the roads, and in the streets of Ie town they laid numerous mines, some converted aircraft bombs powerful enough to flip a thirty-five-ton Sherman tank onto its back, others smaller wood and terra cotta anti-vehicle and anti-personnel devices.

In supplementing his 930 regulars Igawa performed a near-miracle. From the service units attached to the airfields, he armed more than a thousand additional men, including among others 350 from the 50th Airfield Battalion, 120 from the 118th Independent Maintenance Unit of aircraft specialists, and 580 from the Gibo Labor Battalion of Okinawan conscripts drafted originally to help build the airstrips. In addition, more than 1,500 civilians of both sexes of approximately 5,000 on the island joined the force. Igawa organized his garrison of about 3,500 carefully and armed each person, using every weapon on Ie Shima—75 mm. artillery pieces, light and heavy A-A guns, standard infantry mortars and machine guns, stripped from wrecked planes, rifles, pistols, and even sharpened bamboo spears for use by his frightened but determined civilians. Moreover, Igawa trained and indoctrinated his miscellany of fighters so well that GI's attacking could discern no difference between the fanaticism and skill of the regulars and the civilians. Ie Shima truly was an island in arms, a foretaste of what American soldiers could expect when and if they invaded Japan.

When the Okinawan campaign began General Buckner had intended to seize Ie Shima only after southern Okinawa had been secured. On discovering that Ushijima intended no serious defense of the north, he ordered the anticipated Ie Shima landing advanced and designated for the job Major General Andrew Bruce's 77th Division. For some days, however, he deferred specifying the exact date. This proved irksome to the 77th's troops, who had to stay aboard crowded transports circling monotonously south of Okinawa and fret about kamikazes. They recalled too well the hit on the *Henrico* on April 2. To their relief General Bruce received the final go-ahead on April 12, and after two days of hasty staff planning, the transports straightened course for Ie Shima. Landing day was set for the morning of April 16.

Igawa had hoped to trick his enemy into landing on the island's two best beaches which fronted on his strong defenses in Ie town. He had therefore elaborately camouflaged his positions— so well that many officers in Buckner's 10th Army headquarters had become convinced that Ie Shima had been abandoned. This clever ruse failed. General Bruce was suspicious, for on Guam he had encountered Japanese deception before. He therefore protested successfully a 10th Army suggestion to land two companies to reconnoiter the island and insisted on a full-scale landing at the western end to uncover first the airfield and then the beaches near Ie town. He was certain that Iegusugu Yama and Ie town contained the bulk of the 2,500 defenders his intelligence officers insisted were present.

Bruce's landing plan was simple. Embarked in amphibious tractors his 306th Regiment would land across Green Beach on the west end and overrun the airfield. The 305th Regiment would land across Beaches Red 1 and 2 on the south coast and pivot east toward Iegusugu Yama and Ie town, in the process uncovering the two best beaches, Red 3 and 4, over which would have to come the heavy construction equipment necessary to develop the airfield. Standing by aboard ship was the 307th Regiment. General Bruce hoped that he would not have to use it; that the other two regiments could take the island by themselves.

II

A fierce American naval and air bombardment of Ie Shima, beginning on March 25 and carried on intermittently thereafter, had made life most unpleasant for Major Igawa but had not weakened appreciably his defenses, though most of the bombs and shells fell on Iegusugu Yama and Ie town. Attacks intensified on April 13, with battleship *Texas* lobbing in 14-inch projectiles, and continued with but one respite until just before "S" hour on "W" day, as landing hour and day for Ie Shima were designated. In the final bombardment every identifiable target was hit, every likely appearing bit of terrain bombed, shelled, napalmed, rocketed, or strafed. Just before the landing two battalions of 105 mm. howitzers of the 77th Division added their full-throated roar to the din, firing from tiny Minna Shima, a sand islet just off the Motobu Peninsula. Pinned under a blanket of flying steel, Major Igawa's defenders made no effort to reply to the bombardment or fire on the landing craft circling out to sea. Well before S hour, set for 8:00 A.M., smoke and dust blanked out Ie Shima to observers aboard ship.

At exactly 7:58 A.M. the amphibious tractors carrying Lieutenant Colonel Joseph B. Coolidge's 305th Infantry crawled across the western beaches. Nine minutes later others with Colonel Aubrey D. Smith's 306th rumbled across a beach on the southwest end of the island. On jumping from their mounts the troops met slight initial opposition and moved rapidly inland, hampered only by long-range fire from Iegusugu Yama to the east. A few Japanese were inland from the beaches, holding outposts, but a diary entry translated later explained why they remained passive most of the morning. "After fierce naval bombardment," an unidentified Japanese author had penned, "the enemy began landing directly in front of the 4th Company. . . . His firepower is so great we dared not show our hand."

All day the advance went smoothly, with Colonel Smith's men overrunning the airfield. The greatest problem turned out to be the Japanese mines, which the infantry could see and avoid, but which greatly hampered tank and armored tractor movement. Elsewhere the advance was slower, hampered similarly by mines and also by enemy machine gun fire from Ie town. Already it was clear that the battle for Ie Shima would resolve into a fight to seize Ie town and the adjacent miniature mountain, Iegusugu Yama.

Casualties on W day had been light. Early in the action Captain Donald W. Cheff of Waynesboro, Pennsylvania, a medical officer of the 302nd Medical Battalion, had established a collection station on the beach. He then had set out for the front with a pair of jeep ambulances to pick up casualties though warned that the road was mined. After completing a round trip with eight wounded, Cheff went back to load eight more. This time his luck ran out; his lead jeep hit a mine, killing him and his four wounded passengers.

Major Igawa waited until nightfall before attempting a counterattack. Then at 8:00 P.M. he began to probe the American perimeter, following with a company-size counterattack. This last was a vicious affair, mixing Igawa's regulars with auxiliary troops. Many attackers carried with them mortar shells in wooden boxes, intending to rush these into the American lines and blow up themselves and the enemy. A wild night ended with 152 Japanese dead and a number of injuries in Coolidge's battalion. One GI had an arm broken by a leg blown from one of Igawa's human kamikazes.

The next day, April 17, the second of the operation, the GI's began meeting what the military communiqué writers are wont to call "stiffening resistance." Their job was to push straight eastward to uncover Red Beaches 3 and 4 and take Ie town. They reached the area but ran into serious trouble with a nest of caves behind the beaches. Hoping to keep the attack rolling, General Bruce set ashore Colonel Stephen S. Hamilton's 307th Regiment, but evening found the troops heavily engaged in Ie town along a line running from the beach to a ridge on which stood Ie Shima's concrete and steel three-story Government House. Its heavy frame had stolidly endured bomb, shell, and rocket and symbolized the iron resistance that lay ahead from what the men would soon call "Bloody Ridge."

On April 18, the third day of the operation, General Bruce proposed to use Hamilton's infantry in a straight-ahead punch through Ie town and across Bloody Ridge to the base of Iegusugu Yama 700 yards beyond. Smith's regiment he would circle to the other side of the mountain from the north and west. Coolidge would support Hamilton. "This was," says the 77th's official history, "the age-old but still workable plan to forge a ring of steel around the enemy position, then squeeze." It would be mainly a rifleman's fight, for mines and rubble in Ie town barred the use of tanks.

Combat on April 18, and particularly on the approaches to Bloody Ridge, resembled a miniature Battle of Stalingrad. Every house, every street in Ie town became an object of assault. Every yard gained or lost cost both sides dearly. On the morning of the 19th Companies G and F of Hamilton's 307th managed to fight their way up Bloody Ridge toward the key position, the Government House, which lay on a small plateau. Neither company could consolidate a perimeter, both ran low on ammunition, and a heroic group of Igawa's defenders frustrated the advance by dashing from cover to toss a satchel charge into an amphibious tractor bringing more ammunition up the hill. The charge didn't explode, but the driver and his assistant understandably abandoned the vehicle. Both companies then withdrew, carrying their dead and wounded with them.

Under such conditions the fighting became intensely personal. In the center of Ie town Pfc John Polovchak, a member of an intelligence and reconnaissance (I & R) platoon, found himself crawling through masses of rubble to locate the source of some enemy rifle fire. With bullets ricocheting about him, he crawled on until he suddenly spotted three Japanese soldiers in camouflage suits perched in a tree not far away. Taking cover behind a coral pillar, he sighted his BAR, took careful aim, and tumbled all three from the tree.

Earlier this day, the GI's of the 77th had welcomed to Ie Shima the common soldier's spokesman of World War II, the famous war correspondent Ernie Pyle. Ernie had been ill aboard ship after a brief visit ashore with the marines, but had come to the island anyway to meet with an enthusiastic reception and numerous requests for his autograph.

Ernie Pyle hated war, having seen a lot more of it than most frontline GI's. He had covered the invasions of North Africa, Sicily, and Italy before going to Normandy to renew his acquaintance with a favorite outfit, the 16th Infantry of the Big Red One, the 1st Division. His books *Brave Men* and *Here Is Your War* were bestsellers, and perhaps his finest piece of writing was a description of some infantry bringing down from an Italian mountain by mule pack the body of their beloved company commander.

With the war in Europe almost over, Ernie had come to the Pacific ". . . simply because there is a war on and I'm a part of it." His next to last column, written while with the marines, was typical of his homespun Indiana style that had earned for him his reputation as the GI's Boswell.

Ernie had elected to bed down with Corporal Martin Clayton, Jr., and Pfc William Gross, ". . . partly because it was warmer, and also because I wanted to be with the enlisted men." After supper they burned their ration boxes in a little fire they had built and "just sat talking."

Other marines drifted along and after a while there were more than a dozen sitting around. We smoked cigarettes and talked of a hundred things. The first topic was, in all groups, about our surprise at no opposition to our landing. Then they got to asking me what I thought of things over here and how it compared with Europe. And when did I think the war would end? Of course, I didn't know any of the answers but it made conversation. . . . We talked like that for about an hour, and then it grew dark and a shouted order came along the hillside to put out the fires. . . . Gross and I went to bed. There was nothing else to do after dark in blackout country.

Early on April 18 Ernie set out for the front with Lieutenant Colonel Coolidge, the 305th Infantry's commander. Near Ie town Ernie, Coolidge, and the driver dove from the jeep into a ditch when a Japanese machine gun suddenly opened up from behind the American line. Coolidge and Pyle lay still until the firing stopped, then cautiously raised their heads over the rim. At once the enemy gun chattered and Ernie Pyle slumped limply into the ditch. Realizing that Pyle had been hit, Coolidge crawled to him and was shaken to find him dead; the gun's burst had caught Ernie Pyle just below the rim of his helmet killing him instantly.

Coolidge and his men immediately sought revenge on the machine gun but had a difficult time getting it. Tanks could not reach it because of the terrain; an infantry patrol finally blasted the gun and its crew with grenades.

Spreading rapidly, the news of Ernie's death caused more sorrow on Ie Shima. Back home in the United States the shock of it called the island and the Okinawan campaign to the attention of millions.

Ernie Pyle was buried in the 77th Division cemetery in a casket made from salvaged packing crates. A wooden marker set up at the place where he fell recorded simply, "On this spot the 77th Division lost a buddy, Ernie Pyle, 18 April 1945." Later, the engineers erected a permanent concrete monument in the form of a truncated pyramid five feet high and three feet wide bearing a brass plaque with the same inscription. It remains today, one of just three American memorials of the Okinawan campaign.

III

Heavy 77th Division casualties had displeased but not surprised General Bruce and his assistant division commander, Brigadier General Edwin H. Randle, who had been directing the fight on the scene. They had thrown two regiments into a frontal assault on Ie town and Bloody Ridge to keep pressure on the enemy and prevent a counterattack on Red Beaches 3 and 4.

They also wanted to free the beaches from enemy fire and land engineer equipment. Bruce had radioed to General Buckner, "I know emergency exists for air warning service and airfields. My tactical plans...[are] based on necessity of securing Red Beaches 3 and 4...." But now on April 19 both generals realized that frontal attack had failed; that the 77th would have to try something else.

To clarify his division's problem General Bruce examined from the water the eastern approaches to Iegusugu Yama. He decided to attack the next day, the twentieth, from across open terrain north and east of the miniature mountain. Seizure of Iegusugu might well unlock Igawa's fortress. Attack from this direction would also place the main burden on Colonel Smith's 306th Regiment, thus taking some of the pressure from the casualty-ridden 305th and 307th.

Recognizing that their shellfire had been of slight help in earlier assaults, the 77th Division's artillery officers tried a ruse on the twentieth. They laid on a ten-minute barrage at 8:50 A.M., paused—hopefully to draw the Japanese from dugouts and caves—and blasted away for fifteen more minutes, after which all three of the 77th's regiments jumped off.

The main attack was launched by Smith's regiment, attacking from 600 yards northeast of Iegusugu. Companies B and C led, with shells sailing over the men's heads to beat against the mountain and about its base. Divisional 37 mm. antitank guns blasted pillboxes and marked with tracers targets for the larger guns of tanks and M-8 and M-18 self-propelled guns. Where the terrain was open the infantry and accompanying engineers advanced by crawling and creeping. By early afternoon the 306th had secured a small ridge about 200 yards from Iegusugu. Here the line infantry paused and consolidated. For B Company the advance had been rough, having cost the unit twenty-six men and its commanding officer. Much of its success was attributable to Sergeant Harold F. Murray, who had crawled into an extensive Japanese antipersonnel minefield to blast a path through by exploding the mines with accurate bursts from his submachine gun. After B Company reached the ridge First Lieutenant Robert G. Conner, Jr., who had assumed command, moved from platoon to platoon to organize the company positions and provide a secure base for continued advance.

In Ie town on the other side of the mountain, the 307th and 305th had attacked once again. Though resistance initially seemed just as savage as on previous days both regiments kept going. The 305th's 2st Battalion, commanded by Major Eugene Cook, managed to seize a hill overlooking Government House and Bloody Ridge from the east. Private first class Alfred L. Stott of A Company sparked this attack by dashing fifty feet to its top, then tossing grenades and using his BAR to kill six enemies and enable the rest of the company to come up. The 3rd Battalion, commanded by Captain Louis B. Hinson, brutally forced its way through Ie town from the west, street by bloody street, house by house. In the center of the town attacking north toward Iegusugu, two battalions of the 307th once more advanced up Bloody Ridge toward Government House determined this time to seize and hold it.

They made it, occupying the small plateau and hastily consolidating and organizing a perimeter. Machine guns of Company H went onto the second floor of Government House; Company F occupied the center of the ridge; Company E held the east end; and Captain Garrett V. Rickards occupied the west end of the ridge with his Company G. If the 307th could hold Bloody Ridge and the 305th the high ground just to the east, the enemy in the still-uncleared parts of Ie town and on Iegusugu Yama would remain trapped.

Meanwhile, on the other side of Iegusugu, the 306th resumed its advance toward the mountain's north and east face. Crouching in a shell hole was Captain Joseph A. (Kat) Katalinas, C Company's commander. When the last rounds of the preliminary artillery barrage had fallen, he asked an artillery observer with him, "Is that it?" The artilleryman said it was. "O.K.," replied

Katalinas, replacing a stubby cigar in his mouth, "watch our smoke." He leaped up and, followed by his company, sprinted 200 yards across open terrain to the base of Iegusugu. There C Company began at once to systematically attack caves and dugouts. Twenty minutes after gaining the mountain Katalinas' men, joined by others, had worked halfway up, supported from below by direct fire from tanks and M-8's.

M-8

Much of the task of blasting caves fell to the engineers. First Lieutenant Harold S. Atkinson led one such platoon, which first cleared a field of 240 mines from the approaches to Iegusugu, then sealed or blasted 88 caves. Atkinson personally accounted for two enemy mortars and a machine gun. In another action Staff Sergeant Julius Jacobsen, a platoon guide of Company A, found his squad pinned down by an enemy machine gun that wounded a man. Jacobsen crawled to him, pulled him to safety, then noted an enemy soldier carrying a grenade at the mouth of a cave. He shot the Japanese with his BAR, then began crawling to outflank the machine gun, only to hear the "pop" of an enemy knee mortar. Wiggling into an exposed position he dispatched the two-man mortar crew. So it went all afternoon on the steep slopes of Iegusugu.

By nightfall many men had been wounded, "Kat" Katalinas twice, but the 306th had a firm hold on the north face of the mountain. A patrol had scaled the near-vertical upper slopes to toss a colored smoke grenade over the peak to signal their presence to the GI's of the other regiments on the other side.

General Bruce summarized the day's action in a radio message to General Buckner. "Base of Pinnacle completely surrounded despite bitterest fight I have ever witnessed against a veritable fortress."

For the surviving Japanese April 20 had been disastrous. Not only had they lost half of their mountain stronghold, but vital Bloody Ridge and Government House had fallen. Now their only hope was to counterattack, to drive the enemy away from his hard-won key terrain.

Beginning after dark on the night of April 20–21, small groups of Igawa's troops began attacking Bloody Ridge, probing for a soft spot. Finally, they concluded that Captain Garrett V. Rickards' G Company, occupying the left end of the ridge, held the weakest point. At 4:30 A.M. about five hundred attacked, preceded by the densest mortar barrage yet encountered on Ie Shima. As Rickards ran forward through the bursts from his command post to join his men on the perimeter, the leading Japanese overran Rickards' left-flank platoon. The right-flank platoon held, supported by attached heavy machine guns of Company H, the weapons company. Nevertheless, many attackers managed to reach the battalion command post, where everyone, from Lieutenant Colonel Joseph W. Hanna, the battalion commander, down to the lowliest cook, fought desperately for their lives.

Private first class Rune E. Yberg, on duty at an ammo dump to the rear, seized as many grenades and as much ammunition as he could carry and ran to the ridge, bolstering the improvised line. Two machine gunners, Staff Sergeant Anthony J. Cernawsky and Pfc Martin O. May, fired their heavy machine guns until mortars knocked out their weapons. Then both fought for an hour at close quarters with carbines and grenades until May was mortally wounded and the enemy driven off. Nearby Pfc Emiliano Gonzales, a platoon scout from Company G, rose from his foxhole to grenade an enemy squad trying to outflank one of the guns. Knocked down and severely wounded by a mortar burst, he got up and killed six attackers. Finally, Captain Rickards managed to reorganize some of his men, counterattack, and recover the lost ground.

Full daylight revealed 280 Japanese bodies around G Company which itself had only 36 effectives left. Eighty-four more Japanese lay in the areas of F and E Companies, which had managed to hold their ground. Company H had but forty-nine men fit for duty and two of its eight machine guns operable. But it had many heroes, of whom one, Pfc May, was awarded the Congressional Medal of Honor posthumously. Captain Rickards, Staff Sergeant Cernawsky, and Pfc Gonzales were among the many awarded Silver Stars.

Though pressed home with the utmost determination, the enemy's last attack had merely confirmed what a thousand similar episodes had repeatedly demonstrated. Sheer bravery and cover of darkness could not overcome superior firepower. The bodies in the American positions included a high percentage of officers and noncommissioned officers, suggesting that the attackers had been from Major Igawa's headquarters group. Igawa was not among them; according to a POW he had died the day before. The attackers had included eight women, one of whom was armed with a saber and the rest with bamboo spears.

The fighting after daylight on April 21 featured the seizure of the rest of Iegusugu Yama and all of Ie town. In taking the mountain the 77th Division staged an Army version of the Marines' Iwo Jima flag raising. Early in the morning Captain Stephen K. Smith, the regimental intelligence officer of the 306th, improvised mountain-climbing ropes and scaling ladders, and accompanied by four volunteers with mountain-climbing experience, set out to reach the summit. On a ledge halfway up the men encountered sniper fire but kept going to the top, where they unfurled and planted the Stars and Stripes. Then, with enemy bullets zipping viciously past and mortar fragments pelting about, they descended safely to receive Silver Stars. The parallel was more than superficial; like Iwo Jima, where the colors had been raised three months earlier under similar danger, Ie Shima was destined to become an important advance air base from which long-range fighter aircraft could operate over Japan.

By midafternoon of the twenty-first the fighting on Ie Shima had reached the mopping-up stage, which is not to say it was any less merciless. However, the numbers of Japanese killed in proportion to Americans rose very steeply. Now holed up in isolated caves and dugouts, Igawa's survivors could be approached carefully and systematically blasted out. Mopping up continued five more days, the last noteworthy fight occurring on the night of April 22–23, when a mixed group of Japanese soldiers and civilians emerged from caves on Iegusugu Yama to rush the perimeter of the 306th. All were gunned down. Very few Japanese soldiers tried to surrender; only 149 were captured during the entire operation. But some hundreds of civilians allowed themselves to be talked out of caves by the 77th's Nisei interpreters. In all, 4,706 Japanese were counted dead—probably somewhat of an exaggeration—against 77th Division losses of 172 killed, 902 wounded, and 46 missing. In total numbers 77th Division losses approximated those of its Guam campaign, in which the fighting had extended over a much longer period.

In no sense could the Ie Shima invasion be considered a sideshow to the main Okinawan campaign. In arming so many of his soldiers and civilians, in training them to fight so well, Major Igawa raised his combat potential to its highest possible maximum, furnishing to the American commanders a grim prophecy of what they could expect if they invaded the Japanese home islands, where they would meet the desperate fury of a fully mobilized Army and population. On the American side, as Lieutenant General Andrew D. Bruce, U.S.A. (Ret.), recalls, the Ie Shima operation was a "masterpiece of planning and execution" to take a sorely needed bit of ground. Not least, Bruce adds, "It is where we lost Ernie Pyle."

15

BEHIND THE LINES

THE RAPID ADVANCE of the marines and GI's had by mid-April given the engineers and services of supply troops plenty of room in which to operate. Already, a GI sprawl had begun to cover central Okinawa, creeping close to the front lines. Every suitable piece of ground harbored a supply dump, hospital, headquarters, tent city, or encampment. Bulldozers hacked at coral hills, and laden dump trucks rumbled along dusty roads to unload on soft spots or on Kadena or Yomitan airfields, both of which swarmed with engineers and Seabees extending runways, laying down taxiways, and building hardstands. Poles and telephone lines sprouted everywhere as the Signal Corps unraveled a communications network.

I

This hive of activity had a remorseless logic. From the beginning it was aimed not merely to support the conquest of Okinawa but to further the next and final operation of the war in the Pacific, the invasion of Japan. Already, the engineers had discovered that Okinawa would harbor many more than the eight airfields aerial photographs had indicated could be built. By late April Admiral Nimitz at Guam had decided that seizure of Miyako Island in the Sakishimas could be dispensed with; that Okinawa could harbor eighteen airfields and Ie Shima Island four more, enough to handle a whole air force transferred from England with its necessary fighter escort. Six fields would take B-29's, five B-24's, and three more the light and medium bombers, A-20's, A-26's, and B-25's. The remainder would be fighter strips, and one, Naha airfield still in enemy hands, would be reserved for use as an air depot for major overhauls.

Almost of equal importance to the airfields was the Navy's planned operating base at White Beach on Nakagusuku Bay. Its construction by mid-April was only in the survey stage; the main concern of the Engineers and Navy was to clear the Nakagusuku beaches to supplement those at Hagushi. Already, a problem of grave concern had emerged. The stalemate in the ground fighting at Kazazu Ridge had suggested that Naha would not fall on the date specified in the ICEBERG war plan, April 26, but much later, after weeks of fighting. This, in turn, meant that Naha's sheltered port would not be usable, and that the Hagushi beaches, supplemented by those at Nakagusuku and Kin bays, would have to support both the combat operations and the base buildup. Inevitably, the troops must have priority and base and airfield development must suffer.

II

To the Okinawans this strange GI world might as well have been Martian, so alien was it to their experience. But with a fatalism born of centuries of typhoons and adversity they were already beginning to accept it. The end of eighteen days of combat found over one hundred thousand in detention camps with more rapidly coming in as northern Okinawa was cleared.

The American soldiers did not quite know how to regard the Okinawans, whether as nationals of the state that had attacked Pearl Harbor, or as people with separate language and customs who had been exploited by Japan. Their briefings on this subject had been ambiguous, reflecting the uncertainty of the intelligence officers themselves. Contact soon dissolved this largely philosophical question, and the Okinawans simply became to the GI's and marines "Okies."

Certainly they were objects of pity as they trudged along the roads carrying their few belongings, their babies and their small children. The women, barely four feet tall, clad in long black dresses, seemed frail and prematurely aged. The undernourished old men, a little taller, but well below the stature of the average American, trudged with their women in knee-length trousers and bare feet. Their shy smiles showed no evidence of the hostility the Americans had half-expected to meet. To one marine they seemed to be "a very simple and amiable people [who] always think of the old folks first."

In charge of the detainees was Brigadier General William E. Crist's Military Government Section of the Okinawa Island Command. Special military government teams containing officers and enlisted specialists and translators were ready, one for each 10,000 of the population, to establish camps and detention centers and to administer the civil economy. The troops had been severely enjoined to spare and not to molest civilians—General Buckner wanted no rapine to embitter relations—but many officers had feared that when captured the Okinawans would either be hostile or inclined to mass suicide. The first hours of Love Day had dispelled this concern, and by mid-April Buckner knew that the Okinawans would be easy to manage and no threat.

Another concern dispelled was the fear that in addition to feeding its own men the 10th Army would have to supply rations to the civilians. Each division had carried along rice, fish, and other foods for this purpose, but as it turned out unloading crews did not have to be diverted to handle them. The rapid conquest of central Okinawa had hardly touched the fields; as usual, summer had come early and already ripe for harvest were sweet potatoes, rice, sugar cane, and vegetables. The military government teams soon found the Okinawans willing and able to harvest the crops under the direction of their own "honchos" —leaders—picked by the young military government captains in charge of the detention centers. Communication proved to be easy. The Nisei interpreters had little trouble because all of the younger Okinawans understood Japanese. Also, in nearly every center there was an Okinawan or two who had lived in Hawaii and who spoke some English.

The chief problem turned out to be the fearful overcrowding in the villages set aside as internment camps. Visitors to the largest of these, Shimibuku, a town located to the rear of the 96th Division, found it jammed with 14,000 refugees. A jeep picking its way through the narrow, winding streets had to contend with innumerable children and goats. Only women, old men, and children populated the village, which was not encircled with barbed wire. The few men of military age, seventeen to forty-five, had been interned separately as a security measure. Nevertheless, the women and old men worked hard in the adjacent fields, and although food and clothing were by no means plentiful, they acquired enough of both to get by. The medical aid provided by the military government was the best they had ever known. Diarrhea and dysentery were the most common ailments, and tuberculosis the most common serious disease, but the health of the population was not adjudged poor by the medics. Liberal application of DDT decimated the ranks of the people's most ancient enemies, the fleas, flies, and mosquitoes. The chief discipline problem in the village proved to be getting the people—the elderly women in particular—to use latrines. Otherwise, the military government officers had little trouble with the Okinawans, whom they considered to be better disciplined and more easy to manage than Leyte's Filipinos.

The unfamiliarity of Okinawans with American ways and life produced many bizarre incidents, recalled years afterward with amusement. Two upper-class Okinawans, who passed through the lines in the 24th Corps zone, were given occupation scrip by their GI captors with which to buy food. Mistaking the scrip for safe conduct passes, they waved it when they met the next group of soldiers and received more. This continued until they reached Shimibuku. Afterward, they were mortified to discover that the Americans had assumed they were begging.

Few Okinawans thought much of their future, or of the consequences of coming under American rule. "Our main concern," recalls Yasuharu Gibo, who became mayor of Ozato after the war, "was to keep alive." He directed the process of evaporating seawater to provide the civilian camps with salt.

Early in the campaign General Crist established a rate of one yen a day—about eighteen cents, the going 1940 wage—for those Okinawans who elected to work for the U.S. Army. But the lack of able-bodied men in the camps, most having been conscripted by the Japanese, limited civilian labor to ditch maintenance and service in hospitals.

Very few Okinawans elected to join Japanese Army troops in the northern mountains as guerrillas. Had they done so General Buckner might well have faced a serious problem. Guerrilla activity, mostly on the part of scattered troops of Colonel Udo's former Motobu Peninsula command, was a "nuisance," according to General Wallace, the head of the Okinawa Island Command, but not much more. It did keep the 6th Marine Division and then the 27th Division busy sweeping the north with security patrols and engaging in an occasional firefight, but no serious harm was done to the 10th Army's elaborate and vulnerable supply dumps.

A resister was Kazufumi Uechi, a thirty-one-year-old newsman, who left Naha shortly before the American landing with the mission of relocating Okinawa's newspaper, the *Shimpo,* in an abandoned copper mine near Haneji at the base of the Motobu Peninsula. The project died aborning after L day when a Marine Corps tank blew apart the shack near the mine shaft which served as the *Shimpo*'s new quarters. Unwilling to abandon his trade, Uechi joined a guerrilla outfit under Captain Haruo Murakami which called itself the Gokyo (Youth Fighters) unit. Using radio news from Japan as his source, Uechi became the unit's war correspondent and news editor, printing a small newssheet in a shack in the hills. Twice he had close calls. In a skirmish with American troops a shot literally ripped off the top of the head of the man next to him. In another episode, when the unit was caught in a violent storm, he was nearly crushed by falling trees. He survived the campaign to reestablish the paper after the war.

A few Okinawans, either out of fear of Americans or for other reasons, chose to hide out as refugees rather than to surrender and accept American rule. In the hills of northern Okinawa many persons lived a half-starved miserable existence, dodging American patrols, grubbing sweet potatoes from tiny mountainside plots, chewing sugar cane, and making themselves as comfortable at night as they could. The experience of Miss Chiyoko Higa illustrates their lot.

Chiyoko, in contrast to Uechi, wanted no part of the military, either American or Japanese. She, too, fled to Haneji, but took to the hills when her brother-in-law, who had been writing government propaganda, assured her that if caught by the Americans she would be raped and slain. She then began a three-month odyssey, becoming separated from her family, crossing and recrossing steep mountain ranges in search of food, shelter, and safety. Being pretty and fearful of all men she met, she daubed her face with charcoal "to make myself ugly." Her long hair she bound with a piece of rope. She narrowly escaped the amorous attentions of a Japanese soldier hold-out by knocking him down a hillside with a rock, but her first encounter with a GI was reassuring; a soldier helped her to dig sweet potatoes and gave her some canned rations. But recalling her brother-in-law's warning, she could not bring herself to come in. Finally, she was caught by MP's and placed under the care of a family in a northern Motobu village.

For most Okinawans captivity came in a much less spectacular fashion. When their caves were overrun, they were ordered to come out, usually by a Nisei interpreter with the troops. Sometimes American soldiers went after them, and one 7th Division GI, making resourceful use of his Japanese language phrasebook, "talked out" five hundred in the first days of the campaign. When out, they were turned over to MP's who processed them through regular prisoner-of-war channels, first to a civilian detention compound maintained by the combat division, then after screening by counterintelligence (CIC) agents, to a detention village in the rear. Civilians in custody numbered 126,876 by the end of April. Thereafter, the total coming in fell off sharply because of the relatively static fighting line, by June numbering 144,331. This figure in itself was worrisome to General Crist, for it suggested—rightly it turned out—that many civilians remained in the combat zone between the front lines and the end of the island at the steep cliffs near Mabuni. The 1940 population of the island, Crist knew, had been tabulated by the Japanese at 435,000. Every day the fighting continued must bring added suffering to the civilians, for Ushijima's 32nd Army, intent on its own survival, could make little or no effort to feed them or to provide medical care and shelter.

III

Back in Tokyo concern for Okinawa's civil population was probably the furthest thought from the minds of the Imperial General Staff. So far as it was concerned the island was already lost and all its people with it. The best that could be hoped for in late April was that General Ushijima would continue to hold out for a considerable time and that the kamikazes would take a heavy toll of American shipping.

Nowhere was the war news good. The Philippines were collapsing rapidly as General MacArthur's forces continued to take island after island and to clear northern Luzon. Rangoon in Burma was about to be lost. The next logical Allied step was an invasion of the Netherlands East Indies and Malaya, which strategically would make little difference since the invasion of Okinawa had effectively severed Japanese supply routes to the area. Japan must now concentrate on withdrawing and consolidating its position in central China and in Manchuria, hope that Russia would not enter the war, and prepare as best it could to meet a certain American invasion of Japan proper.

In Washington it was time to begin planning for the big show, for Operation Olympic, the invasion of Kyushu, and for Operation Coronet, a landing near Tokyo on Honshu. But much had to be done first. Okinawa had to be cleared and converted into an advance base. Then, as soon as the European war finally had ended, men and materiel must be transferred to the Far East as rapidly as the perpetual worldwide shortage of shipping would allow. All of this would take time, but time was now a factor which worked in the interests of the Allies.

16

THE BLOODY REPULSE

AT 12:00 noon on April 18 Lieutenant General Simon Bolivar Buckner, Jr., closed his command post aboard the *Eldorado*, and opened it near Uchi, a small village 3,500 yards southwest of Kadena airfield. Buckner was reasonably satisfied with the progress of the campaign. Northern Okinawa was falling rapidly to the marines, and his 77th Division was firmly lodged on Ie Shima and must soon conquer it. True, Ushijima's 62nd Division had stalled Major General Hodge's 24th Corps before Shuri, but the Guadalcanal veteran was readying another attack to seize the Shuri fortified zone and end the campaign.

I

This new offensive, for which preparations had been underway several days, was to be a juggernaut. Buckner and Hodge planned to pour on so much artillery that the reorganized 96th and 7th divisions, reinforced by the newly landed 27th Division, could as one artilleryman hopefully put it "walk into Shuri." As yet, Buckner had not seriously considered an alternative tactic, such as landing below Shuri at Minatoga to outflank Ushijima. Sheer weight of metal had won many an earlier battle of the Pacific War; sheer weight of metal should win another.

General Hodge issued his attack order on April 16, specifying H hour as 6:40 A.M. on April 19. Though containing but eight pages of text, it listed objectives for each American division and for the massive artillery bombardment. It also provided for another demonstration off Minatoga, to be supported by aircraft and naval gunfire and feinted by a battalion of the 77th Division, which Buckner had withheld from the Ie Shima operation. Following Ie's conquest, the entire 77th would transfer to Okinawa to serve as 24th Corps reserve, prepared to move to the front line on six hours' notice. The marines, not a part of Hodge's 24th Corps, would continue their separate campaign to overrun northern Okinawa.

The April 19 attack, as Hodge's order envisaged it, would consist of a massive bombardment with every available gun after which the infantry would overrun the Shuri defenses and descend into the valley running between Naha and Yonabaru. Hodge did not expect his infantry to make it in one day. Two days before the attack he told newsmen, "It is going to be really tough; there are 65,000 to 70,000 fighting Japs holed up . . . and I see no way to get them out but to blast them out yard by yard." But he hoped for substantial progress the first day, and as the official action report later put it, to reduce the entire Shuri zone "within a reasonable time." In scope, the attack exceeded anything yet seen in the Pacific War and was comparable to major offensives launched in Europe. In its emphasis on use of massed artillery it would be a miniature version of the British attack at the Somme on July 1, 1916.

To concentrate the maximum of cannon fire on Japanese positions, the attack would begin first in the 7th and 96th division sectors on the left and center of the island. Fifty minutes later, after the artillery had shifted fire to the Kakazu area, the 27th Division would jump off, and following up a surprise night crossing of the Machinato Inlet, would advance two regiments to the west end of the Urasoe-Mura escarpment. Hodge realized that Ushijima might try to disrupt his plan with a spoiling attack of his own but counted on defeating it. If the Japanese should attack, he decreed, the operation would proceed anyway.

Ushijima had contemplated another attack, but ever mindful of the menace of a landing in his rear, had once again dropped the idea, concentrating instead on bolstering his vulnerable right flank near Yonabaru. His observers atop the Urasoe-Mura escarpment, who had a commanding view clear to the Hagushi beaches, could see Hodge's artillery digging in, sure sign, if any were needed of the American determination to have another go at the Shuri defense zone.

The Japanese commander's defenses on Kakazu and eastward across the island were as strong or stronger than ten days earlier when the 96th and 7th divisions had attacked and had been repulsed. Lieutenant General Takeo Fujioka's 62nd Division still had enough men to hold the line by itself, using its reserves to replace or bolster depleted units. Ushijima's ridgetops had no soft spots for General Hodge to hit.

II

Though new to combat on Okinawa, the 27th Division was an old-timer in the Pacific War. Activated before Pearl Harbor, it had gone into action in the Gilbert Islands in 1943 and had suffered heavy losses on Saipan in 1944. Some of its veterans were war-weary and cynical, but its new commanding officer, Major General George W. Griner, Jr., who had reorganized the outfit, had worked hard to improve morale. Intended originally for use on the eastern islands fringing Nakagusuku Bay, and ultimately as the occupation force after Okinawa's fall, General Buckner decided to commit it after General Hodge had requested that it reinforce his understrength corps. Now, in attacking the west flank, the 27th was taking on a task demanding the utmost from every man, from Griner to the greenest nineteen-year-old replacement.

Griner's attack problems, which he knew were tough, duplicated those of his unsuccessful predecessor, Major General Jim Bradley. Somehow getting past Kakazu Ridge, Griner had to break the formidable Urasoc-Mura escarpment. He elected to combine surprise with an outflanking maneuver, sending his 106th Regiment across the Machinato Inlet down Highway 1 in a predawn attack, counting on the 32nd Army's assumption that American troops "seldom take offensive action" at night. Then, as the 106th assailed the west end of the escarpment, his 105th Regiment would cross Kakazu Ridge to hit the escarpment head on.

If successful this exacting maneuver would deprive Ushijima of his best high ground before Shuri. But if the 105th failed to cross Kakazu, Griner risked isolating his 106th, exposing it to fire from its front and left flank and to possible counterattack into its rear from behind Kakazu.

The only unusual activity Japanese observers atop the Urasoe-Mura escarpment might have noticed on the bright afternoon of April 18 was the movement on the American side of the Machinato Inlet of several three-quarter-ton reconnaissance cars. These had carried up observers from 27th Division headquarters. Everything else was normal: the ubiquitous bulldozer that had been working fitfully on the road, the small groups of GI's moving slowly about or lounging under trees, the warships idling offshore and lobbing an occasional shell at the cliffs on the Japanese-held side of the inlet.

Shortly after 3:00 P.M. the soldiers of Company G of Lieutenant Colonel Almerin C. O'Hara's 106th Infantry buckled on their equipment, and in loose, straggling lines began moving to the north bank of the inlet. To maintain the pattern of previous days their movements were exaggeratedly unhurried and casual. At precisely 4:07 P.M. a lone smoke shell burst two hundred yards on the Japanese side of the inlet as if some artilleryman had fired "a tentative, mistaken shot." Other rounds fell, and concealed by the smoke Lieutenant Clarence F. Stoeckley's G Company crossed the 150-foot-wide inlet on a water pipe that remained intact and hid below a 60-foot bluff. G Company's mission: to destroy the Japanese platoon that manned obervation points on the bluff and garrisoned the town of Machinato lying between it and the escarpment on Route 1.

In performing its mission G Company did not arouse the main body of Japanese on the escarpment, who apparently assumed the commotion near the inlet was routine patrol activity. For the single platoon from the 272nd Independent Infantry Battalion, G Company's attack was stark tragedy. Every man was killed. The Japanese unit had arrived the day before, and an unidentified enlisted man had recorded, "With our one platoon we will guard this place to the death." The platoon did; this was his last entry in the diary.

Just after nightfall truckload upon truckload of bridging equipment rolled forward. Company A of the 102nd Engineer Battalion began assembling two Bailey bridges made of prefabricated steel sections, a pontoon bridge, and a footbridge to replace the blown pair of Japanese spans that had carried Highway 1 across the inlet. Working quietly, the engineers finished all except the pontoon bridge before dawn the next morning. By midnight the footbridge was complete, and at 2:00 A.M. on April 19, Lieutenant Colonel O'Hara's 106th started filing across. A gray predawn at 5:35 A.M. found his F Company approaching a road cut where Highway 1 sliced through the west end of the Urasoe-Mura escarpment. Not a shot had sounded.

Shortly before reaching the road cut, F Company's lead platoon, commanded by Lieutenant Robert J. Hyland, Jr., swerved off the highway to the right, climbed the ridge, and angled through scrub pine trees toward the rear of the enemy position. Soon the men spotted the Japanese squatting around little fires in groups, singing and preparing their breakfast, rifles stacked nearby. Immediately, Hyland's men fired, dropping some, sending the others fleeing southward toward the cut. The GI's raced after them, shooting as they went, and digging in above the cut, engaged the enemy on the south side in a firefight until the Japanese abandoned their positions. Hyland had lost just two killed and five wounded in routing an entire enemy company. By 7:00 A.M. Captain Hubert N. Slate, F Company's commander, had another platoon on the ridge and an observer with a radio to call fire on the enemy's ridgetop positions southward along Route 1. Surprise was complete; the opening round had gone to Griner's 27th Division.

III

At 6:00 A.M., as Lieutenant Hyland's platoon was firing at the Japanese infantry at the west end of the escarpment, 324 artillery pieces ranging from 105 mm. to a battery of 8-inch howitzers were beginning the greatest mass bombardment of the Pacific War. Each battery was authorized to expend between 150 and 200 rounds apiece for each gun. This had required a tremendous effort from the 10th Army's beach parties.

For twenty minutes twenty-seven battalions of Army and Marine artillery thundered, plummeting thousands of shells into the enemy areas before the 7th and 96th divisions. The barrage then lifted 500 yards ahead for 10 minutes while the infantry simulated attack, then abruptly shifted back again with "time fire," shells fused to burst just above the ground. The intent was to slaughter with shrapnel any Japanese unwary enough to emerge from caves and tombs. Few apparently did, and Brigadier General Josef R. Sheetz, commanding the artillery, later said that he doubted that the massed barrage had killed as many as 190 Japanese, or one per hundred shells fired. Which may have been true; but Kosei Yokora, an ammunition bearer for the mortar section of the 11th Independent Infantry's gun company (dug in on the reverse slope of Hill 178), told his American interrogators the day after the attack that the barrage had forced his unit to abandon its mortars. On this area of the front, at least, the bombardment had been partially effective.

Both the 7th and 96th divisions had received some replacements, but both still were understrength. The 96th was to take Tombstone, Nishibaru, and Tanabaru ridges in the center of the island. The 7th Division was to seize Hill 178 and Skyline Ridge on the east side.

A feature of the 7th Division's attack—as well as that of the 96th—was the first use in the Pacific of the flamethrowing tank, to which the 715th Tank Battalion had converted just before the campaign began. It consisted of a Sherman tank with a flame projector installed through the tube of its 75 mm. gun. The fuel was a mixture of six percent napalm and gasoline. The purpose of the napalm, a soapy, granular substance, was to absorb the gasoline and cause it to stick, jellylike, to whatever it hit. The result was a frightful device, very effective against caves, pillboxes, camouflaged positions—and men. It was the only weapon from which the Japanese would break and run, abandoning their positions.

The 7th Division's attack began when three flamethrowers, accompanied by two regular tanks, rumbled up to the east end of Skyline Ridge and began squirting long jets of orange flame. Shortly after, at 7:00 A.M., Colonel Mickey Finn's 32nd Infantry began the dirty, dangerous business of assaulting the strong fortifications of Lieutenant Colonel Hideshiro Miura's 11th Independent Infantry Battalion. Though sorely pounded by the bombardment, Miura's men were full of fight and determined not to yield an inch of Skyline; nor did they, except where the flame tanks had incinerated them.

Further westward, a battalion of Finn's men and one of Lieutenant Colonel Green's 184th Regiment approached Ouki Hill, a knob on the east side of Hill 178. Finn intended to wheel his attack companies once the crest was reached and sweep east along Skyline, while Green's turned west and fought to the top of Hill 178. Neither reached Ouki Hill. About 500 yards from jump-off both battalions reached a belt of ground covered by preregistered mortar, artillery, and machine gun fire and found themselves thoroughly pinned down. Miura's defenders had swiftly scuttled the hope of General Arnold that his 7th Division men would have lunch atop Hill 178.

On the extreme right of the 7th Division's sector, where it joined the 96th Division's zone, lay an uneven coral ridge running parallel to the direction of the attack. From it two rough coral knobs rose thirty to forty feet, high enough to dominate lower ground on either flank. These two promontories came to be known as the "Rocky Crags," infamous to this day to 7th Division veterans. Neither had seemed like much, but Arnold's GI's soon discovered that advancing toward Hill 178 was impossible so long as the crags remained in enemy hands. From them the Japanese could interdict all movement eastward and westward as far as their machine guns and mortars could reach. Both crags were miniature fortresses, honeycombed with several layers of tunnels, studded with caves and firing apertures.

The misfortune of discovering precisely how tough the Rocky Crags were fell to Captain James B. Hewette's Company K of the 184th Infantry. Supported by tanks Hewette made several determined attacks and managed to edge two platoons along the east face of the northernmost crag, suffering heavy casualties in the process. He held his men there as long as he could, but early in the afternoon had to pull back.

Nightfall on April 19 found the 7th Division stopped well short of the enemy's main line of defense. Gains had been confined to lightly defended foreground areas, and all four basic features of the enemy's position, Skyline Ridge, Ouki Hill, Hill 178, and the Rocky Crags, remained solidly in the hands of Colonel Miura's 11th Battalion.

If anything, the experience of the 96th Division in the center of the island was more frustrating than that of the Hourglass Division on the east. Attacking there were the Deadeyes of Colonel Dill's 382nd and Halloran's 381st regiments, operating on the left and right respectively, between divisional boundaries that stretched from the Rocky Crags on the east to Kakazu Ridge on the west. The 96th's objective was the Tanabaru-Nishibaru ridge line, which joined with Skyline Ridge, Hill 178, and

Kakazu Ridge to form the 62nd Division's main line of resistance. Repeated attacks, however, netted the Deadeyes little except outpost ground. Their casualties exceeded those for any other single day of the Okinawan campaign.

To describe in detail the actions of individual companies and platoons of the 7th and 96th divisions during the attack would require a full volume. Fairly typical of myriad rugged experiences were those of First Lieutenant Lawrence T. O'Brien, a platoon leader in Company L of Colonel Finn's 32nd Regiment. O'Brien's mission was to push his platoon onto the eastern end of steep Skyline Ridge after the flamethrowing tanks had burned out enemy positions. Then, working along below the crest of the north slope, he was to traverse the ridge toward Hill 178.

Things went relatively well at first. A single exploding shell did cost O'Brien a man killed and three wounded, but he and his men methodically climbed the steep forward slope, and then turned west to traverse Skyline Ridge. After going a hundred yards they came to a dip and kink in the ridge through which a Japanese machine gun was laying down a band of fire. O'Brien had his choice, he could hole up, or dash through the fire area to the shelter of an abandoned pillbox. With his men he ran for it and made the pillbox safely, but then found himself in serious trouble. Japanese just over the crest of the steep ridge above first tossed over grenades, then zeroed in with knee mortars. O'Brien countered by keeping his platoon spread out. Since the range was short, the enemy mortars were firing almost straight up and the projectiles were falling almost straight down. Hearing the "pop" of the mortar on the other side of the ridge, the men would yell when they spotted the black dot hurtling down and drop flat in a circle about the point of impact. To make things worse, a Japanese added a white phosphorus grenade that set afire the dead grass around them.

After some time at this dangerous sport, O'Brien called his company commander, Captain Alfred E. Grantham, and asked for help, but Grantham was wounded while trying to reach him. A platoon from K Company, the battalion reserve, worked its way directly up the slope west of O'Brien, but failing to reach the crest, found itself in a worse fix, exchanging grenades with Japanese on the other side. Casualties reduced this platoon to six unwounded men and drove it down the hill.

In the late afternoon O'Brien's battalion commander, Major

John P. Conner, decided not to expend men on Skyline any longer. He ordered all units, O'Brien's included, to withdraw to the morning's jump-off positions, which they did safely. Once again Okinawan experience had demonstrated how untenable was the forward slope of a hill so long as the Japanese held the reverse side. Altogether, Conner's battalion had lost eighty men, including nine killed and twenty-six wounded in O'Brien's company.

IV

In the 27th Division's sector opposite Kakazu Ridge, the action for most of the day was a repeat of what the 96th Division had undergone ten days before. Colonel Walter S. Winn had planned to send his 105th Infantry directly over Kakazu Ridge into Kakazu village. In the village the infantry would team with a company of tanks which would roll through the road cut on Highway 5 east of the ridge to clear the town and the hill's reverse slope. Then infantry and tanks would advance to the escarpment.

Trouble began at once. Lieutenant Colonel Rayburn H. Miller's 1st Battalion found itself pinned down shortly after leaving the gorge, well short of Kakazu's northern slope. When Major Holeman Grigsby, commanding the 2nd Battalion, which was supposed to follow the first, attempted to reconnoiter ahead of his men, he was hit four times by an enemy machine gun and left for dead. Although he survived and later was rescued, his battalion also failed to advance.

The failure of the infantry to get over Kakazu meant that the tanks—thirty of them, including several flame tanks—had no support. They managed to get around the ridge to burn and blast Kakazu village, but without infantry protection they fell victim to Japanese antitank fire and suicide squads armed with satchel charges.

One 47 mm. gun commanded by Fujio Takeda picked off five of six tanks at 400 yards range with six shots. Watching the satchel-charge teams Takeda thought, "Our infantry really fights!" Only eight tanks returned; twenty-two others were destroyed or immobilized and nineteen tankers killed. Some crews, trapped, dug pits under their disabled machines and remained behind the enemy's lines for as long as three days. The Japanese were elated. They had anticipated just this sort of tank attack and were prepared for it.

While the 105th's 1st and 2nd battalions still were struggling before Kakazu, Major Charles E. De Groff's 3rd Battalion, which had been ordered onto Kakazu West, moved to outflank the enemy. De Groff sent his men around the right (west) side of Kakazu West, hoping to reach the escarpment by sidestepping

Bazooka

the stubborn Kakazu position. He succeeded largely because of one man's initiative. When the battalion stalled because of an enemy machine gun firing from Kakazu West, I Company's Technical Sergeant Richard J. Bean, exasperated, jumped up and methodically drilled eight rockets from a bazooka into the enemy pillbox. Then he grabbed a BAR, charged 150 yards, and completely eliminated it. Freed to move once more, the battalion ducked and scrambled the thousand-odd yards to the escarpment's west end to join the 106th. Shortly after, the 2nd Battalion, now commanded by Captain Ernest J. Fleming, took the same route.

The regimental commander, Colonel Winn, now decided to recall Miller's 1st Battalion from before Kakazu and sent it, too, to the escarpment via De Groff's flanking route around Kakazu West. Since the 1st Battalion had lost seven killed, eighty-two wounded, and sixteen missing, the men were happy enough to go. By dark, the 1st Battalion had joined the 2nd and 3rd on the escarpment.

The day's fighting in the 27th Division sector had developed a bizarre situation, worrisome both to General Griner, the division commander, and to his chief, General Hodge. Virtually no American troops now held the line before Kakazu Ridge. For almost a mile no American infantry faced the Japanese forward positions. In theory a counterattack could strike deep into the rear and cut off the 27th Division. In fact, the danger was slight, for the Japanese forces behind and under Kakazu had no plans to advance, no real knowledge of their enemy's whereabouts, and themselves had been punished severely in the day's fierce fighting.

Overall, the great offensive of April 19 had been most disappointing to General Hodge. Artillery had not appreciably dented the enemy's powers of resistance anywhere. Only the 27th Division, by virtue of a successful night attack, had penetrated the enemy's forward defense zone on the extreme right flank. But in no sense had the 27th scored a breakthrough. It had lodgment on the Urasoe-Mura escarpment but faced fierce opposition either to an advance east along the escarpment or south toward Naha. It had evaded the Kakazu Ridge problem by bypassing this troublesome stronghold. Kakazu remained a salient in the American line and potentially dangerous if Ushijima should try a counterattack.

17
GRINDING AHEAD

THE AMERICAN OFFENSIVE on April 19 marked the beginning of
fourteen days of brutal combat that imposed heavy attrition on
both armies. On Okinawa's eastern side the 7th Division had
uncovered the strongpoints that must be reduced. Skyline Ridge
being obviously too tough, General Arnold's attack would resume against Ouki Hill and the two Rocky Crags which enfilad-
ed the flanks of both the 7th and 96th divisions.

I

On April 20 the Hourglass Division hit and took Ouki Hill,
while Skyline Ridge was kept blanketed with smoke to blind the
enemy mortarmen. Two men, First Lieutenant John J. Holm and
Staff Sergeant James McCarthy, led a final rush to mount the hill
and then perished in an enemy counterattack. Flamethrowing
tanks helped by burning out a mortar position on the hill's
forward slope.

Against the Rocky Crags no headway was made on April 20,
though Colonel Green's 184th Infantry did its best. Because the
strength of these coral pinnacles perturbed General Arnold, he
came up to see them for himself. He then ordered to the front a
155 mm. howitzer to blast the crags with point-blank fire.
Setting up on a small knoll its crew rammed in a 95-pound shell
with a concrete-piercing fuse, loaded a charge 7 behind it, and

let fly at the northernmost crag over open sights from 800 yards. A satisfyingly large chunk of coral flew off. Seven more times the howitzer roared, then the Japanese started spraying the knoll with machine gun fire, wounding two men and forcing everyone, General Arnold included, to take cover. The crew then dug in the weapon, and in the next two days, aided by gun and flame tanks, shot both crags literally to pieces. Twenty-five years later General Arnold could recall that some shells passed right through the top of the crags. Finally both collapsed on themselves.

It still took three days of savage infantry fighting to occupy the crags. Company C of the 17th Infantry closed out the fight on the morning of April 23 after the Japanese had stopped feeding reinforcements into the position.

In the meantime, on April 21, Colonel Finn's 32nd Infantry had unexpectedly managed to clear Skyline Ridge. Finn had about decided to leave Skyline alone until Hill 178 fell and fire could be brought against its reverse slope. He had his E Company well dug in below a twenty-foot embankment on Skyline's north side. On the other side of the embankment, covering the slope and barring further advance, was a Japanese machine gun team in a pillbox. Then, as the 7th Division's official historian, Captain Edmund G. Love, put it, there occurred "... one of those strange incidents peculiar to combat."

With E Company was Sergeant Theodore R. MacDonnell, an observer for the 4.2-inch mortars of the supporting 91st Chemical Mortar Company. MacDonnell habitually observed mortar fire until a fire mission had ended, then joined the infantry on the line. Just after 2:00 P.M. MacDonnell became infuriated after seeing an E Company man killed by the machine gun and impulsively charged over the embankment throwing grenades at the enemy pillbox. Returning, he borrowed a BAR, but it fired one shot and jammed. Sliding down again he grabbed a carbine, climbed back up the embankment, rushed the pillbox, and shot all three enemy gunners inside. Then he grabbed the enemy's machine gun and a knee mortar and heaved them down the embankment to the astounded E Company GI's below. For his feat he won a Distinguished Service Cross.

Presented with this gift Lieutenant Fred Capp immediately sent E Company past the embankment up Skyline Ridge. Colonel Finn dispatched Company F as reinforcement, and both companies traversed Skyline to overrun its crest at a cost of only two killed and eleven wounded. On the next two days patrols methodically blasted enemy caves on Skyline's reverse slope and on the east face of Hill 178. Inspection disclosed two hundred corpses in one cave, a hundred in another, fifty in a third, and forty-five in a fourth, most bearing signs of wounds inflicted by mortar or artillery fire.

Hill 178 now was untenable to Colonel Miura, and on the night of April 22–23 three hundred survivors of his 11th Battalion withdrew to Maeda at the east end of the Urasoe-Mura escarpment. Few soldiers, anywhere, more richly deserved the unit commendation that General Ushijima awarded to them.

II

Facing the 96th Division to the right of the 7th was the Tanabaru-Nishibaru-Tombstone ridge complex. In the heaviest sort of fighting the Deadeyes managed in two days to clear Tombstone and to push several companies onto the crest of Nishibaru Ridge. But on the night of April 21–22 three particularly vicious counterattacks successively hit Lieutenant Colonel Franklin H. Hartline's 3rd Battalion of the 382nd Infantry. When the attacks grew intense Staff Sergeant David N. Dovel, a machine gunner, lifted his 62-pound weapon and fired from the hip, burning his hands severely on the jacket and suffering mortar wounds in both legs. Mortarmen of K Company fired their 60 mm. mortars at 86-degree elevations to drop shells on Japanese just 30 yards to the front. The "Old Man," Lieutenant Colonel Hartline, joined his men, tossing grenades and firing every weapon he could lay his hands on. Hartline and his boys rebuffed the last challenge at 3:15 A.M. and the next morning estimated enemy dead at 198.

The unit that opened the way to Tanabaru Ridge was Hoss Mitchell's L Company "lardtails" now rebuilt with replacements. It succeeded in getting atop Hill 7, a small knoll before Tanabaru Ridge. This was child's play compared to what Mitchell had experienced on Kakazu West but was still bad enough. This time L Company spent three-and-one-half hours exchanging hand grenades with Japanese on the reverse slope. "Hoss" finally picked up three grenades, grabbed his carbine, and rushed the crest, killing two of the enemy and wiping out a machine gun nest. This added a Silver Star to his collection of medals.

By nightfall on April 23, at a cost of 99 killed, 19 missing, and a staggering 660 wounded, the Deadeyes had cleared most of Nishibaru and Tanabaru ridges. Plans for April 24 called for six battalions to attack and polish them off. Similar preparations were underway in the 7th Division zone to complete the seizure of Hill 178. After five days of fierce fighting, from April 19 through April 23, the Hourglass and the Deadeye divisions were about to finish what everyone had hoped on April 19 would be merely a morning's work, the cracking of the initial line of defenses of the Shuri zone. On their part, the Japanese 11th, 12th, and 14th Independent Infantry battalions and units of the 22nd Infantry Regiment had fought as skillful and determined a defensive battle as any waged on Okinawa.

Except for the two battalions of the 105th Infantry bruised at Kakazu Ridge, the 27th Division had had fairly easy going on the nineteenth. But the next day, April 20, all units experienced the kind of resistance the Deadeyes and Hourglass had been getting. General Griner's plan for the twentieth called for the 105th and 106th regiments to expand and consolidate their holds on the western end of the Urasoe-Mura escarpment, while his reserve regiment, Colonel Gerard W. Kelly's 165th Infantry, pushed down Highway 1 to seize the Machinato airstrip.

Unbeknownst to Griner, one of the most cleverly designed of all Japanese positions on Okinawa absolutely barred all movement toward Machinato. Originally intended to cover the seaward flank and the airfield, it served equally well to block Highway 1. The defenders comprised two companies of Lieutenant Colonel Kosuke Nishibayashi's 21st Independent Infantry Battalion with attached mortar, artillery, and antitank units. They numbered about six hundred, plus several hundred attached Okinawan conscripts. Their defensive zone, on which they had labored for months, consisted of

Arisaka Rifle

several small coral and limestone ridges running like spokes from a modest swale at the center. Since the swale lay in the I or "Item" grid square on the official U.S. tactical map, the defense zone became known to the Americans as "Item Pocket." The Japanese called it their Gusukuma position after a nearby town.

The trouble with Item Pocket was that no safe way existed to approach it. Two knocked-out bridges on Highway 1 prevented approach by tanks. Every ridge in the pocket was protected by mortars or machine guns on others. These also blocked any approach from a marshy flatland running along the shore. Vehicles could not carry supplies south until the pocket was eliminated. Colonel Nishibayashi's men had extensively tunneled all ridges, digging openings on either side and at the top. A narrow-gauge railroad threaded some tunnels. Each ridge was a miniature Kakazu, immune to artillery and stocked with food, ammunition, and water adequate to sustain the defenders for some time.

The brutal job of reducing Item Pocket initially fell to the 1st and 2nd battalions of the 165th Regiment. On April 20 neither got fairly started. On the following day, April 21, Technical Sergeant Ernest L. Schoeff and eight men of E Company got into one of the wildest and most vicious night fights of the entire Okinawan campaign in trying to seize one of the ridges. Just after dark the little band found themselves counterattacked by fifty to sixty enemies who yelled "Banzai!" and charged from just forty yards away. The nine Americans stayed in their foxholes and fired everything they had. Private First Class Paul R. Cook expended four cases of ammunition and killed at least ten before being killed himself. The others slew fourteen or more in hand-to-hand fighting. The men used grenades, rifle butts, rocks, and anything else they could grab. Sergeant Schoeff broke his M-1 rifle over a foe's head, threw it away, then snatched an Arisaka rifle from another Japanese, bayoneted him, and shot a third with it. Schoeff counted only two of his own men killed and one missing after the Japanese retired, but he realized that he must retreat if he and his surviving men intended to live much longer. All slipped away to the north and returned to their company at 11:30 P.M.

Schoeff's desperate little action epitomized the battle of Item Pocket until April 25. Company after company approached various ridges, failed, and limped back under fire with severe losses.

The man who finally unlocked the pocket was Captain Bernard Ryan, commander of the 165th's Company F. He moved out on April 25, got two platoons onto a key ridge, and—predictably—got into a terrific fight to hold the crest. But hold his men did, aided by other companies, clearing the ridge and turning the seaward flank of Item Pocket. Nevertheless, it took until April 28 to open Highway 1 to vehicle traffic southward and several days more of demolition work to completely eliminate the last of the defenders.

Eastward from Item Pocket the 27th Division broadened its hold on the Urasoe-Mura escarpment's western end but suffered heavy casualties. On the twentieth two companies fled in disorder and panic—one of the few times this happened in the Okinawan campaign—after advancing too far into the enemy position and becoming surrounded and cut off. By close of day divisional losses had soared to over five hundred. Three more difficult combat days followed before two enemy strongpoints on the escarpment's western end could be cleared.

By the morning of April 24 the 27th Division held the western end of the Urasoe-Mura escarpment as far as the village of Nakama, plus an extensive line running from Iso to Item Pocket. Kakazu Ridge still held out but Brigadier General William B. Bradford, the 27th's assistant division commander, was preparing to attack it with a special "Bradford Force" made up of a battalion each from the 7th and 96th divisions and two from the 27th. His attack, General Hodge fervently hoped, plus full-scale divisional attacks to be launched by the Hourglass and Deadeye divisions, would shatter completely what remained of the enemy's initial line stretching from Kakazu to Skyline Ridges.

III

The savage fighting on land during the attack of April 19 had its parallel at sea and in the air. Following up their initial strikes of April 16, the B-29's repeatedly hammered the kamikaze airfields. These missions were unpopular with 20th Air Force senior officers, who preferred to use their bombers for strategic attacks on Japanese cities, but Admiral Nimitz, realizing the absolute necessity of keeping the kamikazes pounded down, insisted that the B-29's continue.

Admiral Ugaki frequently used his entire force of fighters to try to stop the superfortresses, though this meant canceling kamikaze escort missions and though few of his fighters had the speed at high altitude or the firepower to stop a B-29. Nevertheless, some vicious air duels erupted, becoming intense on April 27 when over a hundred B-29's attacked Kanoya and five other airfields. Afterward pilot Lieutenant Kenneth Hornbeck of St. Louis told war correspondents, "The milk run is over; the cream is curdled." Recalled Lieutenant Philip Van Schuyler, ". . . They went after us. They must have made a hundred attacks on the eleven B-29's that I saw, and thirty on our four plane section." One B-29 turned out of formation trailing smoke, to have four Japanese fighters release white phosphorus bombs across its flight path. Somehow, the plane evaded and got clear. Gunners claimed four defending fighters; one B-29 fell.

The next day, April 28, the B-29's returned, and this time their gunners scored heavily, using their electronic computing gunsights. They claimed thirty-six fighters shot down and thirteen "probables." Again one B-29 fell.

Attacks continued into May, and before they had ended 24 of the B-29's had been destroyed and 233 damaged, with heavy losses, too, to the defending fighters. These raids damaged the Kyushu airfields severely because the B-29's pattern-bombed, blanketing each field with demolition and fragmentation bombs that cratered all runways, parking stands, and taxiways and riddled every standing object. Shops, hangars, planes under repair, and even tools were so cut up that keeping machines flyable became difficult. Moreover, fighters intercepting the B-29's had to land all over Kyushu, augmenting difficulties in assembling escorts for Kikusui attacks.

Despite their problems Admiral Ugaki and General Sugahara had not the slightest intention of abandoning the Kikusui operations. On April 27 and 28 they staged Kikusui 4, consisting of two main attacks on the aforementioned days and a preliminary. The preliminary on April 22, an attack on the Hagushi beachhead,* did more damage than the main event. This day twenty Navy and thirty-six Army kamikazes broke through a haze over the beachhead.

---

*General Sugahara's staff called this the "fourth general attack" and the April 27–28 affair the fifth. To Ugaki's officers both the preliminary and main attacks were Kikusui 4.

One plane crashed and sank a support landing craft in three minutes; another capsized the minesweeper *Swallow* in seven. Still a third hit the destroyer *Isherwood* aft, exploding its depth charges and sending it crawling toward the Kerama haven with a mangled stern. Other ships, including a pair of destroyers, suffered minor damage from near-misses. It would have been still worse but for the Marine air groups at Kadena and Yomitan. Flying his first combat mission in the area, Major George C. Axtell, Jr., of VMF 323 claimed five Vals. Altogether, the marines reported downing thirty-one foes, mostly suicide pilots who made little attempt to evade their firing runs.

On April 28 and 29, despite the B-29 attacks on Kanoya and other airfields, Ugaki and Sugahara managed to get about a hundred special attack planes airborne. Four were Oka piloted bombs. Ugaki intended to make Task Force 58 his target but had to settle, as did Sugahara, for the Okinawa area the first day. The planes struck at dusk with a fighter escort. Four destroyers suffered minor damage from near-misses, but at 8:41 P.M. the naval hospital ship *Comfort* was hit by a fighter while steaming southwest of Okinawa with a full load of patients. The night was clear, the moon full, and the ship was lighted according to the Geneva Convention. The enemy pilot dove over the unarmed ship, pulled up, then dove again, crashing his plane and bomb through three superstructure decks amidships into the surgery compartment.

Chaos followed as a searing explosion ripped the compartment and others near it. An Army nurse, Lieutenant Evelyn Bachelor, was flung onto the stirrups supporting the legs of a patient being operated on for wounds in the pelvis. She was unhurt but he was killed. Major Dorsey Brannan had just completed an operation and was bandaging a patient when he was blown through a window onto the weather deck of the ship, uninjured except for concussion and a cut on his hand. "Fortunately," he observed later, "few patients required further surgery or we would have suffered even worse from the loss of the surgery compartment."

Even so the medical staff had been decimated. Six nurses had been killed outright, all surgeons but two had perished as had several enlisted medical technicians, and the ship's medical commander had been badly hurt. The senior uninjured medic, Major Alexander Silvergrade, quickly improvised a clearing station in the undamaged patients' lounge to treat casualties, and other doctors whose duties were not normally surgical in nature treated wounds and injuries and dug shrapnel from the limbs of Army men and sailors. Despite heavy casualties, thirty killed and thirty-three wounded, there was no panic. The calm and precise manner in which the medical teams circulated amongst the patients, Major Silvergrade reported, quickly spread a feeling of reassurance throughout the ship.

While the Army medics organized casualty treatment, Captain Adin X. Tooker cared for his ship. As a precautionary measure he ordered the undamaged lifeboats on the weather decks slung out and the ship's firefighting and repair crews to deal with fire and flooding. He was quickly reassured about the basic integrity of the ship—the exploding kamikaze had not damaged engines or boilers nor holed the ship's sides below the waterline. Using CO_2 fog, foamite, and water, the crew attacked blazing tanks of nitrous oxide and oxygen in the surgery compartment to such good purpose that in only ten minutes these and other fires were out. Because steering control of the ship from its bridge was lost, Captain Tooker shifted to emergency controls aft, and wishing no further brushes with the kamikaze corps, darkened the ship and set full speed for Guam, arriving five days later without further incident. Except for the smashed hospital spaces, the *Comfort* had not been seriously damaged.

The next day General Curtis Le May's B-29's kept Ugaki and Sugahara occupied during the morning leaving few fighters available to escort the thirty-three kamikazes that sortied. This time the target was Rear Admiral A. W. Radford's T.G. 58.4, one of two fast carrier task groups still off Okinawa. Like Turner's amphibious forces, the fast carriers had installed their version of a radar picket line. Twelve miles north of the task group in the direction of likely enemy attack two suicide Zeros jumped destroyers *Uhlmann* and *Haggard* by diving past a combat air patrol from out of the sun. Before Lieutenant Commander Victor J. Soballe's crew could do much, a 40 mm. shell from the *Uhlmann* hit the *Haggard*'s main gun computer, wounding the gunnery officer, Lieutenant M. E. Wall, and disrupting control of its 5-inch guns. These planes missed, but at 4:57 P.M. a plane crashed the *Haggard*'s starboard side, detonating a 550-pound bomb against the forward engine. Seaman Charles H. Rademaker directed his 40 mm. gun until the Zero crashed below his mount. Fred Pinne and Clarence Peterson, 20 mm.

gunners, continued firing even though it seemed that the plane would hit them. All three received the Bronze Star for heroism, but thirteen shipmates died and thirty-eight were wounded.

With both firerooms and the forward engine room flooded, the ship settled until seas broke over her deck. Yet another suicide pilot dove but missed by ten feet. A little later, another destroyer, the *Hazelwood*, which had been ordered to assist the *Haggard*, took a bad hit on her main deck next to the forward stack. Damage was heavy, and Commander Volckert P. Douw, the skipper, perished with forty-five of his officers and men.

The *Haggard* now suffered the indignity of being towed, barely afloat, to the Keramas. There Commander Soballe and his crew witnessed an amazing sight. Destroyers and other craft in every conceivable state of disrepair crowded the anchorage, masts gone, stacks askew, guns pointing upward where they had jammed in train, superstructures wrecked and burned out. On some ships the bows had vanished or become a twisted mass of steel folded up against the bridge—all this mute evidence of the zeal of Japanese youngsters determined to die for their country.

The *Haggard*'s men discovered that several weeks would pass before the overworked floating dry dock in the anchorage could take their ship—if indeed she could be repaired at all. She would not have survived the flooding of even one more compartment. Refusing to accept defeat Soballe and his men set to work, scrounging from every available source scraps and pieces of lumber and equipment to patch a hole twenty feet long and eighteen feet wide where the kamikaze had hit. Soballe and others put on diving equipment to direct the fitting of a temporary seven-ton patch so that the flooded engine and boiler rooms could be pumped out. The Black Gang, the engine room crew, rebuilt an after boiler from parts of the forward set and used any scraps they could find to repair the steam lines to the engines. Lighting off one boiler, they got the ship underway, and in four months steamed her halfway around the world to the Norfolk Navy Yard.

IV

In the meantime, the GI's ashore on Okinawa had been enjoying a breather. On April 24 Bradford Force jumped off on schedule at 7:30 A.M. to finish Kakazu Ridge. A few minutes later the 7th and 96th divisions attacked, their mission being to smash what was left of Ushijima's initial line. To the amazement of the commanders the wary and cautious infantry encountered few enemies and scarcely fired a shot all along the front. Under cover of an artillery barrage during the night, all Japanese units had retreated south to the next defensible chain of hills. To General Hodge this demonstrated once again his adversary's exceptional skill, for at exactly the moment his line had become untenable, Ushijima had abandoned it to preserve his troops. Hodge knew this meant a hard fight farther south, probably at the high and towering Urasoe-Mura escarpment and adjacent hills extending east. But for the GI's, as the 96th Division's history records, Ushijima's withdrawal was "manna from heaven." They would live at least one more day to sleep in a hole in the ground and to eat cold K and C rations.

The 96th and 7th divisions advanced as much as 1,000 yards on April 24. The 7th on the left worked south from Hill 178 and Skyline Ridge toward its next major obstacle, towering Conical Hill looming above Yonabaru. The 96th in the center worked close to the Urasoe-Mura escarpment and adjacent hills reaching east into the 7th Division sector. Only the 27th Division did not advance. Item Pocket still was holding out strongly, and on the west end of the escarpment the former New York National Guard outfit was nose-to-nose against General Ushijima's new line of defense.

The next two days, April 25 and 26, brought the 24th Corps once again to a full stop. The enemy was firmly entrenched in a new system as elaborate as the old, running from the vicinity of Conical Hill and Kochi Ridge on the east across the Urasoe-Mura escarpment to Item Pocket on the west. As before reverse slopes were better defended than forward slopes. What was different was that the defenders were more numerous. At Ushijima's order the 24th Division was taking over the east half of the line, from the coastal flats to the town of Maeda, while the thinned ranks of the 62nd Division were concentrated on and behind the escarpment. Ushijima also had ordered the 44th Brigade to take station behind the 62nd. This left no major combat unit south of Shuri to combat an enemy landing, but Ushijima could not risk a 10th Army breakthrough of the weakened 62nd.

In the meantime, Lieutenant General Buckner had been worrying about his own personnel problem. Understrength to begin with, his 24th Corps had taken very heavy losses and had not received enough replacements. More were coming but via slow boat.

A fundamental decision confronted Buckner. He now had available the 77th Division, still licking its wounds from the unexpectedly difficult Ie Shima invasion, and also the 1st and 6th Marine divisions, the conquest of northern Okinawa having been completed. Buckner was free to use the 77th Division and the Marines as he chose.

On or about April 22 Major General Andrew D. Bruce, the 77th's commander, had urged Buckner to land his division near Minatoga in southern Okinawa to outflank the Shuri line. From a beachhead at Minatoga, Bruce believed, the 77th could push either to the southern tip of Okinawa or to Yonabaru, where junction could be made with the 7th Division. On the recommendation of his supply officer, Brigadier General David H. Blakelock, Buckner rejected Bruce's proposal. Blakelock had analyzed in detail the difficult reef conditions at Minatoga and was convinced that not enough ammunition to sustain a division could be supplied. Moreover, the loss of two ammunition ships to kamikazes in the Kerama Retto on April 6 and a subsequent period of squally weather had produced a general ammunition shortage. To divert amphibious tractors, DUKW's, cranes, and landing barges from the Hagushi beachhead to Minatoga would further slow operations and might produce a critical supply shortage. Buckner therefore chose to use the 77th Division to relieve the hard-hit Deadeyes of the 96th, who had been in combat continuously and had suffered heavier losses than the troops of any other division.

The question next arose as to the disposition of the marines. Again Buckner rejected a secondary landing, electing instead to use the 1st Marine Division to relieve the 27th Division. Buckner was pleased with the sterling performance of the New Yorkers, who had fought well and very bravely, but the original intent had been to use the 27th as the Okinawa garrison force. Buckner chose to replace the 27th with the 1st Marine Division, fresh and overstrength in troops, then to bolster his right flank with the equally strong 6th Marine Division and continue against Ushijima's Shuri line. The 27th would assume the occupation and mop-up of northern Okinawa.

By April 28 Buckner had firmed up his strategy: The 77th

Division would relieve the 96th the next day; on the day following, April 30, the 1st Marine Division would begin relieving the 27th Division; on or about May 7 the 6th Marine Division would take over the extreme west flank. Together, the two Marine divisions would operate as the 3rd Amphibious Corps under Major General Roy S. Geiger.

Ever since, Buckner's decision has been controversial. Before the Okinawa campaign had ended, beginning on May 30, David Lawrence, the noted syndicated newspaper columnist, criticized Buckner's strategy in the Washington *Star*. He was heatedly answered by *Newsweek*'s commentator, Admiral William V. Pratt, U.S.N. (Ret.). Lawrence took the view that a secondary landing should have been made and seems to have based his opinion on information in articles by the *New York Herald Tribune*'s correspondent on Okinawa, Homer Bigart, and to have had encouragement from Admiral King. Buckner, however, made his decision in the fog of battle on the basis of his best military judgment at a time when logistical considerations seemed paramount. Also, as the 24th Corps official report put it, as late as April 26 at Buckner's headquarters "....there was as yet a general belief that once the next line was taken the Shuri defenses would be quickly overrun."

Had Buckner known that a month of hard fighting before Shuri lay ahead, to be followed by nearly another month of battle in the south of Okinawa, he might have chosen to risk landing either the 77th Division or one of the Marine divisions at Minatoga. Whether this strategy would have worked is still debatable,* though it is true that by May 1 both the Japanese 24th Division and the 44th Brigade were out of the south and

---

*In a letter to the authors Lieutenant General Pedro A. del Valle, U.S.M.C. (Ret.), states his view that a landing in the south would have been advisable. But Lieutenant General Merwin A. Silverthorn, Sr., U.S.M.C. (Ret.), who served as chief of staff of the 3rd Amphibious Corps, indicates that on the basis of his experience at Guam a secondary landing would not have been a good idea. The U.S. Army's historians, in the 24th Corps history, *Okinawa: The Last Battle*, p. 263, hold that a landing at Minatoga would have produced logistical difficulties, and that if made prior to the end of April might have failed or bogged down. If made after May 5, they contend, it would have encountered only a delaying force of two to three thousand troops.

only a weak holding force remained. An alternative strategy might have been to dispose the 10th Army as Buckner did, then to bring up from Guam the 2nd Marine Division—which had its own supply organization—to land at Minatoga.† This would have increased pressure on Ushijima without weakening the drive on Shuri. Suffice to say the issue of the Minatoga landing remains the great "what might have been" of the Okinawa campaign, and one on which historians writing long after the event may do well to avoid hasty judgment.

V

April 26 again found the 24th Corps on the offensive. The 27th Division began the fight at 7:00 A.M. when the 105th and 106th Infantry attacked on the west end of the Urasoe-Mura escarpment into a mass of tangled ridges and draws to the south. The 165th still was bloodily mopping up Item Pocket. It finally cleared most of the pocket and seized the Machinato airstrip, but neither the 106th nor 105th made appreciable gains before May 1. All three regiments were riddled with casualties and their lines stretched dangerously thin.

On the opposite side of Okinawa, the veteran Hourglass Division had moved easily to the forward slope of Kochi Ridge. Then Colonel Francis T. Pachler's 17th infantrymen found that they dared not lift their heads over the rim. Efforts to work around either flank of the 500-yard-long slope were equally dangerous. The Japanese defenders of Lieutenant Colonel Masaru Yoshida's 22nd Infantry Regiment, 24th Division, had worked out in this area an exceptionally effective system of bringing artillery and mortar shells onto any attacking unit. The 17th Infantry had to sweat it out on the forward slope of Kochi Ridge from April 26 through May 3.

---

†General Lemuel C. Shepherd, Jr., U.S.M.C. (Ret.), states in a letter to the authors that he suggested use of the 2nd Marine Division several times to General Buckner. It had, he writes, organic logistic support to sustain itself for at least thirty days. Its use "... would have seriously threatened Ushijima's rear and required him to withdraw troops from the Shuri battle or employ his limited reserve to contain the landing."

On the left in the same period the 32nd Infantry made painful progress amid a complex of hills in front of Conical, but failed to turn the enemy's carefully designed Kochi Ridge flank. Nor could the 32nd move on the coastal flat; so long as the Japanese held the high ground to venture out there was sure death. May 3 found both General Arnold and General Hodge concerned at the 7th Division's lack of progress and neither fully aware as yet of the intrinsic strength of the enemy's new defense system.

As usual the bitterest fighting fell on the Deadeyes. On April 25 Brigadier General Claudius D. Easley, the 96th Division's assistant commander, had come up to Colonel Michael E. Halloran's command post to have a good look-see at the east end of the Urasoe-Mura escarpment a few hundred yards ahead. A single glance convinced the peppery little general that plenty of artillery would be needed. The escarpment was, as the division's history put it, "... an obstacle calculated to chill the blood of the most hardened infantryman."

The escarpment's defenders consisted of remnants of several 62nd Division units stiffened by the fresh 32nd Infantry Regiment of the 24th Division. They held what amounted to a great underground fortress. Caves under the escarpment were large enough to hold entire companies and were linked to one another and to numerous firing ports and apertures on both faces of the ridge. Behind lay the town of Maeda and a few hundred yards to the west a complex of concrete school buildings. Maeda, the school buildings, and lower hills further south contained enemy mortar, machine gun, and artillery positions registered on the top of the escarpment and adjacent hills to the east.

Attacking on April 26 only E Company of Colonel May's 383rd Infantry managed a significant penetration, crossing hills east of the escarpment into Maeda. There the attack was checked, but not before producing near-consternation at General Ushijima's headquarters. Ushijima hastily ordered the 32nd Infantry under Colonel Kakuro Kitazato to reinforce the area. On the escarpment itself the Deadeyes made little progress. They managed to get on top, but found enemy fire so devastating they had to pull back below the northern face.

The next day Captain Louis Reuter, Jr., of the 381st discovered firsthand how extensive the enemy's defenses were. With two of his men he entered a cave on the escarpment's northern face to find a passage within leading straight into the cliff. Cautiously the three crept on until they could see a beam of light. Continuing they found a shaft from which the light was coming, running straight down into the bowels of the escarpment. Reuter noted three levels below and could hear Japanese voices coming from far beneath. Making their way back the men found another passage off to the right. Entering this they emerged into a room with an observation slit hollowed out of the rock. Peering from the slit Reuter was astonished to find that he could see all the way to the Hagushi landing beaches and every road being used by the 24th Corps. Discovering an observation telescope and binoculars, Reuter took these, knowing his own artillerymen could use them, and left.

By April 29 the Deadeyes still had not managed to reduce the escarpment or to fully clear Maeda and the concrete school buildings. They had killed an estimated 2,500 Japanese since renewing their offensive, but the 381st Infantry had lost 536 men and had to be relieved by the 77th Division's 307th Infantry. May's 383rd Infantry was relieved the following day.

Lieutenant Colonel Gerald D. Cooney, commanding the 307th's 1st Battalion, decided that the best way to get atop the escarpment and to stay there was to send Companies A and B right up the face of the cliff. On the night of April 30 he brought up four 50-foot ladders and five cargo nets borrowed from the Navy. The next morning, aided by these, B Company managed to gain a precarious foothold on the narrow top, harassed by enemy machine gun and mortar fire from hills to the south and counterattacks from the enemy on the reverse slope. Under absolutely desperate conditions the men stayed all day, succored only by their medic, Pfc Desmond T. Doss, a Seventh Day Adventist and conscientious objector who would not touch a gun or work on Saturday. When a man was hit, Doss would crawl to him, dress his wound, then drag him to the edge of the cliff. Tying him to a rope sling of his own devising, Doss would lower him the fifty feet down the cliff to safety. To the other men he seemed to bear a charmed life, and many sought to stay near him.

At midnight on May 1 the Japanese counterattacked and drove B Company back to the cliff edge where the men groped in the dark for ropes and cargo nets to get down the face. Some fell; a few jumped. Soldiers at the bottom tried to aid B Company by hurling grenades up over the rim to drive back the Japanese. This was dangerous, for unless a grenade cleared it fell back on its thrower. B Company's 60 mm. mortars, firing almost straight up, finally drove away the attackers by laying in accurate fire all along the crest.

The next morning, with medic Doss still in attendance, B Company again grimly scaled the cliff, got onto the top, and managed to hold through the night. The next day, May 3, its GI's laid on a grenade shower intended to blast out the enemy on the reverse slope by sheer weight of powder and metal. A human chain passed grenades up the cliff which the GI's on top hurled over the south rim as fast as they could. The Japanese responded with grenades of their own and also with knee mortars. So terrible was the fighting that men would come back to the escarpment's north rim sobbing and swearing that they could not go back. "Yet in five minutes' time," said a platoon leader, "these men would go back there tossing grenades as fast as they could pull the pins." They finally made their point. The enemy retired deep inside the escarpment. The next day the 307th began systematically blasting reverse slope caves with what the Japanese called "straddle attacks," demolition operations carried out from above the opening of a cave which they could not effectively counter.

On May 4 Colonel Hamilton expressed the hearty sentiments of everyone in the 307th Regiment in a conversation over the field telephone with Colonel Halloran of the Deadeye's 381st. Said Hamilton, "You can have this goddam thing back any time you want it."

The escarpment battle had demonstrated that the only way the Okinawa fight could be won was by tactics General Buckner had described to newsmen on May 1, "corkscrew and blowtorch," with "corkscrew" being the explosive, "blowtorch" the flamethrower or napalm. Necessarily, the process was slow—and costly.

18

USHIJIMA BIDS FOR VICTORY

ON APRIL 29, the emperor's birthday and Japan's most important holiday, General Ushijima abruptly decided to alter his strategy for the Okinawa campaign. This day a staff meeting had taken place in the 32nd Army's headquarters cave. Ushijima had not attended but the entire staff had, including its impetuous chief, Lieutenant General Cho, and his rival and antagonist, Colonel Yahara.

Cho had hotly led the discussion. For some days, and especially since the 96th Division's penetration into the Maeda area, he had been more impatient than ever with Yahara's defensive strategy. Attrition, he had argued, would make continued 32nd Army resistance impossible after May 25 even if the U.S. 96th Division was stopped. The Japanese Army's only hope was to mount a massive counterattack, one that would pitch two-and-one-half Japanese divisions against five American. Cho agreed that the 32nd Army might not survive the apocalyptic encounter, but neither, he said, would the Americans. Better mutual annihilation than slow attrition and sure defeat.

Of the staff members only Yahara had opposed him. While it was "a stark reality," Yahara agreed, that during the month of fighting the Shuri defense zone had been penetrated to a depth of two kilometers, it was also true that on no other invaded island had Japanese forces held out so long with major elements intact. Also, the Americans had suffered great losses, and the 32nd

240

Army still had intact two major units, the 24th Division and the 44th Brigade, to further prolong resistance. To attack would be folly. The Americans held the high ground before Kakazu and Skyline ridges; to break through would require vastly greater forces than the 32nd Army possessed. "Therefore," concluded Yahara, "the Army must continue its current operations, calmly recognizing its final destiny—for annihilation is inevitable no matter what is done. . . ."

A heated quarrel followed, heightened by the sake which made the rounds freely, not over Yahara's arguments, which made little impression, but over the command of the troops. A proposal to place part of the 62nd Division under 24th Division command failed of approval. The 62nd Division commanders countered effectively that the division was not a "weak tree"; it had earned the right to attack and die under its own leaders.

At about midnight the decision was made; the 32nd Army would take the offensive early on the morning of May 4. The staff's consensus then was taken to General Ushijima who ratified it and indicated his own determination to take sword in hand and fight to the end.

I

As embodied in 32nd Army and 24th Division orders, the attack plan was as ambitious as it was clear and detailed. Its objective was to destroy the 10th Army's combat troops by smashing the American front to a depth of over three-and-one-half miles. The attack would begin just before daylight on "X day," May 4. Initially, the 24th Division would seize the eastern end of the Urasoe-Mura escarpment. Then the 44th Brigade would break through to the sea at Oyama, a town north of the Machinato Inlet, cutting off the 1st and 6th Marine divisions. In finale the battered 62nd Division, holding the line along the escarpment, would attack to aid the 44th Brigade in annihilating the two Marine divisions, while the 24th Division mopped up General Hodge's 24th Corps.

As a preliminary, small amphibious forces would land behind the American lines on both the east and west coasts. On the west coast the 26th Shipping Engineer Regiment would embark in

241

Okinawan canoes and landing boats to put ashore seven hundred men at Oyama. On the east coast the 23rd Shipping Engineer Regiment would land five hundred men behind Skyline Ridge. Both amphibious units would embark about midnight and reach their objectives well before daybreak on X day. Neither force contained first-line infantry, but all men had had infantry training. Also in advance of the main attack, other shock units would launch predawn thrusts in platoon-to-company strength intended to penetrate the American line and "create confusion" in the rear.

The main attack, to be launched by Lieutenant General Tatsumi Amamiya's 24th Division, would follow a heavy half-hour artillery bombardment scheduled to begin at 4:50 A.M. At full daylight the 32nd Infantry Regiment would jump off to recapture the escarpment and the adjacent hills on either side of Highway 5. Across the island on the east the 89th Infantry Regiment would rout the 7th Division from the high ground overlooking the east coast flat. In the center, on either side of Kochi, the 22nd Infantry Regiment would first support by fire and with screening smoke its sister regiments, then attack and break through.

Colonel Kitazato's 32nd Infantry held the key to the success of the whole venture. It had to take the eastern end of the escarpment, the town of Maeda, and the high ground dominating Highway 5. Otherwise, the 44th Brigade could not pass through to cut behind the U.S. Marines in the second phase of the attack. Recognizing this, General Cho reinforced Kitazato by giving him Captain Yasunori Toyofuko's previously uncommitted 26th Independent Infantry Battalion. Cho also arranged to have the strongest artillery support fall into the Maeda area and to have the 27th Tank Regiment under Lieutenant Colonel Todomu Murakami enter the fighting at this point. Murakami's outfit, consisting of a company each of light and medium tanks plus a company of supporting infantry, had not yet seen action.

In placing such a burden on the 24th Division and especially on Colonel Kitazato's 32nd Regiment, General Cho assumed that both division and regiment were fresh and fully ready. This was an optimistic presumption. As early as April 12 the division's 22nd Infantry Regiment had begun to suffer heavy losses, and at least one battalion of its 89th Regiment had gotten into the bloody escarpment fighting. As for the 32nd Infantry, all of its three battalions had already been severely mauled. The 2nd Battalion, commanded by twenty-three-year-old Tsuneo Shimura, had been decimated. With three hundred of his own men and a few survivors from another battalion, Shimura was holed up in a large cave on the south slope of the escarpment from which he could do virtually nothing to support the attack. Not far away near the town of Maeda was the 1st Battalion, commanded by twenty-four-year-old Captain Koichi Ito, a classmate of Shimura's from the Japanese Military Academy's class of 1940. Though personally still a man of fight and determination, anxious to carry out his attack assignment, Ito had lost more than half of his men in defending Maeda and had only 600 left. The 3rd Battalion, under Captain Yasuji Mitsuo, had also gotten into the Maeda fighting and had been reduced to a strength of 420 men. Even the reinforcement of the regiment with the 26th Independent Battalion had not brought it up to full table of organization strength.

Through his air officer, Lieutenant Colonel Naromichi Jin, General Cho made arrangements with General Sugahara, head of the 6th Air Army, and Admiral Ugaki, commanding the 5th Air Fleet, to support for the attack. Beginning at dusk on May 3, bombers from Kyushu would attack Kadena and Yomitan airfields to destroy Marine land-based Corsairs on the ground. Later, other bombers would drop on 10th Army rear areas. After daylight on May 4, X day, kamikazes would attack transports and cargo ships in a major assault.

If all went according to plan, the end of the 32nd Army's attack, three or four days after X day, would find Ushijima's troops holding an east-west line across Okinawa running through Futema, headquarters site for General Bradley's 96th Division, which Cho mistakenly believed was General Buckner's headquarters. Whether or not the 32nd Army would then have enough men to continue fighting, the honor of the Imperial Army would have been preserved. An attack order of the 24th Division enjoined each unit: "Display a combined strength. Each soldier will kill at least one American devil."

One factor worked in Cho's and Ushijima's favor; neither Buckner nor Hodge was expecting an enemy attack. Sound plots on artillery ranging equipment on May 3 locating Japanese artillery pieces south of Shuri had been interpreted as possible Japanese preparation to abandon the Shuri line. In fact, the guns were moving to prepared locations in the open, protected by antiaircraft, offering better arcs of fire. A few days before, Buckner and Hodge had been worried about the 27th Division's open flank in the Kakazu sector, but by May 3 both were inclined to believe that Ushijima had missed his only chance. They did not discount entirely the possibility of a general attack but expected Ushijima to continue his not unsuccessful policy of attrition warfare and stubborn defense of every fixed position— indeed, to continue the only strategy that Colonel Yahara thought feasible. They had reckoned without the firebrand Isamu Cho.

As dusk fell on May 3 a sober mood pervaded the 32nd Army. By now all hands knew their objectives; all units had been reorganized and reinforced. Full darkness would find the hardy little soldiers, in round helmet, brown uniform, and full pack, leaving their caves to brave the nightly harassing artillery and naval gunfire and form up in their assembly areas. A soldier of the 89th Regiment jotted in his diary,

. . . Preparations for the all-out attack have been completed. . . . I do not think our planes will come for none have appeared since the beginning of the campaign. Consequently, I have my doubts as to whether this all-out offensive will succeed. But I will fight fiercely with the thought in mind that this war for the Empire will last a hundred years. I must fight to the bitter end, for a moment ago a comrade died.

Wrote Leading Seaman Sasumu Kanzaki, a Navy man called up with his unit to support the attack,

We are about to set out for the fighting zone. We will annihilate every single soldier in the American 14th [sic 24th] Corps. I am greatly honored to have been granted such an unusual opportunity. . . . I will fight to the utmost of my powers.

However inwardly pessimistic Ushijima's men may have been concerning the outcome of their venture, their determination and fanaticism remained as untouched as if they had been winning rather than losing the struggle for Okinawa.

II

The first indicator that the enemy might be trying something out of the ordinary came at 6:00 P.M. on May 3, X day minus one, when Japanese planes in force raided Kadena and Yomitan airfields. Neither field was put out of action in this or later attacks that hit between 2:00 and 3:00 A.M. In addition to unusual strength these attacks featured widespread use of "window" to produce "snow" on the screens of American radars. Shortly before daylight several enemy planes attacked purely tactical targets, one dropping its bombs into the 7th Division's sector. A gesture, though not much more, had been made by the Army's air squadrons on Kyushu to respond to Colonel Jin's radioed plea for "all-out" air support.

Ground action began at 10:00 P.M. with unusually heavy artillery fire on the 77th Division's forward companies. After peaking in intensity with nine hundred rounds the first hour, it then slackened until rising once more just before the main attack. The red-eyed GI's on the receiving end assumed the fire was another enemy attempt to deny them a night's sleep and to produce more than the usual number of battle-fatigue and concussion cases.

Shortly before midnight the attack began in earnest as the troops of the 23rd and 26th Engineer Shipping Regiments started up the east and west coasts respectively. Simultaneously, twenty motorboats, all that remained of the Japanese suiciders on the east coast, sortied from Yonabaru against American naval craft on "flycatcher" patrol in Nakagusuku Bay. Minutes later both U.S. Navy ships and Army guard units spotted the 23rd Regiment on the water. Mass slaughter followed with at least eight craft sunk. A few troops got ashore alive only to be spotted by the infantry and brought under artillery fire. Sunup at 5:50 A.M. revealed only dead bodies on the water, some bloodstained and discarded clothing on shore, and one POW to be interrogated. None of the Japanese had closed with or attacked American troops. The east coast attack had failed with the virtual annihilation of the 23rd Engineer Shipping Regiment.

The west coast attack fared little better. The 26th Regiment traveled undetected until after 1:00 A.M. when most of its men began landing—not at Oyama—but much farther south opposite Marine infantry and amphtrac units guarding Machinato airfield and the adjacent shoreline. Screeching battle cries merely helped the Marine machine gunners and riflemen to cut down some two hundred on the reef. Others fled south along the reef, and the remainder, numbering about 150, found themselves pinned down at daybreak near Kuwan at the south end of the airstrip. Systematic sweeping by the 1st Marine Division killed most before evening. Only sixty-five Japanese managed to land near the village of Isa five miles up the coast near the attack objective. These scattered inland, but the 96th Division patrols killed all but ten or fifteen by the close of day. Like that of its sister unit, the sacrifice of the 26th Engineer Shipping Regiment had served no useful purpose. Between them the regiments had lost about a thousand valuable men.

Hints of trouble for the GI's of the 77th and 7th divisions came at about 3:00 A.M. when the 184th and 306th Infantry heard Japanese voices and the clatter of approaching tank treads. These sounds heralded—though the men did not know it—the forward deployment of the Japanese 89th and 32nd Infantry regiments and the march toward the front line of the 27th Tank Regiment. Just twenty minutes later infiltration began, as a platoon-sized force began trying to circle the flank of the 306th's I Company.

Leading a team of three men was Second Lieutenant Hiroshi Yamamoto, who tried to slip through the Onaga sector at 3:40 A.M. Seventh Division GI's heard him go and dropped mortar shells on his small party, separating him from his two companions, Corporal Kuooda and Superior Private Hayashi. By 5:30 A.M. with daylight fast breaking, Yamamoto found himself pinned down by his own artillery and unable to move. Later he was able to when fire lifted, but this was the last entry in the little diary he carried. American artillerymen found his body a week later well north of the front line.

As far as can be determined from American records, this and similar infiltrations failed to produce the intended confusion in the 24th Corps's rear. Customary patrolling behind the line by reserve battalions cleaned out those infiltrators who had slipped through.

At 4:30 A.M., a few minutes ahead of schedule, the Japanese artillery, which had been firing sporadically, suddenly broke into heavy volume, thundering about 8,000 rounds into the zone of the 7th Division and another 4,000 on the 77th Division. The experience was terrifying but casualties were light among the deeply entrenched GI's.

"Y hour," set for just before daylight at 5:00 A.M., found the attack underway in earnest. Already, 150 men of an 89th Regiment advance force had slipped into three destroyed towns in the Unaha area, too close to the American lines for the defenders to use artillery. A little later C Company of the 184th Infantry spotted a group of Japanese hand-pulling a pair of 75 mm. field guns to the base of a hill just one hundred yards from the command post of their battalion commander, Lieutenant Colonel Daniel C. Maybury. Fire from medium tanks and machine guns scattered the Japanese, forcing them to abandon the guns.

An observer who also saw the artillery pieces was First Lieutenant Richard S. McCracken. From a position from which he could look onto the east coast flats, McCracken found another target which so excited him that he could hardly talk. In plain sight, milling about in the open—perfect "artillery meat"—was a force of Japanese he estimated at two thousand. McCracken called Colonel Maybury and soon both artillery and mortar fire began thudding into the area. What had happened was that the 89th Infantry's two assault battalions, apparently delayed by transportation problems during darkness, had failed to close the line before first light. Daybreak caught both battalions in the open. In minutes each had lost half of its strength, and before the morning had ended both had been decimated with the loss of almost all officers.

Systematic destruction of the 89th Regiment's advance force in the Unaha area wiped out the only dent in the 7th Division line and concluded what had been for the 32nd Army a terrible fiasco. Much more fortunate than most attackers was Master Sergeant Ichiro Kanamura, a platoon leader of the machine gun unit. Though wounded in the leg by shrapnel, he survived to be taken to the large 32nd Army hospital cave south of Shuri at Kochinda. Ultimately, he fell captive. Few others of the more than 2,000 attackers of the 89th Regiment emerged unscathed.

Near Maeda in Colonel Kitazato's 32nd Infantry's sector, the attack went only slightly better. Here, too, the Japanese infantry failed to close the front line quickly enough to mask the American artillery and mortars. Captain Koichi Ito's weakened 1st Battalion led off the attackers, followed by Captain Yasunori Toyofuko's 26th Independent Battalion, Captain Yasuji Mitsuo's 3rd Battalion, and Lieutenant Colonel Todomu Murakami's tankers of the 27th Regiment. All four Japanese units fell on Colonel Aubrey D. Smith's weary 306th Infantry. Though weakened by casualties and not yet the recipients of replacements, Smith's men had organized the terrain to best advantage.

Heavy fighting developed shortly after 5:00 A.M. and continued for the next two hours. Smith's K Company, perimetered in a small valley, exchanged hand grenades with enemy attackers until dawn, 5:50 A.M. Then the outfit spotted two enemy medium tanks two hundred yards away firing their 47 mm. guns. Private First Class James E. Poore grabbed a bazooka rocket launcher and crawled to within a hundred yards. Triggering off several shaped-charge rockets, he hit and disabled one of the tanks. A

Japanese Medium Tank

shell fragment caught him in the shoulder on his way back for more ammunition, but he picked up the rockets and crawled back. Another hit disabled the second tank. BAR gunners finished off both tank crews as they tried to escape.

Poore, single-handed, had broken up the foray of the only two medium tanks that had closed the front lines. The others had failed to get through along their approach road. Several light tanks had been disabled by artillery fire. Without benefit from the tanks Captain Haruo Hasegawa, commanding the 27th Tank Regiment's Infantry Company, had audaciously attacked the unit that had repulsed the 26th Battalion. He failed to overrun it, lost an entire platoon, and found himself and his men pinned down by GI mortar fire until dark.

By 7:30 A.M. Ushijima's counteroffensive was as good as over. Just one enemy pocket remained for the 77th Division to clear up with tank support.

That the attack had failed was clear enough to the 24th Division's front-line infantry. A platoon leader of the 22nd Infantry wrote, "The front line is somewhere around Utama. . . . It looks as if the battle situation isn't progressing as expected. The enemy seems to be putting up a pretty stiff fight."

Further to the rear, atop the shell-pocked stone walls of Shuri Castle, where Ushijima, Cho, and the assembled staff were straining to see through the smoke with binoculars, the battle's progress at first seemed different, possibly because the initial reports from the 24th Division's regimental commanders were less than candid. A 32nd Army report recorded the staff's early morning impressions.

This day [May 4] our artillery has been so furious since daybreak that it seems as if we have wrested the initiative from the enemy. When observed from the summit of Mt. Shuri, the whole battlefield is covered with the smoke screen which was laid by our forces, and the deafening sound of earth-shaking bombing and artillery fire by both sides presents a glorious sight. Good news has poured in successively and unceasingly since dawn, reporting the success . . . [of] the 24th Division, especially by its right flank troops. An air of optimism filled Army headquarters.

By noon the "air of optimism" had all but evaporated. The staff had learned of the decimation of the 89th Infantry and of the

32nd Infantry's failure to break through in the all-important Maeda area. As a result Ushijima ordered the 44th Brigade, poised to attack, to hold up. The 44th had lost seventy killed and wounded in moving by night into assault position; now, it would stay under cover until Ushijima could be certain it could penetrate the American line. This did not mean that the offensive was off; rather, it would hold up until the 32nd Infantry could try a night attack to punch the necessary hole in the Maeda area.

III

The Japanese offensive carried a different script at sea, where the fifth major Kikusui operation was underway, timed by Admirals Ugaki and Yokoi to coincide with Ushijima's attack. Against land targets the Japanese flyers had accomplished little; but against shipping, and particularly against the radar picket destroyers, they once more demonstrated a deadly effectiveness.

The fifth kamikaze show began off Okinawa at about 6:20 P.M. on May 3, X day minus one, when about twenty Army Sonia light bombers and some late model fighters from Formosa reached Picket Station 10 seventy-five miles east of the Hagushi beaches. Commander William H. Sanders' new destroyer-minesweeper *Aaron Ward* carried the fighter-director team, and destroyer *Little* with four gunboats provided support. Most of the Japanese Army pilots circled to get their bearings, but three eager beavers dove at once, one near-missing, one splashing, and one hitting the *Aaron Ward*, loosing a bomb that exploded in an engine room.

No sooner had Commander Sanders' men put damage-control parties to work controlling fires and flooding than the rest of the pack dove in twenty minutes later. There were too many to stop and no American fighters were around to help. In two minutes four hit Commander Madison Hall's *Little* amidships, wrecking engines and boilers and starting uncontrollable flooding. In five minutes Hall had to order abandon ship, and in five more the *Little* had sunk. Thirty sailors went down with her, and seventy-nine were wounded, mostly burned. Some attackers made for the *Aaron Ward* and three hit, blowing off her second stack, gutting her amidships, and leaving forty-five dead and forty-nine wounded.

The pack also sank a gunboat, LSM (R) 195. The other gunboats rescued survivors. The determined crew of the *Aaron Ward* kept the ship afloat, but when it arrived in the United States, having limped across the ocean on one engine, the ship constructors took one look and ordered it scrapped as beyond repair.

Nearby, an attacker singled out and crashed destroyer *Macomb* on Station 9, making the kamikaze score for the day three destroyers in exchange for only twenty planes, a ratio unacceptable to the U.S. Navy. The first round had gone to the 8th Air Division from Formosa.

Early the next day, May 4, the Kyushu command contributed to Kikusui 5. About 110 planes, Army and Navy, set out for the beachhead. As usual, they ran afoul of the radar pickets north of Okinawa, and although some droned on to attack ships in the Kerama vicinity and off Hagushi, most jumped the pickets despite orders to hit transports.

A single crash on its starboard side finished U.S.S. *Luce* on Station 12. Only a minute after Commander J. W. Waterhouse ordered his destroyer abandoned, the ship abruptly sank, exploding violently underwater before many of the crew could get clear. Losses were consequently very heavy, 149 killed or missing, most of the rest of the crew injured. This feat, accomplished despite a combat air patrol, was followed by four suicide crashes on destroyer *Morrison,* one on the *Ingraham*—these ships on Station 1—and an Oka rocket bomb hit on U.S.S. *Shea* on Station 14. Another pair of suiciders near-missed two destroyers on Station 2. Wracked by explosions in her after powder handling rooms, the *Morrison* flooded aft and sank quickly after the last two hits, taking 153 men down with her. The last two hits had been delivered—ironically—by a pair of ancient naval float biplanes that Admiral Ugaki, short of more modern types, had dispatched. Five others that did not attack brought the admiral word that the antiques had sunk a cruiser. Neither the *Ingraham* nor the *Shea* sank; the hurtling Oka had passed completely through the *Shea*'s superstructure before its warhead exploded in the air. Even so twenty-seven Americans were slain. A suicide hit on the light cruiser *Birmingham* and another—very damaging— on the escort carrier *Sangamon* ended a day of sheer misery for the U.S. Navy off Okinawa.

The worst of it was that the kamikazes had gotten through

despite a strong combat air patrol. Several Val pilots had tried an old German *Luftwaffe* trick of emitting smoke from their tails to deceive attacking Marine pilots, but the leathernecks shot them down anyhow. Much more successful was the tactic of diving promptly on sighting a target. Although the defending Corsair pilots followed an opponent down when they saw him, a head start by the attacking plane too frequently tipped the advantage to the attack. Rueful intelligence analysts at Okinawa Defense Command Headquarters commented, "Helpful as an alert combat air patrol has proved to be, it must be admitted that so long as the enemy can get even a single plane through the barrier, losses of ships must be anticipated."

Admiral Nimitz did not like the news of the actions of May 3 and 4 one bit. He was especially depressed by the casualties: 91 killed, 280 wounded, and 283 missing and presumed lost. But he could do little about it, except to hope that Ugaki and Sugahara would run out of kamikazes before he ran out of destroyers. Reviews of the Kamikaze menace by Nimitz's experts at Guam produced predictable conclusions. The best defense was interception by fighters before the suiciders could dive; after that, good shooting at long range and skillful maneuver by ship's captains. Since everyone knew this already, publication of these conclusions in CINCPAC bulletins merely produced shrugs from destroyer skippers and orders for an extra air defense drill or two.

Southward of Okinawa the British naval contribution to Operation ICEBERG, T.F. 57, had been having its own private war with the Special Attack Corps. Vice Admiral Sir Bernard Rawlings had established a routine to interdict the airfields in the Sakishima Gunto, way stops for kamikazes en route from Formosa to the Hagushi beachhead and the Kerama anchorage. His pattern had been to attack airfields on Miyako and Ishigaki islands for two days, retire for two days to fuel while American escort carriers assumed the task, then return with his fast carriers for another round of strikes. By May 4 Rawlings was back again with three carriers.

Task Force 57 began its strikes, as before, with early morning attacks on Miyako and Ishigaki. A high-flying Japanese Dinah reconnaissance plane picked up the British ships and escaped to report, but Rawlings decided to release the battleships *King George V* and *Howe* with five cruisers to plow up Miyako's three airfields thoroughly with shellfire. His three carriers thus had only cruiser and destroyer antiaircraft protection when the Formosa-based 1st Air Fleet struck.

At about 11:30 A.M. a Zero evaded defending Seafires to dive from great height at the armored flight deck of H.M.S. *Formidable*. Before hitting near the superstructure the plane released a bomb which knocked a two-foot hole in the deck, denting the armor in a ten-foot circle about the hole. Flames broke out among parked Avenger torpedo bombers on the hangar deck below, a splinter either from the bomb or the deck damaged a boiler, and the big carrier slowed to eighteen knots. Eight sailors died and forty-seven were wounded. Four minutes later the *Indomitable* caught it from another Zero which dove from starboard. This plane again proved the value of the armored deck by glancing from it and exploding close aboard with no damage. An hour later more planes came in, but Corsairs and Seafires of the air groups destroyed two Jills and a Val to end the threat for this day. The same disturbing pattern had shown up as in the north; those planes that had broken through the combat air patrol mostly had hit.

Despite the heavy losses inflicted in terms of the number of planes dispatched, the fifth Kikusui operation had in no sense been decisive. Rather, it represented a seagoing variation of the attrition strategy Colonel Yahara had been urging on land and which General Cho had abandoned without success. The radar picket destroyers were not the best targets, but if the kamikazes could deplete Admiral Nimitz's destroyer flotillas, or better still, shatter the morale of their crews, then the American and British navies would find themselves in serious trouble.

IV

As the sun dipped low on May 4 an uneasy calm settled over both Okinawa and the waters offshore. The angry snarl of aircraft engines faded; the roar and thunder of the artillery and naval gunfire died to a mutter. Near Maeda, still the focal point on which all the hopes of the 32nd Army rested, Captains Koichi Ito and Yasunori Toyofuko were busily reorganizing their battalions for renewed attack. Well after dark Ito's 1st Battalion and

Toyofuko's 26th would again move out to seize all-important high ground.

Ito's objective was the high Tanabaru escarpment, a hill mass 1,500 yards behind the American front line which the Japanese had abandoned on April 23. To reach it Ito planned to bypass the enemy's outposts. Toyofuko's men would follow. Afterward, the second attack unit, Captain Mitsuo's 3rd Battalion of the 32nd Infantry, aided by the surviving machines of the 27th Tank Regiment, would overrun the American hilltop positions about Maeda. With Ito and Toyofuko deep in the American rear, and Mitsuo in command of the high ground at the eastern end of the Urasoe-Mura escarpment, the path would be open for the break-through of the 44th Brigade the next morning.

At about midnight on May 4–5, Ito led out his men in a column of twos, each man walking softly to avoid detection. The GI's of the 306th Infantry's C Company heard them pass by along the east side of Highway 5 but held fire thinking they might be Americans. Virtually unmolested Ito and most of his men reached the Tanabaru escarpment, occupied the town of Tanabaru on its southeast face, and surrounded a supply dump of the 7th Division's 17th Infantry Regiment. The escarpment, clifflike to the north, tablelike on top, with a bridge to the south topped by coral knobs, did not dominate Highway 5, which curved away to the west, but it did straddle a secondary road supporting the 17th Infantry.

In the meantime violent fighting had broken out to Ito's rear. Troops of Mitsuo's battalion and others from Toyofuko's battalion had assailed the 306th Infantry. One unit, accompanied by four tanks of the 27th Regiment, had jumped a twenty-man outpost from C Company. Desperate night fighting followed. The GI's manning the outpost called for illumination and 81 mm. mortar fire, which drove the Japanese into the open, and then opened up with machine guns. At dawn the attackers withdrew, leaving a counted 248 dead behind against losses to the Americans of 7 men and an officer wounded.

A half-hour after this clash, at 4:00 A.M., a five-man artillery observation team commanded by Pfc Richard H. Hammond got into a much worse scrape. Hammond had dug his men into the base of a coral knob atop a hill. The knoll overhung them and provided some overhead cover. Hammond's position covered a gap between the 306th's 1st and 3rd battalions, through which a Japanese force intended to penetrate. One of the men spotted a column of Japanese moving below, reported his find via field telephone to battalion, and then all five observers opened fire. Though surprised the Japanese immediately deployed and began rushing the knoll. The observers stopped the first charge with their M-1 rifles, pistols, and their one M-3 submachine gun. Quickly, the enemy reorganized below and rushed again screaming. Private Joseph C. Zinfini fell dead with a bullet through his head. Hammond and the other three were wounded. But with grenades and bullets they once more stopped the charge, this time just five yards from their position.

Undaunted, the Japanese circled the position, some climbing onto the knob behind the Americans to throw grenades. The four survivors tossed these out as fast as they fell. One bounced out of arm's reach, but Pfc John P. Kenny flung his legs over it to smother the blast. One leg was blown to bits, the other shredded. Private First Class Raymond L. Higginbotham then grabbed a pistol in each hand, jumped into the open, and drove the attackers from the knoll above.

Until daylight the four now badly wounded young men hung on, when a patrol from the 306th's 2nd Battalion arrived to drive away the remaining attackers. More than a hundred enemy bodies lay scattered in the area against an American loss of Zinfini killed and the other four wounded.

More than outposts braved the fury of the attack. Companies E, F, G, and K of the 306th all became involved, sometimes at very close range. Captain Edward S. Robbins had dug his E Company into a hill just east of Highway 5 which commanded both the road and the eastern end of the escarpment. His positions were good but his manpower too limited to allow him to hold an unbroken front. At 4:40 A.M. a guard began firing his BAR through an aperture. Robbins stopped him and stuck his head into the two-foot-square embrasure for a look. Just eight feet away he spotted a Japanese officer panting up the hill and waving his sword to what seemed an ocean of faces behind him. Robbins hastily withdrew, ordered the guard to resume firing, and began organizing the rest of his command post group. Within fifteen minutes E Company had checked the Japanese, and in growing daylight it counterattacked. The other companies did the same in mop-up operations that lasted all day and ran the counted total of enemy dead to over 800 plus 6 tanks destroyed. The night attacks on the 306th had failed as disastrously as those of the previous morning. Only Ito had slipped through.

Colonel Francis T. Pachler, commanding the 17th Infantry, was aware that Ito had gotten behind him when told at 4:20 A.M. that Japanese forces were attacking a supply dump and motor pool. At 5:00 A.M. he ordered his 2nd Battalion to patrol the Tanabaru escarpment and find out the enemy's numbers and strength. He did not know that an entire battalion had infiltrated; it seemed more likely that only an infiltration team had slipped past on a raiding mission.

The task of locating the enemy fell to Captain Delmer E. Paugh's E Company. Paugh sent first a platoon, which drew heavy fire, then at 8:30 A.M. attacked up the steep face of the escarpment with his full company. The men almost reached the top before Ito's men drove them back with a sudden burst of fire. Colonel Pachler then sent up Captain Walter C. O'Neill's F Company through the town of Tanabaru over less precipitous ground. O'Neill, too, met heavy fire and had to hold up.

Since neither company could advance, the American effort by midday had turned into an attempt to blast out Ito, a tactic which made life extremely miserable and hazardous for the valiant captain and his 600 men. He had gone into an all-around defense of the top of the escarpment with his own command post on the north side, the better to advance if he was ordered to continue. Nevertheless, Ito knew he was in an extremely dangerous position; he had penetrated into what amounted to a trap well behind the enemy line. Fire was coming in from all sides. Ito found it dangerous to use his radio—the GI's of E and F Companies could hear its hand crank—and communication with his own men was difficult. All hands had to keep their heads below ground level and toss messages tied to a rock from foxhole to foxhole. Nighttime on May 5 found the mini-battle on Tanabaru in stalemate. Pachler's 2nd Battalion had not overrun Ito, but Ito could not move.

Back in his Shuri Castle headquarters General Ushijima early had become discouraged with the result of the second day of the offensive. He knew that Kitazato's 32nd Infantry had suffered further heavy losses, and the fragmentary reports from Captain

Ito furnished him little solid information. With tears in his eyes he summoned Colonel Yahara to his quarters and told him that in the future he would accept the proposals of the chief planning officer. It took somewhat longer for Isamu Cho to lose heart, but by late afternoon he too had given up hope. At 6:00 P.M. Ushijima officially called off the offensive; all units would reorganize and resume their preoffensive dispositions.

To some of the youthful staff this decision hit like a thunderbolt. On learning of it several of them, Colonel Naromichi Jin recalls, ran to Lieutenant General Cho with drawn swords demanding an explanation. The former moving spirit of the Cherry Society turned sadly aside, offered no explanation, and apologized to them. As his former personal secretary recalls, he had given up all hope that the battle for Okinawa could be won.

Daylight on May 6 brought no relief to the trapped Ito. Companies E and F continued relentless pressure against the escarpment and thoroughly cleared Tanabaru town. By the end of the day, though still in position, Ito's small force was badly depleted. His 2nd Company had lost all but two men; his own Headquarters Company had but seventeen left. To stay longer was useless; Ito decided to withdraw under cover of darkness.

In the early morning hours of May 7, Ito returned without incident from Tanabaru over the same route he had come, again in a column of twos with himself in the lead. Only some 230 of his original 600 accompanied him. American units mopping up after daylight would count 355 bodies in and about his former positions, mostly victims of 81 mm. mortar fire.

The attacks of May 4 and 5 must be accounted the only serious Japanese mistakes of the Okinawan campaign. Losses to the 32nd Army totaled approximately 5,000. Both the 89th and 32nd Infantry regiments had suffered grievously and would require heavy reinforcement. The 27th Tank Regiment had expended nearly all of its light tanks and about half of its mediums. The two amphibious landing units had been virtually wiped out. American losses also had been heavy, totaling about 335 killed and wounded in the 7th and 77th divisions on May 4 and another 352 on May 5. But neither had been forced to suspend offensive operations or to give ground. From the American viewpoint the offensive also had an important by-product, the weakening of Ushijima's powerful artillery. Counterbattery fire on May 4 and

5, delivered with air spotter direction, destroyed nineteen enemy guns found unprotected in the open after shellfire had driven the defending antiaircraft crews under cover. These losses, plus others uncounted, noticeably reduced the volume of enemy fire and the number of U.S. battle-fatigue cases. Japanese casualties suffered in the attack probably reduced the overall length of the Japanese resistance on Okinawa; 24th Corps estimates calculating this time as about two weeks may have been correct.

V

While their Army comrades-in-arms were beating off counterattack, the marines of the 1st Division were learning the hard way why the conquest of southern Okinawa was such a slow business. In the tangled ridges, coral hills, draws, and shattered villages just south of the western end of the escarpment, they were experiencing the same frustrations and casualties the Deadeyes had encountered on Kakazu Ridge. Reverse slopes of hills were the problem; a leatherneck company could easily take a forward slope, then lose half its riflemen in the next few hours trying to stay there. Tanks helped but were vulnerable. Japanese 47 mm. antitank guns destroyed three on May 6. The Japanese 62nd Division still could offer stubborn resistance. The 1st Marine Division's casualty reports for May 4 and 5 record 649 marines killed, wounded, and missing, a total not far short of the 687 carried on the lists of the 7th and 77th divisions for the same two days. And the GI's had faced enemy counterattacks.

The severest ordeal fell on Lieutenant Colonel James C. Magee, Jr.'s 2nd Battalion of the 1st Marine Regiment. Magee had been ordered to seize Hill 60 and Nan Hill. Hill 60, an unimpressive hummock of coral about a half-mile southeast of Yafusu, was completely blanketed by fire from other positions, including adjacent Nan Hill 200 yards northward. It took Magee's marines dozens of casualties, thousands of mortar and artillery rounds, and hundreds of gallons of napalm and gasoline plus innumerable TNT charges to completely "process" the two small hills by May 9. "Blowtorch" and "corkscrew" applied by small units operating with artillery and tanks were literally the only methods by which a unit could move forward. Daring rushes accomplished nothing. A hill could quite literally be covered with marines and still be commanded by the Japanese holed up inside. Every cave, hole, aperture, and firing slit had to be burned out and blasted shut.

In the 7th Division's sector on the other side of the island the weakened condition of Ushijima's 89th Infantry made possible an easy advance to Gaja Ridge. But from there resistance began to stiffen after May 8. Before Kochi Ridge, where the Japanese 22nd Infantry still held out, a near-stalemate persisted. Four days of battle finally carried Colonel Pachler's 17th Infantry on May 9 to the crest of the ridge. But the next day the 7th Division was out of it. Rightly judging that its men were battle-weary and not up to their usual high standard of performance, General Hodge ordered the Hourglass Division into reserve for rest and replenishment, to be replaced by the freshened and reinforced Deadeyes.

In the center of the island the 77th Division had been willing and able to move forward after the end of the Japanese counteroffensive but could not do so because of fire from its flanks. Until the returned 96th Division could crack Kochi Ridge and the bogged-down 1st Marine Division clear a pocket in the troublesome Awacha area to the west, an advance by the 77th toward Shuri might propel it into the sort of trap that Captain Ito had experienced on the Tanabaru escarpment.

Major General Andrew D. Bruce, the 77th's commander, therefore seized the opportunity to replace Colonel Stephen S. Hamilton's 307th Infantry with the fresh 305th. No soldiers ever had deserved relief more than Hamilton's. Between April 29 and May 5 they had suffered 87 killed, 413 wounded, 3 missing, and 112 nonbattle casualties. Their line companies had only a handful of men left.

Back in the rear after relief one GI was heard to say, "Plenty of quiet, that's what I like." A wounded man added, "The chow back here is damned good, and there's no shells whining over your head." Men began writing home, amazed at their good fortune to be alive and unhit. Others found a stock of books and magazines and began doing something they had never thought they would again—relaxing and reading. But for company commanders, platoon leaders, and sergeants there was no rest. Rookies were coming who had to be assigned and integrated.

Though Colonel Hamilton's problem of rebuilding his regiment was difficult, that of Colonels Kitazato and Kanayama,

259

commanding respectively the Japanese 24th Division's 32nd and 89th regiments, was much worse. Kanayama had to rebuild completely two battalions and appoint new commanding officers. He did this so expeditiously from rear echelon units that his reorganization was complete by May 10. Kitazato's problem was more difficult; he had to continue to defend a segment of the line with his 32nd Infantry while re-forming all three of its battalions. Levies from service units helped him to fill out his 1st and 3rd battalions, while the entire 29th Independent Infantry Battalion was added and renumbered the 2nd Battalion, replacing Captain Shimura's outfit lost on the Urasoe-Mura escarpment. By May 10 the Japanese 24th Division had been restored to a semblance of its preattack organization and rebuilt to front-line strength, ready to continue a battle that could have but one ending.

19

THE WOUNDED

THE SAVAGERY OF the Okinawan campaign, and especially the fighting up to and including Ushijima's counterattack, had produced casualties in both armies on a scale unprecedented in the Pacific War excepting only Iwo Jima. Not typical, but illustrative of the suffering of the wounded on both sides, was the experience of Private Richard A. McCurdy of E Company, 17th Infantry, an automatic rifleman.

I

A husky six-footer from Boise, Idaho, and former sawmill hand, McCurdy was twenty-five years old, married, with three children, the eldest age six. He was thus typical of the somewhat older soldier drafted in 1944 and sent to the front in 1945. On April 30, with his buddies, McCurdy moved out against a ridge 200 yards to the front. He had not gone 20 yards before encountering machine gun and mortar fire, but with the others he pushed on anyhow. As he recalled the experience later, "I crowded close to the hillside and started making for a little depression. Suddenly, I felt as if my legs were cut off. I collapsed and couldn't move them." A mortar fragment had struck his back near his spine, penetrating to his left lung. He dragged himself toward the depression only to have a bullet rip into his right arm near the elbow. Nevertheless, he reached the hole, slid in, and lay without moving.

His three-day ordeal had begun. "I thought of my wife, my poor kids, and was sorry for them rather than for myself." His wife would have a hard time raising the youngsters alone. "I remember saying the Lord's Prayer and another one, 'The Lord is my shepherd, I shall not want. . . .'" To move was excruciating, so he lay still waiting for the medics to come and pick him up. By lifting his head he could see the bodies of six of his comrades sprawled on the slope, but he didn't lose hope. "The flies were swarming and I could feel them in my back wound."

Night fell and Japanese soldiers came instead of the medics. "They rolled me over but I acted dead. They went through my pockets carelessly. They took my BAR and fired several shots toward our lines, laughing and talking." Then they went away.

The next day McCurdy drank a little water from his canteen. By now maggots had collected in his wounds. Another Japanese group arrived, poking at his eyes, cheek, and stepping on his fingers. The pain was agonizing, but he stayed quiet, held his breath, and the presence of the maggots finally convinced them he was dead. Later, still a third party came but gave him only a cursory examination.

"Most of the third day I was out of my head and can't remember much. Our artillery poured it on almost on top of me, and I got a chunk in the right knee. . . ." When night came he decided to crawl back, "lying flat and pushing myself with my elbows and legs which got their movement back." Rain concealed his efforts and deadened the sound. "Four or five times I had to stop and vomit. But after four hours or so I got to the top of the ridge and yelled at the boys not to shoot." In reply a voice growled, "Get off that skyline." Crawling down, McCurdy was quickly treated by medics and put into the regular routine for handling casualties. When they heard his story later, McCurdy became to the doctors a living miracle. Said one, "I think that his is the most remarkable example of human endurance and self-control I have ever seen."

II

Many hundreds of GI's wounded as badly as McCurdy survived. Most were fortunate enough to receive either immediately or within a few minutes attention from the aid man, the company "medic." The aid man disinfected and bandaged an injured man's wounds, stopping the bleeding if he could, and splinting and immobilizing shattered arms and legs. Then the WIA (wounded in action) was transferred to a stretcher and carried, usually by ambulance jeep, to the battalion aid station located at or near battalion headquarters. There a doctor examined his wounds, tagged him, gave him plasma and morphine to curb the pain, and dispatched him to his next station, the collecting company and clearing company of the division. Often in less than two hours after being hit, and seldom in more than six, the wounded man found himself in either a portable surgical hospital or a field hospital, equipped to operate on him if necessary.

Because of this relatively quick evacuation from the combat area, the mortality rate of the wounded in the Okinawa campaign was half that of other Pacific battles, and comparable to the rate of the European theater, which averaged 2.8 percent. Unless killed outright or fatally hit—that is, wounded so badly death was certain regardless of treatment—a man had a good chance of recovery. The use of whole blood saved many a victim who otherwise would have died. Universal-type whole blood, Type "O," was donated in the United States from as far east as Chicago, flown to San Francisco and Portland under refrigeration, and from there in thirty-six hours to Guam and on to Okinawa. Altogether, the 10th Army used more than 15,000 gallons of whole blood. One badly hurt boy required forty pints.

Once he had recovered somewhat from shock and his recovery prospects seemed good, 10th Army policy was to get the WIA away from Okinawa as soon as possible. Exceptions included patients with abdominal wounds and others hurt too badly to move. Otherwise, as Colonel Frederick V. Westervelt, the 10th Army surgeon, explained to an inquiring newsman, "We evacuate all those who can stand the trip." Some divisional personnel officers questioned Westervelt's policy; they believed some of the less seriously hurt should have been allowed to recover on the island for return to duty.

About half of the patients were evacuated to Guam aboard large, well-equipped hospital ships, complete with good-looking nurses and comfortable beds. The others went in less comfort but much greater speed aboard big, four-engine C-54 transport planes of the Army's Air Transport Command and the Navy's Naval Air Transportation Service. The first plane departed Kadena airfield on April 8 carrying forty-five passengers. Others followed on a regular hourly schedule, and within a few days the planes were lifting out an average of 150 of the more seriously wounded daily. The peak load came on April 21, just after General Hodge's big offensive, when 367 patients left by air. All were bearded and battle-haggard, with eyes dulled from morphine, still clad in fatigues and combat boots. Many had had just enough of their clothing cut away to permit the surgeon to dress their wounds. Otherwise, even to steel helmets, they were just as they had been picked up on the battlefield.

By no means all of the combat casualties on Okinawa suffered from the tearing shrapnel of enemy shell or mortar, or from the ripping jolt of a Nambu or Arisaka bullet. Many—more than in any other campaign of the Pacific War—suffered from psychoneurosis, or, as it was more popularly called, from "combat fatigue." The reason, the doctors believed, was General Ushijima's abundance of artillery and ammunition. As Major Eugene Alexander, a 96th Division doctor, put it, "You know, it's tough. . . . Like the fellow we had in here the other day who saw a mortar shell drop 50 yards away, then another 40 yards away, another 30, and so on until finally one landed in the next foxhole and spilled someone's brains all over him." Plus the normal strain of combat, the constant threat of death from enemy artillery was too much for many of the soldiers and marines; they "cracked up" and had to be evacuated. They were not cowards; some were veterans of Leyte and earlier Pacific campaigns. Okinawa was simply too much for their nervous systems. One observer called them the "walking dead" because of their yellowish pallor.

That Okinawa would produce an unusual number of psychoneurosis cases first became apparent between April 9 and 13 at Kakazu Ridge. By April 15 both the 96th and 7th divisions had established rest camps to deal with these casualties, about forty percent of which could be returned to the line. By the end of April the 10th Army had to reserve for them one entire field hospital.

Men reacted differently according to their individual natures and to the seriousness of their wounds when hit. Some of the lightly wounded seemed apologetic and embarrassed, as if they had been the victims of something that should not have happened to them. The following scene, a true one, was repeated endlessly in the aid stations of the 1st Marine Division. Enter a grinning marine, limping from a mortar tear in the fleshy part of his leg. "They got me, pal," he said to the enlisted corpsman. "How about putting a patch on this so I can go back to my outfit." Then his eyes wandered to the stretcher in the corner of the tent where a young lad lay, white and unconscious. "What happened to him?" "Shrapnel in the stomach," the corpsman replied shortly, leading the marine to a cot and forcing him to lie down. He began removing the hasty dressing on the marine's leg, dusting the wound with sulfa, and replacing it with another bandage, while the marine lay still, his glance wandering again and again to the still form in the corner. At last the corpsman finished. "Thanks," the marine said, and started to get up to retrieve his M-1 rifle, which he had stood in a corner. The medic pushed him down again. "No," he said wearily, "you'll have to stay here. Danger of infection, you know."

Other men had "happy" wounds, not serious enough to cripple or permanently disable, but severe enough to warrant evacuation to the United States. Another scene: a GI showing a deep gash in his arm and shoulder to a surgeon at a battalion aid station and asking anxiously, "Doc, is it a 'homer'?"

In grim truth, to suffer a nonfatal wound was about the best a frontline GI or marine who began the campaign could hope for. His chances of getting through unhit were slight. The man who survived almost ninety days of combat unhurt could consider himself a fugitive from the law of averages. Albert C. Talbod recalls that among "Hoss" Mitchell's L Company "lardtails," besides the "Hoss" himself, he and just seven others of the original company strength of nearly two hundred men remained at the end of the campaign. Everyone else was a replacement. Other companies suffered even more severely, turning over three and sometimes four times. The man evacuated with a reasonably light wound could consider himself lucky.

III

If being wounded was no picnic for an American, it was a manyfold worse experience for his Japanese counterpart. A Japanese soldier badly hurt might well consider himself less fortunate than another killed outright. The 32nd Army's medical facilities were greatly inferior to the 10th Army's, in part because of combat conditions, in part because of a lack of equipment, and in part because of a holdover of a Japanese service tradition that regarded a wound as the individual's misfortune rather than the Army's.

If hit, a Japanese had to rely chiefly on his buddies for immediate aid and evacuation. If he made it to the rear, he could expect to arrive at a hospital cave, such as Kochinda, where crowding was terrible, fleas abundant, and medical facilities rudimentary. Other than amputations, the Japanese doctors performed very few operations. The troops had not been inoculated against tetanus, drugs were scarce, and the death rate correspondingly high. A man with a really bad wound had little chance. Those with light wounds often limped back to their units before they were fully recovered rather than remain in the depressing atmosphere of the hospital cave. But for all Japanese soldiers, wounded and unwounded alike, a common fate seemed to be ahead. None could expect to survive the campaign.

IV

Care for the GI did not end when his lifeless form was stretchered to the rear or a blanket drawn gently over his face in a battalion aid station. The graves registration teams made every effort to identify his body, an easy task if he had been wearing— as he should have—his dog tags with name, rank, and serial number. Then a dog tag could be driven between his front teeth to accompany and identify his body. If he had lost or discarded the tags, then an attempt was made to find somebody who knew him, usually with success.

Each division had established to its rear at least one temporary cemetery. The 96th Division had two, burying 875 men in one and 768 in another before the campaign had ended. All but 31 were identified. Established procedure at the cemetery had the division's assistant chaplain on hand to preside over a brief but dignified religious ceremony. All stood at attention, the chaplain spoke the service while two GI's held a flag over the simple pine coffin. The body was lowered into the grave, and the soldier or marine took his place at the end of a neat row of simple wooden crosses, each of which had a dog tag nailed to it, about three inches from the top. The burial completed, the assistant chaplain would compile the necessary information for a letter of condolence to the man's next-of-kin.

Though brief, the funeral services were not perfunctory and certainly were not regarded lightly. General Buckner frequently visited the divisional cemeteries and often attended services, as did Generals Hodge and Geiger and the division commanders. When a division left the line for a rest, many men would visit the cemeteries and would attend the burials.

Battlefield conditions denied to the Japanese even the luxury of proper treatment of the dead. Custom demanded cremation, after which the soldier's ashes were sent to the family for enshrinement. With Okinawa cut off from Japan proper the ashes could not be returned, and American artillery denied the opportunity for cremation. Dead were therefore either buried or stacked in caves. The Americans, partly for sanitary reasons, counted Japanese dead as quickly as possible, stripped the bodies of dog tags and other items of intelligence value, and buried them.

Today no American cemeteries remain on Okinawa; all dead have been removed and reinterred in the United States. But the Japanese have honored their own with numerous memorials at Kakazu Ridge, on the Urasoe-Mura escarpment, at the southern tip of the island at Mabuni, and elsewhere. In its own way, each nation has honored its fallen.

20

BUCKNER'S MAY OFFENSIVE

USHIJIMA'S COUNTERATTACK coupled with the success of the kamikazes in their fifth Kikusui offensive brought to a head a conflict that had been germinating in ranking American circles. Admiral Turner wanted Okinawa won quickly to allow Task Force 58 and the naval pickets to clear those dangerous waters. But General Buckner preferred not to try to rush the campaign and waste lives, for a rapid conquest would not appreciably hasten the conversion of the island into a base—only shipment of more engineer troops from Europe or the United States would do that. Moreover, a hundred actions from Kakazu Ridge to the seizure of Nan Hill had demonstrated repeatedly that a lavish expenditure of infantry had not resulted in more rapid acquisition of territory. The best results seemed to come from tactics that General Bruce had been using with his 77th Division: to concentrate all available firepower on a limited objective, then seize a forward hill from which the reverse slopes of adjacent hills could be blanketed with fire. In this way, like the tireless inchworm, the 77th was creeping slowly ahead.

I

Yet, as Turner was quick to remind Buckner, the campaign had to be kept moving as rapidly as possible. And Buckner, mindful of Turner's impatience, laid on still another general offensive, this one to begin on May 11. It was, Buckner told his staff, to be a coordinated attack, made all along the line simultaneously, in a continuation of the same tactics used in earlier offensives. There is no evidence that Buckner reconsidered the idea of landing across the Minatoga beaches to take Ushijima in the rear. He did ask Turner to bring to Okinawa from Guam the 2nd Marine Division to provide his 3rd Amphibious Corps with a reserve division.

G hour for the new attack was set for 7:00 A.M. on May 11 after thirty minutes of precision artillery bombardment. Four divisions would jump off, the 96th on the east, the 77th in the center, the 1st Marine Division on the right, and the newly committed 6th Marine Division on the west along the shoreline.

To the 6th Marine Division would fall the task of breaking Ushijima's line on the west. Its leathernecks would attack across the Asa River, advance across fairly level ground to the Asato estuary, then turn east, bypass Naha, and cross the Kokuba Hills into the Kokuba River Valley behind Ushijima's Shuri bastion.

The 1st Marine Division, attacking just to the east of the 6th, would have to smash through a deadly combination of hills and draws directly into Shuri. Dakeshi Ridge, which its men had reached but had not taken on May 10, was the first. Then came Wana Ridge with Wana town just over the crest. Finally came Wana draw, a narrow, rocky cleft which began just north of Shuri and widened at the base onto a coastal flat. The Dakeshi-Wana draw position constituted the corner of Ushijima's Shuri bastion. Hence his order to its defenders, the 62nd Division and the 44th Brigade: "Hold without fail."

The 77th Division would attack south of Maeda in the center of the island across terrain that was much flatter, though jumbled and broken in places. It would have to take terrain south of Maeda, and eastward of that an ugly little wart of a hill alongside another called the "Chocolate Drop." Both were covered by fire from Flattop Hill, 250 yards long, which lay partly in the 77th and partly in the 96th zones of action. If successful in breaking through the Japanese defenders in this area, the 32nd Infantry Regiment and lesser units, the Statue of Liberty Division, as the 77th was known because of its shoulder patch, would seize the enemy's headquarters. Shuri Castle and Ushijima's cave lay

269

some 3,500 yards due south of their positions. Getting this yardage would be tough; no enemy position stood unprotected by others.

The objective of the 96th Division was to break Ushijima's eastern flank. To do this the Deadeyes would have to smash the 89th and 22nd Infantry regiments and take Conical Hill, a round cone rising to nearly 500 feet directly above the narrow east coast flat. Like the Dakeshi-Wana position on the west, Conical anchored Ushijima's line on the east and was equally indispensable. It was tough—and looked it—but hardly more so than the Dick-Oboe hill complex on the division's right flank that tied into Flattop along the divisional boundary.

For every one of the four attacking American divisions, the offensive of May 11 would be Kakazu Ridge all over again. Seizing the forward slopes of the hills would be the first and easiest step. Clearing Ushijima's men from their caves and tunnels would be the next and more costly job. Nor was the enemy, despite his losses, a pushover. The 24th Division, facing the Statue of Liberty and Deadeye divisions, was again at full strength. The 44th Brigade opposite the two leatherneck divisions had hardly been hurt. Even the 62nd Division, though it had only 600 of its original men left, had been filled out with service troops to 6,000 men. A firmly held perimeter, anchored on positions at least as good as the old Kakazu-Skyline line, faced General Buckner's infantry across the island.

The attack problem of the 6th Marine Division poised at the Asa River somewhat resembled that of the 27th Division prior to the April 19 offensive. The marines had to bridge the Asa, carve out a beachhead, then attack across flat ground exposed to enemy artillery for nearly 3,000 yards before encountering Ushijima's next chain of defenses.

At 7:30 A.M. on May 11, General Shepherd sent his tanks across a Bailey bridge built by the 6th Engineer Battalion, and by nightfall his infantry-tank teams had reached the Asato River estuary just across from Naha. Captain Warren F. Lloyd's C Company of the 22nd Marines had the hardest fight of the day. Supported by the gunfire of a heavy cruiser offshore, it seized, at the cost of a third of its men an elaborately tunneled hill which had harbored a battalion of the 44th Brigade. Afterward, twenty-four-year-old Captain Lloyd remarked, "Same old story. We sealed them up on Guadalcanal, too." And he added, "A lot of them probably got away, running through these tunnels and scooting back into the hills."

Elsewhere, the attackers gained much less ground. General del Valle's 1st Marine Division managed to secure a hand grip on Dakeshi Ridge, and General Bruce's 77th Division gained 400 to 500 yards with the aid of liberal quantities of napalm from flame tanks. On the extreme left the Deadeyes of Colonel Eddie May's 383rd Infantry did well to gain 600 yards toward the northwestern approaches to Conical Hill.

Though limited, and won at considerable cost, these gains did not discourage General Buckner. He had not expected an immediate breakthrough on May 11; he did not get one. Only the 22nd Marines of the 6th Division had moved a considerable distance. But from the Asato estuary the 22nd would have to pivot east into the hilly ground between Naha and Shuri. The 1st Marine Division and the 77th Division could account their gains as only scratchings on the hard inner shell of Ushijima's Shuri defenses. The 96th Division's advance toward Conical Hill held promise, but that awesome peak looked like Mt. Everest to May's Deadeyes and just as hard to climb.

In renewing their attack on May 12, the 22nd Marines moved south and east, aiming for the thousand-yard-wide corridor between Naha and Shuri. They could have crossed the Asato estuary into Naha and taken the city, which was not defended in force, but that would have accomplished little other than to make headlines. Instead, they planned to cross the Asato's upper reaches and strike toward Kokuba, from which they could advance up the Kokuba River Valley toward Yonabaru on the east coast to encircle Ushijima's Shuri bastion. But their clever antagonist had anticipated this by digging into three small hills between the Shuri heights and the Asato estuary, a simple yet diabolically clever defense line.

The center of the line was a smallish but precipitous clay hill about fifty feet high which the Americans came to call Sugar Loaf because of its shape. It protected—and was protected by—hills on either side called Horseshoe and Half-Moon (or Crescent). Replete with 47 mm. antitank guns, deep underground tunnels, well-defiladed mortar positions, and pillboxes on both forward and reverse slopes, the Sugar Loaf complex was

Model 1 (1941) 47 mm. Anti-Tank Gun

highly resilient. Its approaches could be blanketed with artillery and mortar fire from the Shuri heights a few hundred yards to the east. Tanks and infantry trying to outflank any of the three hills would come under fire from the others and also from Shuri. The Japanese defenders were from a fresh outfit, Colonel Seiko Mita's 15th Independent Regiment of the 44th Brigade. Counting attached Okinawans they numbered about 2,000 officers and men.

The task of seizing Sugar Loaf Hill, which looked even less impressive at first glance than had Kakazu, fell initially to Lieutenant Colonel Horatio C. Woodhouse, Jr.'s 2nd Battalion of the 22nd Infantry. But probing actions on May 12 and 13 amply revealed Sugar Loaf's strength, and an all-day attack on the fourteenth had carried only through the enemy's outposts by 4:30 P.M. Tanks could not give effective support. Enemy artillery from Shuri and 47 mm. antitank guns knocked out several and forced others to keep their distance. Nevertheless, at 4:30 P.M. Woodhouse ordered his F Company to advance again, hoping that somehow his men might seize the top of the hill by dark.

It required two hours of costly maneuver under fire and many more casualties for F Company's leathernecks to reach the base of Sugar Loaf at sunset—7:08 P.M.—where those still on their feet could find partial shelter. They now numbered just forty enlisted men and four officers. Leading them was Major Harry A Courtney, Jr., Colonel Woodhouse's assistant battalion commander, who had been with the line infantry all day. A soldier's soldier, still wearing bandages over shrapnel wounds inflicted a few days before, Courtney knew his circumstances hardly could be worse. Mortar fire was pelting down; bullets zinging by testified that Japanese riflemen had worked around the hill to shoot into the dimness where they knew the marines had to be. Others on top had begun tumbling grenades down the slope. When twenty-six additional men arrived carrying ammunition and rations, Courtney made up his mind.

Assembling the crouching men about him during a temporary lull, he addressed them calmly. "Men, if we don't take the top of this hill tonight, the Japs will be down here to drive us away in the morning. . . . I want volunteers for a banzai of our own!" After radioing for mortar support he turned and said, "I'm going up to the top of Sugar Loaf Hill. Who's coming along?" All followed, scrambling up the steep slope, carrying their weapons and as many grenades as each man could hold. By 11:00 P.M. the desperate band was on top, digging in and flinging grenades over the far side at surprised Japanese trying to form up for a counterattack. Courtney himself had not lasted long; shortly after reaching the crest a grenade or mortar shell had exploded at his feet mortally wounding him. But the others held out all night in hastily scooped foxholes, drenched by a cold rain that blew in off the East China Sea, until a gray and cheerless dawn began to break.

Less than twenty-five now remained effective amid signs that the Japanese below and on Horseshoe had begun organizing for another attack. Enemy fire intensified. But Colonel Mita's infantry were not having it entirely their own way, for one of the surviving Americans was Corporal Donald (Rusty) Golar, a self-styled "storybook" marine. Golar, a light machine gunner, used to tell his sometimes unbelieving buddies who thought him a blowhard, "I'm one of those glory hunters. I'm looking for glory and I'm looking for Japs." After Guam many began taking him at his word. "You watch that Rusty," they would say. "Just watch that redhead!" Now that redhead was behind a Browning light machine gun, a camouflaged helmet atop it bobbing with each burst as its owner squeezed the trigger. When the Japanese would begin shooting at him from another direction, Golar would boom, "Yeah!" wheel his gun about, and take them on. Finally, Golar had no more ammunition. "Gotta use what I've got left," he yelled to a buddy, Private Donald Kelly of Chicago. He drew his .45 caliber pistol, emptied it, then stood up and pitched the empty weapon toward the spurts of enemy fire. Dashing about, Golar collected hand grenades from the fallen, then hurled them down Sugar Loaf's reverse slope. When he ran out of grenades, Golar found a BAR and fired until it jammed.

"Nothing more to give them," he yelled to Kelly. "Let's get some of these wounded guys down." He bent over a marine with a chest wound. "I'll have you in sick bay in no time." But as he walked with the marine toward the northern rim of the hill a bullet struck him. He staggered, Kelly recalled, "but he put the wounded man down. Then he went over to the ditch with a surprised look on his face. . . . I saw him sit down and push his helmet over his forehead like he was going to sleep. Then he died."

With Golar was Corporal Stephen Stankovitch, a former coal miner from St. Clair, Pennsylvania. He too threw grenades, then switched to antitank missiles, which he pitched into caves halfway down the reverse slope. When daylight came and some men gave way, he yelled after them, "Don't run. We fought like a sonovabitch for this hill and we're going to hold it."

But hold it the men could not. Mita's infantry began counterattacking at about 9:00 A.M., and at 11:36 A.M. the eleven surviving marines withdrew from Sugar Loaf.

On the crest and forward slopes of the hill lay a hundred-odd of the 6th Marine Division's finest; Courtney, who received a posthumous Medal of Honor, Golar, and Lieutenant "Irish George" Murphy, a former Notre Dame football star. The blazing hulks of three Sherman tanks at the approaches to the hill explained much of the story. The enemy's 47 mm. antitank guns had kept them from circling around to shoot up the reverse slope.

Early afternoon of May 15 found Woodhouse's battalion pulling back into reserve—what there was of it. Woodhouse had lost over four hundred men in just three days of fighting. But Colonel Mita's regiment had suffered losses, too, and that night Ushijima sent forward a provisional regiment under Major Kaoru to to give Mita three additional battalions. Ushijima was dipping into his last reserves of well-trained infantry but he had no other choice. He had to hold the Sugar Loaf complex for as long as he could.

On May 16 and 17 the marines remained stalled before Sugar Loaf. Repeated attempts to take the summit of the hill failed, and the sixteenth was, as the divisional history put it, "... as bitter a day the Sixth Division had seen or would see." But on the eighteenth tanks managed to work their way forward, allowing Captain Howard L. Mabie of D Company of the 29th Marines to execute the winning strategy.

Mabie sent eighty of his men under First Lieutenant Francis Xavier Smith, a replacement platoon leader, up Sugar Loaf's forward slope armed with grenades. Taking up an exposed position on the summit, Smith directed a grenade shower on the Japanese caves on the reverse slope. Smith's battalion commander, Lieutenant Colonel William G. Robb, said afterward, "He had control of every man."

Meanwhile, the tanks, protected by infantry against enemy suicide squads, worked their way about either side of the hill. They met little antitank fire and had little trouble. Said Lieutenant Donald R. Pinnow afterward, "We pumped a few more shells into the caves when suddenly the Japs began running down from the crest. There must have been 150 of them. We fired...and blew them all over the landscape." From one cave a Japanese suicide squad ran toward the tanks with satchel charges. Sergeant Charles M. Scott spotted it, opened up with a machine gun, and squarely hit one of the charges, wiping out the team. Others cut down two more suicide teams. Corporal Whalen R. McGarrity, a tank commander, spotted a Japanese officer standing outside a cave pointing with his saber at positions behind rocks for his men to take cover. Wheeling his 75 mm. gun, McGarrity fired and scored a direct hit. Recalled Lieutenant Richard Peterson, "His sword went flying fifty feet through the air. We could see it glittering in the sun."

The tanks, in cooperation with Mabie's infantry, had broken the back of Sugar Loaf's defenses. By nightfall the bloody fight for the hill had become a mop-up action.

Sixth Division losses had been frightful. In the ten days since the Marine unit had crossed the Asa it had lost 2,662 killed and wounded. But Mita's 15th Regiment had been decimated. The best General Ushijima now could do was to send inexperienced Navy troops to bolster a new 44th Brigade line between the Kokuba River estuary and the Shuri heights. When that line fell Ushijima's flank would be turned; the marines could push tank-infantry teams up the Kokuba River Valley behind his Shuri redoubt.

The 6th Marine Division's harsh experiences at Sugar Loaf were paralleled by those of the 1st Marine Division at Dakeshi Ridge and Wana draw. On May 11 and 12 the 7th Marines managed to clear Dakeshi Ridge, breaking the first of the enemy's three defense lines. They destroyed almost completely the remnants of the 62nd Division, capturing the headquarters caves of a brigade commander, Major General Suichi Akikawa. On May 13, with his cave under close attack, Akikawa personally traded grenades inside and outside the cave with attacking marines. That night at Ushijima's order he and a few survivors exfiltrated the Marine lines to re-form at Shuri, once more to try to rebuild the 62nd Division.

The battle's second stage began the next day, the 14th, when the 7th Marines tried to sweep over Wana Ridge, which formed the north wall of Wana draw, while the 1st Marines battled to reach the end of the ridge at the draw's mouth. Neither succeeded and their failure revealed clearly to Major General del Valle that Wana draw could not be taken until tanks could enter and shoot it up.

The first tanks to enter, M-4 Shermans of Colonel Arthur J ("Jeb") Stuart's 1st Tank Battalion, encountered a 47 mm antitank gun and had to withdraw. One tank took five hits before naval gunfire silenced the gun. The next day Stuart renewed the attack, sending three M-4's and one flame tank as far as Wana village, which they shot up and burned out. A pair of 47 mm guns disabled two machines, but the crews spotted the flashes and radioed up a massive rejoinder from the old battleship *Colorado,* whose big projectiles obliterated the caves holding both guns.

Even with the aid of tanks the fighting was rough for the infantry. Lieutenant Colonel Edward H. Hurd's 3rd Battalion of the 7th Marines lost twelve officers, all from rifle companies between May 16 and 19. Eventually, what the marines called "processing" paid dividends. Protected by infantry, the tanks would hammer specific Japanese caves and emplacements selected jointly by the tank commander and infantry platoon leader. This led to steady reduction of the Japanese positions, until all but the more sheltered upper end of the draw was in leatherneck hands. May 21 found the 1st Marine Division preparing for a final push to reduce the end of the draw, cross a final ridge, and break into the rubble that had once been Shuri town. The price had been terrible. The 7th Marines alone had taken 1,174 casualties since May 10.

II

Had it not been for the constant support of the Navy offshore the marines might not have been able to advance at all. Every day, all day, battleships, cruisers, and destroyers closed the reefs, flinging out shells at the direction of Army-Navy fire control parties (JASCOS) with the line battalions.*

Nightfall brought little relief to the destroyers. Unlike the battleships and cruisers which retired seaward, destroyers had to remain off either coast firing star shells containing bright parachute flares to expose Japanese infiltrators. Although the sailors could (and did) learn to sleep soundly through the ear-rending crack of the 5-inch .38 caliber guns, the constant strain of the bombardment and screening work, and the punishing all-hands task of taking on ammunition and supplies every third or fourth day from LST supply ships at the Keramas, gradually wore down the destroyer men. Merely being at sea was tiring on a constantly rolling destroyer; one could seldom walk a straight line down a deck. There were always watches to stand, little maintenance tasks to do. The prospect of the sudden appearance of a kamikaze added mental to physical strain.

For the U.S.S. *Longshaw,* a fire support destroyer operating with the leathernecks off Okinawa's west coast, all these considerations prevailed and more. The vessel was shorthanded; her 291 enlisted men and 22 officers were only just enough to get the

---

*By the end of the campaign the ships had fired 23,210 battleship, 31,550 8-inch, over 45,000 6-inch, and 475,000 5-inch projectiles.

work done. Also, the *Longshaw* had been on station for a long time. Everyone was weary, and the ship's medic, Lieutenant M. N. Manning, estimated that several were on the verge of mental and physical collapse. But only the campaign's end could bring relief to crew and ship.

By mid-May the *Longshaw* had had her share of close calls. On L day a Jill had just missed her with a torpedo. A week later in Nago Bay her gun crews deflected a kamikaze Val which splashed thirty feet away. On May 13 the ship changed skippers—Lieutenant Commander C. W. Becker replacing Commander T. R. Vogeley—but not her strenuous duties. In the next four days her guns expended 1,500 rounds of 5-inch ammunition in fire support, and on the fifth day, May 17, in "more than a day's work" her weary crew replenished magazines in the Keramas while also taking on provisions and fuel. That night found the *Longshaw* as it again, lofting 500 star shells to light up the battlefield.

On the morning of May 18 the *Longshaw* was ordered to screen a cruiser preparatory to firing at enemy positions later in the day. With Lieutenant R. L. Bly navigating the ship as officer of the deck, the *Longshaw* was proceeding routinely at 10 knots off Omine Point south of Naha. Suddenly, with a grinding crash, the ship grounded on two coral heads of Ose Reef, 2,500 yards from the Japanese-held shore. Fatigue plus hazy conditions had misled Bly and the bridge watch into thinking that the reef—which they knew was there—was still a half mile ahead. Ascertaining that his ship's hull had not been ruptured, Commander Becker—who had rushed from his sea cabin—ordered the engines reversed at full power to no avail.

Another destroyer passed a towline, but the *Longshaw* was gripped so firmly on either side by the coral that this effort failed also. Becker now ordered the crew to lighten ship while waiting for the combined effects of a tow from a rescue tug and a high tide to free his ship from its embarrassing perch.

All went well for a time. At 9:30 A.M. the skipper of the fleet tug *Arikara*, Lieutenant John Aitken, conferred with Commander Becker on the best means of extracting the destroyer. An hour-and-a-half later, the tide being at flood, the tug took up slack on a towline, the *Longshaw*'s crew assembled aft to reduce weight forward, and the destroyer backed both engines at full speed to break clear.

Then disaster struck. A concealed Japanese shore battery plunked a medium-caliber shell between the two ships. As *Longshaw* sailors raced to battle stations a second shell crashed amidships on the destroyer, killing several men. Another demolished the CIC, and a fourth hit the bridge, knocking down the mast, wounding Commander Becker seriously, and cutting down others of the bridge watch. In the 5-inch mounts gunners returned the fire, but a fifth Japanese shell hit the *Longshaw* squarely in a forward powder magazine. A terrific explosion converted the destroyer into a mass of twisted, flaming wreckage forward of the bridge.

Radioman 1/C James Zikus, who had come from the *Arikara* to the *Longshaw*'s bridge to relay messages via walkie-talkie, went spinning through the air along with a large steel plate. "I found myself in water coated about four inches deep with [blazing] oil. . . . I reached some wreckage, then got on a little raft with two men. We linked up with another life raft and picked up a few survivors."

The Japanese gun crew then shifted fire to the tug, as the *Longshaw,* obviously finished, blazed on the reef. Shells landed off the port quarter, then straddled the stern as Lieutenant Aitken maneuvered the *Arikara* to evade the battery. He did so, then lowered a whaleboat to rescue *Longshaw* survivors. Several other ships closed to do the same.

Realizing that his ship was a sitting duck, Commander Becker had ordered his crew overside after the second Japanese shell hit. Lieutenant Bly, who found himself one of the few officers not killed or injured, turned to fighting the ship's many fires. Soon giving that up as hopeless, he joined a courageous pharmacist's mate, Loyer by name, in treating the wounded. Slipping empty powder cans under the men's skivvy shirts, Bly and Loyer eased them into the water to await rescue.

Their injured commanding officer did not leave. Standing near a large fire amidships, dazedly waving a .45 caliber pistol, Commander Becker refused treatment, ordering Pharmacist Loyer off the ship—the last anyone saw of him.

When a support landing craft closed later to remove a few remaining injured and to identify the dead, Commander Becker had disappeared. He was carried as "missing in action, presumed dead." Eleven officers and sixty-six men joined their commander in death; a hundred were wounded. So perished the only fire support ship destroyed in the campaign by a shore battery.

III

In the center of the island, attacking along either side of a mile-wide valley, the 77th Division met the same brand of iron resistance that had held up the two Marine divisions. Colonel Joseph B. Coolidge's 305th Infantry had to fight through terrain strikingly similar to the desolate no-man's-land of World War I, ground cratered, chipped, littered with broken coral, churned by fire that had destroyed almost every living plant. In ten days beginning on May 11 the 305th inched from Hill 187 just south of Maeda to the outskirts of Shuri on Highway 5. No one day was spectacular; gains were steady and so were losses. On May 15 the regiment stood at quarter strength; by the twenty-first it was too depleted to continue in action.

Much more dramatic action took place on the other side of the valley, where the 306th and 307th Infantry regiments struggled with three stubborn terrain features, called incongruously—if accurate geographically—the Chocolate Drop, Wart Hill, and Flattop Hill. Into these hills and on others to the south, General Ushijima had woven a barrier as formidable as Sugar Loaf. In addition to mortars, interlocking bands of fire from machine guns, and 47 mm. antitank guns, Ushijima's defense featured extensive minefields that effectively barred tank movement. As at Sugar Loaf the infantry had to fight at first without tanks, suffering very heavy casualties and gaining practically no ground. On May 15 Colonel Aubrey D. Smith was forced to form the survivors of his regiment into a single battalion, after which Colonel Hamilton's 307th Regiment, rested from its punishment on the escarpment, took over. To one observer the line of dead lying on the Chocolate Drop looked like a skirmish line that had lain down to rest.

The evening of May 21 found Hamilton's 307th probing hills to the south of the Drop and Flattop, having finally reduced both, and while so engaged B Company lost the man it considered the most valuable. Forward with the infantry was medic Desmond T. Doss, already a hero many times over for saving lives on the escarpment. When enemy fire pinned down the company, Doss stayed up, crawling from man to man to aid the injured. While so engaged a mortar burst seriously injured his legs. Rather than expose another, Doss treated his own wounds and waited five hours until litter bearers could reach him. On the way back enemy fire drove the bearers to cover. Seeing a seriously wounded man nearby, Doss rolled from the stretcher, crawled to him, and dressed his wounds. While waiting for the bearers to return, Doss was hit again, this time suffering a compound fracture of an arm. With incredible fortitude he splinted the arm with a rifle stock and crawled three hundred yards rearward to an aid station. So ended the war for the conscientious objector from Lynchburg, Virginia.

In the meantime, Colonel Marcey Dill's Deadeyes of the 382nd Infantry had been struggling to subdue the Dick Hill mass just to the left of Flattop. Dill's GI's managed to work their way onto the face of the hill and to seize a lodging on a fifty-foot-diameter circular plateau on the hilltop, but without tank support they could not clear the hill's reverse slope.

The break for both the Deadeyes and the 77th Division GI's came on May 17 when an infantry platoon under Lieutenant Robert L. Fulkerson crawled into a road cut between Dick Hill and Flattop to probe with their bayonets for mines. They found and removed four and blew five caves while losing nineteen men at this risky work. Despite their efforts the first tank attempting to break through hit a mine and had to be winched out to clear the road.

On the eighteenth, recognizing that this road was the key to both Dick and Flattop, Lieutenant Colonel Cyril W. Sterner, commander of the 382nd's 2nd Battalion, had seven tons of bangalore torpedoes—explosives packed in long pipes—laid in a double row along the road, one in each rut in which a tank tread would go. The resulting blast took care of whatever mines may have remained, enabling tanks to get at the rear of both Flattop and Dick. Two flame tanks commanded by Sergeants Victor J. Albera and Ray Achenbach burned out several smaller caves, incinerating an estimated twenty-five enemies. Antitank fire from hills to the south disabled three tanks, and Albera's flame-thrower threw a tread and stalled, but the mechanical monsters shattered the backbone of the enemy's resistance.

One of the few Japanese to survive was Captain Koichi Ito. On May 15 he had taken four hundred men of his reconstituted 1st Battalion, 32nd Infantry, to reinforce Dick Hill and Flattop. Between the fifteenth and nineteenth he lost nearly all of his force, and by the afternoon of the twentieth was holed up in a deep cave on Flattop. Seventy-seventh Division GI's sealed his cave with rocks, but Ito dug out through the top of the cave that night and with twenty-five others escaped to Shuri to once again re-form his battalion.

Dick Hill contained a few civilians as well as Japanese soldiers. Investigating a cave on May 20, Pfc Paul H. Callahan of K Company found assorted boxes, pots, jars, and on the floor of the cave bundles of rags and blankets. On investigating the bundles Callahan found that each contained a blinking, sleepy child, in all four little girls and two boys. He also found several women and a Japanese soldier farther back in the cave, who in rare un-samurai fashion meekly allowed himself to be marched out as a POW. After the children had been removed, T/5 Don Summa gave one of the boys a pencil and paper. Quickly the lad jotted on it. When translated later by a battalion interpreter it was found to read, "Have mercy on us."

By May 21 both the 77th and 96th divisions were ready to move forward again, the 77th directly into Shuri and on Shuri Castle, and the 96th against Oboe, Hector, and Hen Hills. As with the case of the 1st Marine Division, one more push would shatter the enemy's final Shuri defenses.

IV

Conical Hill on the east side of the front had been the problem of the 96th Division's 383rd Infantry under Colonel May. Against such an obstacle as Conical, General Hodge, the 24th Corps commander, had wanted his best regimental commander. If anyone could take that peak, Hodge believed, it would be Eddie May.

Conical, which the Japanese called Utanamori, rose nearly 500 feet to a high round cone. Westward from it a series of ridges and lesser peaks rose toward Oboe and Dick hills in the 382nd Infantry's zone.

Assuming that his troops could somehow get onto Conical, May knew that they would have to fight their way 800 yards down a hogback to another peak called Sugar Hill. Seizure, however, of Conical, the hogback, and Sugar Hill would completely turn Ushijima's line, for immediately south of Sugar Hill was Yonabaru, Okinawa's third largest town, and the highway running from it to Naha. A breakthrough at Conical would lead to a GI advance up the Yonabaru-Shuri highway behind the Japanese defenses to meet the marines.

To defend Conical Ushijima had about a thousand men, including troops from Colonel Hitoshi Kanayama's rebuilt 89th Infantry Regiment and Lieutenant Kensuke Udo's 27th Independent Infantry Battalion. All were well armed and trained, and most had concentrated on and behind the hills and ridges to the west, which the Japanese assumed would be May's approach.

Initially, May had thought that he would have to take Conical from the west. But beginning with the attack of the eleventh, Major Kenny W. Erickson's 1st Battalion had gotten nowhere from this direction. Nor did Erickson advance very far in the next ten days. Charlie Hill, in particular, proved extremely troublesome as did Love Hill which the infantry promptly redesignated "Tiger." May's 3rd Battalion, commanded by Lieutenant Colonel Edward W. Stare, did much better. By the evening of May 12 Stare had cleared so much ground before Conical's steep north face that Generals Hodge and Buckner had become most encouraged by his prospects.

Eleven A.M. the next day, May 13, found General Buckner at Colonel May's command post watching the final softening up of Conical. For two days May had been standing exposed in the open, ignoring enemy artillery fire, worrying his bodyguard, Pfc James B. Becker, studying the hill with binoculars, and watching tanks hammer every nook and cranny on the forward slope of the hill. Now, with Buckner on hand, May decided that the moment had come and ordered Stare to send E and F companies up the north slope.

Company E was slow in getting away, but F Company's 1st and 2nd platoons jumped off, the men climbing swiftly toward some rocks halfway up the face that offered some prospect of shelter. They met very little fire, for the Japanese had retired to caves on Conical's reverse slope to escape the tanks.

On the company's arrival at the rocks, Technical Sergeants Guy J. Dale and Dennis O. Duniphan, the platoon commanders, hastily conferred and on their own initiative decided to climb onto the crest. Their company commander, First Lieutenant Owen R. O'Neill, was not far behind, but his radio was out and the sergeants decided not to take the time to contact him. A few minutes later, amazed at their good fortune, with every man unhit, both platoons found themselves digging in about fifty feet below Conical's high round peak. There was no point in getting on it; it was a small area exposed to fire from all sides.

Dale and Duniphan had caught the Japanese napping, but not for long. Realizing the danger to the entire Shuri bastion if the Americans held, Lieutenant Colonel Udo, the 27th Independent Battalion commander, immediately ordered a company-strength counterattack. The GI's stopped his first assault made directly over the crest. Then Udo launched another around the left flank of Duniphan's platoon. To defeat this one the gritty sergeant grabbed a BAR, stood up, and emptied it into Japanese faces ten feet away, inspiring his men to hold their ground and fire. Meanwhile, Lieutenant O'Neill, F Company's commander, had arrived to reinforce the line, and a few minutes later E Company, commanded by Captain Stanley B. Sutten, panted up to fall in on F Company's right flank. By nightfall the determined Deadeyes had formed a perimeter east of the peak immediately below the crest. A delighted Buckner congratulated May, telling him that this had been one of the most brilliant pieces of small unit tactics that he had ever witnessed. Nor was it luck. May's patient reconnaissance of the previous two days, his willingness to risk his own life to study the terrain, had paid off.

The next three days, May 14, 15, and 16, witnessed E and F companies, joined by G, engage the Japanese in a most desperate battle on Conical's crest. Again and again the enemy counterattacked, again and again the thinning ranks of Americans held them off. On the seventeenth Major General James L. Bradley, the 96th's commander, wisely decided to relieve Stare's battalion with Lieutenant Colonel Daniel A. Nolan's 3rd Battalion of the 381st. Stare's men, he knew, were now too battle-weary to push down the 800 yards of hogback to Sugar Hill.

Jim Bradley had made a good choice. In the next four days the aggressive Nolan methodically pushed his men the length of the hogback and finished up with a charge to seize Sugar Hill on

May 21. By evening some Japanese remained on Conical's reverse slope, but its entire northern and eastern face had been cleared, including the hogback and Sugar Hill.

With the Japanese now unable to fire on the coastal flat from Conical, General Hodge, the 24th Corps commander, realized that Ushijima's flank was open. Adopting a stratagem from American football, he planned to sweep his entire 7th Division, now rested and reinforced, down the corridor in an "end run" around the Japanese. If the men could reach Yonabaru, then turn west along the Yonabaru-Naha road, they would cut off the 32nd Army and make retreat southward to the tip of the island impossible. General Ushijima recognized the danger but could do little to thwart it. He had expended his last reserve, a unit of naval and ordnance troops, in the Sugar Hill battle.

Indeed, in examining the situation along his entire front on the night of May 21, Ushijima could take no comfort anywhere. Only between Hen Hill and the rugged ground west of Conical was his line firm. Everywhere else, at Horseshoe Ridge behind Sugar Loaf, Wana draw before Shuri, and at Conical his enemies were threatening to break through. General Buckner was as encouraged as Ushijima was disconsolate. A final shove, it seemed, and the Shuri bastion must crumble all along the line.

For all concerned, Japanese and American alike, the ten days between May 11 and 21 had been the most terrible of the extraordinarily bitter Okinawan campaign. Fighting of the utmost violence had raged continuously in *every* sector. Nowhere had combat been light or easy. The 77th Division had lost in the 10 days 239 killed, 1,212 wounded, and 16 missing; the 96th Division lost 138 killed, 1,059 wounded, and 9 missing. The best comment on the action came inadvertently from Tokyo a few days later in an English-language broadcast directed to Americans on Okinawa.

Sugar Loaf Hill...Chocolate Drop...Strawberry Hill. Gee, these places sound wonderful! You can just see the candy houses with the white picket fences around them and the candy canes hanging from the trees, their red and white stripes glistening in the sun. But the only thing red about these places is the blood of Americans. Yes, sir, these are the names of hills in southern Okinawa where the fighting's so close that you can get down to bayonets and sometimes your bare fists.... I guess it's natural to idealize the worst places with pretty names to make them seem less awful. Why, Sugar Loaf has changed hands so often it looks like Dante's Inferno. Yes, sir, Sugar Loaf Hill . . . Chocolate Drop . . . Strawberry Hill. They sound good, don't they? Only those who've been there know what they're really like.

21

MUD AND KAMIKAZES

AT 2:00 A.M. on May 22 a column of well-spaced infantry was marching through the misty darkness along Highway 13, the east coast road, rifles slung, ponchos covering shoulders and light packs. Under their feet the road gradually churned to mud as the rain fell steadily. Returning to battle after ten days of rest were the men of Captain Homer C. Graff's Company G of the 7th Division's 184th Infantry. Many were nineteen-year-old rookies, a few wounded veterans returned from field hospitals. During its brief rest and rehabilitation the Hourglass Division had absorbed 1,691 replacements and 546 men returned to duty, making good about half the combat losses of forty days of continuous fighting.

I

Captain Graff's mission was to spearhead the 7th Division's attack down the coastal road to Yonabaru and west toward Naha, throwing a block across the rear of Ushijima's Army, preventing its retreat either to the southern tip of Okinawa or into the rugged Chinen Peninsula. If G Company and others of the 184th could capture the high ground about Yonabaru, blocking enemy counteraction and driving away Japanese mortars and light artillery, then Colonel Mickey Finn's 32nd Infantry could advance through Yonabaru, wheel west, and drive toward Naha with two battalions abreast to join up with General Shepherd's marines.

Crucial to the strategy of General Hodge and General Arnold, commanding the 7th Division, was the use of tanks. Arnold had personally taken to the air in a Cub plane to reconnoiter the terrain west of Yonabaru. He believed that for the first time on Okinawa tanks could be employed en masse, both regular M-4's and the terrible new flamethrowers. With their aid the reverse slopes of such imposing hills as Mabel, a key objective of Finn's 32nd Infantry, could be cleared without too much trouble.

Despite the rain, which continued all of the next day, May 23, the 184th Infantry was completely successful. By nightfall it had followed up its surprise night advance to drive a 2,000-yard fissure into the Japanese position south of Yonabaru and was pushing steadily south two provisional battalions of defenders organized by Ushijima from service units. Colonel Finn's regiment was moving into place, getting set to begin its big push west.

But already a hitch had developed. In their assembly areas near Skyline Ridge the ungainly Sherman tanks lay scattered about like so many ruptured ducks, some mired hull deep in ooze. About them, sunk to their thighs, the crews cursed and sweated trying vainly to break the machines loose. Highway 13 was already a mile-long traffic jam of stalled six-by-six trucks, jeeps, ambulances, recon cars, and other vehicles standing with radiators steaming from engines overheated from spinning tires. Even M-29 tracked cargo carriers and weasels mired in the thick, adhesive mixture of coral and clay that could rip the sole from a combat boot. M-5 heavy artillery tractors could get through regularly to battalion supply dumps, but from there every box of K rations, every mortar round, every belt and clip of .30 caliber ammunition had to be lugged forward by hand. Some marines tried using packtrains of Okinawan ponies—then shot the animals between the eyes when they became mired to their necks.

In every divisional sector across the island the story was the same. The rain and mud had completely frustrated General Buckner's plan to give Ushijima the *coup de grâce*. In the center of the island, fighting in the 77th and 96th divisional zones dropped abruptly to patrol action. Wana draw became a mud lake, impassable to vehicles and almost so for a 1st Division marine on foot. The 6th Marine Division kept going, clearing Naha and advancing south across the swollen Asato River into the Kokuba Hills, but it had to move at a snail's pace because of the supply problem and took heavy casualties from Ushijima's artillery. For a full week, from May 24 through May 29, the rains had given the 32nd Army an indispensable reprieve it could have gained in no other way.

Besides stopping the offensives the rains had slowed further a base development plan already behind schedule. All engineering effort, except for vital airfield maintenance at Kadena, Yomitan, and on Ie Shima, had to be mustered to keep open Highways 1 and 5. On Highway 13 the engineers had to give up, the 7th Division keeping itself supplied from landing craft grounding at Yonabaru.

L-5

Planes flew short hops to air drop supplies, mostly ammunition and rations, to the troops. A squadron of Marine Avengers victualed forward units of the 6th Marine Division, while Army

L-5 light planes used a steel-planked runway at Chatan to haul various light supplies to the GI's.

Troops in the rear echelons had some amenities despite the rain. Foremost were outdoor movies, and rain or no rain the men gathered nightly to huddle under ponchos and stare at flickering 16 mm. versions of late Hollywood hits. Inevitably, the film would break during the performance, to produce muttered oaths, flashlights aimed at the screen, and invective directed at the operator: "Where did you learn to run that thing? Cook and baker school?" At such times it was hard to believe that just a few miles southward, Japanese and Americans were living in desperate peril and extreme discomfort.

II

May brought kamikazes as well as rain. The 5th Air Fleet and 6th Air Army launched three attacks, Kikusui's 6, 7, and 8, the latter pair being a single, continuous operation. Again the hell-birds were destructive, but not—fortunately for Admiral Nimitz's peace of mind—quite so much so as in late April.

More than a month of attacks had made the dispatch of kamikazes almost routine. In Japan a Special Attack Corps had been organized, feeding pilots and planes—often from training organizations—to the Kyushu bases to send out. At first the pilots had been strictly volunteers, but later orders made all Japanese military personnel subject to suicide missions whether they wished to go or not. Frequently, squadron commanders "volunteered" their entire organizations for the duty. Some airmen were enthusiastic, some resentful, others willing to go but anxious to have their sacrifice inflict maximum possible damage to the enemy. Some got "lost" and aborted their missions, returning to base. Others went willingly not once but several times, engine trouble, bad weather, or some other contre-temps having repeatedly frustrated earlier attempts to die. All were indoctrinated and trained as carefully as time permitted, but the American belief that kamikaze pilots were drugged, brainwashed, or simply intoxicated was a myth. Many carefully avoided strong spirits on the night before their mission, the better to be clear-headed during their final dives at the target. Seitoku Kinjo, who at the time was serving as a primary training instructor in the Army Aviation School, says that "kamikaze pilots were just obeying orders," and this seems to have been the prosaic truth.

Nevertheless, in Japan suicide flyers were extolled as national heroes and saviors of the nation. In the press and over the radio their exploits were endowed with romantic glamour and magnified far beyond actual accomplishments. Many kamikaze pilots became caught up with this general fervor. One left the verse, "When I fly the skies/What a fine burial place/Would be the top of a cloud!" Another—a Christian—wrote to a friend:

I do not want a grave. I would feel oppressed if they were to put me into a narrow vault. A vagabond, such as I, has no need of it. Would you tell my parents that?... 11:30 A.M.—the last morning. I shall now have breakfast and go to the airdrome. I am busy with the final briefing and have no time to write any more. So I bid you farewell.... I believe in the victory of Greater Asia. I pray for the happiness of you all, and I beg your forgiveness.

Others were unsure whether their sacrifice was worth it. Wrote one, "I say frankly, I do not die willingly; I die not without regret. My country's future leaves me uneasy.... I am terribly distressed."

Actual operating conditions contrasted sharply with the supposed glamour of the kamikaze's final hours. To be sure there was always a final ceremony, never allowed by commanding officers to become perfunctory. Special attack pilots lined up, listened to last-minute instructions and patriotic exhortations, drank toasts, and received cigarettes of the Imperial Gift. But the air bases themselves were dismal, and by May most had been thoroughly battered by carrier planes and B-29's. At Kanoya, the most important field for naval kamikazes, Captain Motoharu Okamura's 341st Air Group was established in an old primary-school building on the west side of the main airdrome. The windows had been blown out, there were holes in the roof, and all personnel, suicide pilots included, had to sleep on straw pallets on the floor. The radio communication center, which received attack orders from 5th Air Fleet headquarters, was in an air raid shelter a hundred yards distant. When American raids became almost a daily occurrence the pilots slept there.

With little to do except wait for orders which meant their

deaths, the pilots took to helping farmers in nearby fields with their spring planting and weeding. A stream wound through bamboo thickets and grainfields, and white roses along its banks gave the young men, whose senses were sharpened by their destiny, a measure of tranquility and peace. Grateful peasants brought the pilots eggs, chickens, and once even a cow to improve the indifferent fare of their mess. These touches somehow warmed the shabby surroundings of the Kanoya base.

On May 8 Admiral Ugaki learned that Tokyo had decided to dispatch two divisions of ground troops embarked in destroyers, to relieve the 32nd Army. To enable the ships to get through, the kamikazes would undertake to knock out both the American radar pickets and T.F. 58, while airborne troops hit Kadena and Yomitan airfields to destroy the American ground-based planes. Ugaki's part in this was to organize another attack, Kikusui 6, set for May 11.

Surly rain clouds swirled over Kanoya as May 11 dawned, but they remained high enough to permit the first planes to take off at 5:30 A.M. Reconnaissance Dinahs had found T.F. 58 and had radioed the locations of the radar pickets. Ugaki's staff had planned a one-two punch. Interceptor fighters would accompany eighteen Judy dive bombers against the American carriers, while seventy-five long-range fighters escorted a miscellany of sixty-five Army and Navy kamikazes to Okinawa, of which several were brand-new Kawanishi "Kyokko" (Arrow) fighters similar in appearance to Frances bombers. Ugaki swept clean his fields; virtually every serviceable plane on Kyushu was ordered out.

A disaster weakened the attack at its outset. The Judy dive bombers targeted for the U.S. carriers climbed from Kokobu airfield's number two airstrip directly into a formation of Val suicide planes taking off from another runway. Losses from collisions and exploding bombs totaled eight Judys and seven Vals, in what may have been the worst accident of this type of the war.

As the planes continued toward Okinawa and T.F. 58, American fighter-director teams vectored Hellcats and Corsairs from carriers and Okinawan airfields to intercept. Scattered dogfights erupted over Amami O Shima, then over the radar pickets. Many kamikazes dropped very low, hoping to evade both the defending fighters and the radar, a tactic that enjoyed mixed success. Two Okinawa-based Marine flyers, Lieutenants E. C. Keeley and L. N.

Crawley, got three kamikazes apiece that they caught approaching Okinawa on the deck at 8:30 A.M. Only two tried to evade, and all six flamed and crashed as the two marines, firing short bursts to conserve ammunition, methodically shot them down one after another. Crawley also destroyed a fast two-engine plane, possibly an experimental Kawanishi though he identified it as a Dinah. Pilots from T.F. 58 claimed sixty planes and the Okinawa marines nineteen, less of an exaggeration than customary, for Ugaki's headquarters counted losses to defending fighters at about forty. But enough devil-birds got through to give the radar pickets a bad day.

The special attackers arrived over Station 15 at about 7:50 A.M. Below were destroyers *Evans* and *Hugh W. Hadley* commanded by Naval Academy classmates Commanders Robert J. Archer and Baron J. Mullaney. The two skippers watched as fifty of a stream of attackers peeled off to orbit their ships. At first it was easy. *Evans* blasted down fourteen attackers one after another "like fish in a barrel," and *Hadley*'s gunners dropped a dozen more that approached the ship as it maneuvered violently at 30 knots.

At 9:07 A.M. a fast-diving Judy struck the bow of the *Evans*, rattling the ship but not reducing its speed. Two minutes later its gunners picked off a Tony fighter to port but could not stop another plane that approached in a high-speed glide. "We could see the 20 mm. hitting the plane," recalls Admiral Archer, "but it kept coming." Its bomb or torpedo exploded just outside the after fireroom, flooding instantly that space and the after engine room. Two Oscar fighters in succession then crashed the ship amidships, exploding both forward boilers, wrecking the galley, and starting gasoline fires from the bridge aft. The blast of one blew overside and badly injured Lieutenant L. W. Gillen, the ship's executive officer. Seamen Pasquale Constanzo, Pat J. Macciocca, and Carl A. Martin saw a hand drift aft, jumped overboard, swam to Gillen, and later towed him to a life raft and eventual rescue. Seaman Robert J. Stonelake shifted his 40 mm. mount to manual control when its power system failed and single-handedly destroyed a plane which otherwise would have hit the ship. Despite terrible damage, thirty killed, and twenty-nine wounded, the *Evans* survived to be towed to the Kerama haven.

Meanwhile, the *Hugh W. Hadley* was undergoing its ordeal.

At 9:20 A.M. ten planes attacked the ship simultaneously, one an Oka rocket bomb that missed. Three others scored hits that flooded both engine rooms and a fireroom. The wounded totaled sixty-seven, including Commander Mullaney, and the dead twenty-eight. The *Hadley*, too, had to be towed in, but with its partner had absorbed the bulk of the May 11 attacks off Okinawa. As in other cases where picket ships were hit, reserve destroyers promptly steamed up to fill the gap.

Task Force 58 drew attention from about fifty of Ugaki's aerial destroyers. On the bridge of the flagship *Bunker Hill*, Admiral Marc Mitscher paid grudging tribute to the skill of the Japanese pilots as they used rain clouds and "window" to attempt to nullify American radar. Suddenly, at 10:05 A.M., a Zero darted from low clouds on the flagship's starboard quarter, ripped through parked planes, starting fires, and then went overboard and exploded. Its bomb, passing through the flight deck and side of the ship, sprayed it with fragments. Right behind the Zero came a Judy, diving almost straight down from astern. Plane and bomb smashed through the flight deck near the island, augmenting fires started topside by the Zero. Planes armed for a strike and gasoline pouring from broken refueling lines fed a roaring conflagration on the hangar and flight decks. Like the *Franklin* earlier, the *Bunker Hill* had been caught at her most vulnerable moment. Casualties matched the very severe damage; almost 400 were dead or missing and another 264 injured.

As on the *Franklin* little things saved—and cost—lives. Machinist's Mate Jack Salvaggio had often cursed a porthole in the ship's stencil room because of the brisk wind usually blowing through it. Trapped when flames blocked every exit Salvaggio remembered it, and with several others in the stencil room wiggled to safety. Harold Fraught, another machinist, was trapped in suffocating smoke in a passageway. A porthole in a little corridor to one side offered the only way out. "I tried to reach it but couldn't, and I was just about to give up when someone pushed me through." He added, "I sure would like to find who the seaman was who kept pushing every guy through but not going himself." Only seven of the twenty-five in the corridor made it, Fraught's benefactor not among them. Electrician Vincent Benvinetto heard the Zero hit, and thinking that a Hellcat had crashed on the flight deck, ran from the ship's ready room toward his fire station. "A second later the second plane crashed with its bombload and those guys who had been slow in running from the ready room were killed.''

The *Bunker Hill*'s crew battled the flames for five and one-half hours. Able shiphandling by the skipper, Captain George A. Seitz, enabled them to bring the flames under control. On a course designed to blow smoke and flames broadside to the ship, Captain Seitz decided to gamble on a turn, causing the ship to heel despite her dangerous instability to allow the blazing inflammables on the hangar deck to wash overside. He told his signalman, ''. . . Order the destroyers to stand clear.'' Then (to his navigator, Commander Charles J. Oden'hal), ''What course do you recommend?''

''One-three-zero true,'' replied Oden'hal.

''Very well. Make it so,'' ordered Seitz.

Oden'hal told the helmsman: ''Come right very, very carefully. Don't use more than two and one-half degrees rudder. Watch me.'' He rushed outside the pilothouse to watch the heel of the ship, coaching the helmsman into a turn. Slowly the *Bunker Hill* came about, heeling from a list to starboard to port, and at first gradually, then with a roar, the inferno of gasoline, water, oil, and foam on the hangar deck sloshed away from the fire fighters and over the port side into the sea.

The *Bunker Hill* became the second worst hit carrier of World War II to survive—the *Franklin* being the worst. She was out of the war and required many months to repair. Admiral Mitscher, unharmed, transferred his flag to the *Enterprise*. Ugaki's skillful pair had bagged a prime target.

The blows struck on May 11 by Ugaki's airmen did not end Kikusui 6. May 12 found Japanese aircrews preparing to strike again. From Formosa the Navy's 1st Air Fleet managed to scrape together a half-dozen Type 96 biplane dive bombers, and the Army's 8th Air Division dispatched eleven more kamikazes. One plane hit the U.S.S. *Bache*, a radar picket stationed far south of Okinawa, knocking out its power plant and killing forty-one crewmen.

The two days of attacks induced Admiral Spruance to once more work over the kamikaze airfields. He ordered Mitscher to steam northward with two task groups to blast eighteen airfields on Kyushu and five on Shikoku with repeated carrier strikes. Mitscher added a new wrinkle; the *Enterprise*, with night-flying Air Group 90 aboard, would maintain patrols over the Japanese airfields during the hours of darkness to give Ugaki no respite.

The attacks began before daylight on May 13 when Lieutenant C. E. Henderson's Avenger from Air Group 90 approached Kanoya's main airstrip at an altitude of 1,500 feet and an airspeed of 150 knots. Henderson found the runway and obstruction lights on and a control tower operator blinking a light at him—landing instructions, probably. As he crossed directly over the field, additional lights snapped on, etching what may have been a practice outline of a carrier deck on the east side of the north runway. For five minutes the American pilot circled while the puzzled tower controller continued to blinker, then ended the show by dropping his bombs on revetments where he had counted thirty planes, including three Dinahs earmarked for the morning's search for T.F. 58. Night attacks had gotten off to a good start.

While Henderson was returning hundreds of day-flying Corsairs, Hellcats, Avengers, and Helldivers were roaring northward toward the Kyushu and Shikoku fields. Earlier strikes had concentrated on Kyushu's southern fields; now, since the American commanders were rightly convinced that Ugaki was staging some attacks from more northerly fields, these were targeted for heavy blows.

Attacks this day and the next met little opposition other than A-A fire. Marine fighter pilots from the *Bennington* encountered two groups of Tony and Frank fighters being ferried into Kyushu by pilots unaware that an attack was in progress. Two Tonys fell, but the fast Army Franks mostly outran their Corsair attackers. By fire-walling his throttle Lieutenant Carroll V. King tumbled one into Kagoshima Bay, but the others escaped. Meanwhile, bombers attacked all known Kyushu strips, adding to the accumulating wreckage on the ground but erasing few kamikazes.

Spectacularly different were results of the night interdiction flights from the *Enterprise*. In the predawn of May 13 seven fighter pilots shot down eight enemies, Lieutenant O. D. Young bagging three twin-float Paul seaplanes when he found his Hellcat orbiting in their landing pattern near Kanoya. Young then joined Lieutenant K. D. Smith in playing havoc with Japanese planes aligned for a sunrise takeoff, making pass after pass to keep planes from Kanoya's main runways. Smith's left aileron jammed, but he got back to the *Enterprise* after shooting down a Tony fighter which bounced him after daybreak and missed. The handful of night fighters had done almost as well as some hundreds of day fighters in two days of intensive sweeps.

For two nights Avenger bombers operating at carefully spaced intervals stayed constantly over all known operational fields at Kyushu. Their mission was less to destroy enemy planes than to keep the kamikazes pinned to their fields until day strikes could arrive. Sixteen planes flying these "heckler missions," as the *Enterprise* action report described them, covered eighteen fields on May 12–13, and fourteen harassed twenty fields on the night of May 13–14. Using flares the maneuverable Avengers bombed and strafed parked planes, but results were hard to estimate. The Kanoya tower operators still hadn't learned; on the night of May 13–14 they again blinked landing instructions to the first pilot to arrive. Despite ack-ack and blinding searchlights which made the flyers "feel naked" no Avengers fell.

Not all kamikazes stayed grounded, even at Kanoya. Beginning at 6:00 A.M. on May 14 eighty-four fighters began taking off to cover twenty-six Zero suicide planes headed for the carriers. Some fighters met incoming Hellcats and Corsairs escorting American strikes, provoking impromptu dogfights, but the bulk of the suicide planes, ducking from cloud to cloud, headed for T.F. 58. One of the pilots was Tomai Kai, a junior grade lieutenant from Shiboku.

"Get the carriers," Tomai Kai had been briefed, and this the young man was attempting to do, skillfully flying in and out of clouds, searching for the type of weather formations that would produce "nulls" (blanked out spaces) in American radar beams. Selecting the carriers of T.G. 58.3 as his target, Tomai Kai closed to 20 miles at 8,000 feet, continuing on as one by one his fellow pilots fell to the combat air patrol. His Zero bucked and bounced as the 5-inch guns of the *Enterprise* and the other ships of the task group opened up on him, but a cloud favored him in the immediate vicinity of the carrier.

Bursting from the cloud at 1,500 feet, Tomai Kai found himself astern of the "Big E'" as the ship settled on a new course. Pointing the nose of his plane directly at the ship's stern and opening throttle, he dove into a cone of 20 mm. and 40 mm. tracers floating up and past his plane. Aboard the *Enterprise* someone shouted over a bullhorn, "All exposed personnel take cover!" On the flight deck Air Officer Roger M. Van Frank saw the plane heading right for him and started running; others dove flat. On the flag bridge atop the superstructure, fully exposed to debris and flames, Admiral Mitscher calmly watched. There was nothing he could do, no order he could give.

A mere two hundred yards or less from the ship, Tomai Kai in the second to the last motion of his life, adroitly flipped the fighter onto its back, and over the ship, yanked back on the stick to steepen his plunge into the carrier's deck. His Zero hit at a 50-degree angle, crashing through the *Enterprise*'s flight deck just behind the forward elevator. His 250-kilogram bomb, which he had released just before hitting, plunged into the elevator well and exploded, tossing the elevator roof high into the air whence it tumbled lazily into the ocean. Crewmen still on their feet nearby fell sprawling, but since all wore flash-proof gear, most escaped the frightful burns on exposed skin so usual to kamikaze hits. Most of the thirteen slain and sixty-nine wounded fell to flying bomb fragments and wreckage.

The "Big E" was ready for the ordeal that followed. Well in advance of the attack the crew had drained fuel lines and had filled them with CO_2 gas; planes had been struck below, disarmed, and all but four drained of fuel; all watertight doors had been dogged shut and emergency rations stored in all compartments. This was the fruit of bitter experience, the *Enterprise* having been hit several times before. Flames broke out immediately, but because of the precautionary measures remained confined to the vicinity of the forward elevator. In thirty minutes Captain G. B. H. Hall's crew had the fires out. On the flag bridge Admiral Mitscher blinked, stared at the hole Tomai Kai's Zero had made in the flight deck, removed his baseball-type flight cap with long visor, patted a bald pate, and remarked to his staff, "Tell my task group commanders that if the Japanese keep this up they're going to grow hair on my head yet." Recalled Air Officer Van Frank afterward, "That suicide plane went through the deck not twenty feet behind me and it darn near scared me to death. How I missed getting killed I'll never know." Considering where the plane had hit, the *Enterprise* had gotten off pretty easily. Many another carrier hit in the same place had suffered grave damage and loss of life.

Just the same Tomai Kai had done his work well. The *Enterprise* and its Air Group 90 were out of the campaign for Okinawa, and the ship was out of the war. The "Big E" had to pull out for Bremerton for repairs and Admiral Mitscher again had to shift his command, this time to the brand-new U.S.S. *Randolph*, keeping as a souvenir one of Tomai Kai's calling cards found intact on his corpse. Thanks to the heroism and cool-headed skill of one young Japanese, Admiral Ugaki's hard-pressed command had been handed an important relief.

III

As Ugaki had probably expected, the seaborne landing on Okinawa by two division of troops did not materialize during the Kikusui 6 attacks, for neither the ferrying destroyers nor the oil to propel them were available in Japan. Nor was it easy to prepare an airborne attack on Kadena and Yomitan airfields. This feature was postponed until the next round of kamikaze blows, Kikusui operations 7 and 8, which consisted of a series of sorties, launched at Okinawa as weather conditions permitted, between May 23 and 28, coincident with the lull forced on the battlefield by the rains.

The Japanese 6th Air Army called its planned airborne attack on Kadena and Yomitan the Giretsu or GI Operation. A dozen Type 97 Sally bomber-transports of the 3rd Independent Air Unit flew to Kumamoto airfield in central Kyushu for the mission, Kumamoto being a newly built, square grass field not yet discovered and attacked. The twelve Sallys were to ferry a picked detachment of 120 infantry raiders, 12 to a plane, who joined by the aircrew would leap out as the aircraft belly-landed on the airfields to destroy as many American planes as possible with grenades, TNT charges, and hand weapons. Captain Michiro Okuyama the youthful commander of the Giretsu unit, could expect neither relief nor retreat. He and his men would fight until slain.

After several delays the GI Operation began in the late afternoon of May 24. Tetsuji Tamanaha, an Okinawan attached to a bomber unit, and whose home was near the raiders' destination, watched the special ceremony honoring the men and then the dangerous takeoff diagonally across the small field. Silently, he wished the heroes godspeed.

Ill-fortune plagued the Giretsu Operation at the outset. Four of the twelve planes aborted the attack for mechanical reasons and returned to airfields on Kyushu. The others continued, including

Captain Okuyama's plane. American radar picked them up, and as they flew into the vicinity of Kadena and Yomitan airfields, they met a tremendous reception from 40 and 90 mm. A-A batteries surrounding the fields. One plane crashed onto the northeast-southwest runway at Yomitan, either the violence of the impact or defending gunfire killing all hands. Another struck the ground 500 yards west of the field's air defense center, cartwheeled, and burned, killing all aboard. At least three more crashed elsewhere with hundred percent fatalities.

Just one plane made it. Skidding along Yomitan's coral strip with metal screeching, it lurched to a stop at 8:37 P.M., its twelve-man suicide squad and three aircrew piling from it. Hurling grenades and TNT charges into and under planes parked along the runways, the men fought until all were shot down. Marines ran from nearby ground units and antiaircraft positions to join battle. Two pilots from VMF 311 shot two of the infiltrators with their 45's. Bullets, American and Japanese, whizzed in all directions, but because the runway had been built up several feet above the surrounding terrain, the shots passed over the heads of men crouching along the runway. In the control tower of the field, Lieutenant M. C. Kelly, the duty officer, crumpled from a stray shot. He died later as did two other men. Several more were wounded. The attackers managed to burn seven planes and to damage twenty more, results sufficiently destructive to suggest that, had not unusually good shooting by the antiaircraft destroyed all but one of the Sallys, the loss of Marine Corps transports, Corsairs, Avengers, and utility planes might have been fairly serious.

Japanese psychology demanded that General Sugahara's headquarters should believe that the attack was a success and that Captain Okuyama's raiders had gained control of Kadena and Yomitan airfields for that night and all of the next day, May 25. They had not; field operations were not suspended, and this novel operation, while not exactly a failure, worried the American command much less than the continuing "conventional" kamikaze attacks of Kikusui 7 and 8.

Except for minor attacks the next large-scale raid came May 24, initiating Kikusui 7. Planes were by now so short in the 5th Air Fleet that twenty Shirigaku twin-engine aircrew trainers comprised most of the assailants. That night and the next day, the twenty-fifth, about seventy Army planes sortied and inflicted

300

most of the damage incurred, wrecking destroyer-transports *Barry* and *Bates* and blowing a hole in the bottom of the destroyer *Stormes*. The destroyer was repairable, but the *Bates* and the *Barry* was decommissioned at the Kerama anchorage for later use as a kamikaze decoy.

After a day's pause the attack resumed at Kikusui 8 on May 27 and 28. This time most of the approximately eighty-five attackers, Army and Navy, struck at Okinawa after dark. On Picket Station 5 Commander C. J. Van Arsdall's *Anthony* and William W. Fitts' *Braine* fired on invisible attackers under full radar control. Gasoline fires on the water indicated several fell. At dawn a patrol of Army Thunderbolts (P-47's) from Ie Shima appeared over the station, but trouble with a low overcast moved the flight leader to request and to receive permission to secure. In just a few minutes bogies appeared on the radar screens of *Anthony* and *Braine*.

As two enemy planes burst from the overcast, the *Anthony*'s 5-inch salvos wiped out the lead machine. Subsequent bursts exploded behind the second, and although the 20 mm. and 40 mm. gunners knocked away chunks of metal, the plane cleared the destroyer's stacks at fifty feet, flew on a thousand yards, and crashed the *Braine* amidships. A third plane, thrown barely off course by gunfire, near-missed the *Anthony*, hurling motor parts, blazing gasoline, and the pilot's corpse onto the ship. "The pilot's flight jacket," writes Admiral Van Arsdall, recalling the incident, "was completely covered with small dolls, obviously handmade, all alike, black kimono with red sash."

The *Anthony* had received only a small dent and three men injured, but a fourth plane mangled the *Braine* by crashing the uptakes above the boiler rooms. As engineering and boiler compartments blazed and then flooded, the ship went dead. Sixty-six men perished, seventy-eight were injured, and the *Anthony* had to quench the *Braine*'s fires and take her in tow. Picket stations, obviously, were still no place for the fainthearted.

Improving weather the next day, May 28, brought many kamikaze contacts. At 6:50 A.M. four fast suiciders, probably from a flight of Frances bombers which had taken off from Kyushu three hours earlier, swooped in on destroyers *Drexler* and *Lowry*, which were manning Picket Station 15. Following doctrine, the ships swung broadside to the attack to unmask their batteries. Overhead, Marine pilots R. F. Bourne and J. B. Seaman banked their Corsairs northwest to meet the twin-engine planes which were approaching in a loose column at 7,000 feet. Picking the leader who had swung around the destroyers to attack from the southward, Seaman fired and hit the enemy in the cockpit but saw it plunge down to strike the *Drexler* a glancing blow topside. The plane's bomb did not explode and the crew extinguished the fires in a minute. Bourne attacked a second plane, and following the Frances through a bank, hit it in the left wing, engine, and cockpit. The machine lurched on a moment, then exploded.

Now disaster came. As Bourne's opponent burst apart, Seaman fired from 400 feet at the third bomber, and blasting it to pieces, then teamed with Bourne to attack the last Frances. Although both Marine lieutenants closed to a hundred feet, knocking metal off the plane, its pilot somehow retained control and slammed into the *Drexler*. As Bourne and Seaman, cursing futilely, pulled up, the *Drexler* exploded violently, shooting flames several hundred feet into the air. In a minute she had rolled over and sunk, taking down with her 158 men; another 51 were injured, including Commander R. L. Wilson, her skipper.

This lightning-fast disaster, inflicted despite a flawless performance by Seaman and Bourne, produced furrowed brows from Okinawa to Washington, D.C. In Washington fears arose that the Frances might have carried some dangerous new weapon, and twice Commander Wilson had to testify before a board of inquiry about the *Drexler*'s loss. The fears were groundless; a heavy bomb plus exploding magazines could inflict atrocities on a destroyer's hull.

At the beachhead other attackers hit three merchant ships and an attack transport, but none inflicted serious damage. Kikusui 8 then closed with a game of cat and mouse played out between kamikazes and a destroyer a few minutes after midnight on the twenty-eighth.

The ship was Lieutenant Commander John C. Jolly's U.S.S. *Shubrick* en route to Picket Station 16 fifty miles west of Hedo Misaki. "I well remember," writes Admiral Jolly, "the blackness of the night and the false feeling of its being too dark for kamikazes!" But some were there, probably from a group of eleven Shirigaku trainers that had left Kushira airfield. One, unaccountably showing running lights, appeared low on the water to starboard. Jolly slowed his ship, hoping to reduce wake and avoid detection, then increased to flank speed when he saw the pilot reverse course and head for him. Thirteen minutes after midnight the plane hit the destroyer's side over the after engine room. Thirty feet of deck plating blew away, nearly severing the deck of the ship. Power and communications failed, but Jolly's crew worked energetically to fight fires, control flooding, and— because the ship appeared to be dangerously unstable—to jettison topside weight. The *Shubrick* floated, but twenty-eight of its crew were hurt and thirty-two beyond help.

Though Admiral Ugaki had intended to continue the attacks, lack of planes, bad weather over Amami O Shima, and orders detaching General Sugahara's 6th Air Fleet from his command delayed Kikusui 9. Never as enthused as was the Navy about the defense of Okinawa, the Japanese Army command was no longer willing to permit Army planes to fly under Navy control.

Changes also occurred in the American high command. At midnight on May 27, the long rifles of the battleship *Missouri* swung toward Okinawa, jittered delicately on their mounts, then lobbed nine 16-inch shells at Ushijima's defenders. Thus did Admiral William F. Halsey signify his assumption of overall command of the Okinawa operation. Ray Spruance had performed ably, but Admiral Nimitz had adjudged that over two months of highly arduous duty were enough for any commander and staff. Ten days earlier he had replaced Kelly Turner for the same reason, placing Vice Admiral Harry W. Hill in immediate charge at the beachhead. The 5th Fleet was now the 3rd Fleet; T.F. 58 was T.F. 38. Spruance, Turner, and their staffs received a much-needed rest and then a new assignment—planning the invasion of Kyushu.

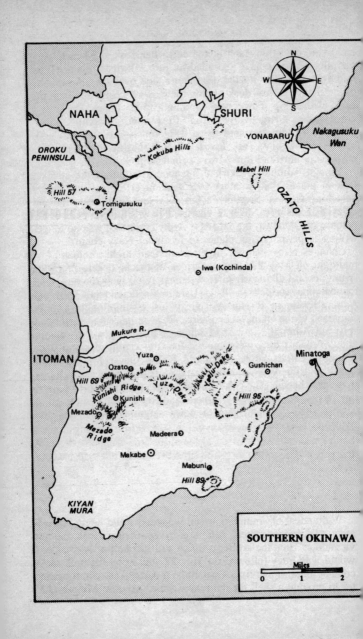

SOUTHERN OKINAWA

Miles
0   1   2

22

USHIJIMA RETREATS FROM SHURI

AT MIDNIGHT ON May 22, as rain began to beat down on Shuri Castle, General Ushijima, his staff, and senior commanders had met once more to debate alternative strategies. They could stay put in Shuri or retreat eleven miles south to Mabuni at the southern tip of the island and hold a new line across the Yaeju Dake–Yuza Dake escarpment. To stay longer in Shuri, the staff agreed, was impossible. Not only was the 10th Army about to break into the bastion, but the shrinking Shuri perimeter could not adequately shelter the 50,000 men it estimated Ushijima had left. The Mabuni area, in contrast, could be reached easily by all-weather roads running directly south and had enough natural and man-dug caves to hold the entire remaining force. The 24th Division, which had garrisoned the area before moving north to battle, had left some of its ammunition and weapons there. At the end of the conference Ushijima elected to retire to Mabuni.

I

Withdrawal of ammunition and wounded could begin immediately, Ushijima decreed, followed by communications and service units. Then the artillery, which still had half of its weapons, would withdraw, followed on May 29 and 30 by the bulk of combat units. Some troops would hold parts of the Shuri perimeter to provide a shell for the retreat. Rear Admiral Minoru Ota's

Navy troops—those that were not holding in the outskirts of Naha—would remain in place for the time being to defend Naha airfield and the Oroku Peninsula, thus denying to Buckner free use of Naha port. Ushijima and his staff would establish their new headquarters in a large natural cave under Hill 89 near Mabuni and right on the sea.

Had not ceiling-zero weather prevailed during most of the week following Ushijima's decision, his elaborate plan for withdrawal probably would have failed completely. As it was, air strikes and naval gunfire took a heavy toll of some of the retreating units and particularly of civilians, who had been ordered by Ushijima into the Chinen Peninsula. Partially clearing weather on May 26 revealed numerous columns both of troops and what appeared to be white-clad civilians on the roads leading south. American pilots strafing the troops noted in their after-action reports that some seemed to explode when hit, suggesting that they were carrying ammunition. At the end of the day intelligence officers more or less arbitrarily set the total of killed at five hundred, though in this instance it probably was much higher. Five tanks and an artillery piece also were accounted destroyed.

Yet American intelligence could make little sense out of the pilots' necessarily fleeting observations. To find white-clad columns moving south seemed appropriate because American propaganda leaflets dropped over Shuri had been urging the civilians to clear the area wearing white, so that attacking planes would not strafe them. Soldiers mingled with the civilians suggested a withdrawal from the Shuri line. But just before dark a column was spotted moving north from the extreme southern tip of Okinawa. The most likely conclusion seemed to be, reinforced by evidence, that the Shuri zone still was being strongly held, that Ushijima had decided to evacuate the civilians, to send south his wounded and battle-weary men, and to bring up to Shuri rested troops from the Mabuni area.

Once again American intelligence had missed, but it made little difference because bad weather was preventing both the 7th Division and the 6th Marine Division from pinching off the escape corridor from Shuri as well as sharply reducing interdiction by air and naval gunfire. The 24th Division was able to shuttle back and forth by day and night over the lightly paved roads its hundred carefully hoarded light trucks to haul munitions and equipment. A total zero ceiling at exactly the right time, on May 29 and 30, completely grounded American planes and allowed Ushijima's staff to note with satisfaction that the withdrawal of the combat troops was "... proceeding in good order without any signs of confusion due to slackened enemy pressure."

Aggregate losses during the withdrawal were nonetheless heavy. When Ushijima was finally able to count his troops once more, he found that he had only 30,000 of the 50,000 that had been at Shuri. Discounting perhaps as many as the 5,000 Buckner's 10th Army estimated as comprising the rear guard, this meant that at least 15,000 more had been lost during the withdrawal—providing that Ushijima was correct in his 50,000-man estimate.

The great tragedy, however, was in the very heavy loss of civilian life. Too frequently civilian columns came under naval gunfire or strafing attack with horrible consequences. Recalls Tokuyu Higashionna, then a teacher at the Nakagusuku school, "The trip from Kochinda to Kyan leaves an impression words are inadequate to describe... utter horror... dead everywhere... everywhere." He saw dead children on the backs of living mothers and living children lying on dead mothers. "It was literally hell."

One of the youngest of the retiring soldiers was Kome Hamishiro, a sixteen-year-old middle school boy who had been drafted into a signal communications unit. He left with his companions on May 25 in a heavy downpour, bearing a 6.5 mm. Model 38 Arisaka rifle that weighed 10 pounds, plus two grenades, communication tools, and such food as he could carry in addition. His group moved only at night and then carefully to avoid stumbling over the bodies that littered the road. Hungry, scared, wet, totally miserable, they found on arrival at their new positions that their lot had scarcely improved. Bombs and shells still pelted down; every hole in the ground was occupied by either soldiers or civilians; food was practically nonexistent and dangerous to acquire by forage from the sugarcane and sweet potato fields.

The irony of the civilian retreat from Shuri was that it was so unnecessary. Had the people done what the American leaflets had recommended many more would have lived. They had been told to wear white, to travel in groups, to stay away from Japanese soldiers, and to assemble at "the nearest point on the [west] seacoast highway." Their failure to heed these instructions and their conviction that the Americans would kill them caused too many to continue south with the Japanese forces, either to die on the roads or in inadequate open shelters in the crowded Mabuni region. Those that obeyed the 32nd Army's order and made the Chinen area were fortunate, provided they stayed there, for the fighting then bypassed them and they evaded the naval and air bombardment. How many civilians perished in the retreat from Shuri can only be conjectured, but losses can hardly have been much less than the estimated 15,000 military deaths.

II

The emergence of a hot sun on May 28 signaled the beginning of the end of General Mud's domination of the Okinawan battlefield. His sticky presence lingered, however, as intermittent showers and low ceilings during the next two days continued to delay the drying of the ground. A general American offensive could not begin until May 30 and then without the tanks, which remained out of action for another full week.

Westward from Conical Hill the GI's of the 96th Division jumped off early on the thirtieth against their bitter nemesis, the stubborn hill complex that included Tiger, Charlie, Oboe, and several others. No one expected an easy time, for the Japanese had been resisting savagely just the day before, but to the infantry's amazement and relief they strolled virtually unopposed across terrain that had been spouting death hours before. Enemy pockets remained only on Charlie Hill and Tiger; these fought till annihilation.

Hen and Hector Hills were different. There Japanese were present in force and full of fight. Against them Companies F and G of the 382nd combined in a dual attack. In the lead, climbing Hen Hill to probe the Japanese position, was a five-man team from Company G which included Pfc Clarence B. Craft from San Bernardino, California, a replacement who had joined the outfit during the 96th's rest period a few days before. The five had gotten but a short way when a heavy barrage of rifle, machine gun, and mortar fire wounded three and pinned Craft and the other man to the ground. After a few moments Craft jumped up, rushed the hill, and drove the Japanese from the crest with accurately thrown grenades. Continuing, he ran on up, straddled a six-foot-deep zigzag trench just over the crest, and with more grenades and his M-1 drove the enemy to cover. Two of Craft's G Company mates now came up, soon joined by others. Standing erect Craft continued to toss grenades which his buddies passed up to him and pointed to places in the trench for others who remained below the crest to throw. The Japanese replied in kind, and for a while grenades flew back and forth over Craft's head as he stood exposed and alone on the crest.

Running down the enemy trench Craft pumped rifle bullets into the crouching defenders—many of whom seemed dazed— knocked out a heavy machine gun with a grenade, and reached the mouth of a cave in which several Japanese had taken cover. Someone brought him a satchel charge, which he tossed into the mouth of the cave. When it failed to explode, Craft went in, retrieved it, relit the fuse, and threw it back into the cave, blasting shut the opening. In his whirlwind attack, which General Hodge commended later as the most remarkable he had heard of in a lifetime of soldiering, Craft had paused just once, to pick up the sword of a fallen Japanese officer. He did so, he explained later, because he knew his Deadeye buddies "... would have stripped that field clean of souvenirs by the time I got back."

Craft had personally accounted for twenty-five to thirty of the defenders and single-handed had broken the foe's resistance on Hen Hill, which together with Hector was fully secured by afternoon. He suffered not a scratch and lived to receive from President Harry S. Truman the nation's highest award, the Congressional Medal of Honor.

Altogether, the 96th Division gained 1,200 yards in its attack of the 30th and by nightfall had pushed elements as far as Bard Hill, 700 yards west of Shuri. Other divisions did equally well. The 77th Division polished off Jane and Tom Hills by nightfall, though on Dorothy Hill the 307th Infantry collided with a strong enemy holding force that required two days to subdue.

Already, Shuri Castle had fallen. On May 29 Captain Julian D. Dusenbury's A Company of the 5th Marines, probing the enemy's lines in the Wana area, had found an opening and had broken through to overrun the ruins of the castle, though it lay within the 77th Division's zone of action. Atop the shattered castle wall, Dusenbury, a patriotic South Carolinian, had raised the Stars and Bars of the Confederacy, soon to be replaced by the division's battle colors. Dusenbury and his men had to stay put for two days, with enemy soldiers still all around, and narrowly escaped being hit by an air strike directed at the area by the 77th Division, which was unaware at first of their presence. Their coup drew a rather bitter complaint from the 77th, which felt, understandably, that it should have had the honor of taking the castle.

On May 30 and 31 the 1st Marine Division cracked completely through the Wana area, now abandoned by the enemy, and tied in with the 96th Division south of Shuri. For its part the 96th had contacted the 7th Division, which finally had taken Mabel Hill south of Shuri after getting support from a platoon of tanks and self-propelled guns. The 6th Marine Division, advancing east from Naha, encountered much stronger resistance than the others, but by June 1 had completely broken through a chain of hilltops manned by naval troops and rear guards to reach the north bank of the Kokuba River and estuary. The advance of the Deadeyes and marines had completely pinched out of action the hard-fighting and casualty-ridden 77th Division which could at last take its turn at rest and replenishment.

Atop and west of Mabel Hill Colonel Finn's 32nd Infantry found clear evidence that the enemy's withdrawal was neither forced nor panicky. Though Japanese corpses lay in profusion, mostly victims of mortar and artillery fire, strewn equipment was notably scarce. The survivors had obviously withdrawn in good order and had taken their gear with them. Throughout the Shuri area it was the same story, a story that told General Buckner that the entire 32nd Army had successfully evacuated its main defense zone, escaping southward—except for appointed rear guards—to live and fight another day.

The admiration of Colonel Cecil Nist, General Hodge's intelligence officer, for General Ushijima's feat was unfeigned and open. In his intelligence summary for the week Nist wrote, "Although the forces of General Ushijima are destined to defeat, his conduct of the defense of Okinawa had been such that his spirit can join those of his ancestors and rest in peace."

Curious GI's and marines poking for souvenirs about the ruins of Shuri and Shuri Castle found little to interest them. An estimated 200,000 rounds of artillery, plus some hundreds of bombs, had fallen on both. Aside from the walls and bell tower of Shuri's little concrete Methodist Church, built in 1937, virtually nothing was recognizable to suggest a town of 17,500 population had stood there. Shellfire had obliterated the streets and reduced all the houses to churned heaps of stone. Even the twenty-foot thick walls of Shuri Castle lay in ruins. In addition to innumerable hits from lighter ordnance, the castle had suffered from the 16-inch guns of the U.S.S. *Colorado*. Everywhere about the castle and town lay unexploded duds, twisted fragments from heavy naval shells, and countless rusting pellets from thousands of rounds from mortars. Blanketing the whole area was the smell of death, of rotting human flesh disintegrating in caves and dugouts below. Yet directly under the castle was Ushijima's headquarters cave entirely intact. With an inferno exploding over his head, this Japanese commander, undetected by his enemy, had carried out one of the most skillful retreats of World War II.

III

To the American fleet offshore of Okinawa the rain and bad weather of May 29, 30, and 31 had contributed to one welcome relief, the absence of kamikazes. But with the resumption of better weather in early June the hell-birds returned, and although Kikusui 9, from June 3 through 7, was much the weakest of the series, it nevertheless was bad enough. To the sailors the various attacks of the TEN-Go Operation had seemed like a continuous process, for hardly a day had passed for over two months without a suicide dive somewhere. To them Kikusui 9—as in the case of the other Kikusui operations—merely represented an intensification.

Admiral Ugaki had intended to launch Kikusui 9 immediately after the end of the eighth attack on May 28, but the bad weather at Okinawa, the lack of suitable planes, the need of establishing new working arrangements with the 6th Air Army—now detached from naval command—had combined with American air attacks on Kyushu to delay a general attack several days.

Commencement in mid-May of sweeps over Kyushu by U.S. Army P-47 Thunderbolts of the 318th Fighter Group operating from Ie Shima gave Ugaki's staff additional problems in assembling planes. At least two of the long-range Thunderbolts usually heckled Kanoya airfield every night, although being without radar, their pilots had trouble finding their prey. Others, sometimes joined by Marine Corsairs with extra drop-tanks, swept Kyushu by day, hoping to catch enemy aircraft shuttling between

P-47

the island's fifty-odd airfields. Their work compelled Ugaki to order Zero and George fighters to fly intercept missions, thus limiting their availability to escort the poorly trained kamikaze pilots to Okinawa. On several occasions dogfights erupted.

One fight of considerable tactical interest took place on May 28 between eight Thunderbolts of the 19th Fighter Squadron led by Captain John E. Vogt and twenty-eight Zeros. On spotting the Americans over Kagoshima Bay a thousand feet below at 15,000 feet, the Japanese leader sought to use the fast-climbing characteristics of the light and agile Zeros to get above Vogt and maneuver into the protection of a Lufberry circle—a tactic that would enable each Japanese pilot to protect the tail of the plane ahead. Discerning the enemy's intent Vogt slammed the throttle of his P-47 wide open and depressed the water-injection switch to give his engine war-emergency power. Climbing steeply the powerful Thunderbolts drew above their opponents at 28,000 feet, then dove to attack, forcing the Zeros to scatter. Vogt himself claimed five that fell, flaming, into Kagoshima Bay. Intelligence officers later credited the squadron with six kills and two "probables," and for his courage and skill in leadership Vogt received the Distinguished Flying Cross. Japanese 5th Air Fleet sources record that on this day fifty-seven Zeros intercepted American raids with four of the Zeros lost, making it one of the few occasions when there was so much as moderate agreement between American claims and officially reported Japanese losses.

The opening installment of much-delayed Kikusui 9 began on June 3 when 64 Zeros set out to accompany 6 old Val Navy dive bombers and 31 Army special attack planes. This group encountered defending Marine Corsairs, whose pilots claimed the shoot-down of 35 Japanese planes in a wide-ranging series of battles. Four pilots of VMF-323 out of Kadena had the liveliest time, engaging 12 Zeros of a group of 25. The Japanese pilots were aggressive, and for this stage of the war surprisingly skilled. One swung onto the tail of Lieutenant C. A. Dolezel's Corsair and thumped 20 mm. and 7.7 mm. slugs into the armor behind its pilot, one shot giving Dolezel's head a bruise by striking directly behind it. Dolezel got away, however, and in revenge blasted down a Zero while his flight mates were claiming 8 more. Interception efforts this day appear to have been exceptionally successful, for no ships recorded attacks.

Despite this unpromising beginning, Ugaki's 5th Air Fleet and the Army's cooperating 3rd Air Division continued the strikes on June 6, launching a handful of Army planes plus six Paul floatplanes from Kanoya. In the early evening one plane, probably a Paul, hit the fast minelayer *J. William Ditter,* blasting a large hole in its side and sending it under tow to the Kerama anchorage. Of the *Ditter*'s crew ten died, twenty-seven suffered wounds.

On the next day the kamikazes came again, but in very light strength. The 5th Air Fleet staff now estimated that 1,270 Japanese aircraft remained on Kyushu—a sizable number—but that 700 needed repair and only 570 were serviceable. Most of those flying had to be reserved to intercept attacks from Okinawa, from Iwo Jima, and from the fast carriers, leaving just 46 available for offensive use against Okinawa. Since most of these were earmarked for conventional attack, only a handful remained for the kamikaze pilots to fly.

This time their target was Commander C. J. Van Arsdall's U.S.S. *Anthony,* operating on Radar Picket Station 1. The Kikusui flyers came in the late afternoon, very low, on the starboard side of the ship. To the surprise of the crew the first pilot pulled up when nicked by gunfire and bailed out, an act which availed him little when his parachute streamed and plunged him into the sea. Another plane dove in, but the 40 mm. gunners of the destroyer shot it up, and it crashed thirty feet from the ship, dousing it first with blazing gasoline and then with saltwater that washed the fuel away. The concussion of the crash knocked four men overboard, but nobody perished except the kamikaze pilot. So ended Kikusui 9, by far the most feeble of the major attacks.

IV

The American change of command may have in part explained the feebleness of Kikusui 9. When on May 27 Admiral William F. Halsey took over the 5th Fleet and T.F. 38, he brought with him an aggressive philosophy in keeping with his restless, dynamic character. Whereas Admiral Spruance had interpreted his mission as close support for Okinawa, keeping fighters from his fast carriers over the beachhead, Halsey believed in attacking the kamikazes at their source, Kyushu. At once he ordered attacks.

On June 2 and 3 Task Group 38.4 under the command of Rear Admiral A. W. Radford hammered Kyushu, while T.G. 38.1 under Rear Admiral "Jocko" Clark supported Okinawa. Halsey detached one of his task groups to replenish and refit at Leyte; to bolster Okinawa he ordered up from the Philippines Marine Air Group 14's land-based Corsairs, after making certain that Okinawa's airfields had room for them. But Halsey, who had fought the Japanese successfully from the opening day of the war, now was to encounter an old enemy that once before had given him serious trouble.

Before the Okinawan operation began many aerologists had

expected that at some time during the operation the Okinawan invaders would experience a typhoon, and that the storm would at the least seriously disrupt unloading at the beachhead. In late May a tropical disturbance was located off the Philippines that developed into a small but dangerous typhoon, measuring about thirty miles from edge to edge of its rotating, hundred-knot winds. Fortunately, it veered away from Okinawa—and into the path of Halsey's T.F. 38.

Halsey was gun-shy of typhoons. In November, 1944, one of those capricious storms had caught his T.F. 38 off Leyte capsizing and sinking three destroyers and damaging dozens of ships. On the evening of June 4, therefore, he steamed T.F. 38 southeast to clear the storm's path.

All went well until late that night. The amphibious force flagship *Ancon,* en route from Leyte to Okinawa, picked up the "eye" of the typhoon on its excellent SP high resolution radar, reported this historic finding, believed to be the first radar fix on a typhoon ever recorded, and maneuvered to avoid the storm. *Ancon's* report placed the storm uncomfortably close to T.F. 38 and caused Halsey and his staff to anxiously reconsider their evasion strategy. Since wave conditions are much less violent on the eastern semicircle of northward-bound typhoons, Halsey at 1:00 A.M. on June 5 ordered T.F. 38 to reverse course, hoping to steer across the path of the whirling little horror into the safer semicircle.

Worsening weather soon made it evident that the typhoon's exact location had been incorrectly estimated. The wind gauge on the big carrier *Lexington* jumped from twenty-seven to forty-one knots in just fifteen minutes. Seas rose to mountainous proportion. Vice Admiral John McCain, T.F. 38's tactical commander, now ordered his ships to change course due north, but as it turned out every ship in T.F. 38 got rough treatment. Many of Admiral Clark's task group ran squarely through the "eye" of the storm, a weird experience for all hands, for the wind suddenly died from over a hundred knots to just twenty-six, then rose abruptly from the other direction. Directly overhead a tiny patch of sky showed amid clouds swirling violently in counterclockwise fashion. Destroyers rolled fifty to sixty degrees and more, but because all had been fueled and sat low in the water none capsized and only one suffered crippling damage.

Probably because the sweep of the waves was widely spaced

from crest to crest, the heavy ships of T.F. 38 suffered most. At about 6:30 A.M. two huge waves bore down on the U.S.S. *Pittsburgh* and slammed the heavy cruiser off course, lifting her so that the water dropped away from under her bow as the wave passed. With a rending crack a full hundred feet of the bow broke away by its own weight, as Captain John E. Gingrich, the ship's skipper, watched in dumbfounded horror. At once he ordered the ship's engines reversed, and the bow, which had threatened to smash the starboard side of the ship, drifted clear. Not a man was in the bow because all hands had been ordered to battle stations just fifteen minutes before; the sixty sailors who berthed in the severed bow section lost their personal gear but not their lives. Frantic work by the crew to shore up the forward end of the ship saved worse trouble. A few days later the fleet tug *Munsee* located the still-floating bow of the cruiser and sent a classic message: "Have sighted the suburb of the *Pittsburgh* and taken it in tow." The bow arrived at Guam not long after the bulk of the heavy cruiser.

No other ship suffered so horrendous an experience, but the cruisers *Baltimore* and *Miami* had their bows twisted, and the large carriers *Bennington* and *Hornet* had thirty feet of their flight decks smashed and drooped downward, which made them look as if some giant had punched each in the nose. In these and other carriers eighty-three planes had been smashed or swept overside.

Halsey was not about to allow a storm to stop his strikes against Kyushu. Immediately afterward he dispatched Radford's T.G. 38.4 to attack Ugaki's airfields once more, while his other carriers, including damaged *Bennington* and *Hornet*, flew combat air patrol and strikes over Okinawa. Ordered to fly a search to locate a pair of hospital ships from a convoy dispersed by the storm, Admiral Clark did so in a unique way. He ordered the damaged *Hornet* to back at sixteen knots and launch its planes over the stern of the ship, since air currents swirling about the damaged bow made conventional launch dangerous. After locating the hospital ships the planes landed normally, dropping in over the stern while the ship steamed ahead.

The typhoon almost cost Halsey his job. A court of inquiry convened at Guam drew an unfavorable parallel between Halsey's experience in the November, 1944, typhoon and the more recent one. It termed his course reversal to avoid the typhoon "ill-advised" and recommended that consideration be given to assigning Admirals Halsey and McCain to "other duty." Secretary of the Navy James V. Forrestal at first intended to retire Halsey but refrained on the ground that the removal of so popular a fighting man would impair public morale in the United States and raise it in Japan. Halsey, for his part, rejoined with some justice that he had successfully evaded other typhoons, and that on this occasion the weather reporting services had served him ill. His recommendation to have planes continuously track dangerous tropical storms was taken up, but not until after Japan's defeat.

His second bout with a typhoon ended the colorful admiral's adventures off Okinawa. Halsey now withdrew the fast carriers, rightly confident that the escort carriers of Admiral Harry Hill and the Marine and Army pilots based on Okinawa and Ie Shima could deal with Ugaki's weakened forces. Halsey wanted to rest his pilots and repair his ships for sweeps throughout the Japanese home islands.

V

Task Force 57, the British contribution to the Okinawan campaign, had preceded Halsey's retirement from the fight. Beginning on May 8 Admiral Rawlings' big carriers had again taken up the job of pounding down the airfields at Ishigaki and Miyako Jima with air strikes and gun bombardments. As before, they fought a private war with the Formosa-based 1st Air Fleet. On May 29 a canny Zero pilot escorting four suiciders lured away the defending Seafires of the combat air patrol, enabling the kamikazes to dive on H.M.S. *Victorious* and *Formidable*. The first merely glanced from the armored flight deck of the *Victorious* into the sea, but the second struck near the forward elevator, holing the deck and disabling the lift. Gunners picked off the third, but the fourth, selecting the *Formidable* as its target, hit the carrier aft and fired planes parked on the deck. The impact popped a rivet on the armored flight deck, permitting burning gasoline to trickle into the hangar deck below. Jack-tars quickly extinguished fires topside and below but eighteen planes burned. Thanks to the armored flight decks neither carrier had to discontinue operations.

Rawlings continued strikes until May 28, when a progressive

loss of planes, mostly to accident, plus mounting evidence that the Japanese had stopped flying from Ishigaki and Miyako, caused him to pull out for Leyte Gulf. Task Force 57 had proven its capacity to operate in the Pacific and had given the U.S. Navy an object lesson in the value of the armored flight deck on a carrier.

The American escort carriers that periodically had relieved T.F. 57 were from escort carrier (baby flattop) group T.G. 51.1 commanded by Rear Admiral C. T. Durgin. Three units of these little carriers had been in the thick of the fight from the beginning, adding FM-2 "Wildcat" fighters to Okinawa's fighter defenses, flying boring but necessary antisubmarine patrols with their embarked TBM Avenger squadrons, and using both types of aircraft to attack ground targets on Okinawa.

Their hard-flying pilots faced many hazards, not the least that of landing planes on the small flight decks of these converted merchant ships. One hapless Wildcat pilot was shot down three times by "friendly" antiaircraft fire. Kamikazes sometimes attacked the jeep carriers, but their normal operating area southeast of Okinawa was hard for the devil-birds to reach, especially those launched from Kyushu. Several had close calls—an alert gun crew on the U.S.S. *Fanshaw Bay* blew the wing from a plane just astern of the ship—but none was sunk and only one, the *Sangamon*, seriously damaged. After the large carriers left the Okinawa area the escort carriers remained, receiving little of the publicity but many of the dangers that the glamour ships, the fast carriers, had faced.

23

USHIJIMA'S FINAL STAND

THE EARLY MORNING hours of June 1 found the GI's of Major General Archibald V. Arnold's 7th Hourglass Division finishing their instant coffee, buckling on gear, checking the actions of BAR's and M-1's, preparing for what everyone hoped would be a nonstop push to Okinawa's southern tip. General Buckner still believed that Ushijima had withdrawn too late; that the 10th Army would overrun the canny Japanese before Ushijima could make a stand. "It's all over now but cleaning up pockets of resistance," he had predicted to correspondents the day before. "This doesn't mean there won't be stiff fighting but [Ushijima] won't be able to organize another line."

I

Beginning on June 1, Buckner's drive to finish the 32nd Army jumped off, GI's on the left, marines on the right as before. Arnold's 7th Division struck due south past the base of the Chinen Peninsula, its immediate goal to prevent Ushijima's forces from escaping into Chinen's rugged hills. The 96th Division pushed toward high ground above the road center of Iwa, while the 1st Marine Division crossed the Kokuba River, secured a bridgehead, and prepared to seal off the Oroku Peninsula in the same way that the 7th Division was isolating the Chinen Peninsula on the opposite side of Okinawa.

319

Rain resuming on the night of June 1–2 swelled streams and muddied roads, but at first did not interfere materially with the new drive south. Nor were the Japanese rear guard units as difficult as the superb 62nd Division had been earlier in the campaign. Often the retreating Japanese seemed poorly trained in elementary maneuver and concealment, tended to shoot prematurely at advancing patrols, and if flushed from positions, ran until cut down. Thus could "Hoss" Mitchell, still alive, unhurt, and in command of his L Company "lardtails," grab a machine gun to fell seventeen enemies crossing a skyline on June 3. The day previous Staff Sergeant Lowell E. McSpadden of Company E had slipped behind two defenders manning an outpost, tapped one on the shoulder, and dispatched both with two quick shots from his .45 pistol. His contemptuous derring-do reflected the disdain that some veteran Deadeye infantrymen had developed for General Ushijima's ill-trained replacements.

II

In the meantime, the 6th Marine Division was embarking on the important secondary mission of seizing the Oroku Peninsula, which jutted into the water just south of Naha. Until it was cleared Naha Harbor would not be usable and engineers could not begin reconstructing its piers and basins and removing sunken Japanese shipping.

Guessing that the enemy's strongest defenses would be across the base of the peninsula facing landward, Geiger decided to outflank them by landing General Shepherd's 6th Marine Division across two small beaches at Oroku's northern tip. He knew that Shepherd had only seventy-two amphibious tractors (LVT's) serviceable because so many had worn out hauling supplies overland during the rains, but he calculated these would suffice to shuttle in the division. Preparations went rapidly, and by June 3, the 4th Marine Regiment was ready to embark.

The defenders of the Oroku Peninsula consisted of the remnant of a force under Rear Admiral Minoru Ota, who commanded all Japanese naval forces on the island. Once nearly 10,000 strong, counting attached Okinawans, Ota's Navy troops had been committed piecemeal to other actions until only some 2,000 were left. They were, nevertheless, well armed with more than two hundred machine guns and light cannon taken from antiaircraft positions and wrecked planes.

On the afternoon of June 3, with H Hour set for the next morning, Lieutenant Colonel Denig's 6th Tank Battalion boarded LCT's, ships big and well stocked enough to serve them a supper of meat, vegetables, olives, and catchup—a welcome change from their usual canned C ration diet. Afterward, lounging on deck, they listened to the Okinawa Armed Forces Radio rebroadcast several regular Sunday night radio programs: Jack Benny, Edgar Bergen and Charlie McCarthy, the Great Gildersleeve. When Lena Horne sang, "My Country 'Tis of Thee," conversation flagged and the men stared pensively across the darkening water at ships etched against the fading light in the west. When full darkness came the tankers curled up in GI blankets and ponchos on steel decks, making themselves as comfortable as possible. Tomorrow would bring another battle and one of the last amphibious landings of World War II.

At 4:45 A.M. the world abruptly burst apart with the crash of naval gunfire. At first light LVT's started for shore, carrying the 4th Marines. Shortly before 6:00 A.M. the first amphtracs waddled across the beaches, and the lead platoons jumped out and jog-trotted toward the low hills.

For the first three days the advance went fairly easily, with the marines overrunning Naha airfield. Then they discovered that Ota had concentrated his men in a rectangular area about a ridgeline running from Hill 57 west of Oroku town to Tomigusuku near his headquarters cave at the southeast corner of the peninsula. In this jumbled region every hill and ridge was fortified in a coordinated defense similar to that encountered earlier in Item Pocket by the 27th Division. With his full force of 10,000 Admiral Ota might have stalled the marines for weeks; as it was he held out for ten rugged days.

The fighting was strictly "blowtorch and corkscrew," and the marines would not have made it without the aggressive tankers of Colonel Denig's battalion. They suffered losses, even though Ota lacked 47 mm. antitank guns. One tank fell victim to a point-blank shot from an 8-inch coast defense gun. Twenty-nine others were disabled by mines or satchel charges. Steady, hard fighting compressed Ota into a smaller and smaller area, until on June 11 he found himself squeezed into a small section between Oroku town and Tomigusuku. To General Ushijima at 32nd

321

Army headquarters, now located near Mabuni, he radioed a final message:

Enemy tank groups are now attacking our cave headquarters. The Naval Base Force is dying gloriously at this moment. . . . We are grateful for your past kindnesses and pray for the success of the Army.

The next day, June 12, saw the breakup. The 4th and 29th Marines advanced until only one hill lay between them and Naha Harbor. Sixth Marine Division losses had been tragically high, 1,608 killed and wounded, proportionately greater than before Shuri and comparable to those of the 27th Division at Item Pocket.

After mopping up June 13 the marines undertook a special search for Admiral Ota's headquarters, finally locating it under a hill near Tomigusuku. Though not the largest in the Oroku complex, what the marines called "Admiral's Hill" had a pair of main tunnels passing 300 yards entirely through it. Dozens of corridors ran at right angles and in long, sweeping curves. The cave complex was equipped with electricity, hot and cold running water, quarters for officers and enlisted men, a communications center, and hospital facilities. So elaborate was it that an American patrol took two days to find Admiral Ota's corpse which was in a concrete-lined room at the center of the complex.

Ota and five of his officers, including Captain Maikawa, Captain Hanada, and Commander Tanamachi, all were lying on a Japanese-style sleeping platform, their bodies obviously arranged by aides, feet outboard from the wall. Each wore a freshly pressed uniform, with sword and naval dress saber slung from a Sam Browne style military belt. Each lay on his back, throat slit, hands behind the head. According to a prisoner they had taken drugs before the gruesome finale.

III

The rain that had interfered with the Oroku landing also had hampered the advance south toward Okinawa's tip. Supply still gave difficulties as the advance continued on June 5. Ahead lay the enemy's final defense line, anchored atop interconnected ridges and escarpments extending completely across Okinawa. A solid wall of coral faced Buckner's 10th Army.

On the wall's east side two imposing terrain features, Hill 95 and the Yaeju Dake escarpment, confronted the 7th Division. Hill 95, which terminated on the east coast in a sheer 300-foot cliff, was high, bold, and rough, a small escarpment of itself. Behind it a broken coral plateau ran southeastward two miles to Mabuni and to Hill 89, under which General Ushijima maintained his new headquarters in a huge natural cave. Between Hill 95 and the Yaeju Dake a V-shaped valley containing three small towns rose at the apex of the V to Hill 155, which stood slightly higher than the broken plateau behind and to either side of it. Under this hill the 44th Brigade's commander, Major General Shigeru Suzuki, maintained his headquarters. Though a natural attack route, the valley was a welter of broken coral easily defensible from the higher ground at either flank and Hill 155 at the head.

On the western side of the valley the Yaeju Dake escarpment rose in an extended semicircle to become a 170-foot cliff. About half lay in the 7th Division's zone, the rest in the path of the 96th Division. A dominant feature 60 feet above the escarpment's rim was the Yaeju Dake proper, which the Deadeyes called "the Big Apple" because of its shape. Rising in two shelves, a massive saddle lay between it and the Yuza Dake, another little peak. From the Yuza Dake the escarpment sloped off westward along Kunishi Ridge to terminate near the sea just south of Itoman.

At no point was Ushijima's final line vulnerable. Nearly everywhere Buckner's troops would have to cross exposed terrain through enemy fire to attack high ground that in places became a vertical cliff every whit as awesome as the Urasoe-Mura escarpment. General Ushijima had to count on this line holding. There was no further range of hills to retreat to. In a final, summary order he admonished his troops:

... The present position will be defended to the death, even to the last man. Needless to say, retreat is forbidden. All troops disposed in depth will lose no opportunity to successively strengthen this principal zone of resistance.

The Japanese commander's main problem was that he lacked enough first-class fighting men to effectively man this escarpment line. A muster counted approximately 30,000, of whom 12,000 were in the 24th Division, 7,000 in the 62nd Division, 3,000 in the 44th Brigade, and 8,000 in miscellaneous units. Only a fifth of these men were combat trained, the bulk being service troops of Okinawan *boetai*. In placing his units Ushijima put the 24th Division, his strongest, on the Yaeju and Yuza Dake and along Kunishi Ridge to the west coast. On Hill 95 he placed the 44th Brigade. In the rear, with his surviving artillery and a few service units, he placed his 62nd Division as Army reserve.

It took a full week for the GI's of the 7th and 96th divisions and the 1st Division Marines to reach Ushijima's final line. Resumption of the rains, sodden ground, swollen streams, and mired roads made the supply problem acute. Tanks had to wait until roads dried and bridges could go in across a number of rivulets. By June 6 the soldiers had advanced to within a thousand yards of the enemy, but then they had to pause until June 9 while supplies and munitions accumulated. This same day found the 5th and 7th Marines at the Mukue Gawa, a stream north of Itoman, preparing to advance through strong enemy outpost positions to formidable Kunishi Ridge.

Though overall combat losses had been light, June 5 had brought grief to the Deadeyes. A Japanese machine gunner on a bypassed hill had put a bullet through the heart of Colonel Edwin T. May, commander of the 383rd Infantry. Described by his divisional commander, Major General Jim Bradley, as "the finest soldier I have ever known," May had stood exposed once too often at his C.P. Posthumously he received a Distinguished Service Cross.

By evening on June 8 General Arnold believed that he had enough supplies amassed to allow the 7th Division to strike an initial blow the next morning. He planned to use his 32nd Infantry along the east coast and his 17th Infantry further inland to seize Hill 95 and the eastern end of the Yaeju Dake. A frontal attack was mandatory; Ushijima could not be outflanked. On its seaward side Hill 95 was vertical, and in the 17th Infantry's sector the Yaeju Dake rose into cliffs. First necessity, however, was to seize an 800-yard-long coral hogback projecting forward from the line which led up toward Hill 95 from along the coast.

At 7:30 A.M. on June 9 Captain Robert Washnok's Company C of the 32nd Infantry moved against the hogback to begin two of its worst days on Okinawa. The coral contained literally thousands of niches to hide enemy riflemen and machine gunners, was highly porous and resistant to shell and mortar fire, and so sharp as to make crawling torture for the infantry. Defending was at least a company of infantry.

Washnok's GI's quickly discovered they could not lift their heads up; every time they tried it they drew fire. After losing five killed and twelve wounded, they had to give up for the day and try again the next morning. This time Captain Washnok expanded his front, sending one platoon down among rocks near the sea. All day his men fought for one rock after another. One man would stick his head up, squeeze off a couple of shots, and then another would take his turn. At a cost of five more killed and another twenty-one wounded, the unit secured the ridge. But the ridge proved to be useless as a means of getting onto Hill 95. No feasible method of advance across a small, fire-swept saddle between ridge and hill could be found.

In the meantime, Colonel Finn, the 32nd Infantry's commander, had noticed that some Okinawan civilians had descended the near-vertical face of Hill 95 along a narrow path. Conferring with his subordinate commanders, Finn decided to work a flame tank of Company C of the 713th Flame Tank Battalion close to the cliff to burn out the path and cliff top using a hose attachment to its flame gun. Company C's commander, six-foot-four-inch Captain Tony Niemeyer, had daringly used the flame hose to sear pillboxes in the path of Washnok's GI's, thus demonstrating simultaneously the practicality of the attachment, which was a new device, and his own personal courage.

Ordering Washnok to hold in place, Finn on June 11 sent Niemeyer up Hill 95 via the Okinawan path at the nozzle of a 200-foot flame hose with Lieutenant Frank A. Davis, a platoon leader of B Company. Davis' men dragged the hose along the steep trail behind them. Observers below literally held their breaths, for although mortars, artillery, and machine guns were pounding Hill 95 it seemed certain that Japanese snipers must shoot the totally exposed men from its face. Forty-five minutes of physically punishing work brought Niemeyer and Davis to a small ledge just below the top. Neither was hit nor were any of Davis' platoon, strung out on the trail below.

Niemeyer first sprayed the hill above to discourage a possible enemy reception committee, then scrambled onto the top and burned the area as far as his flame would reach. Right behind

325

came Davis' platoon followed quickly by Captain Dallas D. Thomas and the rest of B Company. Moving fast, the infantrymen cleared the hillcrest on either side of the trail, then shoved south across the rough plateau for 200 yards before encountering twenty to thirty Japanese holed up in a large pile of coral rock. Two platoons of A Company joined, and by evening on June 11 a secure perimeter had been organized, giving Colonel Finn a firm lodgment on the extreme eastern end of General Ushijima's terminal defense line. Captain Thomas' men were delighted with the success of what they called "Mickey Finn's scorched earth policy" and greatly impressed with the sheer grit of Niemeyer.

But Niemeyer was not through. The next day his tanks began burning their way up a road leading along the base of and around the west end of Hill 95. He also used his flame hose to sear a pair of troublesome pillboxes on the hillcrest. By day's end tanks could ascend the hill.

In the meantime, Colonel Francis T. Pachler's 17th Infantry had been having their troubles with the east side of the Yaeju Dake escarpment and the jumbled valley that lay between it and Hill 95. Pachler's basic difficulty was that his men had no natural cover to shield their approach across the valley before the escarpment. On June 9 Lieutenant Colonel Lee Wallace's 3rd Battalion had attacked by dint of crawling through rice paddies on their bellies, sometimes with noses underwater to escape enemy grazing fire. But a mere handful of men had managed to reach high ground and prepare an all-around defense. Further west, where the broad face of the escarpment rose abruptly 170 feet from the valley floor, Major Maynard Weaver's 1st Battalion got no farther than the base of the cliff.

To resolve his dilemma Colonel Pachler elected to try a night attack. Hopefully the Japanese would not be expecting one; his men needed darkness and poor visibility to make their approach; and in the interim tanks and self-propelled guns would have an opportunity to shell every opening visible in the escarpment's face. To insure no slip-ups Pachler had his commanders study carefully their routes of approach, using low-level, oblique aerial photos. The men were not reluctant to make the night attack. As Major Weaver explained, they had been "... looking at the escarpment so long that they were anxious to get on top so they could look at something else." To insure surprise the artillery would remain silent during the advance, but Pachler had twenty-one battalions register their fires so that they could box in the area and defeat a counterattack after the infantry had seized it. Three companies of the 17th Infantry were to attack; Company A under Lieutenant Howard F. Hall, Company B under Lieutenant George Wyatt, and Company L under Captain Walter E. Conway. The first two companies would take commanding hillocks atop the escarpment proper; Company L was to take Hill 5, a red-topped hill lying between the escarpment's east end and Hill 95, which by now had been fully overrun by Colonel Finn's 32nd Infantry.

At 3:30 A.M. on June 12 Conway's men walked silently out, and a half-hour later Hall's and Wyatt's followed. Providentially, a dense fog had blanketed the area, reducing visibility to ten feet. Within a half-hour Conway's L Company had reached the escarpment's top, and as dawn broke Hall's A Company and Wyatt's B Company had secured their hillocks. Staff Sergeant Charles F. Sanders leading a B Company platoon had encountered three Japanese soldiers on reaching the crest, but not wanting to arouse the foe he had simply walked quietly on past, his entire platoon accepting his cue. The men found very few enemies. To evade artillery fire, the Japanese had evacuated the escarpment's top the night before, intending to return after daybreak before the Americans began the "expected" attack at 7:30 A.M.

In L Company's area Captain Conway sent a platoon forward fifty yards to a small hill to expand his perimeter. The platoon leader had arrived and was checking in with Captain Conway via walkie-talkie, when he suddenly hollered, "For Christ's sake give me mortar fire!" He had glimpsed fifty Japanese approaching in a column of twos, intent on reoccupying Hill 5. The platoon opened up with BAR's and M-1's, killing thirty-seven and sending others fleeing in what the men later called a "turkey shoot." In the B and A company areas to the west other Japanese defenders dribbled back in small groups, many to meet instant death. Four approaching together toppled to a like number of rifle shots.

By 8:30 A.M. most of the excitement was over, and all three companies consolidated while others joined them to exploit this second break in Ushijima's final line. The men sniped all day at individual Japanese spotted on the rough coral plateau behind the scarpment. B Company suffered one killed and eight wounded while bagging sixty-three enemies. A and L companies had it easier, but that night Japanese artillery dropped twenty-four accurate rounds into Conway's L Company area, wounding two dozen men, one for each round fired.

By dusk on June 12 the 7th Division had completely breached the line in southern Okinawa that Ushijima had enjoined to be held unto death. In appearance the terrain had been every whit as defensible as the Urasoe-Mura escarpment, yet it had been seized with comparative ease. Part of the explanation probably lay in the lesser skill—though not bravery—of Ushijima's troops, the defending 15th Infantry Regiment having been heavily fleshed out with service troops. Part also lay, so some American officers thought, in the energy and willingness to brave fire of the young replacements that the assaulting companies had absorbed during the 7th Division's ten days off the line in early May. Part lay too in an exceptionally aggressive use of tanks, particularly of Captain Tony Niemeyer's flame tanks.

IV

Drawn up west of the 7th Division were the Deadeyes of the 96th, facing the strongest portion of Ushijima's fortified coral wall. Ahead of Colonel Halloran's 381st Infantry was the Yaeju Dake itself. Westward and bending south from it, across a saddle that formed a shelf between the peaks, was the Yuza Dake, also called Hill 167. The veteran 383rd Regiment, since Eddie May's death under the command of Lieutenant Colonel DeWitt Ballard, faced this obstacle.

On June 10 both regiments had attacked this formidable terrain, with results far less successful than those scored by the Hourglass Division. Ballard's 383rd failed to reach the escarpment's base, bogging down instead in a nasty fight to clear the town of Yuza. Companies B and C of Colonel Halloran's 381st managed to surmount the shelf between the Yaeju Dake and Yuza Dake but found themselves under such vicious flanking fires as to require smoke screen concealment to organize their perimeter for the night. Leftward along the high forward wall of the escarpment directly below the Big Apple, Halloran's 3rd Battalion seized a small hill but had to dig foxholes short of the escarpment itself.

Laying the smoke screen produced an unexpected result. Its billowing presence fooled the Japanese 89th Regiment's uni-

commander into believing that his foes were retreating. He therefore assembled his company about a nearby small building into which his men began entering to emerge wearing civilian garb. His evident intent was to pose his command as civilians for a night infiltration of the American line. Captain Philip D. Newell, C Company's commander, watched for a time, then adjusted artillery fire that killed most of the would-be infiltrators. Enough lived, however, to give C Company a miserable, sleepless night.

The next day neither attacking regiment moved. Ballard's 383rd stayed bogged down near Yuza, and Halloran's 381st neither could scale the 250-foot cliffs leading up to the Big Apple nor make headway on the shelf where B and C companies still clung on. But all companies blasted caves and pillboxes, each of which had to be sealed or demolished before its vicinity was safe. Bypassing Japanese, the Deadeyes had long since learned, did not suffice. Refusing to accept the logic that they were defeated when trapped, Ushijima's men would stay in place and keep on fighting. For this reason neither the Yaeju Dake nor the Yuza Dake could be bypassed. Both peaks had to be taken—the hard way—before southern Okinawa could be considered secure for base development.

From the GI standpoint the most interesting of the day's events occurred back in divisional reserve in the 382nd Regiment's zone, where its E Company was sitting directly above a Japanese cave. Hearing the rattle of pots and pans beneath them, three soldiers grabbed a satchel charge, found the opening, and tossed it in, but it failed to explode. Private First Class James Bolain then cautiously peered into the opening, to be greeted with a shower of pots and pans from within. Behind came a Japanese soldier clad in khaki shorts and talking volubly. The soldier understood only the terms "Hawaii" and "soldier," but gathered his plea was to return inside and bring out a companion. They let him go and were astonished when he emerged with an attractive young lady, dressed in Occidental clothes and sporting a pair of neatly plucked eyebrows. His motive for surrender was obvious.

The 7th Division's success in seizing Hill 95 and part of the Yaeju Dake escarpment gave the Deadeyes the break they now needed. On June 12 Colonel Halloran sent Company L from his 3rd Battalion up to the top of the escarpment through the 7th Division's zone, from whence it fought westward to a position directly above its sister outfit, K Company, at the bottom of the cliff. Halloran's intention was to clear a roadway running diagonally up the cliff which tanks could use to ascend the escarpment. This road, plus a stone stairway carved into the cliff, was the sole way up in this area. But despite their best efforts neither L nor K company could immediately reduce a chain of Japanese caves covering roadway and stairway. It took both companies till dusk the next day to blow the entrances. When the men finally were ready to go, they fell into a column of twos and marched away briskly for the benefit of a news service camera that had recorded them in action all day. Nightfall found the entire 3rd Battalion atop the cliff, ready to begin reducing the Big Apple itself.

In the meantime neither the other companies of the 381st, nor those of the 383rd and newly committed 382nd, could make significant headway against the Yuza Dake. When Ballard's 383rd attempted to shift into the 1st Marine Division's zone to flank the Yuza Dake from the west, its forward companies detonated so many antipersonnel mines and met such strong opposition in the town of Ozato that the entire attack stalled; this despite effective use of two new weapons brought up by a special team from Guam and put to combat test. These were 57 mm. and 75 mm. recoilless rifles, lightweight artillery pieces that could be manhandled into position to blast caves and pillboxes with rifle shot accuracy. Both weapons performed excellently, but their experimental ammunition, limited to 275 rounds per gun, was insufficient to reduce the 500-odd caves dotting the ridge above Ozato. Nor had the fierceness of combat abated. Though the 96th Division on June 12 took nine prisoners, a considerable number by Pacific War standards, there was not the slightest sign of a collapse of enemy morale. Instead, the prisoners, who came from nine different units, spoke of hearing stories of an impending landing on Okinawa on the night of June 20 to restore the situation. These may have been rumors inspired by a leak of Tokyo's grandiose plan of a month earlier to land two combat divisions on Okinawa or tales planted to encourage the troops.

By June 12 General Ushijima, who doubtless had little faith in such nonsense, understood that the 32nd Army was finished unless by its own efforts it could restore the broken eastern end of his escarpment wall. Ushijima knew that his 44th Brigade had been severely mauled and was greatly disturbed that it had expended so many men trying to defend the base rather than the crest of the Yaeju Dake. During two days he had fed into action a reserve withheld near his own headquarters composed of six companies of service, signal, and artillery troops. Now, he had no alternative to committing his general reserves as well, the 13th and 15th independent battalions of the 62nd Division.

One of the reinforcing units was the 1st Company of the 80th Field Artillery Battalion, now converted to infantry. Its morale

75 mm. Recoilless Rifle

was low; many of the men, as Lance Corporal Shoji Take said, "...had come to feel that they had suffered enough." Only half carried rifles, the others being given grenades and satchel charges and told to pick up the weapons of fallen comrades or to find enemy weapons. Yet urged on by their NCO's they fought hard before Mabuni trying to check the advance of the 7th Division. Dug into caves and under coral heads, they stayed in place until annihilated. Take, a graduate of the Tokyo middle school and possessing some knowledge of English, himself fought until his rifle was literally blown from his hands. Then he surrendered.

Some of the reinforcing companies launched attacks on the nights of April 12 and 13. None regained the rim of the escarpment or seriously hindered GI fighting capacity. In the 96th Division's zone at 2:30 A.M. on April 13, Pfc Willard J. Clary charged ten attackers after expending his ammunition, driving them away with his bayonet. Altogether, L Company killed sixty, of which thirty-five fell to a platoon commanded by Staff Sergeant George T. Frazier.

V

The southern Okinawa fighting saw the 1st Marine Division, drawn up along the Mukue Gawa, again drawing the toughest deal, as it had earlier at Wana Ridge and Wana draw. It confronted Ushijima's best armed and trained troops, the 22nd and 32nd regiments of the 24th Division, plus considerable artillery and positions that offered the enemy the important advantage of reverse slope warfare, something denied the defenders elsewhere because of relatively level ground south of the escarpment's rim.

Beginning on June 10 the marines required two days to break through Ushijima's outposts before the main defense line, anchored on Kunishi Ridge, and to seize the town of Itoman. Several companies were hard hit. "Charlie" Company of the 1st Marines lost every officer and over seventy men in taking Yuza Hill, and by day's end was under the command of its ranking noncom, the mess sergeant. Lieutenant Marcus H. Jaffe's F Company also had a nasty fight in taking Hill 69, a pile of coral just west of Ozato, where the Deadeyes were bogged down.

"Entertainment" that evening began in First Lieutenant Richard B. Watkins' E Company area after it had moved onto Hill 69 to reinforce F Company. Well after dark a line of Okinawan civilians started walking through the company perimeter. Mindful of instructions to spare civilians the men withheld fire until they realized that every fifth "Okinawan" was a Japanese soldier, and that the whole maneuver was a ruse to penetrate their lines, with the Okinawans being pressed into use as decoys. The marines then started shooting, attracting fifteen to eighteen more Japanese waving sabers and charging with bayonets. From the opposite side of the perimeter, possibly by coincidence, a like number of Japanese emerged from a cave and started dashing through the company line. Bullets and grenades flew in all directions, Japanese were everywhere, and Lieutenant Watkins shot two while talking on a field telephone with his battalion commander, Lieutenant Colonel James C. Magee. The bizarre action ended when two women jumped from a cave and began running. Several marines shouted and held fire but others farther away opened up, dropping both. On examining their bodies the next morning, the marines found that one appeared to be a nurse, and that the pair had been carrying a satchel charge and grenades. Forty bodies of Japanese soldiers lay sprawled about, plus several civilians, against losses to E Company of just five wounded and none killed.

This costly slugging of June 11 and 12 had cleared all outposts before the western anchor of Ushijima's final line. Ahead of the 1st Marine Division across a completely open valley was Kunishi Ridge, a high, rugged, tomb-dotted slope riddled with caves and elaborate defenses. Kunishi's defenders were the 32nd Infantry, the best armed regiment remaining to the 32nd Army. The 32nd still had some 47 mm. antitank guns in support, sited to cover the only road leading to the ridge. Artillery behind covered the entire valley. Kunishi's reverse slope was more abundantly patterned with fire from automatic weapons than its forward slope, many guns being emplaced on Mezado Ridge, 500 to 600 yards rearward.

General del Valle's most immediate problem was how to get his men alive across that 800 yards of open ground. As General Arnold was deciding at approximately the same time, he concluded that the best method would be by predawn assault. Colonel Snedeker was ordered to send out a company each from his 1st and 2nd battalions of his 7th Marines at 3:30 A.M. on June 12, before dawn but late enough to provide light soon after the men arrived atop the ridge. Tapped to lead were Captain Richard E. Rohrer's C Company and First Lieutenant John W. Huff's F Company. B and G companies would follow after daybreak.

At first the attack prospered, C Company surprising some Japanese caught atop the ridge preparing breakfast. But after daylight Rohrer's and Huff's companies found themselves isolated when enemy fire pinned down both reinforcing companies.

A situation remarkably like that at Kakazu Ridge had developed; two companies were caught on a ridge, with the Japanese commanding the reverse slope and all forward approaches, thereby making impossible either reinforcement or retreat. Only tanks could cross the fireswept plain. By late afternoon General del Valle and Colonel Snedeker knew that their tanks would not only have to blast the forward slope of the ridge but also bring up supplies and reinforcements and evacuate wounded. Beginning at about 4:00 P.M., the tanks loaded in concealment, then braved 47 mm. fire to discharge men and supplies near the base of the hill through their bottom escape hatches. By dusk nine tanks had ferried up a reinforced platoon of fifty-four men and had evacuated twenty-two seriously wounded.

The next day, June 13, brought no essential change. Tanks continued to reinforce, resupply, and evacuate despite several losses to 47 mm. guns. All day artillery and warships hammered Japanese positions rearward of Kunishi Ridge. Every enemy movement spotted by the assault companies brought a concentrated pasting, and before the day closed battleship *Idaho* was dropping 14-inch shells as close as 250 yards from the embattled marines.

On June 14 the situation still did not change. Two more companies, E and G of Lieutenant Colonel Magee's 2nd Battalion, managed to mount the ridge to the eastward, but they too were pinned in place. Tanks continued to be used to haul up supplies. For an infantryman to rise up meant certain death or a bad wound.

Tanks shooting up the reverse slope finally broke the enemy's resistance. With their aid the 5th and 7th Marines slowly cleared the ridge's caves, the hamlet of Kunishi just beyond, and enemy positions on Mezado Ridge to the south. By June 18 a battalion of the 22nd Marines of the 6th Marine Division had arrived from Oroku to take over the seaward flank of the advance. By day's end the Japanese 22nd Infantry Regiment, sent to reinforce the 32nd, had been totally destroyed, everyone from battalion and regimental staffs downward being killed, and a rapid advance along the coast was threatening to encircle the remains of the 32nd Infantry Regiment as well as 24th Division headquarters located further inland. In fighting as violent, bloody, and sustained as Okinawa had yet offered, the marines had overpowered the western end of Ushijima's escarpment line.

VI

Difficult fighting still lay ahead for both marines and GI's. From Hill 95 and the eastern end of the Yaeju Dake the 7th Division advanced south over rough coral ground studded with spikes and outcroppings to take Hills 115 and 155, the latter the headquarters of the 44th Brigade, by June 17. The advance was slow, for some companies costly, but it would have been infinitely worse had not General Arnold elected to use his regular and flame tanks lavishly. The flamethrowers expended more than 37,000 gallons of napalm, in some instances literally burning a path for the infantry. In the 96th Division the same story prevailed, except that the Deadeyes of the 381st and 382nd regiments had to do without as much tank support in overrunning the Yaeju Dake, which fell on June 14, and the Yuza Dake, which held out very stubbornly for two more days. The 382nd had to clear the ridge above Ozato several times. To it from the Yuza Dake the Japanese had dug a 2,500-yard tunnel through which they had kept dispatching reinforcements.

June 16 featured perhaps the most devastating single artillery concentration of the Pacific War. At about dusk Deadeye observers spotted in Makabe a large gathering of enemy troops. Ringing up the artillery, they arranged a time-on-target (TOT) concentration in which 264 guns—10 battalions of Army and 12 of Marine artillery—all fired together. Simultaneous arrival of 264 shells bursting just off the ground obliterated all soldiers, a distressingly large number of intermingled civilians, and most of the town.

By nightfall of June 17 General Buckner's 10th Army held a solidly anchored line from the crest of Kunishi Ridge directly across Okinawa to the cliffs on the east coast a few hundred yards north of General Ushijima's headquarters. This time Buckner was correct in predicting to newsmen, "We have passed the speculative phase of the campaign and are down to the final kill."

24

SUICIDE AND SURRENDER

JUNE 18 FOUND Lieutenant General "Buck" Buckner at the front visiting a newly arrived combat unit, Colonel Clarence R. Wallace's 8th Marine Regiment of the 2nd Marine Division. The 8th had come to the Okinawa area in early June to seize without loss or incident two small offshore islands, Iheya and Aguni, that Admiral Turner had wanted for radar warning stations to lift some of the burden from his hard-pressed picket destroyers. On June 15 it had been attached to the 1st Marine Division, and now General del Valle had committed it to action in the hope that its fresh men would break quickly through the Japanese lines to the south coast. Buckner had come up to see the leathernecks jump off.

After watching the marines advance across a valley for about an hour, Buckner decided to visit another front. He had just announced his intention at 1:15 P.M., when five Japanese artillery shells, among the very last fired in the campaign, suddenly began bursting nearby. Jagged hunks of coral flew viciously about, one catching the American Army commander squarely in the chest. With his face still wreathed in a smile, Buckner died quietly a few minutes later. As senior officer present Lieutenant General Roy S. Geiger, U.S.M.C., replaced Buckner temporarily as 10th Army Commander.

On Okinawa, where so many had met a like fate, General Buckner's passing seemed not inappropriate. In the United States the news came as a shock and served to further focus attention on the Okinawa campaign. All leading newspapers ran long obituaries recounting Buckner's career and added human interest stories on the simple but dignified burial services held for the fallen leader in an Army cemetery. With the European War over, editors were no longer blue-penciling detailed stories filed by the battalion-sized press corps on the island. Each new advance by the 10th Army now furnished raw material for the front pages. At long last the Okinawa campaign was getting its just due in the press.

I

A few thousand yards from the scene of Buckner's death, deep under Hill 89 south of Mabuni, Lieutenant General Mitsuru Ushijima realized that the doom of his 32nd Army and of himself was finally at hand. Couriers arriving by foot having braved terrible dangers from American artillery and air strikes reported that his surviving troops now were concentrated into two major groups. One, centering about Mabuni and Hill 89, consisted of the headquarters staffs of the 32nd Army and the 62nd Division plus miscellaneous troops; the other, located in a pocket about the town of Medeera, included the 24th Division headquarters group and attached units. Elsewhere, except for local pockets, resistance had become disorganized. The largest surviving local pocket, some 400 men under the command of Colonel Kikuji Hongo, commander of the 32nd Infantry, had gone into hiding in caves under Kunishi Ridge after being overrun by the marines of the 1st Division.

Stiff fighting continued as the marines and GI's of the 10th Army strove to reduce Ushijima's two pockets. It took Colonel Mickey Finn's 32nd Regiment three days, until nightfall on June 21, to completely overrun the town of Mabuni and Hill 89. Even then Ushijima and his staff survived, deep under the coral rock, the main entrance to their cave being sealed shut. The arrival of the 7th Division's tanks to blast cave openings on the hill had coincided with a dinner that Ushijima had held for his staff officers before dispatching most of them to try to break through the American lines and become guerrillas in the north. To his able chief operations officer, Colonel Hiromichi Yahara, he gave the special mission of reaching Japan to report to Imperial

Headquarters, a mission the Colonel could not fulfill because he was taken captive while trying to pose as a civilian.

Reducing the Medeera pocket proved much more difficult than seizing Hill 89. The 7th Division's 184th Regiment enveloped the area from the south, establishing blocking points to prevent the enemy from escaping to the cliffs along the coast. From the west the 5th Marines of the 1st Division finally reduced two stubbornly resisting outlying points, Hills 79 and 81, by June 21. The 96th Division closed from the north, cracking through the town of Medeera and into some fanatically defended ridges beyond by the close of the same day. It took two more days of heavy fighting, however, to annihilate several small pockets holed up in Medeera and in its outskirts. The grand finale of the Medeera pocket came June 26 when a detail from the 321st Engineers opened a sealed cave which a POW had reported was the headquarters of Lieutenant General Amamiya, the 24th Division's commander, who had with him two hundred of his surviving men. After an interpreter had failed to move Amamiya to surrender, the Deadeye engineers poured in 1,700 gallons of gasoline and touched off 300 pounds of dynamite to seal the cave permanently.

Losses in the 96th Division had not been light in its final days of action. So depleted had its line battalions become that General Hodge had attached to it the 305th Infantry of the 77th Division to keep its attack rolling. A final Deadeye KIA was its spark plug, the courageous little assistant division commander, Brigadier General Claudius M. Easley. On June 19 Easley had been on an inspection tour when a hidden Japanese machine gun fired and wounded his aide, Lieutenant John G. Turbeville. Typically, Easley had crawled forward to the top of a small hillock to look for the gun, only to attract a burst that caught him squarely in the forehead. Easley met instant death in circumstances remarkably similar to those that had taken Ernie Pyle.

In the 7th Division sector, also on June 19, Sergeant Dewey R. Boughan had fitted a hose attachment to his flame tank to burn out the top of a low escarpment holding up Colonel Finn's infantry. Though the leaking hose soaked him with napalm, Boughan continued until he had expended his fuel. On leaving the area Boughan spotted a Japanese 75 mm. gun that had just knocked out a tank. Jumping into another machine he guided it into position to blast the gun and finish off the crew.

June 19 brought a final Medal of Honor feat. Technical Sergeant John Meagher of the 305th Infantry, 77th Division, mounted on a tank to direct gunfire in the Medeera pocket area, jumped from the vehicle to bayonet a Japanese running at the tank with a satchel charge. Then he ran back to the tank, grabbed a machine gun, and firing from the hip rushed a pair of enemy machine guns, finishing off the last of the second gun's crew by wielding his empty weapon from the barrel like a club.

Somewhat prematurely, General Geiger, as acting commander of the 10th Army, had reported all organized resistance ended on June 21 and on the next day had raised the Stars and Stripes in an official ceremony. The following day, the twenty-third, he organized a ten-day sweep northward up the island with his combat divisions to clear all enemy resistance, mop up stragglers, salvage equipment, and blast shut all caves the enemy might use as hiding places. Forming a gigantic skirmish line across the island all four divisions worked their way slowly north, searching every square yard, killing many hundreds of enemy stragglers and capturing others. Completion of this mop-up by the end of the month finally rendered Okinawa safe enough, in the opinion of the new 10th Army commander, Lieutenant General Joseph W. Stilwell, to carry on base development even though an estimated 2,500 Japanese still remained at large. On July 2 Stilwell decreed the Okinawan campaign officially closed.

For both contestants and for the Okinawan civil populace the campaign had been costly.* United States losses, Army, Navy, and Marine, tallied 12,274 dead, 36,707 wounded, and over 26,000 nonbattle (injury, illness) casualties. Japanese postwar tabulations count 75,000 dead in Ushijima's army, to which approximately 20,000 Okinawan *boetai* must be added. Estimates of Okinawan civilian dead vary from 42,000 to 147,000, but the figure of 60,000 obtained from Okinawan sources by Dr. George Kerr may be nearly correct.

The heavy American loss, especially to kamikazes, gravely concerned many American leaders, both military and civil. Taken together with Iwo Jima, on which 6,812 marines and sailors had been killed and 19,920 wounded, there seemed to

---

*Except for U.S. battle casualties precise figures cannot be given. The 10th U.S. Army lost 7,374 killed or dead of wounds, 31,807 wounded or injured in action, and 239 missing.

many to be an upward trend in the casualty rate of the Pacific War. Others argued that Okinawa and Iwo Jima were exceptional cases. Where the enemy did not have to be pried cave by cave from a flankless front, they asserted, more moderate losses would again be the rule. On Guam, for example, where the attacking troops could outmaneuver the 18,000 Japanese defenders, nearly all the Japanese had been slain at a cost of about 1,500 Americans killed in action and 6,000 wounded.

II

While General Ushijima and his men had been struggling to maintain their resistance in southern Okinawa, Admiral Ugaki on Kyushu had been trying to muster yet another kamikaze offensive. In two interim attacks launched after the end of Kikusui 9 on June 7, his flyers had bagged two more destroyers. On June 10 a kamikaze had near-missed the *William D. Porter* occupying Radar Picket Station 15. None of the crew was badly injured, but the force of the explosion fatally ruptured the ship's hull. Six days later a torpedo plane launched a tin fish at the U.S.S. *Twiggs* two hours after sundown, scoring a hit that touched off a magazine between the two forward 5-inch gun mounts. This was quite enough to sink the ship and kill 152 bluejackets.

It was not until June 21 and 22, with the 32nd Army's resistance fading away, that Admiral Ugaki finally got away Kikusui 10, the last of his massed kamikaze attacks. Some fifty-eight kamikazes reached the Okinawa area, though as usual many more had been dispatched only to abort their missions. Because it was becoming harder to convince pilots that their expenditure at Okinawa would produce maximum results, the rate of "aborts" had risen sharply. First blood came at about 6:30 P.M. on June 21 when an Army fighter crashed the large seaplane tender *Curtiss*, starting a fire that gutted the ship and killed forty-one and injured twenty-eight crewmen. The only other successful attacks came while the previously kamikazed *Barry* was en route to a new career as a kamikaze decoy under tow of LSM-59. Planes hit and sank both ships. Near-misses damaged others elsewhere.

The intended *pièce de résistance* of Kikusui 10 fizzled; this was an attack by six Oka-manned rocket bombs. Two Oka failed to release and returned in their Betty mother planes. The others either missed or were lost when U.S. fighters shot down the mother planes. An American and a Japanese pilot each reported one Oka streaking at 500 knots over the city of Naha, no target in sight. Second Lieutenant H. L. Priece, a Marine Corsair pilot operating over Picket Station 15, jumped a Betty that had just released its Oka, the missile diving harmlessly into the sea ahead of a destroyer below. The Betty got away when an escorting Zero drilled a stream of 20 mm. bullets into Priece's cockpit. Lieutenants W. L. Milne and J. W. Leaper each destroyed a Betty, and the aggressive Leaper then bagged an Oscar fighter by chewing off its tail with his propeller, a rash act that forced him to bail out into the sea to be rescued from the ocean by the cruiser U.S.S. *Cheyenne*. Pilots claimed two other Bettys damaged; these may have been the pair that returned to Kyushu.

By this stage of the campaign Okinawa's air defense squadrons had become much stronger, with day-flying defenders numbering 272 Corsairs and 104 Thunderbolts (P-47's) from 18 squadrons. Night defense had become better, too. Night sorties by Ugaki's 5th Air Fleet and the 6th Air Army, which at first had encountered little opposition other than antiaircraft, had become increasingly costly. Three of the four Marine Air Groups contained a Hellcat (F6F5N) squadron of fifteen radar-equipped fighters. In June the Army added to its Ie Shima Thunderbolt groups the 548th Night Fighter Squadron equipped with fourteen new twin-tailed, twin-engine Black Widow (P-61) heavy night fighters with range sufficient to fly interdiction missions over Kyushu.

Both types acquitted themselves during Kikusui 10 on the night of June 21–22. A pioneer in Marine Corps night fighting, Colonel Marion M. Magruder, added to his impressive tally of victories at 2:45 A.M. on June 22 when "Ringtail Control," a radar station in northern Okinawa, vectored him against a Betty bomber sneaking in at 1,400 feet. Closing unseen, Magruder picked up the Betty in his scope, gained visual contact at 800 feet, and from 100 yards back set it afire with five short bursts.

Anxious to prove the worth of his twin-engine long-range P-61 was Army Captain William Dames flying out of Ie Shima. Although slower than the Hellcat, his Black Widow carried a superior model airborne radar that could track a target at a dozen miles or more, independently of a ground station. Dames was after a contact that "Delegate," the air controller at the beachhead, had reported orbiting 60 miles southwest of Okinawa. Six miles away the Army captain got a blip on his scope, closed, and dove from above on an agile Zero fighter equipped as a floatplane. At 210 miles per hour indicated airspeed, Dames followed his prey through violent jogs right and left, finally loosing a destructive blast from his four 20 mm. cannon at 200-yard range. A wing sailed from the Zero, its tail flamed, and the machine—one of sixteen from Kanoya—tumbled into the ocean. This was the first of several "kills" recorded by the P-61's, which got most of the others during interdiction missions over Kyushu in a resumption of the tactics used briefly earlier by the night flyers from the U.S.S. *Enterprise*.

The score of the night attacks of June 21–22 was almost but not quite one-sided. A few Japanese planes broke through to drop bombs, one of which hit a tree near the Okinawa Command telephone exchange, cutting electric wires and silencing the radios of Commo Central for thirty minutes. Five men sleeping in nearby tents suffered wounds, none serious.

Kikusui 10 ended the series of massed attacks by Admiral Ugaki's Kyushu command, although no admission was made then or later that the Kikusui operations had been discontinued. A sprinkling of suicide attacks continued, as on June 25 when fourteen Shirigaku trainers took off and half returned to base. The other seven apparently hit nothing, for American records list no damage on this day. After June 21 Ugaki seems to have adopted a deliberate policy of withholding planes, pulling them back from his Kyushu airfields, conserving his strength for the invasion of Japan proper he now knew was coming.

Though he had failed to stop the American invasion of Okinawa, Ugaki, aided by the Japanese Army and Navy commands on Formosa, had inflicted enormous damage. Sixteen destroyer-type ships had been sunk. Twenty-two other warships had sunk, none larger than a destroyer, and 368 other naval vessels ranging in size from battleships and carriers down to small landing craft had been damaged. A few merchantmen not carried on the Navy Register had been hit or sunk but not many. Loss of American life had been very heavy; over 4,900 bluejackets had been killed or drowned and another 4,824 wounded or injured, more by far than in any previous naval campaign in any war the United States had fought. Okinawa was one action in which the number of Navy dead rivaled that of the Army.

Japanese losses incurred during the kamikaze attacks can only be estimated, since accurate date was not kept by Japanese naval commands during World War II. A conservative postwar estimate cites 1,896 planes and pilots dispatched on suicide sorties of which 889 were expended at Okinawa. To this figure must be added 134 Army planes from Formosa and probably other Army planes dispatched from commands on Kyushu not under Navy control. Total losses of all planes, suicide or other, ran to about 1,600 planes in the Okinawa campaign, the loss rate per mission being about 20 percent.*

None who have not experienced it can possibly imagine the full fury of a kamikaze attack or the day-in-day-out nervous strain induced by the hell-birds. Perhaps only a first-rate poet could do it, as Samuel Eliot Morison suggests. Writes Rear Admiral Joseph A. McGoldrick, who commanded the U.S.S. *Rooks* throughout the battle on fire support duty and picket line but whose ship was not hit:

---

*Other Japanese estimates of kamikaze losses are higher and two are lower. Rear Admiral Yokoi, the 5th Air Fleet chief of staff, states that losses were "more than" 700 of 3,000 planes taking part in the Okinawa campaign. Tadashi Nakajima, a naval officer stationed at Kanoya, says that "almost 1,700" Army and Navy pilots flew kamikaze sorties in the Okinawa area but does not indicate whether this total included aborted missions. Two former pilots, Masatake Okumija and Jiro Horikoshi, put the Okinawa kamikaze losses at 914 planes. Official American estimates of 7,800 enemy planes destroyed cannot possibly be reconciled with Japanese figures, even after taking into account Japanese plane losses on Kyushu fields. Double counting of kills seems to have occurred on the basis of pilot reports, and sailors on the business end of kamikaze dives understandably were inclined to exaggerate. In July, 1956, the U.S. Strategic Bombing Survey reduced this figure to 3,000 combat losses and reconciling various Japanese data, counts 1,900 suicide missions down against Okinawa. But this tally does not seem to include "aborts." Japanese estimates of American ships sunk were astronomically high, even in classified reports. Claimed sinkings of dozens of battleships and cruisers suggest that the Japanese pilots commonly mistook the destroyers they attacked for larger game.

Probably the most vivid three months of my life still remain those spent during the Okinawa campaign. I used to compare it to two champion boxers who fought toe to toe for not 15 but for 115 gruelling rounds. . . .

III

That the discipline and morale of the 32nd Army finally collapsed in its last hours of combat is perhaps less surprising than the fact that it held up for so long. Between June 12 and 18, after Ushijima's final line was breached, prisoners had averaged only about fifty per day. On June 19 the POW total suddenly jumped to 343, and the next day to 977, indicating that the discipline and will to fight of the Japanese soldier finally had weakened. Nevertheless, those Japanese willing to accept captivity were a distinct minority compared to those who preferred death. Tenth Army KIA estimates for the same three days numbered nearly 2,000 on June 19, 3,000 on June 20, and a whopping 4,000 on June 21. In many cases Japanese soldiers would jump from hiding before advancing tanks and infantry and stand passively until shot down.

One of the most fruitful sources of both civilian and military prisoners were the numerous caves near Mabuni in the 7th Division's zone. A prisoner who was cooperative, convinced that the war was a mistake, and that as captives Japanese soldiers would be making a contribution to postwar Japan, proved to be the most persuasive "lure" to induce civilians and soldiers to emerge from the caves. Over a loud-hailer he would persuasively testify to the good treatment his comrades could expect. In some cases, using his ex-sergeant manners, he would simply order the occupants from a cave. In this manner he induced about 2,000 to give up.

No accurate count seems to have been made of the numbers of Okinawan civilians who surrendered. The official 24th Corps history guesses that about 80,000 civilians, a third to a half of whom had been wounded, emerged from caves in Okinawa's south tip in the last two weeks in June. A pitiful sight they were as they walked stoically north from the combat area, chewing on sticks of sugarcane and carrying children on their backs. Many more thousands perished, killed by artillery fire, by American soldiers at night near perimeters, and by suffocation in caves blasted shut. The most famous episode of this sort, one whose details now are obscured in Okinawan folklore, was the death in a cave near Mabuni of a party of Okinawan schoolgirls serving as nurses in the Japanese Army in what is today called the "cave of the virgins."

Any number of personal narratives could be related of the experiences of surviving Japanese soldiers and Okinawan civilians. A few will perhaps suffice by way of illustration.

Lieutenant Shonosuke Mizusaki, a graduate of Tokyo University who had majored in Malay and minored in English, an officer of the 62nd Division, lay wounded at the close of the fighting in one of the caves in the 3rd Amphibious Corps sector on the southwest coast. As the marines had neared, Mizusaki had received an order to take his twenty remaining men and escape to the north. He found this impossible and so remained in his cave.

When the marines began their mop-up back to the north, Mizusaki was discovered. A marine tossed in a grenade which killed three men and put out the lieutenant's right eye. He then crawled farther back into the cave—a good thing because three more grenades fell in and exploded. Then silence; the mop-up had passed him by.

Some days later only eight men remained alive in the cave. To eliminate the stench Mizusaki and his seven remaining men had buried the dead by night. Scrounging for American rations left on the battlefield provided just enough food to keep them alive. After three weeks American soldiers again found the cave, this time in company with an interpreter who informed the party that Japan had lost the war, and who left a copy of *Life* magazine showing aerial photos of bomb-ravaged Tokyo to prove his case. If they would not surrender, he said, the cave would be blasted shut the next day.

For a day the survivors debated. Opinions varied. Finally Mizusaki cut off debate by declaring firmly that all must go out and that when the Americans came he would emerge first. He did so, being seized by the arms and lifted bodily out. On being blindfolded for passage to the rear, he assumed he was to be shot, and as his rusty English had escaped him, he requested a pad and pencil, explaining his desire to live. To his surprise he was taken to a camp near Kadena and his wounded eye treated, something he had not expected.

The story of Kome Hamishiro, a sixteen-year-old Okinawan junior high school student assigned to a signal unit, illustrates the stark tragedy faced by most of the Okinawan *boetai* and conscripts. At the end of the campaign just eight of his original group of forty-eight students remained alive in a cave near Mabuni. When a corporal who had been supervising them died of tetanus, the eight lads decided to slip north through the American line to Yonabaru. They made it, walking by night and hiding by day, to a village near the base of the Chinen Peninsula, where three were challenged by American troops and shot. The five survivors stumbled over a trip wire, setting off a flare, but their lives were saved when one remembered enough of his schoolboy English to shout, "What time is it?" The American troops held fire and took them prisoner. Even though they were in uniform none was held as a regular POW because their captors could not believe such striplings could be soldiers.

Seihan Yamashiro, a *boetai* at seventeen years of age but large for his age, finished the campaign in a cave along the shore. In trying to slip north, he was fired on from a P.T. boat offshore because of his army uniform and wounded in sixteen places from bits of shrapnel. Two women cared for him in a cave for several days, stripping from him his blood-soaked uniform and wrapping him in a kimono. Convinced that he would lose his life, he told the women to give up to the Americans.

In this he was mistaken. Two days later 7th Division troops found him, still in the kimono, put him on a litter, and took him to an aid station. Offered food, Yamashiro refused to eat, fearing like most captured Okinawans that it was poisoned. Hunger eventually overcame his fears and he ate. Later, when two Okinawan girls working as aides at the station offered him rice, he contemptuously flung it aside, disgusted that they would serve the Yankee enemy. Still later, he was transferred to a field station and interrogated by American CIC agents, who were suspicious of his insistence that he was a civilian. But he persisted in his story and on discharge from the hospital won release to return to his home on one of the small islands rimming Kin Bay.

Altogether, the 10th Army recorded the capture of 10,988 combat and 3,842 labor troops, the latter mostly Okinawans or Koreans. Japanese demobilization records indicate that about 10,000 Japanese Army and Navy and some 8,000 conscripted Okinawans survived the battle.

IV

To Lieutenant General Mitsuru Ushijima and his chief of staff, Lieutenant General Isamu Cho, surrender was unthinkable. When informed in mid-June of a courteously worded letter from General Buckner assuring him that further resistance was useless and inviting him to negotiate and save the lives of his men, Ushijima had merely laughed. For him defeat must mean either death in battle or ceremonial suicide to expunge the stigma of defeat. Buckner's assurance that "The forces under your command have fought bravely and well, and your infantry tactics have merited the respect of your opponents" could not be accepted as adequate saving of face to justify surrender.

Even so Ushijima and Cho waited until the last possible moment to perform the ceremony demanded by samurai convention. The evening of June 21 found both still in their headquarters under Hill 95 with Colonel Finn's infantry of the 32nd Regiment in perimeter directly above their heads. Both knew all was finished; grenades dropping through a vertical shaft leading from the top of the hill that afternoon had killed or wounded ten officers and men near General Cho's office.

That evening Ushijima's cook, Tetsuo Nakamuta, prepared as ordered an extra-large dinner to be served at 10:00 P.M. He produced a bountiful meal of rice, canned meats, potatoes, fried fish cakes, bean curd soup, fresh cabbage, pineapple, tea, and sake. Generals Cho and Ushijima toasted one another with the remains of a bottle of Black and White Scotch whiskey Cho had carried from Shuri. After dinner, which had included as guests the remaining officers of the staff, Ushijima made his final decision. Before moonrise, in the early morning hours, most of the remaining officers and men would make a climbing charge up the cliff to retake Hill 95 and after that Mabuni. The others would stand guard while Ushijima and Cho committed suicide.

At 3:00 P.M. on June 22, while Tetsuo Nakamuta still was busy in the kitchen, Ushijima's orderly came and whispered that the commanding general and the chief of staff were about to commit hara-kiri. Deeper inside the cave, as Lieutenant Kiyoshi Haginouchi recalls, the assembled staff was singing the national anthem, the grimly martial "Umi Yukaba." Then those staff members appointed to the attack left the cave and started up the cliff.

An hour later, at 4:00 P.M., Ushijima and Cho appeared at a natural fissure in the rock six feet wide and six feet high opening onto a small ledge overlooking the sea. Each was dressed in full field uniform, with sword and medals. Across the ledge a heavy white comforter was laid and over it a white sheet symbolizing death. Said Cho, as Lieutenant Haginouchi recalls, "Well, Commanding General Ushijima, as the way may be dark, I, Cho, will lead the way." Replied Ushijima with perfect composure, "Please do so, and I'll take along my fan since it is getting warm."

Both knelt on the sheet, facing the ocean, since room was lacking on the ledge to perform the ceremony facing north toward the Imperial Palace. Silently each opened his tunic, baring his abdomen. At General Ushijima's side stood his aide, Lieutenant Yoshino, holding two knives with half the blade wrapped in white cloth. The adjutant, Captain Sakaguchi, stood on Ushijima's right, saber drawn. Yoshino handed a blade to Ushijima who took it with both hands and with a shout, thrust. Simultaneously Sakaguchi's saber fell on his neck as prescribed, severing his spinal column. Ushijima's corpse lurched forward onto the sheet. Then General Cho took his turn and the ceremony was repeated. Cook Tetsuo Nakamuta, who had been watching from the entrance to the cave, turned silently away.

Seventh Division GI's, mopping up along the bottom of the cliff several days later, found both corpses, still in their uniforms, in shallow graves below the ledge. Buried with Cho was his white silk mattress cover on which he had written his own epitaph: "I depart without regret, shame, or obligations." So had Cho and Ushijima fulfilled in the ancient way their ritual propitiation.

25

THE "ENGLAND" OF THE PACIFIC

COMPLETION OF THE mop-up of the last remnants of the 32nd Army permitted the 10th Army's service troops to accelerate conversion of Okinawa into an "England" for the invasion of Japan. Despite a naval blockade that had tightened to the point where next to nothing could enter or leave the Japanese home islands, despite a B-29 bombing campaign that had incinerated most of Japan's major cities, despite the destruction of Ushijima's 32nd Army, the island empire still held out. The U.S. High Command in Washington had to assume that blockade and bombing would not be enough, that Japan proper would have to be conquered foot by bloody foot, starting first with the handiest target, the southernmost island of Kyushu. As the British Isles had served as base for the invasion of France, so must Okinawa serve as advance base for the invasion of Japan proper.

When the fighting ended, General Wallace's Okinawa Island Command controlled 95,000 men engaged in construction work. Kadena, Yomitan, and Plum Field on Ie Shima had long since become all-weather airports capable of handling any aircraft except a laden B-29. Fighter strips were operational at Awase and Chimu, and work was progressing on bomber strips at six other locations. Newly arrived aviation engineers, though they had grimaced at news cameras and pointed angrily at rows of "overseas bars" denoting their European service, had made excellent progress and continued to so do in the summer months.

Excellent progress was also being made on living quarters for a garrison of nearly a half-million soldiers, sailors, airmen, and marines. Engineers were surveying for millions of square feet of supply depots, ammunition dumps, and bivouacs. Seabees were building port facilities at White Beach and Kin Bay, and were taking initial steps to convert Naha into a deep-water port. Roads were now adequate. General Wallace had good reason to believe that his Base Command would complete the Okinawan advance base for the invasion of Japan on schedule.

I

Occasional aerial photographs and (probably) intercepted American radio communications kept Admiral Ugaki conscious of the buildup of Okinawa's air bases, ports, and depots. In fact, from the end of June the 5th Air Fleet expected at virtually any moment a preliminary American attack on some one of the Ryuku Islands south of Kyushu. The strategy of defeating the occupation of Okinawa had long since faded from the minds of staff officers; now it was necessary to defend Japan proper while continuing what still could be done at Okinawa, namely, bombing the operational airfields in conventional night attacks. Targets were tempting. As new U.S. air squadrons arrived they were jammed onto Yomitan, Kadena, and Plum fields until, wing tip to wing tip, planes occupied every available space. A well-placed fragmentation or incendiary bomb could have caused havoc.

But as Japanese night bomber pilots found to their sorrow, placing that bomb on an Okinawan airfield had become astoundingly difficult. Despite use by the Japanese aircrews of radar jamming, decoy flights, window, and other countermeasures, the effectiveness of American night fighters and A-A crews steadily increased. Moreover, conditions at Kyushu further deteriorated in July when day and night fighter and bomber strikes became daily occurrences.

Japanese flyers exercised every ingenuity in their attempts to break through to Okinawa. Commander Naomasa Tohme, a slight, engaging Navy pilot, had been posted to Kanoya Air Station from metropolitan Japan where he had shot down seven American planes of several types. Being much too valuable to expend on a suicide mission, Tohme flew late-model Zero (Zeke 52) fighters on reconnaissance missions, scouting the weather and radioing cruise-control information to kamikaze pilots. His technique in reconnoitering Okinawa—which he did successfully on several flights—was to approach high at night, then dive at maximum permissible speed to gather his intelligence in a low, fast pass over the target. Defending Hellcat and Black Widow fighters never caught up with him.

Tetsuji Tamanaha, the Okinawan pilot who had seen the Geritsu flight depart from Kumamoto airfield on Kyushu, flew twice as a co-pilot from this airfield when some factory-fresh Ki 67, Type 4, "Peggy" bombers finally reached his squadron. Because of the delay in transition to the new planes, Tamanaha flew his two missions to Yomitan shortly before the end of the war, on August 4 and 7. His squadron had discovered that during bombing runs of 310 miles per hour or more American searchlights could not get a fix on the planes. Squadron technique was to fly the Peggy to great height, 27,000 feet, and then dive at more than 310 mph over the target. Night fighters they hoped to avoid by the use of one of two evasive courses and by having the tail gunner throw "window" from the tail turret.

In the first attack everything went perfectly. Tamanaha's crew made a bombing run on Yomitan airfield, noting that lights continued to outline the runways until the bombs hit. He be-

P-61 Night Fighter

lieved that the attack destroyed a dozen planes. A Black Widow made a firing run but missed. The second occasion turned out differently. En route Tamanaha's plane commander, Kakeo Kuroki, passed out when his oxygen supply failed at high altitude. Tamanaha took over the controls, diving in an ear-bursting descent to lower altitude and orbiting while the other crew members labored to bring Kuroki back to consciousness. They eventually succeeded, but Tamanaha found that he had expended too much fuel to continue the mission. He and Kuroki had to fly back to Kumamoto. Because his parents lived near Yomitan airfield, Tamanaha had had the curious feeling that he was attacking his home. He did not worry about his parents, however, because he believed that they had long since been slain by the Americans. He was overjoyed, later, to learn that they had survived. Tamanaha's third scheduled mission was scrubbed by Emperor Hirohito's message on August 16 surrendering Japan.

Captain Howard L. Naslund, a blondish twenty-one-year-old who flew eighty-six combat missions with the famous "Grim Reapers," the Army Air Force's 3rd Attack Group, had an experience utterly different from Tamanaha's. As the group's assistant operations officer, Naslund flew in July and August several "on the deck" strikes at Kyushu. In contrast to Tamanaha he met absolutely no opposition, not even from antiaircraft. Not that Naslund's low-level attacks were milk runs; flying A-20 attack bombers at an altitude of 40 feet and 260 mph was tricky business whether or not an enemy fired.

"We were shocked," recalls Naslund, "when we learned the type of missions to be flown." With military targets all destroyed (so the Air Intelligence officers believed) several bomber groups were detailed to burn out Kyushu's medium-sized cities with napalm and thermite bombs. "None of us were impressed by the need to hit such targets," Naslund continues. "Usually, after our previous strikes on purely military targets, such as ships or airfields, the crews talked excitedly about what they had seen, what they had hit. But after these strikes the men were absolutely silent, none of the usual talk."

Orders being orders they went, flying the last mission on August 12, their target the east coast city of Akume on Kyushu. As group navigator, Naslund led twenty-seven A-20's of three squadrons inland behind the city to gain the cover of low hills on its eastern outskirts. Skimming twenty to forty feet over the trees, the planes could scarcely be seen much less hit by defending gunners. To pull up even to a hundred feet was to invite fatal damage from antiaircraft if the gunners could catch the planes silhouetted against the sky. Naslund therefore kept the prop wash from his group rustling the trees. "As I skimmed the foothills and led the first three planes through a shallow saddle, I saw Akume straight ahead. From our forty-foot altitude we could see residents in the streets, on sidewalks, looking in windows, paying no attention until our combined eighteen Cal. 50 machine guns opened fire." Each squadron took a portion of the town, and as they re-formed over the sea all of Akume lay behind enveloped in flames.

Fortunately, this was the last such attack for Naslund and the "Grim Reapers." To their relief they received no more "city-busting" orders and remained inactive during the few remaining days of the war. The Reapers had not lost a plane in operations from Okinawa, and other outfits had lost only twenty planes in July and twenty-three in August, mostly to antiaircraft, in attacking airfields, ports, and other targets.

II

Captain Naslund's impression that Kyushu's defenders had nothing left with which to fight was totally mistaken. The enemy was lying low, moving only at night, conserving planes, men, guns, ammunition, and equipment for a showdown later. Though unsuccessful, Okinawa's defense had bought Japan valuable time to prepare main island defenses. Kyushu had been virtually defenseless when the Okinawa operation began. By the end of the campaign enough troops, guns, supplies, even planes had arrived for a vigorous fight. More were steadily trickling in, and by fall the island would have been a veritable hornet's nest for invaders.

The code name for Japan's final battle in the homeland reflected the feeling of every Japanese; it was called the Ketsu (Decisive) Operation. By the fall of 1945 Japan's leaders planned to mobilize in Japan proper 50 divisions, 27 brigades, 16,000 aircraft (all potential kamikazes), and 8,940 suicide small craft. As the most likely points of U.S. attack, the Kanto (Tokyo) Plain and Kyushu were to be most heavily defended. Despite prior defeats and with considerable justification, the Army and Navy staff officers of Imperial General Headquarters remained confident that this time the Yankee could be beaten off. Kamikazes and suicide boats would maul transports, cargo ships, and landing craft off Japan's beaches; violent counterattacks by elite troops would repulse the assault battalions at the water's edge. If the enemy broke through, twenty million Japanese civilians enrolled in a National Resistance Program would expend their lives to slay the invader and save the empire. Every last person, male or female, would—if necessary—become a kamikaze. As Japan's premier, Baron Kantoro Suzuki, the seventy-nine-year-old hero of the Russo-Japanese War, had admonished the people, "Now is the time for every one of the hundred million . . . to become glorious shields for the defense of the national structure."

Imperial Headquarters in Tokyo had correctly divined American intentions. Plans called for U.S. forces under General MacArthur to land on November 1, 1945, on the southern part of Kyushu, and in the spring of 1946 to assault in massive strength Tokyo's Kanto Plain. Operation Olympic, as the Kyushu landing was code-named, would place six divisions, three Marine and three Army, on either side of the twin peninsulas bounding Kagoshima Bay. Three more Army divisions would land north of Kagoshima Bay at Miyazaki on Kyushu's east coast where a large coastal flat offered sites for a nest of airfields. Two divisions, Operation Olympic's floating reserve, would stand by to reinforce any of the three separate American landing points as needed. To meet the expected swarm of kamikazes, fighters would cover from Okinawa and from Navy carriers.

The atomic bomb did not influence these plans. Nobody could yet be certain that the bomb would work, and knowledge of it was confined to a handful of planners.

As the fighting on Okinawa neared its end, President Truman approved Operation Olympic on June 18, 1945. The Joint Chiefs of Staff did not have an easy time securing the presidential consent. Concerned about the heavy casualties incurred on Okinawa and Iwo Jima, Mr. Truman insisted that the Chiefs first supply definite answers on the number of losses to be expected. At a White House conference that settled the matter, General Marshall and Admiral King finally convinced Truman that the casualties incurred in taking Kyushu probably would not exceed those of Luzon, about 31,000 men. They did not expect a repeat of the heavier Okinawan losses because the terrain on Kyushu would offer the troops more room to maneuver and less need for costly head-on attacks.

Actually this casualty figure might have proved to have been a serious underestimate. MacArthur's headquarters expected to meet seven Japanese divisions and two or three independent mixed brigades, or about 206,000 defenders in all. In fact the Japanese had mustered eleven divisions, three mixed brigades, and three tank brigades. Reinforcements could have been dispatched from other units stationed in northern Kyushu. Anywhere from 8,500 to 10,000 planes could have been fed into Kyushu's defense. Had the hell-birds scored as well as at Okinawa—a reasonable expectation—the U.S. Navy could have lost some 90 ships sunk, 900 more damaged, and 21,000 sailors killed in action. Years later Admiral Spruance could express heartfelt relief that he had not had to command an amphibious assault on Kyushu. Had ground force losses been three times as great as at Okinawa—a not unreasonable expectation in light of Japanese strength in numbers of military and mobilized civilians—an additional 22,000 troops would have been killed and nearly 100,000 wounded. And there is every reason to suppose that a landing on the Kanto Plain before Tokyo would have been much worse. To conquer Japan might have cost a million American casualties and twenty million Japanese. Fortunately, Emperor Hirohito decreed this should not come to pass.

III

With the end of the battle for Okinawa most Japanese in positions of authority understood that Japan could not win the war. Some had realized this after the failure at Guadalcanal, others when Saipan was lost, still more when Luzon and Manila fell. But not many would admit that Japan could *lose* the war and virtually none thought that Japan should surrender unconditionally. Yet President Roosevelt had announced, and the Cairo Conference of 1943 Allied leaders had affirmed, that unconditional surrender was the only acceptable formula for peace. Unless someone yielded, a fight to utter extinction seemed assured.

The break came first in Washington, D.C. Joseph C. Grew, America's prewar ambassador to Japan, believed that invading the home islands was neither desirable nor essential. Mr. Grew possessed the prestige, and in his capacity as undersecretary of state, the official authority, to bring to President Truman and his inner circle of advisers a reconsideration of the long-standing unconditional surrender formula. He found allies in the Secretaries of War and Navy, Henry L. Stimson and James V. Forrestal, who seconded to Truman the estimate that to dismantle the Japanese government and rule Japan through a military administration—as was being attempted in Germany—would be a mistake.

Stimson was of particular help. At the June 18 White House conference which had approved the Kyushu invasion plan, Stimson had gone along because he felt he had no choice. But Okinawa's casualty rate, thirty-five percent of the troops engaged, bothered him, and the prospects of a final apocalyptic encounter between the youth of Japan and America on the Kanto Plain left him sick at heart. On July 2, 1945, therefore, he expressed these forebodings to President Truman and urged Grew's proposal that a message be sent to Japan's leaders pointing out the destructive effects of continuing the war and—in effect—vitiating the severity of "unconditional surrender."

After a heated debate within the upper circles of the policymaking establishment, President Truman decided to take the chance that an Allied declaration, which—in effect—abandoned "unconditional surrender," would not be interpreted in Japan as indication that America's will to continue the fight was eroding. After clearing with the British and Chinese governments, the President on July 26, 1945, issued a statement from Potsdam, Germany, whence he had gone to consult with Premier Stalin of the Soviet Union. According to this Potsdam Declaration Japan would be stripped of all except the four main islands and would remain occupied until a peacefully inclined postwar government was assured. Except for war criminals its population would not be punished. A military government would not directly rule Japan; rather, a Japanese administration would function under the supervision of an Allied supreme commander. Reflecting differences of opinion within the U.S. State Department on the future of the emperor, the declaration was vague, neither explicitly denying nor affirming that Hirohito would remain as official chief of state.

When the Potsdam Declaration reached the attention of Japan's leaders, the reaction was diverse. Among staff officers at the War

Ministry the message received precisely the contempt and misestimate—that the United States was war-weary—that objectors in Washington had feared it might. On the other hand a group of Japanese "doves," mostly civilians, saw in the message a chance to end the war with some semblance of honor. Nevertheless, the omission of a clear statement concerning the future role (if any) of the emperor bothered them, and they urged Premier Suzuki to ask the United States to clarify the Potsdam statement. Before they could convince this venerable statesman, however, Suzuki held a press conference at which he declared that Japan would treat the Potsdam message with "contemptuous silence." This official rejoinder, promptly broadcast by Tokyo Radio, led President Truman to conclude that Tokyo's leaders still intended a bitter-end fight.

The Potsdam Declaration had included a warning that "the utter devastation of the Japanese homeland" would follow a rejection. That these words were not an idle boast should already have been apparent while B-29's continued to rain destruction on city after city, while the "Grim Reapers" attacked Kyushu towns, and while carrier planes ranged over metropolitan Japan, blasting airfields, factories, coastal shipping—anything worthwhile left to hit. Halsey's battleships steamed close along shore, shelling steel plants and other targets with high-capacity ammunition from their big guns. An aerial minelaying campaign to close ports on Japan's western side had virtually isolated Japan proper from Korea and Manchuria.

Severe as this punishment was and had been, it was as nothing compared to the genie now loosed over Japan. Implementing the declaration's threat, on August 6, 1945, the B-29 "Enola Gay" dropped over Hiroshima the "Thin Boy," a U-235 atomic bomb as powerful as three shiploads of TNT. In a blinding flash of light many thousands perished instantly. Three days later Kyushu's major city of Nagasaki fell victim to the "Fat Man," a squat, bulky, even more powerful missile containing plutonium as its explosive component. Again thousands vaporized in an eye blink. Power akin to the source of light from the sun had been released on Japan.

To maximize its effect, Mr. Truman had delayed the release of the Potsdam Declaration until tests had proved it certain that the atomic bomb would work. Nevertheless, the dropping of the bombs did not overwhelm Japan's military hierarchs or markedly stir them from their determination to have a showdown battle on Kyushu's beaches. Perhaps more shocking to them than the atomic bomb—even after local physicists had explained it—was the sudden entry of Stalin's Russia into the conflict. By the close of August 8 (August 9 in the Far East), Soviet tanks were driving south into Manchuria against light opposition from the Kwantung Army. The Japanese Army staff had hoped that negotiations with the Soviet Union might ease the Allied blockade or perhaps divide Allied councils.

To Japan's civilian leaders and to Emperor Hirohito, the Hiroshima bomb was the last straw; Japan *must* end the war on the terms of the Potsdam Declaration. However, the civilians, with Foreign Minister Shigenori Togo playing the lead role, had to be careful, because Japan still was ruled largely by hard-line middle-grade military officers, intellectual kin of Isamu Cho, who had many times summarily murdered dissenters. Carefully and delicately the Japanese "doves" worked out a plot to cause the emperor to command the Japanese cabinet to accept the Potsdam Declaration.

The climax came even as the news of the Nagasaki bomb and the Soviet invasion of Manchuria reached Tokyo. A hastily summoned War Cabinet meeting of the six major Japanese leaders deadlocked, three including Foreign Minister Togo favoring, three opposing the acceptance of the Potsdam terms. Admiral Soemu Toyoda, the Navy staff chief, and General Korechika Anami, the Army chief, wished dearly to have one more contest with the Americans on Kyushu. They would win, so they believed, and better terms than Potsdam's would then be forthcoming. The meeting continued all afternoon and far into the night in the subterranean gloom of the air raid shelter beneath the Imperial Palace. Finally, in the presence of the full cabinet, Premier Suzuki turned to the emperor to regret that the cabinet could not reach a consensus. "Your Imperial Majesty's decision is requested."

As all present bowed respectfully, Hirohito rose from his chair and in a voice tremulous with heartbreak said, "I cannot bear to see my innocent people suffer any longer. . . . There are those who say that the key to national survival lies in a decisive battle in the homeland . . . [but] there has always been a discrepancy between plans and performance. . . . How can we repel the invaders? . . . I swallow my own tears and give my sanction to the proposal to accept the Allied proclamation on the basis proposed by the Foreign Minister."

There was a single reservation in Hirohito's acceptance. The broadcast by Radio Tokyo, confirmed by diplomatic radiogram later, specified that the Japanese understood that the Potsdam Declaration did not propose disestablishing the emperor as chief of state. After debate in Washington President Truman agreed to continue Hirohito as titular but not the actual ruler of Japan.

Even this imperial word did not immediately bring peace. The American reply accepting the emperor had declared that he would be subject to orders of the Allied Supreme Commander, and that the ultimate form of government in Japan would be determined by free vote of the Japanese people. Those who favored one more battle reopened the issue and continued the debate. Curiously, seven American B-29's resolved the matter. They dropped five million leaflets over Tokyo and elsewhere containing the text of the Potsdam Declaration, the Japanese reply, and the U.S. acceptance. Fearing disorder among the military units distributed about Japan's coastal defenses when the leaflets were read, the leaders once more convoked a meeting in the Imperial Presence. On August 14, 1945, Emperor Hirohito indicated his wish that the cabinet accept the American reply. He would broadcast the war's end to his people the next day.

That night some frenzied young officers tried to seize at Radio Tokyo the imprint of the wax recording of the imperial rescript ending the war. They failed, and failed also to rally a following to overturn the cabinet. Had Isamu Cho been present to lead them and not been dead on Okinawa, the outcome might well have been different.

Early on the morning of August 15, 1945, every Japanese stopped in his tracks and bowed reverently. Said Radio Tokyo, "The next voice you hear will be that of the Emperor." Then it came, reedy, a bit squeaky, in a speech—the language of the court—difficult for most citizens to comprehend. They had never heard this voice before.

We have ordered our government to communicate to the governments of the United States, Great Britain, and the Soviet Union that Our Empire accepts the provisions of their Joint Declaration. . . . Having been able to safeguard and maintain the structure of the Imperial State, We are always with ye, Our good and loyal subjects, relying on your sincerity and integrity. Beware most strictly of any outbursts of emotion which may endanger needless complications, or cause ye to lose the confidence of the world. Let the entire nation continue as one family from generation to generation.... Cultivate the ways of rectitude; foster nobility of spirit; and work with resolution so that ye may enhance the glory of the Imperial State and keep pace with the progress of the world.

As one, Japan wept. The war was over.

IV

On Okinawa that night Captain Naslund stepped to the door of his tent to gaze wonderingly at the sky. From batteries ashore, from ships at sea, every A-A gun that would fire spurted tracers aimlessly into the sky. Naslund and the pilots of the "Grim Reapers" watched for a while, then quietly organized their own celebration of the end of World War II.

For others on Okinawa the pyrotechnic display raised uncertainties. These puzzled observers of the antiaircraft display were Japanese holdouts, several hundreds of them, who had been overlooked in the American mop-up of southern Okinawa or who had become guerrillas in the rugged northern hills. The ranking leader, Colonel Kikuji Hongo, commander of the 32nd Regiment, 24th Division, had managed to establish a virtual Japanese enclave in caves in the Itoman-Kunishi Ridge area. A half-truce had prevailed in which American soldiers stayed away from the area, and the Japanese, most of whom were sick or wounded, did not attack the GI's.

Among Hongo's 55 officer and 342 enlisted survivors was valiant young Captain Koichi Ito, commander of his 1st Battalion. Ito had been overrun by marines on Kunishi Ridge on June 17 and 18. His decimated companies and platoons had scattered to various caves, out of touch with one another. Ill, suffering with dysentery, Ito was very weak, but he evaded the mop-up, and later had managed to contact Colonel Hongo by messenger. Organizing an attack or even escaping northward being impossible, he and his men had remained in place all summer, scrounging food to stay alive.

Ito had observed the American celebration of the war's end and wondered about it, but when Island Command light planes later flew over the area dropping leaflets announcing Japan's surrender, he dismissed their messages as propaganda. On August 22, 1945, however, an American language officer of the 7th Division, Captain Howard Moss, came to Ito's cave in company with a noncom from Ito's battalion. The Japanese corporal called out respectfully, informing Ito that the war was over. At this Ito emerged from the cave and spoke with Moss, but he still was not convinced. Finally, he asked Moss to return two days later which the American readily agreed to do.

In the interim Ito visited Colonel Hongo, who appointed him to investigate the American claim. After the prescribed two days Captain Moss returned with a jeep and driver, offering to take Ito to Kadena airfield where he could hear for himself a recording of Emperor Hirohito's broadcast. Ito still believed that Moss was deceiving him, but was puzzled by the American's attitude; Moss was very relaxed, as if he did not greatly care whether Ito believed him or not.

At the airfield Ito listened to the imperial rescript twice, half-convinced that it sounded authentic and that no American propagandist could have made it up. After that Moss took him to see Colonel Yahara, who had been discovered by American CIC men while trying to pose as a civilian in an internment camp. Yahara told Ito that he personally believed the news of the war's end; that Russia had entered the war and that to attempt further offensive action would be foolish. Then—Moss being very accommodating—Ito listened to Japanese enlisted men in a POW camp, and their conversations with one another supported Yahara's conclusion. With many stops because of the Japanese's dysentery, Ito and Moss returned to Kunishi via Hill 95, where Moss showed Ito the spot where Generals Cho and Ushijima had committed suicide.

Finally convinced, Captain Ito reported to Colonel Hongo that Japan had evidently lost the war, and informed him of the imperial message requiring Japanese troops to lay down their arms. Officers at the regimental cave debated the matter, and in the end Colonel Hongo, also convinced, decided that the emperor's wish could not be disobeyed; all must surrender. On the night of August 28 Ito and Hongo burned the 32nd Regiment's colors, saw to it that the sick and wounded were removed in American ambulances, and the next day formally surrendered 55 officers, 342 enlisted men, and 105 civilians.

A little later Ito found that he had another surrender to arrange. His good friend and fellow member of the Japanese Military Academy's Class of 1940, Captain Tsuneo Shimura, had like himself survived the battle with a handful of soldiers from the 2nd Battalion of the 32nd Regiment. Overrun in the fighting for the Urasoe-Mura escarpment, Shimura had simply remained in place in a deep, well-supplied cavern until the end of June. Then he slipped north to Arakashi near Ginowan, hoping to gather more men and to engage in guerrilla warfare.

Others joined his band until he had about 300 including Air Force and Navy men. Shumura planned to organize them, to hijack some GI trucks, and escape in these to the wilds of northern Okinawa, it being impossible to consider guerrilla warfare where he was in an area literally swarming with Americans. But the war had ended before he could carry out his bold plan. At this point Ito contacted him, told him of the imperial rescript ordering surrender, and Shimura, after personally disarming his men, haughtily mounted a jeep to pass into detention at Kadena. With Colonel Hongo's group, Ito's was the largest detachment to surrender, though many smaller groups and individuals continued to come in piecemeal for months afterward.

V

The typhoon of steel that descended on Okinawa in 1945 is now nearly forty years past. Yet as one today flies the 972 miles between Tokyo and Naha much the same panorama unfolds below that greeted Japan's young kamikaze pilots. The seas retain their intense blue, the beaches of tiny islets their sharply contrasting bleached whiteness. Clouds hover low in random fashion, and here and there one towers to the height of the speeding jet airliner. A shimmery luminescence in the air marks the dividing line between the temperate and tropic zones.

As the plane lets down over northern Okinawa's steep hills, military roads along the ridges attest its present utility as a U.S. Marine Corps training area. On the right the Motobu Peninsula drifts past, and Ie Shima slides quickly by the starboard wing, showing its pinnacle, Iegusugu Yama, but no sign, now, of an airfield. Ahead and to the left Nakagusuku Bay appears festooned with shoals and guardian islets and across a narrow neck of land the unbroken sweep of the Hagushi beaches bespeak their choice as the American landing site. Military installations by the dozen and the distinctive patterns of four airfields now emerge. Warehouses and communications facilities of all sorts attest the still martial role the island performs in an age of international tension.

Naha today surprises one who recalls only its wartime visage. Engulfing Shuri, the metropolis extends almost to the wartime beachhead. Lined with businesses of all sorts, Highways 1 and 5 swarm with taxis and private autos. New construction has all but obliterated signs of wartime combat; hardly a trace of an old bunker remains. Tombs still abound, though, testifying to the durability of Okinawan religious beliefs. New ones, built at considerable expense, adorn many hillocks.

Kakazu Ridge remains, but below its northern face a neat row of new apartments, stoutly built to withstand typhoons, lies between it and the infamous gorge. Beyond Kakazu Ridge the escarpment glowers as menacingly as ever to the knowing eye, the Sho family tombs still carefully maintained in the face of its cliffs. Simple yet somehow appropriate Japanese memorials line its crest.

The middle of the Shuri fighting zone is as confusing as before. Only a surveyor's transit, carefully sighted from a known reference point, could identify many hills of bitter memory, such as Zebra, the Chocolate Drop, Flattop, and Dick Right.

On the east coast Nakagusuku Castle still impresses with its terraced slopes and grand vista. Beyond, the Pinnacle is identifiable, but otherwise the crazy quilt of hills offers no sure guide to either tourist or expert. Conical Hill, looming above Yonabaru and Highway 13, intrigues the observer as it did Eddie May; one wonders how the GI's of E and F companies surmounted it. Beyond Yonabaru on the Chinen Peninsula and southward, small villages remain much as in prewar days. Pairs of little Shi Shi, or Lion Dogs, one at either end of the tile rooftops, guard the tiny houses from evil spirits, while in the bushes in the yards cicadas sing a monotonous refrain. Here and there a burst of color reveals a bougainvillea or hibiscus.

Perhaps the Suicide Cliff near Hill 89 and Mabuni is the most impressive sight on the island. Dozens of memorials of marble, the product of talented modern sculptors, line a roadway and parking area at the end of the cliffs. Every prefecture in Japan honored its fallen. Below, the rich blue sea strikes the rocks to explode into white foam. No *Götterdämmerung* setting this; there is something classic about it, a union of old and new, symbolic both of a war and an island where spirits feudal clashed with modern arms.

A NOTE ON SOURCES

IN RESEARCHING this volume the authors have explored all available sources of information. In Washington, D.C., they have used the extensive documentary collections at the World War II Records Center of the National Archives, selected materials at the Department of the Army's Office of the Chief of Military History (OCMH), war diaries and other data at the Navy Department's Naval History Division, and records held at the Historical Branch, Headquarters, U.S. Marine Corps. They have extensively used the U.S. Naval Academy Library, the Library of Congress, and the New York Public Library.

The sheer volume of source material staggers the imagination. Each major unit, from 5th Fleet and 10th Army down to sub-task force and regiment, has submitted an after-action report. Every ship kept a war diary of its daily activities. In addition to the published campaign histories, official historians prepared manuscripts and published histories for each division, Army and Marine. Yet gaps exist. Except for the 7th U.S. Army Division, reports do not exist for company-level action, and the divisional histories do not focus primarily on the individual rifleman in his foxhole. Nor do the naval histories dwell extensively on the exploits of the individual gob. To see the battle through the eyes of the participant, the authors had to supplement the written record with interviews with veterans of the Okinawa campaign and to search the press and unofficial literature.

For the Japanese side written material, though understandably less abundant, is surprisingly voluminous. Most useful have been the various Japanese monographs prepared for General MacArthur's occupation forces after the war. A correction and supplement to these is the Japanese Ministry of Defense's official history, which appeared while the authors were engaged in their research. Yet for the Japanese as for the American side individual exploits tend to be slighted, and interviews with Japanese veterans were also necessary.

In the List of Contributors which follows, the name, and where appropriate, the rank and the individual's vantage point during the campaign are indicated. The Bibliography describing the written sources is divided into two parts for convenience. The first relates to the American side of the campaign; the second to the Japanese.

The authors wish to express their thanks to the following publishers for permission to quote briefly from the following works: to Little, Brown for Admiral Samuel Eliot Morison's *U.S. Navy in World War II*, Vol 14 *Victory in the Pacific;* to Holt, Rinehart & Winston for Ernie Pyle's *Last Chapter;* to the Exposition Press for Edward T. Higgins' *Webfooted Warriors;* to the Infantry Journal Press for *Uncommon Valor: Marine Divisions in Action;* and to the U.S. Naval Institute for articles in the *Proceedings* by Mitsuru Yoshida and J. Davis Scott.

APPENDIX A

LIST OF CONTRIBUTORS

Adams, Capt. Henry, U.S.N.R.—T.F.-58
Archer, R./Adm. Robert J., U.S.N. (Ret.)—*Evans*
Armstrong, William S.—898 Sig. Co.
Arnold, Maj. Gen. Archibald V.—7th Division
Barnum, Col. Allen T., U.S.M.C. (Ret.)—VMF-224
Becton, R./Adm. F. Julian, U.S.N. (Ret.)—*Laffey*
Benedict, Col. William E., U.S.M.C. (Ret.)—5th Marines
Blakelock, Brig. Gen. David H., U.S.A. (Ret.)—10th Army
Brown, Donald C.—96th Division
Brown, James S.—*Hornet*
Brown, Maj. Gen. Wilburt S., U.S.M.C. (Ret.)—11th Marines
Bruce, Lt. Gen. Andrew D., U.S.A. (Ret.)—77th Division
Brunson, William I., Jr.—96th Division
Burke, Maj. Francis T., U.S.M.C. (Ret.)—1st Marines
Ciola, Frank—2nd Marine Air Wing
Crocker, Col. David—27th Division
Dane, Arnold S.—4th Amphib. Tractor Bn.
Deakin, Brig. Gen. Harold O., U.S.M.C. (Ret.)—1st Marine Divison
del Valle, Lt. Gen. Pedro A., U.S.M.C. (Ret.)—1st Marine Division
Denig, Brig. Gen. Robert L., Jr., U.S.M.C. (Ret.)—6th Tank Bn.
Donohoo, Col. Malcolm "O," U.S.M.C. (Ret.)—22nd Marines

Dornin, Capt. R.E., U.S.N. (Ret.)—Office of CNO
Easley, Mrs. Claudius M.—96th Division
England, CWO John J., U.S.A.—77th Division
Evans, Capt. William D., U.S.M.C.R. (Ret.)—8th Phib. Tractor Bn.
Gard, Maj. Gen. R. G., U.S.A. (Ret.)—96th Division
Genda, Gen. Minoru—Kamikazes
Gibo, the Hon. Yasuharu—Okinawa civilian
Halloran, Col. Michael E., U.S.A. (Ret.)—381st Infantry
Hamamatsu, Akira—Kamikazes
Hamilton, Col. Stephen S., U.S.A. (Ret.)—307th Infantry
Hamishiro, Kome—Okinawan *boetai*
Higashionna, Tokuyu—Okimawa civilian
Higgins, Lt. Col. William W., U.S.A.—152nd Combat Engineers
Hill, Admiral Harry W., U.S.N. (Ret.)—Okinawa naval forces
Holbrow, William—383rd Infantry, L Company, Kakazu
Hubbard, Earl O.—Kamikazes, radar pickets
Ito, Koichi—1st Bn., 32nd Infantry (Japanese)
Ito, Tsuneo—32nd Army
Jin, Lt. Col. Naromichi—Hq., 32nd Army
Johnson, R./Adm. Frank L., U.S.N.—*Purdy*
Jolly, Capt. John C., U.S.N. (Ret.)—*Shubrick*
Katano, Sakae—*Yamato*
Kauffmann, R./Adm. Draper L., U.S.N.—UDT's
Kijima, Yoshitaka—63rd Brigade, 62nd Division
Kinjo, Seitoku—Kamikazes
Klassen, Richard—383rd Infantry
Kobayashi, Nobuyuki—*Yamato*
Koiner, F. K. ("Dixie")—1st Marines
London, Daniel E.—San Francisco Conference
Lyon, Chiyoko Higa—Okinawa civilian
Lyon, John G.—1st War Dog Platoon
Makimano, Tokuzo—Okinawa civilian
Matayoshi, the Hon. Kosuke—Okinawa civilian
McFarland, Comdr. Alan R., U.S.N. (Ret.)—*Bache*
McGoldrick, R./Adm. J.A., U.S.N. (Ret.)—*Rooks*
Minoru, Capt. Toyohiro—Shinyo boats
Mitchell, Willard M. ("Hoss")—L Company, 383rd Infantry
Mizusaki, Shonosuke—15th Independent Inf. Bn., 62nd Div.
Momm, Capt. Albert O., U.S.N. (Ret.)—*Mullany*
Moreau, Col. Jean W., U.S.M.C. (Ret.)—29th Marines

Moriwaki, Koji—44th Brigade
Muncie, Lt. Col. John C., U.S.M.C. (Ret.)—5th Marines
Naslund, Col. Howard L., U.S.A.F. (Ret.)—"Grim Reapers"
Nelson, M./Sgt. Johnnie N., U.S.A.F.—Amphibious tractors
Nimitz, Fleet Admiral Chester W.— CINCPAC
Nolan, Lt. Col. Martin E., U.S.A.—27th Division, "Item Pocket"
Norgaard, R./Adm. Rollo N., U.S.N. (Ret.)—*Hyman*
Palaia, Maj. Gerald E., U.S.M.C.R. (Ret.)—9th Phib. Trac. Bn.
Parker, Capt. Alton E., U.S.N. (Ret.)—*Mannert L. Abele*
Parker, Lt. Col. Marvin D., U.S.A.—*Fanshaw Bay*
Parran, Lt. Col. Thomas, Jr., U.S.M.C. (Ret.)—22nd Marines
Phoutrides, Aristides S.—*Laffey*
Poland, Mrs. Frank W., Jr.—5th Marines
Potter, Comdr. E. B.—CINCPAC staff
Pulsifer, B./Gen. Arthur, U.S.A. (Ret.)—10th Army
Puryear, Herman A.—381st Inf., Kakazu
Rector, Robert E.—382nd Infantry
Robbins, Edward S.—306th Inf., 77th Division
Roth, Col. Martin C., U.S.M.C. (Ret.)—5th Marines
Shapley, Lt. Gen. Alan, U.S.M.C. (Ret.)—4th Marines
Shaw, Samuel R.—22nd Marines
Shepherd, Gen. Lemuel C., U.S.M.C. (Ret.)—6th Marine Division
Shepsky, Milton—L Co., 383rd Infantry, Kakazu
Shimura, Col. Tsuneo—2nd Bn., 32nd Infantry (Japanese)
Silverthorn, Lt. Gen. M. H., Sr., U.S.M.C. (Ret.)—Hq., 3rd Phib. Corps
Smith, Gen. Oliver P., U.S.M.C. (Ret.)—10th Army Hq.
Smoot, V./Adm. R.N., U.S.N. (Ret.)—*Newcomb*
Soballe, Capt. V. J., U.S.N.—*Haggard*
Solomon, Chief M./Sgt. Hubert B., U.S.A.F.—10th Army
Spruance, Adm. Raymond A., U.S.N. (Ret.)—5th Fleet
Stare, Col. Edward W., U.S.A. (Ret.)—383rd Infantry, Kakazu
Strother, Col. K.C., U.S.A. (Ret.)—Hq. 24th Corps
Stump, Adm. Felix B., U.S.N. (Ret.)—Baby Flattops
Talbot, Albert C.—L Co., 383rd Infantry, Kakazu
Tamanaha, Tetsuji—6th Air Army, Kyushu
Tanaka, Kunishige—63rd Brigade, 62nd Division
Thorne, Oakleigh L.—San Francisco Conference
Tohme, Cmdr. Naomasa—5th Air Fleet, Kyushu
Tomasello, Mrs. W. P.—10th Army
Tschirgi, B./Gen. H. C., U.S.M.C. (Ret.)—1st Marine Division

Tsunoda, Dr. Jun—32nd Army and Kamikazes
Uechi, Kazufumi—*Okinawa Shimpo*
Uema, Seiyu—32nd Army Hq.
Van Arsdall, R./Adm. C. J., Jr., U.S.N.—*Anthony*
Vincent, William W.—10th Army
Von Holle, Alvin E.—383rd Infantry, Kakazu
Wallace, Lt. Gen. W. J., U.S.M.C. (Ret.)—Okinawa Air Defense
Wallin, Dr. Franklin W.—Radar pickets
Westholm, Captain Rollin E., U.S.N. (Ret.)—*Bush*
Whaling, Maj. Gen. W. J., U.S.M.C. (Ret.)—29th Marines
Whitney, Thomas H.—Radar pickets
Whitworth, Thomas H.—29th Marines
Williams, W.O. Raymond J., U.S.A.—96th Division
Wilson, Col. Tyson, U.S.M.C. (Ret.)—8th Marines
Winn, Col. Walter S., U.S.A. (Ret.)—105th Infantry
Yahara, Col. Hiromichi—32nd Army Hq.
Yamashiro, Seihan—Okinawa *boetai*

APPENDIX B

MAJOR COMBAT UNITS ENGAGED IN THE CAMPAIGN

American Forces, Fleet Adm. Chester W. Nimitz

10th Army, Lt. Gen. Simon B. Buckner, Jr.
  24th Corps, Maj. Gen. John R. Hodge
    7th Infantry Division, Maj. Gen. Archibald V. Arnold
      17th, 32nd, 184th Infantry Regiments
    27th Infantry Division, Maj. Gen. George W. Griner, Jr.
      105th, 106th, 165th Infantry Regiments
    77th Infantry Division, Maj. Gen. Andrew D. Bruce
      305th, 306th, 307th Infantry Regiments
    96th Infantry Division, Maj. Gen. James L. Bradley
      381st, 382nd, 383rd Infantry Regiments
  3rd Amphibious Corps (Marine), Lt. Gen. Roy S. Geiger
    1st Marine Division, Maj. Gen. Pedro A. del Valle
      1st, 5th, 7th Marine Regiments
    6th Marine Division, Maj. Gen. Lemuel C. Shepherd, Jr.
      4th, 22nd, 29th Marine Regiments
  Tactical Air Force, Maj. Gen. Francis P. Mulcahy, U.S.M.C. 5th
Fleet, Admiral Raymond A. Spruance
  T.F.-51, Joint Expeditionary Force, V./Adm. R.K. Turner

T.F.-52, Amphibious Support Force, R./Adm. W. H. P. Blandy
T.F.-53, Northern Attack Force, R./Adm. L. F. Reifsnider
T.F.-54, Gunfire and Covering Force, R./Adm. M. L. Deyo
T.F.-57, British Carrier Force, V./Adm. Sir H. B. Rawlings, R.N.
T.F.-58, Fast Carrier Force, Pacific Fleet, V./Adm. M. A. Mitscher

Japanese Forces

32nd Army, Lt. Gen. Mitsuru Ushijima
  62nd Division, Lt. Gen. Takeo Fujioka
    11th, 12th, 13th, 14th, 15th, 21st, 22nd, 23rd, 272nd, 273rd Independent Infantry Battalions
  24th Division, Lt. Gen. Tatsumi Amamiya
    22nd, 32nd, 89th Infantry Regiments
  44th Independent Mixed Brigade, Maj. Gen. Shigeru Suzuki
    2nd Infantry Unit, 15th Independent Mixed Regiment
  27th Tank Regiment, Lt. Col. Todoru Murakami
  Independent Battalions (under 32nd Army control) 1st, 2nd, 3rd, 26th, 27th, 28th, 29th
Naval Forces on Okinawa, R./Adm. Minoru Ota
5th Air Fleet, V./Adm. Matome Ugaki
6th Air Army, Lt. Gen. Michio Sugahara
1st Air Fleet (Formosa)
8th Air Division (Army, Formosa)
Yamato Task Force, V./Adm. Seiichi Ito

BIBLIOGRAPHY

1. SOURCES COVERING THE ACTION OF U.S. FORCES:

Unit Histories:

Appleman, Roy E., James M. Burns, Russell A Gugeler, and John Stevens, *Okinawa: The Last Battle,* Historical Division, U.S. Department of the Army, *The United States Army in World War II: The War in the Pacific,* Vol. I. Washington, D.C.: Govt. Print. Off., 1948. This is the official Army history of the campaign. The historians who wrote the volume were attached to the 10th Army. Detailed and hard to follow for the average reader.

Carleton, Major Phillips D., *The Conquest of Okinawa: An Account of the Sixth Marine Division.* Historical Branch, H.Q. U.S. Marine Corps, Washington, D.C., 1947.

Cass, Bevan (ed.), *History of the Sixth Marine Division.* Washington, D.C.: Infantry Journal Press, 1948.

Condit, Kenneth W., and Edwin T. Turnbladh, *Hold High the Torch: A History of the 4th Marines.* Historical Branch, H.Q. U.S. Marine Corps, Washington, D.C.: Govt. Print. Off., 1960. Especially good for Motobu action.

Craven, W. F., and J. L. Cate, *The Pacific: Matterhorn to Nagasaki, June 1944 to August 1945, The Army Air Forces in*

World War II, Vol. 5. Chicago: Univ. of Chicago Press, 1953. The official Air Force history. Good for B-29 attacks on Kyushu.

Davidson, Orlando R., Jr., Carl Willems, and Joseph Kahl, *The Deadeyes: The Story of the 96th Infantry Division*. Washington D.C.: Infantry Journal Press, 1947. Davidson was the division's historian.

Frank, Benis M., and Henry I. Shaw, Jr., *Victory and Occupation*, Historical Branch, H.Q. U.S. Marine Corps, *History of U.S. Marine Corps Operations in World War II*, Vol. 5. Washington, D.C.: Govt. Print. Off., 1968. The most recent of the official U.S. Marine Corps series on World War II.

Love, Edmund G., *The 27th Infantry Division in World War II*. Washington, D.C.: Infantry Journal Press, 1949.

——,*The Hourglass: A History of the 7th Infantry Division in World War II*. Washington, D.C.: Infantry Journal Press, 1950. Both volumes by Love are detailed, thorough, and well written. The author served as a 10th Army historian during the campaign.

McMillan, George J., *The Old Breed: A History of the First Marine Division in World War II*. Washington, D.C.: Infantry Journal Press, 1949. McMillan was a Marine combat correspondent and former reporter. Colorfully written.

Meyers, Lt. Col. Max, (ed.), *Ours to Hold It High: The 77th Infantry Division in World War II*. Washington: Infantry Journal Press, 1947. Not up to the standard of the other divisional histories, but very useful.

Morison, R./Adm. Samuel Eliot, *History of United States Naval Operations in World War II*, Vol. 14, *Victory in the Pacific*. Boston: Little, Brown, 1960. Admiral Morison's last volume. Very well written, but needs to be supplemented by additional material. Excellent account of Japanese surrender.

Nichols, Major Charles S., Jr., and Henry I. Shaw, Jr., *Okinawa Victory in the Pacific*. Historical Branch, H.Q. U.S. Marine Corps. Washington D.C.: Govt. Print. Off., 1955. The standard Marine Corps history until the appearance of the Frank and Shaw volume above. Not easy to read and follow.

Sherrod, Robert A., *History of Marine Corps Aviation in World War II*. Washington, D.C.: Combat Forces Press, 1952. Includes material on Marine fighter units on Okinawa.

Stockman, Capt. James R., U.S.M.C., *The First Marine Divi-*

sion on Okinawa. Historical Branch, H.Q. U.S. Marine Corps. Washington, D.C.: Govt. Print. Off., 1946.

———, *The Sixth Marine Division on Okinawa*. Historical Branch, H.Q. U.S. Marine Corps, Washington, D.C.: Govt. Print. Off., n.d. Captain Stockman served in the 1st Marine Division. Brief accounts.

Thacker, Joel D., *The First Marine Division, 1941–1945*. Historical Branch, H.Q. U.S. Marine Corps, Washington, D.C.: Govt. Print. Off., 1945. A short monograph by a Marine historian.

United States Naval Chronology, World War II. Division of Naval History, Department of the Navy, Washington, D.C.: Govt. Print. Off., 1955.

Books:

Baker, Botts, *et al.*, *Baker, Botts in World War II*. Privately printed, Houston, 1947. Personal experiences.

Blakeney, Jane, *Heroes U.S. Marine Corps 1861–1955*. Washington, D.C., 1958. Includes a list of all Silver Star winners on Okinawa.

Brown, David Tucker, *The Letters of David Tucker Brown, USMC*. Privately printed by Barbara Trigg Brown, Alexandria, Virginia, 1946. David Brown killed in action, Okinawa.

Buchanan, Lt. A. R., U.S.N.R. (ed.), *The Navy's Air War: A Mission Completed*. New York: Harper & Row, 1945. Prepared by men of Aviation History Unit, Deputy Chief of Naval Operations (Air). Copy available in Division of Naval History.

Butow, Robert J. C., *Japan's Decision to Surrender*. Stanford: Stanford Univ. Press, 1954. The standard work.

Carter, R./Adm. Worrall Reed, U.S.N. (Ret.), *Beans, Bullets and Black Oil: The Story of Fleet Logistics Afloat in the Pacific During World War II*. Washington, D.C.: Govt. Print. Off., 1953. An excellent book.

Chapelle, Dickey, *What's a Woman Doing Here?* New York: William Morrow, 1962. Dickey sneaked ashore and caused an uproar before being dispatched in disgrace to Guam.

Clark, Adm. J. J., U.S.N. (Ret.), with Clark G. Reynolds, *Carrier Admiral*. New York: David McKay, 1967.

Craig, William, *The Fall of Japan*. New York: Dial Press, 1967. The most readable account of Japan's surrender.

Davis, Kenneth S., *Experience of War*. Garden City, N.Y.: Doubleday, 1965. Personal narratives.

Davis, Russell G. *Marine at War*. Boston: Little, Brown, 1961. An enlisted marine's story.

Fane, Cmdr. Francis D., with Don Moore, *The Naked Warriors*. New York: Appleton-Century-Crofts, 1956. Includes a chapter on the Frogmen at Okinawa.

Feis, Herbert, *The Atomic Bomb and the End of World War II*. Princeton: Princeton Univ. Press, 1966. Excellent.

Forrestel, V./Adm. E. P., U.S.N. (Ret.), *Admiral Raymond A. Spruance, A Study in Command*. Division of Naval History, U.S. Dept. of Navy. Washington, D.C.: Govt. Print. Off., 1966.

Hall, Captain Basil, R.N., *Account of a Voyage of Discovery to the West Coast of Corea and the Great Loo-Choo Island*. London: John Murray, 1818. A classic account.

Halsey, Fleet Adm. William F., and Lt. Cmdr. Joseph Bryan III, U.S.N.R., *Admiral Halsey's Story*. New York: Whittlesey House, 1947.

Hawks, Francis L., *Narrative of the expedition of a Squadron to the China Seas and Japan performed in the years 1852, 1853, and 1854 under the command of Commodore M. C. Perry . . . at his request and under his supervision*. Published by order of the Congress of the United States. Washington, D.C., 1856.

Heinl, Col. Robert D., Jr., *Soldiers of the Sea: The United States Marine Corps, 1775–1962*. Annapolis: U.S. Naval Institute, 1962. Takes the view that a landing in the south of Okinawa would have quickly ended the campaign.

Higgins, Edward T., and Dean Phillips, *Webfooted Warriors: The Story of a Frogman in World War II*. New York: Exposition Press, 1955.

Hough, Frank O., *The Island War: The United States Marine Corps in the Pacific*. Philadelphia and New York: Lippincott, 1947. Good brief account of Okinawa campaign.

Huie, William B., *From Omaha to Okinawa: The Story of the Seabees*. New York: E. P. Dutton, 1945.

Isely, Jeter A., and P. A. Crowl, *The U.S. Marines and Amphibious War: Its Theory and Its Practice in the Pacific*. Princeton:

Princeton Univ. Press, 1951. A scholarly book. Good critique of naval gunfire and air support on Okinawa.

Jenkins, William E., *Okinawa: Isle of Smiles*. New York: Twayne, 1951.

Johnston, Richard W., *Follow Me: The Story of the Second Marine Division in World War II*. New York: Random House, 1948.

Karig, Walter, with Russell L. Harris and F. A. Manson, *Victory in the Pacific, Battle Report*, Vol. 5. New York: Holt, Rinehart, and Winston, 1949. Not scholarly, but good photographs and action description.

Kerr, George H., *Okinawa: The History of an Island People*. Rutland, Vt., Tokyo, Japan: Tuttle, 1958. A fine, scholarly history, by far the best on the subject.

King, Fleet Adm. Ernest J., and Cmdr. W. M. Whitehill, *Fleet Admiral King: A Naval Record*, New York: W. W. Norton, 1952.

Leahy, Fleet Adm. William D., *I Was There*. New York: Whittlesey House, 1950.

Lebra, William P., *Okinawan Religion: Belief, Ritual, and Social Structure*. Honolulu: Univ. of Hawaii Press, 1966. Scholarly.

Leckie, Robert, *Strong Men Armed: The United States Marines Against Japan*. New York: Random House, 1962. Well-written popular account.

Litz, Leo M., *Report from the Pacific*. Indianapolis: Indianapolis *News*, 1946. Stories of home state boys.

Lott, Cmdr. Arnold S., U.S.N. (Ret.), *Brave Ship, Brave Men*. Indianapolis: Bobbs-Merrill, 1964. Excellent account of the life—and death—of the U.S.S. *Aaron Ward*.

Love, Edmund G., *War Is a Private Affair*. New York: Harcourt, Brace, 1959.

McCahill, William P. (ed.), *Hit the Beach! Your Marine Corps in Action*. New York: William H. Wise, 1948.

McMillan, George, *et al.*, *Uncommon Valor: Marine Divisions in Action*. Washington, D.C.: Infantry Journal Press, 1946. See the accounts of McMillan and Herman Kogan.

Morison, R./Adm. Samuel Eliot, *The Liberation of the Philippines: Luzon, Mindanao, the Visayas 1944–1945, History of United States Naval Operations in World War II*, Vol. 13. Boston: Little, Brown, 1959. See for raid on Naha of Oct. 10, 1944.

O'Callahan, Father Joseph T., S.J., *I Was Chaplain on the Franklin*. New York: Macmillan, 1956. Vivid description of the agony of ship and crew.

O'Sheel, Capt. Patrick, and S./Sgt. Gene Cook (eds.), *Semper Fidelis: The U.S. Marines in the Pacific, 1942–1945*. New York: William Sloane, 1947. Collection of articles and short accounts written by Marine Corps combat correspondents assigned to each Marine regiment. Several on Okinawan campaign.

Passaic (New Jersey) *Herald News, Anybody Here from Jersey?* Passaic, N.J.: *Herald News*, 1945. Personal narratives.

Pyle, Ernie, *Last Chapter*. New York: Holt, Rinehart and Winston. Collects his wartime dispatches from the Pacific.

Reynolds, Clark G., *The Fast Carriers: The Forging of an Air Navy*. New York: McGraw-Hill, 1968. Some pertinent information on command relationships.

Roscoe, Theodore, *U.S. Destroyer Operations in World War II*. Annapolis: U.S. Naval Institute, 1957. Excellent photos.

Schuon, Karl (ed.), *The Leathernecks*. New York: Franklin Watts, 1963. See "Surrender or Die" by Herman Kogan and "Key to the Castle" by Ralph Meyers.

Sherman, Adm. F. C., U.S.N. (Ret.), *Combat Command: The American Aircraft Carriers in the Pacific War*. New York: E. P. Dutton, 1950. Personal narrative of a T.F.-58 task group commander.

Sherrod, Robert, *On to Westward*. New York: Duell, Sloan & Pearce, 1945. Much pertinent material.

Smith, S. E. (ed.), *The United States Marine Corps in World War II*. New York: Random House, 1969. Compendium of articles and extracts. Some on Okinawa.

Stafford, Cmdr. Edward P., U.S.N., *The Big E: The Story of the U.S.S. Enterprise*. New York: Random House, 1962.

Tantum, W. H., and E. J. Hoffschmidt (eds.), *Second World War Combat Weapons, Japanese*. Old Greenwich, Conn.: WE, Inc., 1968. Appears to be a reprint of U.S. Army's handbook of Japanese weapons, perhaps with some emendations.

Taylor, Theodore, *The Magnificent Mitscher*. New York: W. W. Norton, 1954.

Walworth, Arthur, *Black Ships off Japan: The Story of Commodore Perry's Expedition*. New York: Alfred A. Knopf, 1946.

Articles:

Bergren, Maj. Orville V., U.S.M.C., "School Solutions on Motobu," *Marine Corps Gazette*, December, 1945.

Braman, Sgt. Don, U.S.M.C., "Miracle on Okinawa," *Leatherneck*, July, 1945. An account of shelling of Kadena, with effects considerably exaggerated.

del Valle, Maj. Gen. Pedro A., "Old Glory on Shuri," *Marine Corps Gazette*, August, 1945.

——, "Southward from Shuri," *Marine Corps Gazette*, October, 1945.

Finan, Sgt. James, U.S.M.C., "Damndest Battlefield," *Leatherneck*, June, 1945. Good account of L day.

Kogan, S./Sgt. Herman, "Glory Kid," *Leatherneck*, September, 1945. The story of Rusty Golar on Sugar Loaf.

Lardner, John, "A Reporter on Okinawa," *New Yorker*, May 26, 1945. Perhaps the most informative of his articles, which are better literature than history.

Mason, Col. Arthur T., "Battle of Wana Draw," *Marine Corps Gazette*, October, 1945.

Meyers, Sgt. Ralph W., "Admiral's Hill," *Leatherneck*, October, 1945. Description of R./Adm. Ota's underground headquarters.

——, "Ammo from Heaven," *Leatherneck*, July, 1945. The story of airdrops to the marines.

Pratt, W. V., "Reply to the Okinawa Critics," *Newsweek*, July 2, 1945.

Scott, Cmdr. J. Davis, U.S.N.R., "No Hiding Place—Off Okinawa," U.S. Naval Institute, *Proceedings*, November, 1957.

Shepherd, Maj. Gen. Lemuel C., "Battle for Motobu Peninsula," *Marine Corps Gazette*, August, 1945.

Shilan, First Lt. Alan, U.S.M.C., "To Yontan and Beyond," *Marine Corps Gazette*, July, 1945.

Smith, Cmdr. Edward L., II, M.C., U.S.N.R., "The Navy Hospital Corpsman, Okinawa," *Hospital Corps Quarterly*, March, 1946. Account of treatment of sick, injured, and wounded civilians.

Soth, L. K., "Hacksaw Ridge on Okinawa Island," *Infantry Journal*, August, 1945.

Stockman, James R., "Night Operations on Okinawa," *Marine Corps Gazette*, September, 1946.

Tomlinson, Maj. L. A., Jr., "Tank-Artillery on Okinawa," *Marine Corps Gazette*, September, 1946.

Waterman, Col. Bernard S., U.S.A., "The Battle of Okinawa: An Artillery Angle," *Field Artillery Journal*, September, 1945.

Williams, Lt. Col. Thomas E., U.S.M.C., "Jap Tactics on Okinawa," *Marine Corps Gazette*, October, 1945.

Newspapers:

The authors have used the files of the following newspapers for the entire period of the Okinawa campaign. Stories are brief and lack detail until about May 15, when other news finally stopped dominating the columns.

Atlanta *Constitution*, Chicago *Daily News*, Chicago *Sun*, Chicago *Tribune*, *Christian Science Monitor*, Cleveland *Plain Dealer*, Honolulu *Advertiser*, Los Angeles *Times*, Portland *Oregonian*, New Orleans *Times-Picayune*, New York *Herald Tribune*, New York *Sun*, *New York Times*, Salt Lake City *Tribune*, San Francisco *Examiner*, Seattle *Post Intelligencer*, Seattle *Times*, Washington *Evening Star*, *Washington Post*.

Two newspaper stories deserve special mention. Article by Homer Bigart appearing in the New York *Herald Tribune*, May 28, 1945. Article by David Lawrence, "Inquiry into Battle of Okinawa Proposed," Washington *Evening Star*, January 10, 1946. Both are critical of Buckner's Okinawa strategy.

Documents:

Manuscript histories written by 10th Army historians:

Appleman, Maj. Roy E., "The XXIV Corps in the Conquest of Okinawa, 1 April–22 June 1945," 4 vols., Dec. 1945.

Gugeler, Capt. Russell A., "The Operations of the 7th Infantry Division on Okinawa, 1 April to 22 June 1945," 3 vols., n.d.

Leach, First Lt. Paul R., "Narrative of the Operations of the 77th Division on Okinawa," 3 vols., n.d. Vol. I, *Keramas,* Vol. II, *Okinawa,* Vol. III, *Ie Shima.*

Mulford, Capt. Donald, and First Lt. Jesse Rogers, "The 96th Division on Okinawa," 4 parts, n.d. These documents are of exceptional value. They were the primary basis of the Army and unit histories cited above. They include many descriptions of exploits of personal bravery and other combat incidents not mentioned in unit after action reports. They also contain some mistakes and must be used with caution.

After action reports, Army and Marine Corps:

After action reports exist for 10th Army Headquarters, for 24th and 3rd Amphibious Corps Headquarters, and for each division and regiment engaged in the Okinawa campaign. Separate battalions (such as the 713th Tank Battalion, Armored Flame Thrower, Provisional) also submitted reports, and on some occasions battalions reported to their regiments. In addition, all units down through battalion level maintained daily staff journals, message files, maps, and special and periodic reports that occupy many feet of filing space at the World War II Records Center of the National Archives and at the Historical Branch, Headquarters, U.S. Marine Corps. The authors have examined all of the major after action reports and selected items from the various journals, message files, and other special reports.

After action reports, Navy:

Reports exist for Admiral Nimitz's CINCPAC Headquarters, for Admiral Spruance's 5th and Admiral Halsey's 3rd Fleets, and for all task groups, task forces, and individual ships that participated in the campaign. Besides maintaining logs, damaged ships filed special war damage reports, of which a few remain classified if the ship is still in active service. The authors have examined CINCPAC, 3rd and 5th Fleets, and the task force reports, and many individual ships' reports. The physical location of most of these is at the U.S. Navy's Classified Records Branch, Washington Navy Yard.

Citations for awards:

Citations for awards on file with the Office of the Adjutant General, U.S. Army, constitute about the only official source of information—other than the unit histories—for the exploits of individual soldiers. See citations for award of the Distinguished Service Cross, Silver Star, and Bronze Star issued by the 7th, 77th, 27th, and 96th Infantry Divisions.

Unofficial company narratives for companies of the 7th Division:

These are after action accounts obtained from company-grade officers and NCO's by the division's historian. They exist *only* for the 7th Division.

Fact sheet on Okinawan civilian casualties:

Prepared by Mr. Norman D. King, December 28, 1965. A useful round-up of all of the conflicting information on this difficult and controversial subject. Available at Office of Chief of Military History.

Divisional newsletters:

The authors have used the *Gunto Graphic,* 10th Army newsletter, the *Galla Briefs,* the 27th Division newsletter, and the *Deadeye Dispatch,* the 96th Division newsletter.

Operation plans:

Commander-in-Chief, 5th Fleet, Operation Plan I-45, 3 January 1945. This is the basic plan for Operation ICEBERG.

XXIV Corps Operation Plan. XXIV Corps Field Order 45, ICEBERG, 8 February 1945.

III Amphibious Corps Operation Plan I-45, 1 February and 22 February 1945.

Report of Task Force 57, British Carrier Force, Pacific:

This report was not available as such to the authors. However, most of it is available in Sir Bruce A. Frazier, "The Contributions of the British Pacific Fleet to the Assault on Okinawa, 1945," *The London Gazette, Supplements, 1946–1951*, Vol. 2, Item 19. It includes documents as well as a summary of the operation. Very useful, thorough, and accurate.

Tape-recorded interviews at the Division of Naval History:

The authors have used those for Lt. Theodore Arnow, Cmdr. F. J. Becton, Cmdr. C. M. Bertholf, Lt. R. L. Bly, Lt. Sheldon Briggs, Cmdr. Arleigh A. Burke, Lt. John R. Griffin, Cmdr. C. M. Keyes, Lt. Oscar N. Pederson, Lt. Paul J. Schmitz, R./Adm. F. C. Sherman, Lt. Cmdr. V. J. Soballe, Lt. F. H. Sontag, V./Adm. R. K. Turner, Cmdr. G. R. Wilson. Tape recordings made in 1945 and ranks given as of that date.

Unofficial ships' histories, prepared for officers and men:

Many available in U.S. Naval Academy Library; others at the U.S. Navy Library, Washington, D.C. The authors have used those for *Arkansas* (BB), *Maryland* (BB), *Texas* (BB), *Bataan* (CVL), *Bennington* (CV), *Bunker Hill* (CV), *Enterprise* (CV), *Hancock* (CV), *Louisville* (CA), and *Pensacola* (CA).

II. SOURCES COVERING THE ACTION OF JAPANESE FORCES:

Official History:

Okinawa Homen Rikugun Sakusen (Okinawa District Army Operations). War History Branch, Defense Research Department, Defense Agency Japan. Tokyo, 1968. This is the official Japanese history of the land warfare aspects of the Okinawa campaign. The authors have used this, with Monograph No. 135, as their major Japanese source for the ground action of the Okinawa campaign.

Books:

Hattori, Takushiro, *Dai Toa Senso Zenshi* ("The Complete History of the Greater East Asia War"), 4 vols., Tokyo: Matsu Pub. Co., 1953. Has very little on the Okinawa campaign. Useful for homeland strategy and plans.

Hayashi, Col. Saburo, I.J.A. (Ret.), with Alvin D. Coox, *Kogun: The Japanese Army in the Pacific*. Quantico, Va.: Marine Corps Assoc., 1959. First published in Tokyo, 1951. Sketchy on Okinawa campaign.

Kato, Masuo, *The Lost War: A Japanese Reporter's Inside Story*. New York: Alfred A. Knopf, 1946. Good for homeland views.

Konoye, Prince Fumimaro, *The Memoirs of Prince Fumimaro Konoye*. Translated from the *Ashi Shimbun*, Dec. 20–30, 1945, by Okuyama Service.

Kuwahara, Yasuo, and Gordon T. Alfred, *Kamikaze*. New York: Ballantine, 1957. Good on kamikaze background.

Inoguchi, Rikihei, Tadashi Nakajima, and Roger Pineau, *The Divine Wind*. Annapolis: U.S. Naval Institute, 1958. Good on all aspects but especially on origins and early operations of the kamikazes.

Makiminato, Tokuzo, *Tetsu No Bofu* ("The Metal Typhoon"). Tokyo: Asahi Shimbun Sha, 1950. The campaign from the Okinawan side by a member of the staff of the Okinawa *Times*.

Okumiya, Masatake, and Jiro Horikoshi, with Martin Caldin, *Zero: The Inside Story of Japan's Air War in the Pacific*. New York: Ballantine, 1956. Good information on the famous Zero fighter, still in use in Okinawan campaign.

Shigemitsu, Mamoru, *Japan and Her Destiny: My Struggle for Peace*. New York: E. P. Dutton, 1958.

Uechi, Kazufumi, *Okinawa Senshi* ("War History of Okinawa"). Tokyo: Jiji Press, 1959. Based largely on the official U.S. Army history, supplemented by personal recollections of Okinawans.

Yoshida, Shigeru, *The Yoshida Memoirs: The Story of Japan in Crisis*. Boston: Houghton Mifflin, 1962.

Japanese Monographs:

These monographs constitute collectively the major Japanese source on World War II from the Japanese side. They will be supplemented, but not supplanted by, the official histories now appearing. They were written by former Japanese officers for U.S. Army Forces Far East, Japanese Research Division, Military History Section, and translated into English. Sources were diaries, whatever operational records were available, and the memories of participants. The quality of the monographs vary tremendously, they are extremely difficult to use and follow, but are rewarding if treated with care and patience. All are available in the Library of Congress, the U.S. Naval Academy Library, and at OCMH. The authors used the monographs listed below.

Japanese Monograph No. 51, *Air Operations Record of Iwo Island and the Southwestern Islands from Japan Proper (the 6th Army Air Force)*, Aug. 1946.

Japanese Monograph No. 53, *Okinawa Operations Record of the 32nd Army*. Aug, 1946. Brief, but not entirely supplanted by Monograph No. 135.

Japanese Monograph No. 83, *Okinawa Area Naval Operations*,

January–June, 1945. Naval Air Operations. Includes a supplement with statistical charts for kamikaze operations.

Japanese Monograph No. 85, *Preparations for Operations in Defense of the Homeland, July 1944–July 1945.* Covers Japanese planning for defense of Japan proper.

Japanese Monograph No. 86, *Fifth Air Fleet Operations, February–August, 1945. Naval Air Operations.* Major written source of kamikaze operations.

Japanese Monograph No. 123, *Homeland Defense Naval Operations, Part II, March 1943–August 1945.*

Japanese Monograph No. 124, *Homeland Defense Naval Operations, Part III, June 1944–August 1945.* Deals with naval air operations.

Japanese Monograph No. 135, *Okinawa Operations Record of the 32nd Army, 24th Division, and the 8th* [Formosa-based] *Air Division* [Army], Nov., 1949. A revised edition of Monograph No. 53 and much more complete. Views campaign from level of 32nd Army Headquarters. Good for planning and intra-staff quarrels.

United States Strategic Bombing Survey Pamphlets:

These are based on Japanese documents and postwar interrogations. *Campaigns of the Pacific War,* 1946. Reproduces log and track of *Yamato* on her final voyage.

Interrogations of Japanese Officials, 2 vols., 1946.

Japanese Air Power, Report No. 62, 1946. Has widely accepted statistics on kamikazes that are *not* correct. Must be supplemented with Japanese Monograph No. 83.

Japan's Struggle to End the War, 1946.

Mission Accomplished: Interrogations of Japanese Industrial, Military and Civil Leaders of World War II, 1946.

Reports and Monographs Prepared by U.S. Army Forces Far East, Japanese Research Division, Military History Section:

The Brocade Banner: The Story of Japanese Nationalism, 1946. Must be used with caution.

Interrogations of Japanese Officials, 2 vols., n.d.

Major Actions and Decisions of the Army General Staff, n.d.

Personal History Statements, 2 vols., n.d.

Reports of General MacArthur. The Campaigns of MacArthur in the Pacific. 2 vols., Washington, D.C.: Govt. Print. Off., 1966. This is the so-called "MacArthur history," now available in published edition. Volume II represents the "... contributions of Japanese officers employed to tell their story of operations against MacArthur's forces." Supplements the Japanese monographs.

Special Studies, 4 vols.

Statements of Japanese Officials on World War II, 4 vols.

Translations of Japanese Documents, 7 vols.

Articles:

Inoguchi, Captain Rikihei, and Cmdr. Tadashi Nakajima, "The Kamikaze Attack Corps," U.S. Naval Institute, *Proceedings,* September, 1953.

Matsumoto, Capt. Kitaro, and Cmdr. Matsataka Chihaya, "Design and Construction of the *Yamato* and *Musashi*." U.S. Naval Institute, *Proceedings,* Oct., 1953.

Vogel, Bertram, "Who Were the Kamikaze?" U.S. Naval Institute, *Proceedings,* July, 1947.

Yokoi, R./Adm. Toshiyuki, "Kamikazes and the Okinawa Campaign," U.S. Naval Institute, *Proceedings,* May, 1954.

Yoshida, Mitsuru, "The End of the *Yamato*," U.S. Naval Institute, *Proceedings,* Feb., 1952.

Newspaper:

The Japan Times, files, March–Aug., 1945. This is Tokyo's English-language newspaper, published throughout the war. Of interest mainly for insight into Japanese homeland conditions and for articles giving personal experiences—albeit heavily propagandized—of Japanese aircrew.

Documents:

10th U.S. Army, G-2 Section. Counterintelligence Collecting Agency Substation Translations Nos. 4-308, 17 April–11 July 1945. Other sources of Japanese 32nd Army documents are Japanese Monograph No. 135 and the U.S. official histories. A great deal of material was captured and translated on the battlefield, and much of it was preserved in the above collection.

Prisoner of War Interrogations:

POW interrogations and reports were published and preserved by CINCPAC, 10th Army, 24th Corps, 3rd Corps, and all of the combat divisions. The authors have reviewed hundreds of these in World War II Records Center. Of special interest is the interrogation of Col. Hiromichi Yahara, Chief Planning Officer 32nd Army.

Japanese Order of Battle Reports:

10th U.S. Army, 24th Corps. G-2 Weekly Intelligence Summaries Nos. 4-15, 12 April–26 June 1945. Weekly reports of Col. Cecil W. Nist, 24th Corps G-2.

INDEX

ABOUT THE AUTHORS

WILLIAM AND JAMES BELOTE are twins, born in Bellevue, Washington. Both attended the University of Washington, where they obtained their B.A. and M.A. degrees. They received their doctorates at the University of California.

William Belote was Assistant Professor of European History at Mississippi State College from 1953–56. He then accepted an appointment at the United States Naval Academy, Annapolis, where he is currently a professor of naval history. He is co-author of a textbook, *Sea Power, A Naval History*. A trade version, titled *The Great Sea War*, has received numerous foreign translations and adaptations. William Belote lives in Annapolis, Md.

James Belote was a teaching assistant at the University of California, and a military-affairs analyst with a government agency in Washington, D.C., from 1954–60. Since 1960, he has been on the faculty of Principia College in Elsah, Illinois. He is now chairman of the history department.

James and William Belote are co-authors of *Corregidor: The Saga of a Fortress* published in 1968, *Typhoon of Steel: The Battle for Okinawa*, published in 1970, and *Titans of the Seas*, published in 1975.

Drs. William and James Belote are now retired.

Join the Allies on the Road to Victory
BANTAM WAR BOOKS